Literature
of the
American Indian

Princess Red Wing of the Seven Crescents

Literature
of the
American Indian

THOMAS E. SANDERS

Nippawanock—Cherokee

University of South Florida

WALTER W. PEEK

Metacomet—Narragansett-Wampanoag

East Bay High School, Riverview, Florida

GLENCOE PRESS

A division of Benziger Bruce & Glencoe, Inc.
Beverly Hills
Collier-Macmillan Publishers
London

Glencoe Press

A division of Benziger Bruce & Glencoe, Inc.
8701 Wilshire Boulevard
Beverly Hills, California 90211

Collier-Macmillan Canada, Ltd., Toronto, Ontario

Library of Congress catalog card number: 72-89050

4 5 6 7 8 9 MAL 80 79 78 77 76 75

ACKNOWLEDGMENTS

Acknowledgment is gratefully made to the following authors, agents, and publishers who have granted
permission to use selections from their publications.

American Council for Nationalities Service, for: "Chee's Daughter" by Juanita Platero and Siyowin
Miller, from *Common Ground*, vol. VIII, no. 2 (Winter 1948), pp. 22-31. Reprinted from *Common
Ground* with the permission of the American Council for Nationalities Service.

The American Folklore Society, Inc., for: "The Origin of Corn," article by Mrs. Wallace Brown from the
Journal of American Folklore, vol. III, 1890. Reprinted by permission of The American Folklore
Society, Inc.;

Excerpt on page 61, from "Mythology of the Mission Indians," article by Constance G. DuBois in *Journal
of American Folklore*, vol. XIX, 1906. Reprinted by permission of The American Folklore Society, Inc.;
"The Emergence (Hopi)," pp. 5-11 in *Indian Tales of North America*, by Tristram P. Coffin (1961).
Reprinted by permission of The American Folklore Society, Inc.

Associated Press, for: "Sing a Song in Praise of Mother Earth," pp. 117-18, article by George W. Cornell
from *The Tampa Tribune*, April 22, 1972. Reprinted by permission of the Associated Press.

University of California Press, for: "Creation of the Yakima World," pp. 142-43 of *Indian Legends of
the Pacific Northwest* edited by Ella E. Clark, University of California Press, 1953. Originally published
by the University of California Press; reprinted by permission of The Regents of the University of
California.

Jonathan Cape Ltd, for: "Presence," by Ted Berrigan from *In The Early Morning Rain*, published by
Cape Goliard Press. Reprinted by permission of Jonathan Cape Ltd.

The Council on Interracial Books for Children, for: Statements on the Alcatraz Action by Richard
Oakes and Carol Williams, from *Chronicles of American Indian Protest* by The Council on Interracial
Books for Children. A Fawcett Premier Book. Fawcett Publications, Inc., Greenwich, Conn., 1971.

Thomas Y. Crowell Company, Inc., for: "How The World Was Made—Cheyenne," pp. 22-26 from
American Indian Mythology by Alice Marriott and Carol K. Rachlin, copyright © 1968 by Alice Marriott and Carol K. Rachlin, reprinted with permission from Thomas Y. Crowell Co., Inc., Publishers
and with permission from Alice Marriott and Carol K. Rachlin.

Dover Publications, for: 11 poems ("Lullaby," p. 134; "Lullaby," p. 138; "Song of the Rain Chant,"
p. 139; "Corn-Grinding Song," p. 141; "Corn-Grinding Song," p. 142; "We Must Part," p. 149; "Wind
Song," p. 149; "Friendship," p. 157; "Morning Song," p. 162; "The Old Warrior," p. 162; "Hunting-song,"
p. 171) from *The Indians' Book*, recorded and edited by Natalie Curtis, Dover Publications, Inc., New
York, 1950. Reprinted through the permission of the publisher.

DEDICATED WITH GREAT GRATITUDE TO
PRINCESS RED WING OF THE SEVEN CRESCENTS
and
JOHN ALLEN McALISTER

Contents

Chapter 2

The Trickster, Heroes, and the Folk   63

Chapter 3

The Soul of the Indian: Pre-Columbian Poetry   103

Chapter 4

The Liberated and the League:
The Law of the Great Peace and the American Epic   *183*

Chapter 5

The Golden Word Unheard:
Oratory   *241*

Chapter 6

To Golgotha and Back: Native American Religions After the Christian Invasion   313

Chapter 7

Memories Miserable and Magnificent:
Biography and Autobiography   409

Chapter 8

Anguished, Angry, Articulate:
Current Voices in Poetry, Prose, and Protest   445

Foreword

Native American peoples know the Power of their songs, legends, history, stories, oratory—those things which a "literate" society calls its "literature." Listening to an elder talk during a winter evening or responding to the rhythm of the drum and the melodies of the singers is more than just entertainment or social pastime for the People of this Land. It is "literature" which passes on advice and knowledge, which gives the eye a framework of beauty and peace through which to view the world, which binds together individuals into that web of extended family and clan and tribe and Membership in the Creation which Western Civilization knows of, but seldom experiences.

In the interests of "civilization," "progress," "education," and "religion," the culture—and thus the literature—of Native Americans has been mocked, suppressed, and destroyed. Spanish conquistadores spent weeks throwing volumes of Mayan literature into massive pyres until the great libraries stood empty. So effective was their work that only a few specialized scholars today even know the libraries existed. Grandfathers found that the children who used to sit about their lodges to hear the accumulated wisdom of the ages were away in boarding schools operated by the government or the churches—and when they did return to their homes, the children could no longer understand the only language Grandfather spoke.

Missionaries painted dreadful pictures of the Fires of Hell which would meet all who followed the "pagan and heathenish" ways of the "devil-worshippers." It was ridiculous, they said, that people should believe such nonsense as twins, one good and one evil, born to a virgin mother. Instead, they said, only the Gospels contained the Truth of Cain and Abel and Mary, Mother of Jesus. Native medicine people and orators were hard-pressed to compete with the mission people who could "prove" their way by pointing to the text of a printed book said to be the Word of God—especially when children had been taught that writing of any kind could hardly be questioned—"It must be true if it's printed" is an adage that prevails today.

The little respect that was given to Native American literature came from those strange and possessive scholars known as "anthropologists." While music departments of a university teach the intricacies of Italian operas, while historians expound on the Crusades and the French Revolution and while Spanish novelists and poets are interpreted and discussed in Humanities classrooms, Native Americans are always shuffled off to Anthropology. There the greatest of poetry is dissected for its "cultural insights" and songs and legends are burdened with faithfully applied footnotes.

Nippawanock and Metacomet do a tremendous service in changing that unfortunate and unpleasant relationship by their compilation of this volume and their insistence that it be accepted at face value as literature. As non-native people get their first glimpse of the philosophy and wisdom of the peoples whom they have displaced, they need a context and encouragement to bridge the gap from their own isolated culture, hemmed in by feelings of superiority, over to the culture of a people who are viewed as the pitiful remainders of the Stone Age.

For Native Americans, this volume will be a source of strength, adding depth and status to their knowledge and belief that their ways and wisdom are indeed of value. To non-native people, this volume can be an indication of what has been denied to them by Manifest Destiny and what has remained undiscovered because of the Doctrine of Discovery. For non-native people, it will be something which they can appreciate—for native people, it is a volume in which they can participate.

This anthology also offers hope, as it points the way to that Universal Anthology of the Creation, which speaks a language that all sensitive and thoughtful observers can understand—birds and insects as well as human observers. The voice of the waters, the whisper of the winds, the tale of the mountains, the patterns of the stars are the source of this "literature." Hopefully, as other peoples share this land with the native peoples, they will grow to respect and honor her as their Mother. It is in this Library of the Creation that native peoples take the greatest pride in their literacy.

—Rarihokwats

(Rarihokwats is editor of *Akwesasne Notes,* produced by the Mohawk Nation at Akwesasne, via Rooseveltown, N.Y. 13683.)

Prolog and Epilog
by Way of a Preface

Ours has been a rich and varied heritage—just how rich and varied we had no idea until we gave ourselves over to this book. Metacomet (Walter Peek) was born to a Narragansett-Wampanoag mother and a Tama father; his stepfather was a Mohegan. His Rhode Island boyhood was a blend of acculturation, assimilation, and Indianization, for time had made the remnants of the early inhabitants a part of the society—but apart from the society. The Native Americans of the area were, generally speaking, Christian citizens who periodically recalled their past with pageants and ceremonies which, he felt, displayed the Indian as some sort of anachronistic freak. For many years, he anguished over being forced to don "those damned costumes" and perform before crowds. As a result of the early feeling of being some sort of side-show attraction, he was not anxious to acknowledge his Native American origin and would do so only if asked direct questions. Nippawanock (Thomas Sanders), on the other hand, was led to believe his parentage was lily white, an evasion that was damaging indeed, for, born on Quapaw land in northeast Oklahoma, his only male authority figure was the Cherokee stepfather who never divulged the secret but raised the boy as an Indian child would have been raised. Thus, he became "the stepson of that halfbreed" in a society that had no more denigrating word than "halfbreed" in its vocabulary. Longing to be an Indian because his stepfather had more dignity and bearing than anyone else in the town of Picher, he existed in neither world. Many years later when his mother "confessed" the guilty secret that his great-grandfather was a Cherokee, Nippawanock knew why he had always "felt" Indian.

After many years of friendship, Metacomet and Nippawanock became blood brothers when Nippawanock was adopted into the Narragansett tribe. Their mother, Red Wing, had only one son by birth but now she had one by adoption, and that son had a mother who carried her Indianness proudly, for she was a descendant of Metacomet, King Philip of Pokanoket. In time, Metacomet became very proud of his heritage even as Nippawanock learned to be less ashamed of the white blood that flows in his veins. And this book is a kind of testimonial to the pride they both feel in their great heritage.

The work that has gone into the book has been phenomenal, and it could never have been accomplished without the aid of the many Whites and Indians of the past who set down, however imperfectly and out of whatever motives, the material that would otherwise have been lost forever. Nor would it have been accomplished without the aid and encouragement of certain friends of both cultures who are, even before they are Indian or White, human beings of the highest order. For that reason, we prefer to thank them as representatives of the best in both worlds. George Gath, Frank Urbanowski, and Marie Enders know exactly why the book could not exist without them—and so do we. Paige Graham, Christopher Thiessen, Gabe and Linda Horn, and Faye Ayala all made contributions that cannot adequately be recognized. And Grace McAlister knows how much her ultimate truthfulness added to this work—and to the love her son bears her.

The great mass of material and the demands of space have created problems of an unbelievable nature. One day, perhaps, the definitive anthology of American Indian literature can be compiled. We hope we are a part of the compilation process. And, until that time, we hope this collection will serve to reveal the great riches that are the literature. We think it represents a cross section of the very best of that literature, even though it is a very small part.

Thomas E. Sanders (Nippawanock)
Walter W. Peek (Metacomet)

An Historical Overview
by Way of Introduction:
Who Are We?
Where Did We Come From?
What Makes Us Endure?

The white man in America is a recorder of "educated guesses," facts, dates, deeds, promises, and items to be sent to the laundry or purchased at the store. He counts, records, and rationalizes or estimates everything which may supply a clue to some overwhelming question that he seeks to articulate through the as yet undiscovered answer. Some part of that question must concern itself with origins and identity, for he probes the earth, violates burial chambers, and reads history in rocks and bones that he may speculate endlessly on his findings. And, perhaps one day he *will* find the answer, ask the question, and turn his attention to his present—a present that his unanswered, unasked question seems to make uncomfortably confining.

One part of the endless pursuit is an effort to learn where man came from—and how long ago. A kind of archaeological one-upmanship accompanies each new "find," for his quest leads always to the "great tomb of man" and the unstated though implicit hope that some toe in that eternal morgue will bear the tag: "Adam. Husband of Eve. Father of Cain and Abel." The archaeologist who discovers that tagged toe will win the game, for no competitor can say, "My fossil remain is older than yours," or "My creature is a man; yours is an ape." That fossil will prove or disprove all arguments about the origin of man and supply the answer to the questions that really terrify him: "Are we supposed to be going somewhere— and why?"

Rummaging through the ruins of Troy, scrabbling about in Olduvai Gorge, the Heinrich Schliemanns and Mary Leakeys force the earth to yield its stored oddments, then examine them to see where they fit into the chronological jigsaw puzzle that, once completed, will tell us unequivocally whether or not we were created and whether or not we are the present but changing result of some evolutionary experiment of an ongoing nature. The intellectual reason: Man needs to know the details of his past if he is to chart the course of his future. The emotional reason: *Someone* has to be wrong in the chronic confrontation between history and religion, and the dedicated scientist can serve as arbiter only if his proofs are unassailable.

Utilizing both his religion and his concept of history to justify his initial incursions, succeeding conquest, and consequent appropriation of the Western Hemisphere, the European and his American descendants proffered a variety of hypotheses, apologies, and explanations for the presence and nature of the nuisance primitives who momentarily blocked their progress and manifest destiny but who might ultimately have to be eradicated because, as Benjamin Franklin observed, it may be "the design of Providence to extirpate these Savages in order to make room for cultivators of the Earth."[1] Among the early "explanations" for the presence of the Native Americans: (1) They were survivors of Plato's lost continent of Atlantis. (2) They were descendants of shipwrecked Phoenician mariners. (3) They were descendants of a band of Welsh subjects who crossed the Atlantic with Prince Madoc in 1170 A.D. (4) They were descendants of the Ten Lost Tribes of Israel. The Church of Jesus Christ of Latter-day Saints retains this last belief even today.

Certainly the architectural achievements of the Aztec, Inca, and Maya, the literature of any number of tribes, the agricultural and medical achievements of divers peoples, and the political sophistication of the League of the Five Nations could scarcely be attributed to "savages" or "primitives" who were to be dispossessed of their lands. "Inferior" and "uncivilized" because they lacked property and possession concepts (Did they not share their wives and daughters with guests even as they felt all people were granted use without ownership of land by greater power than man possessed?), they nevertheless had achieved culturally desirable capacities which obviously indicated contact with men of the Judeo-Christian tradition. Logic is absent from such reasoning, but when a people con-

---

[1] Benjamin Franklin, *The Autobiography of Benjamin Franklin,* ed. Leonard W. Labaree et al. (New Haven, 1964), p. 199.

sider themselves the inheritors of someone else's earth, in perpetuity, by divine right, intellectual dishonesty demands rationalization even as it breeds almost paranoid fear that some stronger people of alien ideology and equally irrational claim is momentarily ready to dispossess them.

Until the twentieth century, speculation and controversy centered around the geographical origin of the people Columbus had mistakenly labeled "Los Indios" in 1492 and John Cabot had nomenclatured "red men" in 1497, probably after encountering the now extinct Beothuk of Newfoundland, a people about whom we know little *except* that they colored their skins with red ochre. As early as 1590, the Spanish priest José de Acosta suggested that, at some place in the unexplored North, Asia and America were joined or, at any rate, "not altogether severed and disjoined." That place is what we know as the Bering Strait—today a fifty-six-mile stretch of water between Siberia and Alaska in which the Diomedes sit like giant stepping stones so that the greatest expanse of open water is only twenty-three miles, an expanse that would be of little consequence to the most primitive sea craft. In addition, winter freezes the strait so that even today men cross on an ice bridge. However, if the majority of speculators are right, the Asian migration began during the last Ice Age, and the immigrants walked across on land that was lifted above the water by the Wisconsin Glaciation. They agree, further, that those waves of migration probably ended with the arrival of the Eskimo about 2000 years ago.

That, generally speaking, American Indians have prominent cheekbones, yellowish-brown skin, broad-headed skulls, and shovel-shaped incisors places them in the Mongoloid race. Many Indians even retain the epicanthic fold that creates the slant common to Oriental eyes. Some Indians of the Northeast and of the Plains are long-headed—not as extremely long-, narrow-headed or as beetle-browed as some of the oldest skulls yet found in America (dated at 10,000 B.C.) but more nearly like them than like their broad-headed neighbors.

Scientifically, an early chronology—still controversial but of growing validity—dates the Native American on this continent, the dates being fixed by relative or absolute dating or by a combination of the two since, happily, the estimated dates usually coincide.

About 27,000 B.C.   Santa Rosa Island dwarf mammoth bones indicate man was butchering and cooking food.

About 20,000 B.C.   Sandia Cave in New Mexico yielded Pueblo Indian artifacts at the top layer; Folsom points among the bones of ground sloth, bison, mammoth, and wolf below a layer of travertine; camel, bison, and other animal bones obviously cracked open for their marrow, ash-filled fireplaces, flint knives and scrapers, and spear points beneath a layer of yellow ochre.

About 19,500 B.C. The oldest complete skeleton yet found in the Western Hemisphere (thirty miles southwest of El Centro, California, in the Yuba Desert) indicates burial practices at that early date. The skeleton, found by amateur archaeologist Morlin Childers and carbon dated by Geochron Laboratories in Cambridge, Massachusetts, was buried in a shallow grave topped by rocks that Childers notes "had to have been placed there by man, not nature."

About 9000 B.C. Folsom Man (identified through his spear points) was hunting and killing the bison that became extinct 10,000 years ago. That the skeletal remains of the bison lacked tail bones indicates man was also skinning the animals for their hides.

"Interesting but tenuous evidence," the pragmatist and the fundamentalist demur. "And even if some primitive, uncivilized creature was on this land that long ago, so what? The inheritors of the earth in Benjamin Franklin's terms are men who early developed artistic concepts and aesthetic responses that make them superior." Their self-aggrandizing complacency may be momentarily shaken by the findings of Dr. Juan Armenta, the Mexican anthropologist who unearthed four fragments of mammoth bones near Puebla, Mexico, in 1959. Hunting scenes depicting catlike figures, mammoths, camels, and serpents of an incredible artistic skill decorate the fragments which are carbon dated at about 27,000 B.C. and may have been—no, probably were—carved on bones of freshly killed animals.

Theoretically at least, man crossed the Bering Strait as early as 30,000 years ago and had arrived at the Straits of Magellan by at least 8000 B.C., for in Fell's Cave, Chile, long-headed human skulls and charred animal bones have been carbon-14 dated to that time. And along the way, he developed his arts and crafts. Early copper work has long distinguished the Egyptians and the people of the Sinai Desert, but radiocarbon tests have pushed back the relatively arbitrary 600–700 A.D. date of the Wisconsin Old Copper Culture to about 5000 B.C., a date indicating the Native American of the time was as "civilized" as his old world counterparts. Nor was he as slow to develop his agricultural talents as the old world apologists held for many years in the absence of scientific proof. At Whitewater Creek outside Cochise, Arizona, grinding stones possibly 12,000 years old indicate a food-gathering people were grinding the seeds, berries, and roots they found around the shores of a long-vanished lake. These early mortars and pestles are stones hollowed to hold the vegetable matter which is pounded or ground with a rounded stone to create a paste or flour. And at nearby Bat Cave in New

Mexico, a cultivated species of corn has been radiocarbon dated at about 3500 B.C. Louis S. B. Leakey's 1968 excavations in California produced the oldest artifacts yet found in the Western Hemisphere. These primitive stone tools are called pebble choppers, and Leakey dated them at at least 40,000—possibly even 100,000—years old. Not that the Native American is excited or even concerned with such gamesmanship. He is content to wait until, ultimately, the white man will realize the truth of his unshakable belief: "The Creator put us here on this land. He made us from the mountains and the rivers."

What did these early Americans look like? Certainly not like the busts on Indian head pennies or buffalo nickels. Anthropologist Ernest A. Hooton is as authoritative as anyone in his 1930 "Indians of Pecos Pueblos." His basic conclusion:

At a rather remote period, probably soon after the last glacial retreat, there straggled into the New World from Asia by way of the Bering Strait groups of dolichocephals in which were blended at least three strains: one very closely allied to the fundamental brunet European and African long-headed stock called "Mediterranean"; another a more primitive form with heavy brow-ridges, low broad face and wide nose…thirdly, an element certainly Negroid (not Negro).

These people, already racially mixed, spread over the New World carrying with them a primitive fishing and hunting culture. Their coming must have preceded the occupation of eastern Asia by the presently predominantly Mongoloid peoples, since the purer types of these dolichocephals do not show the characteristic Mongoloid features.

At a somewhat later period there began to arrive in the New World groups of Mongoloids coming by the same route as their predecessors…capable of higher cultural development than the early pioneers and…responsible for the development of agriculture and for the notable achievements of the New World civilization. In some places they may have driven out and supplanted the early long-heads, but often they seem to have interbred with them producing the multiple and varied types of the present American Indians—types which are Mongoloid to a varying extent, but never purely Mongoloid. Last of all came the Eskimo, a culturally primitive Mongoloid group….

Consequently, and for comparative purposes, by the traditional date of the historically undocumented Abraham (1500 B.C.) and his immigration from Ur of the Chaldeans to Canaan, the Native Americans had been on this continent for some 20,000 years, the Algonquians arriving at the Atlantic coast as early as 7000 B.C. and there growing on religious and political paths that led to an incredibly personal and private communication between man and theological entity on the one hand, a greater but still minimal political institutionalization of loose, short-lived confederations on the other. In short, an individual awareness of needs and responsibilities solidified the group so that it was singularly free of one man's impositions on another. Neighboring Iroquoians (Cayuga, Mohawk, Oneida, Onondaga, and Seneca) were much more complex both religiously and politically, their virgin-born Dekanawidah of the Huron came among them and, possessing great spiritual power or genius, with the aid of the great orator Hiawatha, organized what can only be called a constitutional convention that produced the code beginning, "I, Dekanawidah, and the Confederate Chiefs, now uproot the tallest pine tree, and into the cavity thereby made we cast all weapons of war. Into the depths of the earth, deep down into the underearth currents of water flowing to unknown regions, we cast all weapons of strife. We bury them from sight and we plant again the tree. Thus shall the Great Peace be established."

And established it was, for Benjamin Franklin, that paragon of white wisdom and honor, was to advise the Albany Congress in 1754 to examine and heed the wisdom written into that document. Ten years earlier at the meeting of the colonial governors in Lancaster, Canasatego of the Iroquois had suggested:

Our Wise Forefathers established Union and Amity between the Five Nations. This has made us formidable; this has given us great Weight and Authority with our neighboring Nations. We are a powerful Confederacy; and by your observing the same Methods, our Wise Forefathers have taken, you will acquire such Strength and Power. Therefore whatever befalls you, never fall out with one another.[2]

Franklin reinforced that suggestion when he advised his colleagues at Albany:

It would be a strange thing if Six Nations of ignorant savages should be capable of forming a scheme for such an union, and be able to execute it in such a manner as that it has subsisted ages and appears indissoluble; and yet that a like union should be impracticable for ten or a dozen English colonies, to whom it is more necessary and must be more advantageous, and who cannot be supposed to want an equal understanding of their interests.[3]

A comparison of the Constitution of the Iroquois Confederacy and the Constitution of the United States of America serves as its own best argument for the extent to which the colonists followed European or Native American political thought. In matters

---

[2]See Walter H. Cohen and Philip L. Manle, "The Indian, the Forgotten American," *Harvard Law Review,* June, 1968, p. 1820.

[3]Quoted in Alvin M. Josephy, Jr., *The Indian Heritage of America* (New York, 1969), p. 33.

of political power for women, the colonists certainly followed European custom, but the white man is catching up in this area in the twentieth century—his primitive concept of male absolutism suffering anguishing growth pains toward civilized thought.

Far to the south in what is now Central and South America, the Maya, Inca, and Aztec rivaled "the glory that was Greece and the grandeur that was Rome" as well as the religious-political-scientific supremacy that was Egypt. Between the geographical points occupied by the Algonquians and the great architects of the South, cultures of varying degrees of development existed. The inhabitants of southern California were simple people of simple pursuits not unlike those of any people in areas where nature supplies adequate vegetable food, moderate need of protection, and little reason for elaborate political development. They concentrated on their simple art forms and the development of religions that in no way glorified war or violence—religions that were to cause them to be decimated by the Christian concept of peace on earth and good will to all men. In the Northwest, from northern California to Alaska, sea people developed rigid class and ancestor codes, while the people of the Southwest developed elaborate irrigation systems that may not have turned the deserts to lands of milk and honey but which did coax enough growth from them to cause us to consider the Gila River canals of the Hohokem among the wonders of the Western Hemisphere. The three- and four-story apartment houses they built around 1300 A.D. also attest to their engineering genius, while the desirable pima cotton grown today in Egypt was the agricultural development of their remnant survivors, the Pima, a people so peaceful they quarantined warriors who had killed in battle for sixteen days of prayer and purification. The Anasazi who lived in the area where Colorado, Arizona, Utah, and New Mexico meet were also architecturally so advanced that between 919 A.D. and 1067 A.D. they built Pueblo Bonito in the valley of the Chaco Canyon in New Mexico. Rising in terraces, its five stories contain over 800 rooms and cover more than three acres. No multi-family dwelling rivaled it until the 1880s when an apartment house in New York City outsized it. Pueblo Bonito is only one of a dozen such houses in the valley, and each has its own chapel—the "kiva," a circular room with roof access where prayers were offered up. The Great Plains people (Siouan, Caddoan, Cheyenne, Arapaho, Comanche) fought the intrusive, land-hungry white man so fiercely and bravely that they are popularly held to be the bloodthirsty savages of John Wayne motion pictures, but when war is a way of life, heroes to their own people are vicious killers to their enemies—that's what makes them heroes. Hunting, personal valor, and honor were paramount to these people with their stringent family protection codes that required a young man to remain single until he had distinguished himself for his people and to take all his wife's sisters into his home and care for all his brothers' or cousins' widows as his own wives. The people of the Southeast (Cherokees, Creeks, Seminoles) built temples to the sun, established strong political alliances, and achieved in a few years what Europeans had taken centuries to accomplish. Disproving any notion that the Native American lacks adaptability when he desires to adapt, the Cherokees foreswore fighting in 1788, learned the techniques of farming, formed a republic with a written constitution, courts, bicameral legislature, and police force. Sequoia is credited with inventing a syllabary that allowed the language to be written. However, Traveller Bird, descendant of Sequoia, asserts in his study, *Tell Them They Lie*, that the syllabary had long existed in the custody of the Scribes of the Seven Clans and was merely taught to the people by Sequoia, who was horribly disfigured by Cherokee puppets as punishment. At any rate, the Cherokees established a printing press and a newspaper and achieved literacy in an incredibly short time. Gold was discovered on their lands sometime before 1830 and the Indian Removal Act resulted in the Trail of Tears. When U.S. Supreme Court Chief Justice John Marshall ruled that the State of Georgia had no right to abrogate the treaty rights of Indians who could, therefore, continue to occupy their land, President Andrew Jackson supported the ultimate law of the land with his infamous pronouncement, "John Marshall has made his decision: now let him enforce it."

In all, the Native Americans were an ancient people with an infinite variety of cultural patterns. In 1492, they numbered an estimated one million in what is now the continental United States; their present number is impossible to authenticate. Of the people encountered by Columbus and other Europeans, some half a million are special charges of the Government of the United States. The number of non-tribal, non-reservation Native Americans is impossible to estimate because the U.S. census lists them as white along with the six million Mexican-Americans and Spanish-Americans— many of whom were officially Indians in Mexico. The Puerto Rican, certainly, has Native American blood, and one of every three American Negroes, according to the studies of Melville J. Herskovits,[4] is part Native American, a confusion exemplified in the person of

[4]See *The American Negro* (New York, 1928) and *The Myth of the Negro Past* (New York, 1951).

Crispus Attucks, the first person killed in the Boston Massacre of March 5, 1770. A slave owned by William Brown of Framingham, Massachusetts, he had escaped in 1750. The *Boston Gazette* advertisement for his return read: "Ran away from his master William Brown of Framingham, on the 30th of September last, a Mulatto Fellow, about 27 Years of Age, named Crispas...." His surname, Attucks, belonged to his Indian mother and means "small deer."

The policy of termination has raised the necessity of identifying the American Indian; yet, it has merely focused attention on America's inability to see her most invisible man. The California State Senate Interim Committee on Indian Affairs held meetings in 1954 to determine the effect of certain bills pending in the United States Congress. California Senator A. W. Way asked Sacramento Area Director of the Bureau of Indian Affairs, Leonard M. Hill: "What is the proper definition of an Indian who will come under this act?"

Leonard M. Hill's reply:

To answer that, Senator, there is no definition contemplated under this act. I think that I mentioned at Redding the other day that the government itself has that question before it, trying to find some definition of an Indian. There was a bill presented to Congress last session which made a definition that anyone with less than half-blood was not an Indian and would not be entitled to any services. They are still talking about it in the Department of Interior, and in the congressional committees, as to how to define an Indian...and it is not possible under our multiplicity of laws and regulations to define it. You have to look to the purpose for which you're trying to define an Indian...; for some purposes...he must be a quarter-blood and live on trust land. For educational purposes...he must be a quarter-blood or more....I just don't think there is any definition that you can give to an Indian....He is an Indian for some purposes and for other purposes he isn't an Indian, so there just isn't any clear definition.

SENATOR WAY: I think that we should have a definition of an Indian who would come within this act.

MR. HILL: Well, sir, a definition in...the act defines a tribe or group of Indians and I believe it states those Indians who reside on or have an interest in trust property.

SENATOR WAY: I still don't know what is a person who is described as an Indian....

MR. HILL: I am sorry. I cannot make a definition....We in the Indian Bureau are concerned with it also. We don't know how to define an Indian.[5]

At least the U.S. Immigration and Naturalization Service knows how to deal with the problem, however. It recommends a

[5]*Progress Report to the Legislature by the Senate Interim Committee on Indian Affairs* (Sacramento: California State Senate, 1955), pp. 241–42, 407–08.

pamphlet, "Twenty-five Lessons in Citizenship" by D. L. Hennessey, to all persons filing applications to become U.S. citizens in California. Printed in Berkeley in 1969, the pamphlet contains this succinct history of the 30,000 years of Native American accomplishment:

A few hundred years ago there were no white people in this country. The only inhabitants of the United States were the Indians. These Indians usually lived in small bands and wandered about from place to place. They lived mostly by hunting and fishing. They were often quarrelsome. Some of the different tribes or bands had settled homes and were partly civilized, but most of them were wandering savages who did nothing to develop this great country.

Art and architecture, music, the world's food supply, cotton, tobacco, at least fifty-nine major drugs, social, philosophical, and political concepts, child psychology, games—the list is endless. Only Mr. Hennessey's pamphlet is limited.

To define the Native American is as impossible as it is to define the Jew—for many of the same reasons. However, just as a Jew knows he is a Jew because he recognizes himself within the framework of an historical-cultural setting that allows him identity, the Native American, the Indian, the Navajo—call him what you will—knows he is an Indian because the mystic tie to the land, the dim memory of his people's literature that has been denied him, the awareness of his relationship to Sakoiatison, Manitou, Huaca, Wakan (depending on his being Iroquois, Algonquian, Inca, or Sioux) somehow all manifest themselves within him and consistently call him back to his ancestors. The white man may have forced an alien concept of "the Great Spirit" on the Native American's ancestors, but—like most of them—he does not associate it with human realities and he dismisses it from daily considerations.

In the vast body of his religious literature, pre-Columbian poetry, oratory, political documents, autobiographical literature, white forms, and voices of protest, he hears that sum total of spiritual power of his people—Orenda—or that collective awareness William Butler Yeats called *spiritus mundi*, Carl Jung called the collective unconscious, and Sigmund Freud called racial memory. And, in some few schools, colleges, and universities in America, his white neighbor is beginning to hear it too, for he is disillusioned with his religious institutions, his destructive land policies, his shattered *hubris*, and his fragmented identity. Seeing American Indian literature for the first time as the great cultural and philosophical riches it has always been, he is asking for—even demanding—courses that will help him read, understand, and utilize that literature for whatever truths it contains for him. It is our hope this book will lead him to some of those truths; it is our hope his own heritage has not damaged him so badly that he cannot hear truths.

When a man is ashamed of his heritage, ashamed of the large group that encompasses him whether or not he feels a part of it, he is, indeed, alienated. He can, through renunciation of his citizenship in one country and naturalization in another, exchange national allegiance; but he cannot doff his old heritage, don a new one. If he was not born Irish, he cannot become Irish; he can only so identify with the Irish that he allies himself with them. Always his heritage will betray him in a moment of cultural crisis. But birth is not necessarily the natal moment; it is also the moment of awareness of allegiance beyond intellectual choice. LaDonna Harris, Comanche, summarized that allegiance when, speaking to a group of students at the University of South Florida on May 4, 1972, she was asked to define the Indian. She said, "I can't define the Indian for you anymore than you can define what you are. Different governmental agencies define him by amount of blood. I had a Comanche mother and an Irish father. But I am Comanche. I'm not Irish. And I'm not Indian *first*. I'm Comanche first, Indian second. When the Comanche took in someone, he became Comanche. He wasn't part this, part that. He was *all* Comanche or he wasn't Comanche at all. Blood runs the heart. The *heart* knows what it is."

In a rather curious way, the United States Department of Health, Education and Welfare agrees. In a recent case[6] the U.S. District Court for Middle Florida had ordered Flagler County schools integrated by August 7, 1970. The school board argued it did not know what the terms "race" and "ethnic origin" meant. HEW issued this definition: "Negro: Persons considered by themselves, by the school, or by the community to be of African or Negro origin." It issued similar qualifications to identify American Indians, Orientals, Mexican-Americans, and others.

At least by HEW standards, anyone can be white or Indian or Chicano if he, the school, or the community so considers him. Nor, seemingly, do all three entities have to agree. It is doubtful that many Native Americans will consider themselves white. We have too much difficulty with draft boards and schools now, for if we are non-reservation Indians, we may be either "black" or "white" in those little boxes demanding a statement of race. We are not allowed to be "American Indians." At least, not by the unique laws governing those

[6]See UPI release, New Orleans, March 30, 1972, in *The Tampa Tribune*, Tampa, Florida, March 30, 1972, p. 11A, cols. 1–2.

little boxes. And we don't care for either of the two choices granted us. When we refuse to use either, the box is filled in for us. We become "white," for to be "black" would qualify us for certain scholarship privileges accorded only the black minority. Therefore, we are white. The confusion, however, is not ours. We know who and what we are. And the knowledge does not come from blood or legislation or a school or community's consideration. In LaDonna Harris's words, it comes from "the heart" and "the heart knows what it is."

One of the ways it learned is recorded in this book. It listened to a collective voice. And that voice spoke the word. And the word is magic. At least it is magic enough to give the Native American identity. In this century, that is potent magic indeed.

Chapter 1

Pre-Columbian Religions: From Wah'kon-tah, the Great Mystery...

"Civilized man" seems a curious creature to the "primitive man" who would not willingly trade places with him because the resultant loss would be too great. In process of becoming civilized, man must learn to surpass other animals—which accounts for his developing tools that give him physical equality or superiority—but the nature of his intellect is such that he then begins to assume *he* is a superior creature because he begins to rationalize the power of his instruments into being his own power. He does not see his technological achievements as merely *artificial* extensions of himself; he becomes so dependent on them that they seem to be *actual* extensions. Then, having become equal or superior to the creatures he originally sought merely to survive among, he begins to see them as inferior creatures and makes a distinction between himself and them. They are the "brutes"; he is "man." In his irrational logic, he *is* superior because he has an instinct for aggression beyond survival, an intellectually developed killer instinct. That the loss of his technological instruments would reduce him to a weaker state and lesser position than he originally held seems not to occur to him. Perhaps he dare not let it occur.

With his arbitrary distinction between brutes and men, he begins to attempt domination not only of the creatures in their environment (that total natural backdrop against which all things live out their brief lives) but also of the environment itself. From weaker animal with limited possibilities of survival, he progresses to equalized animal with equal chances of survival, continues to technologically superior animal with a developed instinct for using technologically inferior animals, and arrives at a point where "use" becomes "deserved luxury." This rationalization allows him the "right" to wasteful excess, to brutal conduct, to deliberate abuse of the environment he cannot escape, cannot change beyond whatever laws or intelligence govern it. Yet he cannot live happily in this environment because he has separated himself from its essence with a wall of technological, artificial, self-weakening tools that extend him beyond his physical capacities as a unique entity, blur his vision of self without extensions, and make him dependent on those created elements that make the natural world in which he earlier found himself inimical to him because his extensions damage it.

Cut off from a natural response to it, he cannot generate a natural response to his created world; and he spins out his days in a limbo of discontent, ease, and frustration. Life becomes a mystery that must be solved with unassailable logic leading to unequivocal answers. And he becomes so unaware of himself in relation to the original environment he has lost that the questions he is forced to pose concern themselves with his self-created world, itself a phantasmagoria clouding the face of the natural world he has lost. When he reads his poets, he feels vaguely disquieted, for, like Gerard Manley Hopkins, they tell him that "the dearest freshness deep down things" still exists but he cannot feel it, his "foot being shod."[1] Truth seems to reside in the assertion, but it is truth he dare not understand for he cannot act on it except he lose that artificial, created world that has become his only reality.

When William Butler Yeats tells him a "voice out of *Spiritus Mundi*"[2] speaks, he nervously acknowledges the intellectual possibility but rejects the emotional possibility because it is as unnerving as that Jungian concept of the "collective unconscious" or the Freudian "racial memory," both of which suggest the primordial pull of the totality of man, and he has lost identification with that corporate body, for it consists, in part, of the soil beneath the cement on which his temporary home rests. It reminds him of his learned response of condescension to nomadic, waste-prowling ancestors seeking survival in a hostile world. Nor does he recognize the analogy between his life and theirs, for to do so would necessitate his realization that they adapted to their world, that he cannot adapt to the one

[1]"God's Grandeur."
[2]"The Second Coming."

he adapted to himself. All he can do is create endless dreams that tomorrow will be better because he is evolving toward some ultimate utopia. After all, is he not superior to the primitive who retains that tie with the technologically unimproved world?

Ambition to achieve an indefinable goal drives him relentlessly, and he studies the primitive as if he were the alien creature on earth and might contain the secret to civilized man's present dilemma. That *civilized* man can never know the spiritual peace that comes from the unquestioning acceptance of the belief: "That which the children of the Earth do not comprehend as they travel the roads of the Earth and which becomes clear to them only when they have passed on to the great mysteries in Wah'kon-tah."

This statement, couched in different forms, is at the heart of most Native American religions—those religions that flourished in the Western Hemisphere before the intrusion of Judeo-Christianity, that survived its imposition, that co-mingled with it, and that have resurfaced as Judeo-Christianity weakens and undergoes social transformation in the United States today. It is a belief that cannot be equated with the Judeo-Christian acceptance inherent in "Thy will be done on Earth as it is in Heaven," for that acceptance presupposes an imposition of a divine will embodied in an infinite intelligence beyond man's comprehension, therefore conceivable only as finite. The resultant theological relationship is of God to man, but the god is anthropomorphic in emotional conception because the intellectual conception of a disembodied will is beyond the abstracting powers of most men.

It has been stated by a plethora of commentators that the Native American lacks the power of abstraction, that he sees things only in concrete, realistic terms; yet the concept of Wah'kon-tah (or Sakoiatison or Wakonda or Nesaru or Awonawilona or Manito—there are many names among various peoples but they all mean the same thing) is so great an abstraction that the non-Indian has seldom been able to grasp the concept. It is "the Great Mystery," somewhat akin to Ralph Waldo Emerson's concept of the Over-Soul, that transcendental concept derived from Eastern mysticism and chronically misunderstood by American literature students, completely unfamiliar to the great mass of Americans: "The soul knows only the soul; the web of events is the flowing robe in which she is clothed....One made of the divine teaching is the incarnation of the spirit in a form,—in forms, like my own. I live in society; with persons who answer to thoughts in my own mind, or express a certain obedience to the great instincts to which I live. I see its presence in them, I am certified of a common nature; and these other souls, these separated selves, draw me as nothing else can."[3] In "Brahma," Emerson was to come perhaps a little closer to the concept of Wah'kon-tah than he had ten years earlier in the revision of "The Over-Soul." A statement of Brahma, the Hindu supreme soul of the universe—the essence of being, uncreated, illimitable, timeless—the poem includes the lines, "When me they fly, I am the wings;/I am the doubter and the doubt." That is an approximation of the idea—at least as close an approximation as a Judeo-Christian in the European tradition has come. It lacks the essential quality of Wah'kon-tah, however, for that quality is totality, allness, inseparability. "The doubter *and* the doubt" implies a sundering, a cutting away, a lack of cohesive oneness because the parts are distinguishable. The Christian concept of the trinity of Elohim, Christ, and Holy Ghost seems beyond even the devout fundamentalist as he flounders in the references to the Holy Spirit's descending on Christ when John baptized him or the forlorn cry of the crucified Christ, "My God, My God, why hast thou forsaken me?"

Wah'kon-tah is the sum total of all things, the collective totality that always was—without beginning, without end. Neither a force nor a spirit, it is the inexplicable sharing-togetherness that makes all things, animate and inanimate, of equal value, equal importance, and equal consequence because they are all Wah'kon-tah simultaneously, their forms collectively creating the form of Wah'kon-tah which is, obviously, incapable of being anthropomorphized.

Huhuseca-ska (White Bone), Zintkala Maza (Iron Bird), and Mato-nažin (Standing Bear) assert there are two kinds of songs: "songs made by man, and songs that come in dreams or in visions through the spirits from Wakan-Tanka." Those from the Great Mystery "have power to work wonders." Further, "Everything that has life has spirit as well as fleshly form. All things have *nagi*—soul. Rocks and animals have the power to appear in the form of man, and to speak to man in dream or in vision. It is from Wakan-Tanka that they have power and wisdom."[4]

Natalie Curtis in her dedication to recording the literature and music of the American Indian cannot be faulted. Her understanding was, beyond question, incredible. Yet her footnote to this passage reads, "Thus the Indian learns from nature, from the animals, and from elemental forces, whose power to teach him is from the Supreme Being." Even such a sincere, dedicated scholar-humanitarian as Miss Curtis could not escape the Judeo-Christian concept of a

[3]"The Over-Soul" from the 1887 edition of *Essays.*
[4]"Songs of the Dakotas," *The Indians' Book,* ed. Natalie Curtis (New York, 1968), pp. 60–61.

limited, anthropomorphic, Jehovah-like deity or, at least, a Zeus-like god. That widespread failure among white people had, much earlier, debased the idea into the words "Great Spirit," a phenomenon noted by Miss Curtis in an introductory essay, "The Holy Man, or 'Medicine-Man.'"

The English word "medicine" has come to be applied to what the Dakota Indian calls *wakan*. Wakan means both mystery and holiness, and is used by the Indian to designate all that is sacred, mysterious, spiritual, or supernatural.

The Supreme Being of the Dakotas is called Wakan-Tanka. In English this name is commonly rendered "The Great Spirit," but it would be translated more correctly as "The Great Holy-Mystery."

Wakan-Tanka is an omniscient force. This conception of an impersonal, spiritual, and life-giving power is held by many Indian tribes as well as by the Dakotas, and would seem in no way to be a product of early missionary teaching, but rather an intense and integral part of the Indian's nature. Besides the Great Mystery, the Indians recognize lesser spiritual beings who are personifications of certain elements in nature, in animals, and in man; but these, like all else, owe their existence and their power to the Supreme One.[5]

If such an Indian-oriented white person as this remarkable women could not understand the complete abstracting process that is at the heart of such a basic, animistic belief, it is not strange that the fervor of the ghost dances so mystified the American white man that he released all his resultant frustration at Wounded Knee.

Wah'kon-tah is not a "Supreme One" any more than the Greek Moira is a supreme being. If you will recall, Moira is "the necessary connection of things," an English-synonym-defying concept. Even the gods were subject to Moira but Moira willed nothing; Moira was the inevitability factor that all things working in equal cosmic importance could not escape, for the interrelatedness of all things created the necessity of choice in their responses to life situations and those choices established the pattern of their fate or destiny.

Such is the nature of the Great Mystery, Wah'kon-tah. The "spiritual beings who are personifications of certain elements in nature, in animals, and in man" are neither more nor less hierarchical elements under the domination of Wah'kon-tah than are the lesser divine beings called angels and named Satan, Gabriel, Michael, etc., under the rule of Jehovah. Wah'kon-tah is not, however, the personifiable deity as is Elohim. All things exist *in* Wah'kon-tah and Wah'kon-tah exists *in* all things.

In 1871, Sir Edward Tylor, professor of anthropology at Oxford, propounded the theory that Animism is the minimum defi-

[5]Ibid., p. 32.

nition of religion because all religions begin in Animism. The ensuing arguments are of no concern here. His statement is:

It seems as though thinking men, as yet at a low level of culture, were deeply impressed by two groups of biological problems. In the first place, what is it that makes the difference between a living body and a dead one; what causes waking, sleep, trance, disease, death? In the second place, what are those human shapes which appear in dreams and visions? Looking at these two groups of phenomena, the ancient savage philosophers probably made their first step by the obvious inference that every man has two things belonging to him, namely, a life and a phantom. These two are evidently in close connexion with the body, the life as enabling it to feel and think and act, the phantom as being its image or second self; both, also, are perceived to be things separable from the body, the life as being able to go away and leave it insensible or dead, the phantom as appearing to people at a distance from it....

It is a thin unsubstantial human image, in its nature a sort of vapour, film, or shadow; the cause of life and thought in the individual it animates; independently possessing the personal consciousness and volition of its corporeal owner, past or present; capable of leaving the body far behind, to flash swiftly from place to place; mostly impalpable and invisible, yet also manifesting physical power, and especially appearing to men waking or asleep as a phantasm separate from the body of which it bears the likeness; continuing to exist and appear to men after the death of that body; able to enter into, possess, and act in the bodies of other men, of animals, and even of things.[6]

Tylor's concept of the phantom was apparent in the two movements in the Ghost Dance Religion under Tàvibo (1870) and Wovoka (1890) even though the prophets had been strongly influenced by the messianic teachings of Christianity and spoke of God rather than the Great Mystery. That the Wakan objects (the medicine bundles, ceremonial peace pipes, and sacred body paint) were everywhere in evidence suggests the rigid tie to Wah'kon-tah. Even those tribes such as the Navajo who refused to participate in the Ghost Dance did not refuse because they lacked belief in the ghost. Rather, like the Pueblo, they believed that to look upon the faces of the dead (either the corporeal body or the ghost) meant sudden death to the beholder.

Body, spirit, ghost—the three components of animistic man. The body is its animation, an animation that resides elsewhere than among men when the body returns to grass but which may return to the living as a nonphysical entity or ghost under certain desirable or undesirable circumstances. The spirit is the "life breath" that is the Great Mystery—not separated from it at any time, but *it* inexhaustibly, *it* undiminished, *it* undiminishing.

[6]Cited in *Man, Myth & Magic*, Vol. 1, ed. Richard Cavendish (New York, 1970), p. 94.

Ohiyesa (Dr. Charles Alexander Eastman) attempted, in several books, to explain some aspects of the religious beliefs and conduct of the Indian, especially among his own Dakota. In *The Soul of the Indian,* he distinguishes between the spirit (which is Wah'kon-tah) and the ghost (which is that recallable aspect of man):

I recall a touching custom among us, which was designed to keep the memory of the departed near and warm in the bereaved household. A lock of hair of the beloved dead was wrapped in pretty clothing, such as it was supposed that he or she would like to wear if living. This "spirit bundle," as it was called, was suspended from a tripod, and occupied a certain place in the lodge which was the place of honor. At every meal time, a dish of food was placed under it, and some person of the same sex and age as the one who was gone must afterward be invited in to partake of the food. At the end of a year from the time of death, the relatives made a public feast and gave away the clothing and other gifts, while the lock of hair was interred with appropriate ceremonies.

Certainly the Indian never doubted the immortal nature of the spirit or soul of man, but neither did he care to speculate upon its probable state or condition in a future life. The idea of a "happy hunting-ground" is modern and probably borrowed, or invented by the white man. The primitive Indian was content to believe that the spirit which the "Great Mystery" breathed into man returns to Him who gave it, and that after it is freed from the body, it is everywhere and pervades all nature, yet often lingers near the grave or "spirit bundle" for the consolation of friends, and is able to hear prayers. So much of reverence was due the disembodied spirit, that it was not customary with us even to name the dead aloud.[7]

Unfortunately, Ohiyesa knew that the capacity of the white Christian is limited, that "They spoke much of spiritual things, while seeking only the material," a realization that led him to conclude:

It is my personal belief, after thirty-five years' experience of it, that there is no such thing as "Christian civilization." I believe that Christianity and modern civilization are opposed and irreconcilable, and that the spirit of Christianity and of our ancient religion is essentially the same.[8]

The Great Mystery, that animistic concept, pervades all of the creation accounts in some way though they differ in many respects as a result of the cultural history and the geographical location of the various Native Americans. Such variation should not trouble the average Judeo-Christian who has grown up with two distinct and seemingly irreconcilable accounts of creation in his own religious book. Unfortunately, he is not often conversant with Genesis

[7]Charles Alexander Eastman, *The Soul of the Indian* (Boston, 1911), pp. 154–56.
[8]Ibid., p. 24.

nor very clear about his religious beliefs beyond vague generalities. Unable to recount the incidents of his own religion, he becomes remarkably pragmatic about another man's, insisting on consistency, denigrating the poetic, metaphoric, mistily historic account because it is not ordered in that logical pattern he has been taught to expect of material presented for instant assimilation.

Happily, not all white Americans are so limited. Any number (among them such speculative fiction authors as Robert Silverberg, Arthur C. Clarke, and Robert Heinlein) think they see very distant history recorded in the accounts among various tribes of "star people," "sky dwellers," and "Havmusuvs (Little People)" who came to earth in "flying boats." The motives of these authors are not in question, for their concern for all men is apparent in their work; their respect for the religious belief of the Native American is obvious. Perhaps Ohiyesa's words of caution are pertinent here:

There are to be found here and there superficial accounts of strange customs and ceremonies, of which the symbolism or inner meaning was largely hidden from the observer; and there has been a great deal of material collected in recent years which is without value because it is modern and hybrid, inextricably mixed with Biblical legend and Caucasian philosophy. Some of it has even been invented for commercial purposes. Give a reservation Indian a present, and he will possibly provide you with sacred songs, a mythology, and folk-lore to order![9]

Or perhaps George Bird Grennell's admonition is more to the point:

It is not easy for a white man, unless he has had some special training, to place himself on a level with the Indian, and learn how he thinks. Yet this must be done before we can understand him. To fully comprehend him, the investigator must cast aside all that he has been taught, and all that he has absorbed since childhood, must cease to be *artificial* and become *natural*. If one takes part with them in their daily lives, listening to the solemn prayers which they offer when they light the pipe, and joining with eye, ear and voice in the conversation that passes between those who form the circle, he (the white man) will gain an insight into a life and a method of thought that he did not suppose existed![10]

Whether the religious accounts of any people are "attempts to explain the inexplicable" or dim, racial memories oral transmission has embellished poetically into metaphor, the obvious similarities and comparative features remain and can, viewed intel-

[9]Ibid., pp. xi–xii.
[10]*Indians of Today.* Cited by George Hunt Williamson in *Road in the Sky* (London, 1959), p. 207.

ligently, help the reader understand his response to his own religion's accounts.

      It might be well to reflect for one moment on the nature of Judeo-Christianity and its concept of God. Most Christians blithely assert their religion is monotheistic, most other religions are polytheistic. Asked to define *monotheism,* they respond immediately, "Having one god." Asked what Satan and Michael and Gabriel are, they are somewhat at a loss, for those minor divinities are obviously immortal, Elohim himself lacking the power to kill them. Judeo-Christianity has more than one god. But it is, nevertheless, monotheistic. By definition, monotheism is the belief that only one "first cause" or "prime mover" existed without being created, that the first cause brought all other things into existence. Elohim existed. He created Satan and the other angels, man, other animals, and so on. The divine nature of Satan et al. does not make Judeo-Christianity any less monotheistic. Polytheism, on the other hand, holds no "first cause" or "prime mover" responsible for the lesser gods. The Greeks, for instance, were polytheistic because the gods simply came into existence through a process of interrelationships, the major pantheon being the offspring of earlier gods.

      The Native American religions encountered by the white man were every bit as monotheistic as is Judeo-Christianity and, perhaps, more subtle, more complex in that Wah'kon-tah is incapable of being anthropomorphized as is Elohim who created man in his own image. Wah'kon-tah lacks image, being all things. The European's lack of capacity to abstract to that degree, however, caused him to assume the Native American was polytheistic, his religious tenets barbaric and uncivilized. Nothing can be done about the barbaric ignorance of the conquering hordes, but a compounding of their narrowness and stupidity is unforgivable.

      The Native American creation accounts presented here are exemplary of the various religious beliefs of the people of the dawn. It is not necessary to *understand* them (unless you *understand* the Judeo-Christian accounts) for they are a part of Wah'kon-tah. The insights and methods of thought they offer will give the unbiased reader a new dimension in his life. For the reader who seeks to reduce them to the level of "mythology" that his own religious accounts remain the only "true" impartings, the Great Mystery will only become more mysterious—the loss great to both the reader and Wah'kon-tah.

The Cheyenne Account
of How
the World Was Made

as told by Mary Little Bear Inkanish

In the beginning there was nothing, and Maheo, the All Spirit, lived in the void. He looked around him, but there was nothing to see. He listened, but there was nothing to hear. There was only Maheo, alone in nothingness.

Because of the greatness of his Power, Maheo was not lonesome. His being was a Universe. But as he moved through the endless time of nothingness, it seemed to Maheo that his Power should be put to use. What good is Power, Maheo asked himself, if it is not used to make a world and people to live in it?

With his Power, Maheo created a great water, like a lake, but salty. Out of this salty water, Maheo knew, he could bring all life that ever was to be. The lake itself was life, if Maheo so commanded it. In the darkness of nothingness, Maheo could feel the coolness of the water and taste on his lips the tang of the salt.

"There should be water beings," Maheo told his Power. And so it was. First the fish, swimming in the deep water, and then the mussels and snails and crawfish, lying on the sand and mud Maheo had formed so his lake should have a bottom.

Let us also create something that lives on the water, Maheo thought to his Power.

And so it was. For now there were snow geese and mallards and teal and coots and terns and loons living and swimming about on the water's surface. Maheo could hear the splashing of their feet and the flapping of their wings in the darkness.

I should like to see the things that have been created, Maheo decided.

And, again, so it was. Light began to grow and spread, first white and bleached in the east, then golden and strong till it filled the middle of the sky and extended all around the horizon. Maheo watched the light, and he saw the birds and fishes, and the shellfish lying on the bottom of the lake as the light showed them to him.

How beautiful it all is, Maheo thought in his heart.

Then the snow goose paddled over to where she thought Maheo was, in the space above the lake. "I do not see You, but I know that You exist," the goose began. "I do not know where You are, but I know You must be everywhere. Listen to me, Maheo. This is good water that You have made, on which we live. But birds are not like fish. Sometimes we get tired swimming. Sometimes we would like to get out of the water."

"Then fly," said Maheo, and he waved his arms, and all the water birds flew, skittering along the surface of the lake until they had speed enough to rise in the air. The skies were darkened with them.

"How beautiful their wings are in the light," Maheo said to his Power, as the birds wheeled and turned, and became living patterns against the sky.

The loon was the first to drop back to the surface of the lake. "Maheo," he said, looking around, for he knew that Maheo was all about him, "You have made us sky and light to fly in, and You have made us water to swim in. It sounds ungrateful to want something else, yet still we do. When we are tired of swimming and tired of flying, we should like a dry solid place where we could walk and rest. Give us a place to build our nests, please, Maheo."

"So be it," answered Maheo, "but to make such a place I must have your help, all of you. By myself, I have made four things: the water, the light, the sky air, and the peoples of the water. Now I must have help if I am to create more, for my Power will only let me make four things by myself."

"Tell us how we can help You," said all the water peoples. "We are ready to do what You say."

Maheo stretched out his hand and beckoned. "Let the biggest and the swiftest try to find land first," he said, and the snow goose came to him.

"I am ready to try," the snow goose said, and she drove herself along the water until the white wake behind her grew and grew to a sharp white point that drove her up into the air as the feathers drive an arrow. She flew high into the sky, until she was only a dark spot against the clearness of the light. Then the goose turned, and down she plunged, faster than any arrow, and dived into the water. She pierced the surface with her beak as if it were the point of a spear.

The snow goose was gone a long time. Maheo counted to four four hundred times before she rose to the surface of the water and lay there floating, her beak half open as she gasped for air.

"What have you brought us?" Maheo asked her, and the snow goose sighed sadly, and answered, "Nothing. I brought nothing back."

Then the loon tried, and after him, the mallard. Each in turn rose until he was a speck against the light, and turned and dived with the speed of a flashing arrow into the water. And each in turn rose wearily, and wearily answered, "Nothing," when Maheo asked him what he had brought.

At last there came the little coot, paddling across the surface of the water very quietly, dipping his head sometimes to catch a tiny fish, and shaking the water beads from his scalp lock whenever he rose.

"Maheo," the little coot said softly, "when I put my head beneath the water, it seems to me that I see something there, far below. Perhaps I can swim down to it—I don't know. I can't fly or dive like my sister and brothers. All I can do is swim, but I will swim down the best I know how, and go as deep as I can. May I try, please, Maheo?"

"Little brother," said Maheo, "no man can do more than his best, and I have asked for the help of all the water peoples. Certainly you shall try. Perhaps swimming will be better than diving, after all. Try, little brother, and see what you can do."

"Hah-ho!" the little coot said. "Thank you, Maheo," and he put his head under the water and swam down and down and down and down, until he was out of sight.

The coot was gone a long, long, long, long time, Then Maheo and the other birds could see a little dark spot beneath the water's surface, slowly rising toward them. It seemed as if they would never see the coot himself, but at last the spot began to have a shape. Still it rose and rose, and at last Maheo and the water peoples could surely see who it was. The little coot was swimming up from the bottom of the salty lake.

When the coot reached the surface, he stretched his closed beak upward into the light, but he did not open it.

"Give me what you have brought," Maheo said, and the coot let his beak fall open, so a little ball of mud could fall from his tongue into Maheo's hand, for when Maheo wanted to, he could become like a man.

"Go, little brother," Maheo said. "Thank you, and may what you have brought always protect you."

And so it was and so it is, for the coot's flesh still tastes of mud, and neither man nor animal will eat a coot unless there is nothing else to eat.

Maheo rolled the ball of mud between the palms of his hands, and it began to grow larger, until there was almost too much mud for Maheo to hold. He looked around for a place to put the mud, but there was nothing but water or air anywhere around him.

"Come and help me again, water peoples," Maheo called. "I must put this mud somewhere. One of you must let me place it on his back."

All the fish and all the other water creatures came swimming to Maheo, and he tried to find the right one to carry the mud. The mussels and snails and crawfish were too small, although they all had solid backs, and they lived too deep in the water for the mud to rest on them. The fish were too narrow, and their back fins stuck up through the mud and cut it to pieces. Finally only one water person was left.

"Grandmother Turtle," Maheo asked, "do you think that you can help me?"

"I'm very old and very slow, but I will try," the turtle answered. She swam over to Maheo, and he piled the mud on her rounded back, until he had made a hill. Under Maheo's hands the hill grew and spread and flattened out, until the Grandmother Turtle was hidden from sight.

"So be it," Maheo said once again. "Let the earth be known as our Grandmother, and let the Grandmother who carries the earth be the only being who is at home beneath the water, or within the earth, or above the ground; the only one who can go anywhere by swimming or by walking as she chooses."

And so it was, and so it is. Grandmother Turtle and all her descendants must walk very slowly, for they carry the whole weight of the whole world and all its peoples on their backs.

Now there was earth as well as water, but the earth was barren. And Maheo said to his Power, "Our Grandmother Earth is like a woman; she should be fruitful. Let her begin to bear life. Help me, my Power."

When Maheo said that, trees and grass sprang up to become the Grandmother's hair. The flowers became her bright ornaments, and the fruits and the seeds were the gifts that the earth offered back to Maheo. The birds came to rest on her hands when they were tired, and the fish came close to her sides. Maheo looked at the Earth Woman and he thought she was very beautiful; the most beautiful thing he had made so far.

She should not be alone, Maheo thought. Let me give her something of myself, so she will know that I am near her and that I love her.

Maheo reached into his right side, and pulled out a rib bone. He breathed on the bone, and laid it softly on the bosom of the Earth Woman. The bone moved and stirred, stood upright and walked. The first man had come to be.

"He is alone with the Grandmother Earth as I once was alone with the void," said Maheo. "It is not good for anyone to be alone." So Maheo fashioned a human woman from his left rib, and set her with the man. Then there were two persons on the Grandmother Earth, her children and Maheo's. They were happy together, and Maheo was happy as he watched them.

After a year, in the springtime, the first child was born. As the years passed, there were other children. They went their ways, and founded many tribes.

From time to time, after that, Maheo realized that his people walking on the earth had certain needs. At those times, Maheo, with the help of his Power, created animals to feed and care for the people. He gave them deer for clothing and food, porcupines to make their ornaments, the swift antelopes on the open plains, and the prairie dogs that burrowed in the earth.

At last Maheo thought to his Power, Why, one animal can take the place of all the others put together, and then he made the buffalo.

Maheo is still with us. He is everywhere, watching all his people, and all the creation he has made. Maheo is all good and all life; he is the creator, the guardian, and the teacher. We are all here because of Maheo.

The Ojibwa Account
of the
Origin of the Indians

Sikas'sigé, one of the officiating priests of the Midē' society of the Ojibwa at White Earth, Minnesota, gives the following explanation of Fig. 1, which is a reduced copy of a pictorial representation of a tradition explaining the origin of the Indians:

In the beginning, Ki'tshi Man'idō—Dzhe Man'idō (a)—made the Midē' Man'idōs. He first created two men (b and c) and two women (d and e), but they had no power of thought or reason. Then Dzhe Man'idō made them reasoning beings. He then took them in his hands so that they should multiply; he paired them, and from this sprung the Indians. Then, when there were people, he placed them upon the earth; but he soon observed that they were subject to sickness, misery, and death, and that unless he provided them with the sacred medicine they would soon become extinct.

Between the position occupied by Dzhe Man'idō and the earth were four lesser spirits, f, g, h, and i, with whom Dzhe Man'idō decided to commune, and to impart the mysteries by which the Indians could be benefited; so he first spoke to a spirit at f, and told him all he had to say, who in turn communicated the same information to g, and he in turn to h, who also communed with i. Then they all met in council and determined to call in the four wind gods at j, k, l, and m. After consulting as to what would be best for the comfort and welfare of the Indians, these spirits agreed to ask Dzhe Man'idō to communicate the mystery of the sacred medicine to the people.

Dzhe Man'idō then went to the Sun Spirit (o) and asked him to go to the earth and instruct the people as had been decided upon by the council. The Sun Spirit, in the form of a little boy, went to the earth and lived with a woman (p) who had a little boy of her own.

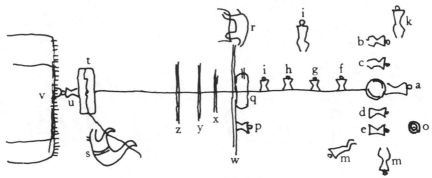

Fig. 1. Origin of the Indians

This family went away in the autumn to hunt, and during the winter this woman's son died. The parents were so much distressed that they decided to return to the village and bury the body there; so they made preparations to return, and as they traveled along they would each evening erect several poles upon which the body was placed to prevent the wild beasts from devouring it. When the dead boy was thus hanging upon the poles the adopted child—who was the Sun Spirit—would play about the camp and amuse himself, and finally told his adopted father he pitied him, and his mother, for their sorrow. The adopted son said he could bring his dead brother to life, whereupon the parents expressed great surprise and desired to know how that could be accomplished.

The adopted boy then had the party hasten to the village, when he said, "Get the women to make a wig'iwam of bark (*q*), put the dead boy in a covering of birch bark and place the body on the ground in the middle of the wig'iwam." On the next morning, when this had been done, the family and friends went into this lodge and seated themselves around the corpse.

After they had all been sitting quietly for some time they saw, through the doorway, the approach of a bear (*r*), which gradually came toward the wig'iwam, entered it, and placed itself before the dead body, and said hŭ′, hŭ′, hŭ′, hŭ′, when he passed around it toward the left side, with a trembling motion, and as he did so the body began quivering, which increased as the bear continued, until he had passed around four times, when the body came to life and stood up. Then the bear called to the father, who was sitting in the distant right-hand corner of the wig'iwam, and addressed to him the following words:

Nōs Ka-wi′-na ni′-shi-nâ′-bi wis′-si a-ya′wi-an′ man′-i-do nin-gi′-sis.
My father is not   an Indian   not   you are   a spirit   son.
Be-mai′-a-mi′-nik ni′-dzhi man′-i-do mi′-a-zhi′-gwa tshi-gi′-a-we-an′.
Insomuch   my fellow   spirit   now   as you are.

Nōs   a-zhi′-gwa   a-se′-ma   tshi-a′-to-yek′.   Â′-mi-kun′-dem   mi-e′-ta
My father now   tobacco   you shall put.   He speaks of   only

a-wi-dink′   dzhi-gŏsh′-kwi-tōt′   wen′-dzhi-bĭ-mâ′-di-zid′-o-ma′   a-ga′-wa
once   to be able to do it   why he shall live here   now

bi-mâ′-di-zid′-mi-o-ma′;   ni′-dzhi   man′-i-do   mi′-a-zhi′-gwa   tshi-gi′-we-an′.
that he scarcely lives;   my fellow   spirit   now I shall go   home.

The little bear boy (*r*) was the one who did this. He then remained among the Indians (*s*) and taught them the mysteries of the Grand Medicine (*t*), and after he had finished he told his adopted father that as his mission had been fulfilled, that he was to return to his kindred spirits, the Indians would have no need to fear sickness, as they now possessed the Grand Medicine which would assist them to live. He also said that his spirit could bring a body to life but once, and he would now return to the sun from which they would feel his influence.

This is called Kwi′-wi-sĕns′ wed-di′-shi-tshi′ ge′-wi-nip′—"Little boy, his work."

From subsequent information it was learned that the line (*w*) denotes the earth, and that, being considered as one step in the course of initiation into the Midē′wiwin, three others must be taken before a candidate can be admitted. These steps, or rests, as they are denominated, are typified by four distinct gifts of goods, which must be remitted to the Midē′ priests before the ceremony can take place.

The characters *s* and *t* are repetitions of the figures alluded to in the tradition (*q* and *r*) to signify that the candidate must personate the Makwa′ Man′-idō—bear spirit—when entering the Midē′wiwin (*t*); *t* is the Midē′ Man′idō, as Ki′tshi Man′idō is termed by the Midē′ priests. The device of horns, attached to the head, is a common symbol of superior power, found in connection with the figures of human and divine forms of many Midē′ songs and other mnemonic records; *v* represents the earth's surface, similar to that designated as *w. w, x, y,* and *z* represent the four degrees of the grand medicine.

The Ojibwa Story
of the First Earth

The first earth was called Ca'ca. It was in this part of the country. The people who lived there were not wise. They had no clothing, but they sat around and did nothing. Then the spirit of the creator sent a man to teach them. This man was called ockabe'wĭs (messenger). Some of those early people lived in the south where they did not need any clothing. But the people around here were cold and began to worry about what they should do. The ockabewis saw the southern people naked and homeless and left them to themselves. He came farther north where the people were suffering and in need of his assistance. He said, "Why are you sitting here with no clothing on?" They replied, "Because we do not know what to do." The first thing he taught them was how to make a fire by means of a bow and stick and a bit of decayed wood.

Then he taught them how to cook meat by the fire. They had no axes, but he took a pole and burned it in two over the fire. He taught them to boil meat in fresh birch bark. It was a long time before they had things as he wanted them, but after a while they were made comfortable by his help. They had no minds or ideas of their own, only to do as the ockabewis told them to do. This was long before Winabojo.

The ockabewis told them that they must fast and find out things by dreams and that if they paid attention to these dreams they would learn how to heal the sick. The people listened and fasted and found in dreams how to teach their children and do everything. The young men were taught that they must regulate their lives by dreams, they must live moral lives, be industrious, and be moderate in the use of tobacco when it should be given to them. They were especially taught that their minds would not be clear if they ate and drank too much. Tobacco and corn were given them, but it was the ockabewis who taught them how to use them.

Navajo Creation Accounts

CREATION OF THE SUN

The first three worlds were neither good nor healthful. They moved all the time and made the people dizzy. Upon ascending into this world the Navajo found only darkness and they said "We must have light."

In the Ute Mountain lived two women, Ahsonnutli, the turquoise hermaphrodite, and Yolaikaiason, the white-shell woman. These two women were sent for by the Navajo, who told them they wished light. The Navajo had already partially separated light into its several colors. Next to the floor was white indicating dawn, upon the white blue was spread for morning, and on the blue yellow for sunset, and next was black representing night. They had prayed long and continuously over these, but their prayers had availed nothing. The two women on arriving told the people to have patience and their prayers would eventually be answered.

Night had a familiar, who was always at his ear. This person said, "Send for the youth at the great falls." Night sent his messenger a shooting star. The youth soon appeared and said, "Ahsonnutli, the ahstjeohltoi (hermaphrodite), has white beads in her right breast and turquoise in her left. We will tell her to lay them on darkness and see what she can do with her prayers." This she did. The youth from the great falls said to Ahsonnutli, "You have carried the white-shell beads and turquoise a long time; you should know what to say." Then with a crystal dipped in pollen she marked eyes and mouth on the turquoise and on the white-shell beads, and forming a circle around these with the crystal she produced a slight light from the white-shell bead and a greater light from the turquoise, but the light was insufficient.

Twelve men lived at each of the cardinal points. The forty-eight men were sent for. After their arrival Ahsonnutli sang a song, the men sitting opposite to her; yet even with their presence the song failed to secure the needed light. Two eagle plumes were placed upon each cheek of the turquoise and two on the cheeks of the white-shell beads and one at each of the cardinal points. The twelve men of the east

placed twelve turquoises at the east of the faces. The twelve men of
the south placed twelve white-shell beads at the south. The twelve men
of the west placed twelve turquoises at the west. Those of the north
placed twelve white-shell beads at that point. Then with the crystal
dipped in corn pollen they made a circle embracing the whole. The
wish still remained unrealized. Then Ahsonnutli held the crystal over
the turquoise face, whereupon it lighted into a blaze. The people retreated far back on account of the great heat, which continued increasing. The men from the four points found the heat so intense that they
arose, but they could hardly stand, as the heavens were so close to
them. They looked up and saw two rainbows, one across the other from
east to west, and from north to south. The heads and feet of the rainbows almost touched the men's heads. The men tried to raise the great
light, but each time they failed. Finally a man and woman appeared,
whence they knew not. The man's name was Atseatsine and the woman's
name was Atseatsan. They were asked "How can this sun be got up."
They replied, "We know; we heard the people down here trying to raise
it, and this is why we came." "Chanteen" (sun's rays), exclaimed the man,
"I have the chanteen; I have a crystal from which I can light the chanteen,
and I have the rainbow; with these three I can raise the sun." The people
said, "Go ahead and raise it." When he had elevated the sun a short distance it tipped a little and burned vegetation and scorched the people,
for it was still too near. Then the people said to Atseatsine and Atseatsan, "Raise the sun higher," and they continued to elevate it, and yet
it continued to burn everything. They were then called upon to "lift
it higher still, as high as possible," but after a certain height was reached
their power failed; it would go no farther.

The couple then made four poles, two of turquoise and two
of white-shell beads, and each was put under the sun, and with these
poles the twelve men at each of the cardinal points raised it. They could
not get it high enough to prevent the people and grass from burning.
The people then said, "Let us stretch the world"; so the twelve men at
each point expanded the world. The sun continued to rise as the world
expanded, and began to shine with less heat, but when it reached the
meridian the heat became great and the people suffered much. They
crawled everywhere to find shade. Then the voice of Darkness went
four times around the world telling the men at the cardinal points to
go on expanding the world. "I want all this trouble stopped," said Darkness; "the people are suffering and all is burning; you must continue
stretching." And the men blew and stretched, and after a time they saw
the sun rise beautifully, and when the sun again reached the meridian
it was only tropical. It was then just right, and as far as the eye could
reach the earth was encircled first with the white dawn of day, then with
the blue of early morning, and all things were perfect. And Ahsonnutli
commanded the twelve men to go to the east, south, west, and north,

to hold up the heavens (Yiyanitsinni, the holders up of the heavens), which office they are supposed to perform to this day.

HASJELTI AND HOSTJOGHON

Hasjelti and Hostjoghon were the children of Ahsonnutli, the turquoise, and Yolaikaiason (white-shell woman, wife of the sun). Ahsonnutli placed an ear of white corn and Yolaikaiason an ear of yellow corn on the mountain where the fogs meet. The corn conceived, the white corn giving birth to Hasjelti and the yellow corn to Hostjoghon. These two became the great song-makers of the world. They gave to the mountain of their nativity (Henry Mountain in Utah) two songs and two prayers; they then went to Sierra Blanca (Colorado) and made two songs and prayers and dressed the mountain in clothing of white shell with two eagle plumes placed upright upon the head. From here they visited San Mateo Mountain (New Mexico) and gave to it two songs and prayers, and dressed it in turquoise, even to the leggings and moccasins, and placed two eagle plumes on the head. Hence they went to San Francisco Mountain (Arizona) and made two songs and prayers and dressed that mountain in abalone shells with two eagle plumes upon the head. They then visited Ute Mountain and gave to it two songs and prayers and dressed it in black beads. This mountain also had two eagle plumes on its head. They then returned to the mountain of their nativity to meditate, "We two have made all these songs."

Upon inquiring of their mothers how they came into existence, and being informed, they said, "Well, let our number be increased; we can not get along with only two of us." The woman placed more yellow and white corn on the mountain and children were conceived as before. A sufficient number were born so that two brothers were placed on each of the four mountains, and to these genii of the mountains the clouds come first. All the brothers consulted together as to what they should live upon and they concluded to make game, and so all game was created.

NAIYENESGONY AND TOBAIDISCHINNI

This world was destroyed five times. The first time by a whirlwind; the second, by immense hail stones; the third, by smallpox, when each pustule covered a whole cheek; the fourth, all was destroyed by coughing; the fifth time Naiyenesgony and Tobaidischinni went over the earth slaying all enemies.

These two boys were born at Tohatkle (where the waters are mated), near Ute Mountain, in Utah; they were the children of Ahsonnutli. Ahsonnutli and Yolaikaiason (the white-shell woman) were the creators of shells. Ahsonnutli had a beard under her right arm and Yolaikaiason had a small ball of flesh under her left arm from which they made all shells. The eyes of Naiyenesgony and Tobaidischinni were shells placed on their faces by Ahsonnutli; the shells immediately becoming brilliant the boys could look upon all things and see any distance without their eyes becoming weary. A stick colored black was placed to the forehead of Naiyenesgony and one colored blue to that of Tobaidischinni. When Naiyenesgony shook his head the stick remained firm on the forehead, but he felt something in the palm of his hand, which proved to be three kinds of seeds, and he said, "We must go by this." When Tobaidischinni shook his head the stick dropped off the forehead and they thought a long time and said, "We must go by this." This is why the deer sheds his horns. In ceremonials the breath is drawn from sticks which are made to represent the originals; the sticks are also held to wounds as a curative.

These two boys grew from infancy to manhood in four days and on the fourth day they made bows and arrows; on the fifth day they began using them. Although they were the children of Ahsonnutli they did not know her as their mother, but supposed her to be their aunt. Frequently they inquired of her where they could find their father. She always told them to stop their inquiries, for they had no father. Finally they said to her, "We know we have a father and we intend to go and look for him." She again denied that they had a father, but they were determined and they journeyed far to the east and came to the house of the sun. The house was of white shell, and the wife of the sun (Yolaikaiason) was also of white shell. The wife inquired of the youths where they were from, and, said she, "What do you want here?" They replied, "We came to hunt our father." When the sun returned to his home in the evening he discovered the youths as soon as he entered his house and he asked, "Where are those two boys from?" The wife replied, "You say you never do anything wrong when you travel; these two boys call you father and I know they are your children." The wife was very angry. The sun sent the boys off a distance and threw a great roll of black clouds at them intending to kill them, but they were not injured, and they returned to the house. He then pushed them against a sharp stone knife, but they slipped by uninjured. Four times they were thrust against the knife, but without injury. The sun finding his attempts unsuccessful said, "It is so, you are my sons." The sun then ordered Hasjelti and Toneennili (these two were special attendants upon the sun) to build a sweat house and put the boys in, that they might die from the heat. Toneennili made an excavation inside of the sweat house, put the boys into the hole, and placed a rock over the hole and built a fire over the rock. When the rock became very hot the sun ordered Toneennili to sprinkle it four times with water, being careful to keep the entrance to the sweat house closely covered. After a time he uncovered the entrance and removing the rock the sun commanded the boys to come out. He did not expect to be obeyed, as he thought and hoped the boys were dead, but they came out unharmed. The sun then said, "You are indeed my own children; I have tried in vain to destroy you." The boys wished to return to the woman whom they supposed to be their aunt. Before departing the sun asked them what they wished; they said, "We want bows and arrows, knives, and good leggings. There are people around the world eating our people (the Navajo). Some of these people are great giants and some are as small as flies; we wish to kill them with lightning." The sun gave the youths clothing that was invulnerable, and he gave them lightning with which to destroy all enemies, and a great stone knife. They then went over the world. Naiyenesgony killed with the lightning arrows and Tobaidischinni scalped with his knife. After all enemies had been destroyed Naiyenesgony and Tobaidischinni said to the Navajo, "Now we will leave you and return to our home in the Ute Mountains, where the waters are mated, but before leaving you we will give to you the ten songs and prayers that will bring health and good fortune to your people." Tobaidischinni is the parent of all waters.

The Winnebago
Origin Account

In the beginning Earthmaker was sitting in space. When he came to consciousness, nothing was there anywhere. He began to think of what he should do, and finally he began to cry and tears flowed from his eyes and fell below him. After a while he looked below him and saw something bright. The bright object below him represented his tears. As they fell they formed the present waters. When the tears flowed below they became the seas as they are now. Earthmaker began to think again. He thought, "It is thus: If I wish anything it will become as I wish, just as my tears have become seas." Thus he thought. So he wished for light and it became light. Then he thought: "It is as I thought, the things that I wished for have come into existence as I desired." Then again he thought and wished for the earth, and this earth came into existence. Earthmaker looked at the earth and he liked it; but it was not quiet. It moved about as do the waters of the sea. Then he made the trees and he liked them but they did not make the earth quiet. Then he made some grass but it likewise did not cause the earth to become quiet. Then he made rocks and stones but still the earth was not quiet. It was however almost quiet. Then he made the four directions and the four winds. At the four corners of the earth he placed them as great and powerful people, to act as island weights. Yet still the earth was not quiet. Then he made four large beings and threw them down toward the earth, and they pierced through the earth with their heads eastward. They were snakes. Then the earth became very still and quiet. Then he looked at the earth and he liked it.

Then again he thought of how it was that things came into being just as he desired. Then for the first time he began to talk and he said, "As things are just as I wish them I shall make a being in my own likeness." So he took a piece of clay and made it like himself. Then he talked to what he had created but it did not answer. He looked at it and saw that it had no mind or thought. So he made a mind for it. Again he talked to it but it did not answer. So he looked at it again and saw that it had no tongue. Then he made it a tongue. Then he spoke to it but still it did not answer. He looked at it and saw that it had no soul. So he made a soul. Then he talked to it again and it very nearly said something, but it could not make itself intelligible. So Earthmaker breathed into its mouth and then talked to it and it answered.

The Blackfeet Genesis

All animals of the Plains at one time heard and knew him, and all birds of the air heard and knew him. All things that he had made understood him when he spoke to them—the birds, the animals, and the people.

Old Man was traveling about, south of here, making the people. He came from the south, traveling north, making animals and birds as he passed along. He made the mountains, prairies, timber, and brush first. So he went along, traveling northward, making things as he went, putting rivers here and there, and falls on them, putting red paints here and there in the ground—fixing up the world as we see it today. He made the Milk River [the Teton] and crossed it, and, being tired, went up on a little hill and lay down to rest. As he lay on his back, stretched out on the ground, with arms extended, he marked himself out with stones—the shape of his body, head, legs, arms, and everything. There you can see those rocks today. After he had rested, he went on northward, and stumbled over a knoll and fell down on his knees. Then he said, "You are a bad thing to be stumbling against"; so he raised up two large buttes there, and named them the Knees, and they are called so to this day. He went on farther north, and with some of the rocks he carried with him he built the Sweet Grass Hills.

Old Man covered the plains with grass for the animals to feed on. He marked off a piece of ground, and in it he made to grow all kinds of roots and berries—camas, wild carrots, wild turnips, sweetroot, bitterroot, sarvis berries, bull berries, cherries, plums, and rosebuds. He put trees in the ground. He put all kinds of animals on the ground. When he made the bighorn with its big head and horns, he made it out on the prairie. It did not seem to travel easily on the prairie; it was awkward and could not go fast. So he took it by one of its horns, and led it up into the mountains, and turned it loose; and it skipped about among the rocks and went up fearful places with ease. So he said, "This is the place that suits you; this is what you are fitted for, the rocks, and the mountains." While he was in the mountains, he made the antelope out of dirt, and turned it loose, to see how it would go. It ran so fast that it fell over some rocks and hurt itself. He saw that this would not do, and took the antelope down on the prairie, and turned it loose; and it ran away fast and gracefully, and he said, "This is what you are suited to."

One day Old Man determined that he would make a woman and a child; so he formed them both—the woman and the child, her son—of clay. After he had moulded the clay in human shape, he said to the clay, "You must be people," and then he covered it up and left it, and went away. The next morning he went to the place and took the covering off, and saw that the clay shapes had changed a little. The second morning there was still more change, and the third still more. The fourth morning he went to the place, took the covering off, looked at the images, and told them to rise and walk; and they did so. They walked down to the river with their Maker, and then he told them that his name was Na'pi [Old Man].

As they were standing by the river, the woman said to him, "How is it? will we always live, will there be no end to it?" He said: "I have never thought of that. We will have to decide it. I will take this buffalo chip and throw it in the river. If it floats, when people die, in four days they will become alive again; they will die for only four days. But if it sinks, there will be an end to them." He threw the chip into the river, and it floated. The woman turned and picked up a stone, and said: "No, I will throw this stone in the river; if it floats we will always live, if it sinks people must die, that they may always be sorry for each other." The woman threw the stone into the water, and it sank. "There," said Old Man, "you have chosen. There will be an end to them."

It was not many nights after that the woman's child died, and she cried a great deal for it. She said to Old Man: "Let us change this. The law that you first made, let that be a law." He said: "Not so. What is made law must be law. We will undo nothing that we have done. The child is dead, but it cannot be changed. People will have to die."

That is how we came to be people. It is he who made us.

The first people were poor and naked, and did not know how to get a living. Old Man showed them the roots and berries, and told them that they could peel the bark off some trees and eat it, that it was good. He told the people that the animals should be their food, and gave them to the people, saying, "These are your herds." He said: "All these little animals that live in the ground—rats, squirrels, skunks, beavers—are good to eat. You need not fear to eat of their flesh." He made all the birds that fly, and told the people that there was no harm in their flesh, that it could be eaten. The first people that he created he used to take about through the timber and swamps and over the prairies, and show them the different plants. Of a certain plant he would say, "The root of this plant, if gathered in a certain month of the year, is good for certain sickness." So they learned the power of all herbs.

In those days there were buffalo. Now the people had no arms, but those black animals with long beards were armed; and once, as the people were moving about, the buffalo saw them, and ran after them, and hooked them, and killed and ate them. One day, as the Maker of the people was traveling over the country, he saw some of his children, that he had made, lying dead, torn to pieces and partly eaten by the buffalo. When he saw this he was very sad. He said: "This will not do. I will change this. The people shall eat the buffalo."

He went to some of the people who were left, and said to them, "How is it that you people do nothing to these animals that are killing you?" The people said: "What can we do? We have no way to kill these animals, while they are armed and can kill us." Then said the Maker: "That is not hard. I will make you a weapon that will kill those animals." So he went out, and cut some sarvis berry shoots, and brought them in, and peeled the bark off them. He took a larger piece of wood, and flattened it, and tied a string to it, and made a bow. Now, as he was the master of all birds and could do with them as he wished, he went out and caught one, and took feathers from its wing, and split them, and tied them to the shaft of wood. He tied four feathers along the shaft, and tried the arrow at a mark, and found that it did not fly well. He took these feathers off, and put on three; and when he tried it again, he found that it was good. He went out and began to break sharp pieces off the stones. He tried them, and found that the black flint stones made the best arrow points, and some white flints. Then he taught the people how to use these things.

Then he said: "The next time you go out, take these things with you, and use them as I tell you, and do not run from these animals. When they run at you, as soon as they get pretty close, shoot the arrows at them, as I have taught you; and you will see that they will run from you or will run in a circle around you."

Now, as people became plenty, one day three men went out onto the plain to see the buffalo, but they had no arms. They saw the animals, but when the buffalo saw the men, they ran after them and killed two of them, but one got away. One day after this, the people went on a little hill to look about, and the buffalo saw them, and said, "Saiyah, there is some more of our food," and they rushed on them. This time the people did not run. They began to shoot at the buffalo with the bows and arrows Na'pi had given them, and the buffalo began to fall; but in the fight a person was killed.

At this time these people had flint knives given them, and they cut up the bodies of the dead buffalo. It is not healthful to eat the meat raw, so Old Man gathered soft, dry, rotten driftwood and made punk of it, and then got a piece of hard wood, and drilled a hole in it with an arrow point; and gave them a pointed piece of hard wood, and taught them how to make a fire with fire sticks, and to cook the flesh of these animals and eat it.

They got a kind of stone that was in the land, and then took another harder stone and worked one upon the other, and hollowed out the softer one, and made a kettle of it. This was the fashion of their dishes.

Also Old Man said to the people: "Now, if you are overcome, you may go and sleep, and get power. Something will come to you in your dream that will help you. Whatever these animals tell you to do, you must obey them, as they appear to you in your sleep. Be guided by them. If anybody wants help, if you are alone and traveling, and cry aloud for help, your prayer will be answered. It may be by the eagles, perhaps by the buffalo, or by the bears. Whatever animal answers your prayer, you must listen to him."

That was how the first people got through the world, by the power of their dreams.

After this, Old Man kept on, traveling north. Many of the animals that he had made followed him as he went. The animals understood him when he spoke to them, and he used them as his servants. When he got to the north point of the Porcupine Mountains, there he made some more mud images of people, and blew breath upon them, and they became people. He made men and women. They asked him, "What are we to eat?" He made many images of clay in the form of buffalo. Then he blew breath on these, and they stood up; and when he made signs to them, they started to run. Then he said to the people, "Those are your food." They said to him, "Well, now, we have those animals; how are we to kill them?" "I will show you," he said. He took them to the cliff, and made them build rock piles...; and he taught them how to drive buffalo over a cliff....

After he had taught those people these things, he started off again, traveling north, until he came to where Bow and Elbow rivers meet. There he made some more people, and taught them the same things. From here he again went on northward. When he had come nearly to the Red Deer's River, he reached the hill where the Old Man sleeps. There he lay down and rested himself. The form of his body is to be seen there yet.

When he awoke from his sleep, he traveled farther northward and came to a fine high hill. He climbed to the top of it, and there sat down to rest. He looked over the country below him, and it pleased him. Before him the hill was steep, and he said to himself, "Well, this is a fine place for sliding; I will have some fun," and he began to slide down the hill. The marks where he slid down are to be seen yet, and the place is known to all people as the "Old Man's Sliding Ground."

This is as far as the Blackfeet followed Old Man. The Crees know what he did farther north.

In later times once, Na'pi said, "Here I will mark you off a piece of ground," and he did so. Then he said: "There is your land, and it is full of all kinds of animals, and many things grow in this land. Let no other people come into it. This is for you five tribes [Blackfeet, Bloods, Piegans, Gros Ventres, Sarcees]. When people come to cross the line, take your bows and arrows, your lances and your battle axes, and give them battle and keep them out. If they gain a footing, trouble will come to you."

Our forefathers gave battle to all people who came to cross these lines, and kept them out. Of late years we have let our friends, the white people, come in, and you know the result. We, his children, have failed to obey his laws.

The Woman Who Fell from the Sky

A Seneca Account

A long time ago human beings lived high up in what is now called heaven. They had a great and illustrious chief.

It so happened that this chief's daughter was taken very ill with a strange affliction. All the people were very anxious as to the outcome of her illness. Every known remedy was tried in an attempt to cure her, but none had any effect.

Near the lodge of this chief stood a great tree, which every year bore corn used for food. One of the friends of the chief had a dream in which he was advised to tell the chief that, in order to cure his daughter, he must lay her beside this tree, and that he must have the tree dug up. This advice was carried out to the letter. While the people were at work and the young woman lay there, a young man came along. He was very angry and said: "It is not at all right to destroy this tree. Its fruit is all that we have to live on." With this remark he gave the young woman who lay there ill a shove with his foot, causing her to fall into the hole that had been dug.

Now, that hole opened into this world, which was then all water, on which floated waterfowl of many kinds. There was no land at that time. It came to pass that as these waterfowl saw this young woman falling they shouted, "Let us receive her," whereupon they, at least some of them, joined their bodies together, and the young woman fell on this platform of bodies. When these were wearied they asked, "Who will volunteer to care for this woman?" The great Turtle then took her, and when he got tired of holding her, he in turn asked who would take his place. At last the question arose as to what they should do to provide her with a permanent resting place in this world. Finally it was decided to prepare the earth, on which she would live in the future. To do this it was determined that soil from the bottom of the primal sea should be brought up and placed on the broad, firm carapace of the Turtle, where it would increase in size to such an extent that it would accommodate all the creatures that should be produced thereafter. After much discussion the toad was finally persuaded to dive to the bottom of the waters in search of soil. Bravely making the attempt, he succeeded in bringing up soil from the depths of the sea. This was carefully spread over the carapace of the Turtle, and at once both began to grow in size and depth.

After the young woman recovered from the illness from which she suffered when she was cast down from the upper world, she built herself a shelter, in which she lived quite contentedly. In the course of time she brought forth a girl baby, who grew rapidly in size and intelligence.

When the daughter had grown to young womanhood, the mother and she were accustomed to go out to dig wild potatoes. Her mother had said to her that in doing this she must face the west at all times. Before long the young daughter gave signs that she was about to become a mother. Her mother reproved her, saying that she had violated the injunction not to face the east, as her condition showed that she had faced the wrong way while digging potatoes. It is said that the breath of the West Wind had entered her person, causing conception. When the days of her delivery were at hand, she overheard twins within her body in a hot debate as to which should be born first and as to the proper place of exit, one declaring that he was going to emerge through the armpit of his mother, the other saying that he would emerge in the natural way. The first one born, who was of a reddish color, was called Othagwenda, that is, Flint. The other, who was light in color, was called Djuskaha, that is, the Little Sprout.

The grandmother of the twins liked Djuskaha and hated the other; so they cast Othagwenda into a hollow tree some distance from the lodge.

The boy who remained in the lodge grew very rapidly, and soon was able to make himself bows and arrows and to go out to hunt in the vicinity. Finally, for several days he returned home without his bow and arrows. At last he was asked why he had to have a new bow and arrows every morning. He replied that there was a young boy in a hollow tree in the neighborhood who used them. The grandmother inquired where the tree stood, and he told her; whereupon then they went there and brought the other boy home again.

When the boys had grown to man's estate, they decided that it was necessary for them to increase the size of their island, so they agreed to start out together, afterward separating to create forests and lakes and other things. They parted as agreed, Othagwenda going westward and Djuskaha eastward. In the course of time, on returning, they met in their shelter or lodge at night, then agreeing to go the next day to see what each had made. First they went west to see what Othagwenda had made. It was found that he had made the country all rocks and full of ledges, and also a mosquito that was very large. Djuskaha asked the mosquito to run, in order that he might see whether the insect could fight. The mosquito ran, and sticking his bill through a sapling, thereby made it fall, at which Djuskaha said, "That will not be right, for you would kill the people who are about to come." So, seizing him, he rubbed him down in his hands, causing him to become very small; then he blew on the mosquito, whereupon he flew away. He also modified some of the other animals that his brother had made. After returning to their lodge, they agreed to go the next day to see what Djuskaha had fashioned. On visiting the east the next day, they found that Djuskaha had made a large number of animals which were so fat that they could hardly move; that he had made the sugar-maple trees to drop syrup; that he had made the sycamore tree to bear fine fruit; that the rivers were so formed that half the water flowed upstream and the other half downstream. Then the reddish-colored brother, Othagwenda, was greatly displeased with what his brother had made, saying that the people who were about to come would live too easily and be too happy. So he shook violently the various animals—the bears, deer, and turkeys—causing them to become small at once, a characteristic that attached itself to their descendants. He also caused the sugar maple to drop sweetened water only, and the fruit of the sycamore to become small and useless; and lastly he caused the water of the rivers to flow in only one direction, because the original plan would make it too easy for the human beings who were about to come to navigate the streams.

The inspection of each other's work resulted in a deadly disagreement between the brothers, who finally came to grips and blows, and Othagwenda was killed in the fierce struggle.

The Osage
Creation Account

Way beyond, a part of the Wazha'zhe lived in the sky. They desired to know their origin, the source from which they came into existence. They went to the sun. He told them that they were his children. Then they wandered still farther and came to the moon. She told them that she gave birth to them, and that the sun was their father. She told them that they must leave their present abode and go down to the earth and dwell there. They came to the earth, but found it covered with water. They could not return to the place they had left, so they wept, but no answer came to them from anywhere. They floated about in the air, seeking in every direction for help from some god; but they found none. The animals were with them, and of all these the elk was the finest and most stately, and inspired all the creatures with confidence; so they appealed to the elk for help. He dropped into the water and began to sink. Then he called to the winds, and the winds came from all quarters and blew until the waters went upward as in a mist.

At first rocks only were exposed, and the people traveled on the rocky places that produced no plants, and there was nothing to eat. Then the waters began to go down until the soft earth was exposed. When this happened, the elk in his joy rolled over and over on the soft earth, and all his loose hairs clung to the soil. The hairs grew, and from them sprang beans, corns, potatoes, and wild turnips, and then all the grasses and trees.

Standing Buffalo of the Wazhazhe gens of the Omaha recounted this version about 1900.

The Omaha Creation Account

When I was a boy I often asked my mother where my people came from, but she would not tell me, until one day she said, "I will give you the story as it has been handed down from generation to generation.

"In the real beginning Wako^{n}da made the Wazha'zhe—men, women, and children. After they were made he said 'Go!' So the people took all they had, carried their children, and started toward the setting sun. They traveled until they came to a great water. Seeing they could go no farther, they halted. Again Wako^{n}da said 'Go!' And once more they started, and wondered what would happen to them. As they were about to step into the water there appeared from under the water rocks. These projected just above the surface, and there were others barely covered with water. Upon these stones the people walked, stepping from stone to stone until they came to land. When they stood on dry land the wind blew, the water became violent and threw the rocks upon the land, and they became great cliffs. Therefore when men enter the sweat lodge they thank the stones for preserving their lives and ask for a continuation of their help that their lives may be prolonged. Here on the shore the people dwelt; but again Wako^{n}da said 'Go!' And again they started and traveled on until they came to a people whose appearance was like their own; but not knowing whether they were friends or foes, the people rushed at each other for combat. In the midst of the confusion Wako^{n}da said, 'Stand still!' The people obeyed. They questioned each other, found they spoke the same language, and became friends.

"Wako^{n}da gave the people a bow, a dog, and a grain of corn. The people made other bows like the one given them and learned to use them for killing wild animals for food and to make clothing out of their skins. The dogs gave increase and were used as burden bearers

45

and for hunting. The corn they planted, and when it grew they found it good to eat, and they continued to plant it.

"The people traveled on and came to a lake. There the Omaha found a Sacred Tree and took it with them. The people (Ponca) went on and came to a river now called Nishu'de (the Missouri). They traveled along its banks until they came to a place where they could step over the water. From there they went across the land and came to a river now called Nibtha'çka (the Platte). This river they followed, and it led them back to the Missouri.

"Again they went up this river until they came to a river now called Niobrara, where we live to-day."

This account was related to Major J. W. MacMurray in 1884 or 1885 by Coteeakun, the son of Chief Kamiakin. Coteeakun was a friend and assistant of Smohalla, the prophet of the Dreamers.

Creation of the Yakima World

In the beginning of the world, all was water. Whee-me-me-ow-ah, the Great Chief Above, lived in the sky, above the water, all alone. When he decided to make the world, he went down to the shallow places and began to throw up great handfuls of mud. Thus he made the land.

He piled some of the mud up so high that it froze hard and made the mountains. The rain, when it came, was turned into ice and snow on top of the high mountains. Some of the mud was made hard, into rocks. Since that time the rocks have not changed, except that they have become harder.

We did not know all this by ourselves; we were told it by our fathers and grandfathers, who learned it from their fathers and grandfathers. We were told that the Great Chief Above made many mountains. He made everything just as our fathers told us. When we are hunting for game or berries in the mountains, we can see that what they said is true.

The Great Chief Above made trees grow on the earth, and also roots and berries. He made a man out of a ball of mud and told him what he should do. He should get fish from the waters, and deer and other game in the forests. When the man became lonely the Great Chief Above made a woman, to be a companion to him, and told her what she should do. He taught her how to dress skins, and how to make baskets out of bark and roots which he showed her how to find. He taught her which berries to gather for food and how to pick them and dry them. He showed her how to cook the salmon and the game which the man brought.

One time when she was asleep, she had a dream. In her dream she wondered what more she could do to please the man. She prayed to the Great Chief Above for help. He answered her prayer by blowing his breath on her and giving her something which she could not see or hear, smell or touch. This invisible something was preserved in a basket. Through it, the first woman taught her daughters and granddaughters the designs and skills which had been taught her.

But in spite of all the things the Great Chief Above did for them, the new people quarreled. They quarreled so much that Mother Earth was angry. In her anger, she shook the mountains so hard that those hanging over the narrow part of Big River fell down. The rocks, falling into the water, dammed the stream and also made the rapids and waterfalls there. Many people and animals were killed and buried under the rocks and mountains.

Some day the Great Chief Above will overturn those mountains and rocks. Then the spirits that once lived in the bones buried there will go back into them. Now, those spirits live in the tops of the mountains, watching their children on the earth and waiting for the great change which is to come. The voices of these spirits can be heard in the mountains at all times. Mourners who wail for their dead hear spirit voices reply to them, and thus they know that their lost ones are always near.

No one knows when the Great Chief Above will overturn the mountains. But we do know this: the spirits will return only to the bones of people who in life kept the beliefs of their grandfathers. Only their bones will be preserved under the mountains.

The Emergence according to the Hopi

In the Underworld all the people were fools. Youths copulated with the wives of elder men, and the elder men attacked virgins. All was confusion, and the chief was unhappy. He thought, and at sunset proclaimed that on the next day all the people should assemble around him. On the following morning all came. They said, "We heard you announce, you have sent for us. What do you wish; perhaps you wish to tell us something." "Yes," said the chief, "I want to tell you that I have been thinking much, and I am saddened by your evil ways. Now, I announce that tomorrow morning early, all the women, virgins, and female children and infants, all females, shall remain here in the village, and all the men, youths, and male infants, all males, shall cross the broad river and remain there on the other side." Neither the men or the women were displeased by this announcement, and discussed it overnight. "Now it will be seen who the lazy ones are, perhaps the women, perhaps the men; we will see." On the following morning, the males all swam the river, carrying the infants on their backs, and leaving the women in the houses which belonged to them. Before the men swam the river, the men and women divided all kinds of seeds between them, all the store of seeds was divided.

   The men carried their hunting weapons with them and caught deer and antelope. They nursed the infants by cutting up small bits of venison which they gave to the infants to suck, and it was as good as mother's milk. They grew fat and strong. The men built houses and planted, and at the end of one year gathered large harvests. The women had but little skill in field work and only obtained a small harvest. The men came down to the river bank and displayed their abundant field fruits and taunted the women. It was an evil time and both men and women were foolish. When they became amorous they resorted to artificial means to satisfy themselves. The women used sticks and cactus and the men used liver of deer and squashes and gourds. In six moons, one of these gourds gave birth to Gourd Girl, a very beautiful maid. Also during this separation of sexes, a young woman, not a virgin, imitated intercourse by using the primary wing feather of an eagle. She conceived and was carried to the San Francisco Mountains where she gave birth to Giant Eagle, a monster.

Another young woman, not a virgin either, was sitting in her house in great misery. Her body was barely covered, for her gown only hung over her in ragged shreds. She was very lousy and was picking the vermin off and was scratching herself. While she was doing this, almost all of her body was exposed. The rays of the sun coming through a crack in the wall fell upon her. She moved in pleasure; then fell asleep. She told some elder women of this experience. It began to rain, and the water started to drip through the roof. The elder women said to her, "Lie over there and let the raindrops fall upon you." She went over and lay down. The raindrops fell upon her body; again she moved in pleasure and fell asleep. She conceived and gave birth to twins. In four days they were able to walk and run around. They were foolish and full of mischief, breaking and destroying food vessels and cooking utensils. They were very dirty and their noses were always snotty.

When the Twins had grown to be the size of a twelve-year-old boy, they frequently asked their grandmother, Spider Woman, who their father was and where he lived. But Spider Woman would say, "How should I know?" At last, she told them that Sun was their father, that he lived at the place of Sunrise, and she would go with them and they should see him. She perched on the ear of one of the Twins. She spurted some medicine and a filament spread before them, making a smooth pathway to the door of the house of Sun. There sat Lion, Bear, and Rattlesnake; Serpent sat on the hatchway. The Twins successively spurted medicine upon these watchers as they came to them, saying as they did so, "Our friend, do not be angry," and each watcher in turn lay down quietly, and they passed on and stood looking down the hatchway. There were many beautiful young women and virgins down there. They were the daughters of Sun. Some of them looked up and said, "Who are these dirty, snotty-nosed young ones, I wonder?" The Wife of Sun said, "Come in you two," and they went down the ladder. In the middle of the floor was a mound of turquoise and on its top was a large abalone. This was the seat of Sun. Around the floor were many other smaller turquoise mounds on which were seated the Wife of Sun and his daughters. The Wife of Sun got angry at the Twins. The daughters asked them who they were and where they came from. But the Twins sat in silence. Then the daughters said, "You may sit there, on these two mounds, and be brothers until our father comes home; then we will know." The Sun came home, from the below, coming up a ladder leading through a hatchway in the floor. He always entered with a great noise. As he emerged, he said, "What do I smell? There are some strange ones in here." The daughters had put the Twins away in the cloud altar before Sun came in, and when Sun demanded that the strangers be brought forth, the daughters brought the Twins from the beautiful cloud altar where they had been covered with clouds of all colors. The Twins ran to Sun, claiming him as their father, but Sun said, "Wait a while." Sun brought out his great pipe of turquoise, with clouds painted on the sides. Filling it with tobacco and ramming it with a stick, he lit it and gave it to the Twins, who smoked it, passing it from one to the other. They swallowed the smoke, which now appears as clouds in the sky.

After they had smoked the pipe, the Twins again claimed Sun as their father. But he said, "Wait a while." There was a high mountain, its top almost touching the sky. Sun showed this to the Twins and told them to go to its top and sleep there. Spider Woman tied a turkey feather to the right side of one Twin and another turkey feather to the left side of the other Twin. They went up to the top of the mountain and the wind blew cold from the North. The wind brought ice around them, and except for the feathers they would have perished. As it was, they were almost frozen and sat there through the night with chattering teeth. In the morning Sun called up to them, "Are you dead yet?" They came running down and on the advice of Spider Woman said, "Oh, no, we had a fine place to sleep, except it was too hot. It made us sweat." They pretended to be wiping sweat from their brows. "Now surely you know we are your sons." But Sun said, "Wait a while."

He led them to a place where there was a smooth path, and there were four large hollow spheres of flint. In each of these spheres was a hot fire. Sun bowled one of the spheres along the trail and told one of the Twins to run after it and catch it. He then bowled the other and told the other Twin to run and catch it. Then he bowled the other two spheres at them, crying to them to be sure and stop them. They did. He next told them to pick them up and bring them to him. They were very heavy, but the Twins spurted medicine on them and they became light. They took them up in their hands and brought them to Sun.

Then Sun recognized them as his sons. He cleansed and decorated them, and his wife was no longer angry at them. He sat each of them on a turquoise mound. He showed them beautiful clouds in one room, asking them if they wished to take some of these. The Twins said, "No." He showed them beautiful shells and ornaments of all kinds, and beautiful garments, and all manner of animals. These he offered as gifts to them. But the Twins did not want them. "Well," he said, "you must desire something. Tell me what it is." So they said they wanted weapons to destroy the monsters that ravaged their mother's land. Sun then gave them bow and arrow and resilient lightning.

Meanwhile, the separation had been going on for three years. The woman's gowns had grown ragged and their fields were poorly cultivated. On the fourth year the men again had abundant harvests, but the women obtained little from the fields, and they were hungry and unhappy. On the morning of the fifth Winter solstice ceremony after separation, the woman chief came to the river bank and called across to the men, "I want to tell you something." A youth heard her and told the elder men and one of them went to the river bank and called, "What is it you have to say?" The woman chief was all in rags and looked miserable. She said, "I have been thinking, let all the men and youths assemble on your side and all the women and virgins on this side and let us discuss." This was agreed to and they all assembled. The woman chief spoke first, "We are all in rags, and we have only a few ears of corn left to eat. We have no meat, no copulation, no childbearing. We are sad." "True," said the chief. The woman chief said, "Let some men come over here." "Let the women come over here," said the chief. The women were all glad of this and ran into the water and swam across. The men received them gladly. The men had built fine houses, and these they gave to the women. They had also woven many fine gowns and girdles, and these they gave to the women also, and there was an abundance of corn, and plenty of elk, deer, bear, and antelope.

At that time, at sunrise the sky was wide. The horizon was far around. But at noon, the sky vibrated. It alternately compressed and distended. The horizon was not so far around as it is in this world. In the daytime, in the Underworld, it was beautiful. There was bubbling water, all around the landscape. But at night the sky contracted and it was disagreeable. There were both sun and moon at that time. Then the bubbling waters increased and encroached upon the dry land and pressed close towards the people. They became sad. The chief thought and said, "Perhaps there is a doorway to this sky."

There were four mountains at the cardinal points. At the mountain at the Northeast lived Spider Woman and the Twins. The Hopi War chief made a war prayer-stick for Spider Woman and a club for the Twins, and prayer-feathers, and sent a youth with these to the mountain. Spider Woman thanked the youth for the prayer-stick and prayer-feathers and asked what he wanted. The Twins danced with joy over their presents. "What do you wish for these things?" asked Spider Woman. The youth said, "We are surrounded by bubbling water, and it is covering all our land. Where is a good place to go to, the good houses. Perhaps you know." "Yes," she said, "I know. In the above is a good place; tell your people to hurry and come here." The youth returned, and after the elders assembled and smoked, he told all. Women prepared food for the journey, and then all the people started, carrying altar slabs on their backs, and went to the mountain. They all went up the mountain to its peak, and the water followed close behind them. The water covered everything, but the mountain grew a little faster than the rise of the water, and after a time the mountain summit was almost touching the sky. Spider Woman planted spruce plant and it grew up against the sky, but the sky was hard and the spruce could not penetrate it. Again Spider Woman thought, "Perhaps reed will pass through." So she planted a reed, and it grew four days and reached the sky and found a small crevice which it penetrated. Badger climbed its stalk and reached its tip, but he could not get through to see anything, so he returned saying, "I am very tired. I can see nothing but earth." The elders thought, "What man knows? Perhaps Locust." So they asked him, and he said, "Yes, I know." Locust is very brave. He never winks his eyes. So he climbed the stalk and went through and reached the tasselled tip of the reed, and looked around, and there was water everywhere. Locust carried a flute, slung on his back. He drew it out and began to play on it. At the Northwest the Yellow Cloud chief appeared. He was angry and darted yellow lightning which went close past the eyes of Locust. But Locust never winked, and went on playing his flute. Yellow Cloud said, "What kind of man have we here? Surely he is brave, surely he is a man!" Next at the Southwest Blue Cloud chief appeared, and he was angry too and flung blue lightning at Locust and it passed through him from side to side. But Locust continued to play as before, and Blue Cloud said the same about him as had Yellow Cloud. Then at the Southeast, Red Cloud came up very angry and darted red lightning which passed through Locust from belly to back, and he continued playing as if nothing had happened. Red Cloud expressed his wonder and said what the other Clouds had said. At the Northeast White Cloud arose and cast white lightning which passed through Locust from head to tail, and he continued playing as if nothing had happened to him. The four Cloud chiefs came close to Locust and talked with him, demanding to know where he came from. They said, "This is the land of the Clouds. What are you doing here? You are a good and brave man. Perhaps you are an orphan." "No," said Locust. "I have many people behind me in the Underworld." "It is well," said the Cloud chiefs. "You are brave and deathless. Your heart and those of your people must be good. Go tell them to come and all this land shall be theirs." "Thanks," said Locust, and he then returned and told his people. Then Badger went up and widened the opening so that the people could pass through. While he was doing this, Locust told of his adventures to the people and said that the place above was just like the place they were then at, all water. The people were saddened at this, but the chiefs thought, and said, "Well, it is no worse than here and may be better. Let's go up and see." The people climbed the reed for eight days, stopping each night at a joint from which a great leaf grew out, and the people slept on it. That is why these leaves are called "sleeps."

When all had emerged, the Twins who each had the resilient lightning shot it in every direction and made canyons through which the water flowed away. The Twins then made all the rocks of mud and made all the mountains and made everything that is of stone. Later they slew the Giant Eagle and the Giant Elk and other monsters.

The Earthdiver

A Western Mono Account

In the beginning, Prairie Falcon and Crow were sitting on a log which projected above the waters that covered the world. They asked Duck what number he had dreamed of, and Duck replied, "Two." Prairie Falcon assigned him the number three and told him to dive into the water and bring up some sand from the bottom. Duck dived to get the sand, but before he reached the bottom, the three days he had been allotted expired. He awoke from his dream, died, and floated to the surface. Prairie Falcon brought him back to life, however, and asked him what the trouble was. Duck said that he had come out of his dream, died, and then floated to the top.

Prairie Falcon now asked Coot what number he had dreamed of. Coot replied, "Four." Then Prairie Falcon assigned him the number two and ordered him to dive for sand. Before Coot reached the bottom, two days elapsed, and he came out of his dream. He too died, and his body floated to the surface of the waters. Prairie Falcon saw the corpse, recovered it, and brought Coot back to life. He asked Coot what had been the trouble, and Coot replied that he had passed out of his dream.

Then Prairie Falcon asked Grebe what number he had dreamed of. Grebe replied that he had dreamed of five. Prairie Falcon assigned him the number four, and told him that was the number of days he had to bring sand from the bottom of the waters. Grebe was successful. He dived all the way to the bottom of the waters and secured some sand in each hand. As he was returning to the surface, he passed out of his dream, died, and floated to the surface. Prairie Falcon brought him back to life and asked if he had secured any sand. Grebe said that he had, so Prairie Falcon wanted to know what he had done with it. Grebe explained that it had all slipped from his grasp when he died. Prairie Falcon and Crow both laughed at him and said that they didn't believe him. Then they looked at his hands and found sand under the fingernails. They took that sand and threw it in every direction. This is the way in which they made the world.

The Genesis of the Worlds, or the Beginning of Newness, according to the Zuñi

Before the beginning of the new-making, Áwonawílona (the Maker and Container of All, the All-father Father), solely had being. There was nothing else whatsoever throughout the great space of the ages save everywhere black darkness in it, and everywhere void desolation.

In the beginning of the new-made, Áwonawílona conceived within himself and thought outward in space, whereby mists of increase, steams potent of growth, were evolved and uplifted. Thus, by means of his innate knowledge, the All-container made himself in person and form of the Sun whom we hold to be our father and who thus came to exist and appear. With his appearance came the brightening of the spaces with light, and with the brightening of the spaces the great mist-clouds were thickened together and fell, whereby was evolved water in water; yea, and the world-holding sea.

With his substance of flesh (*yépnane*) outdrawn from the surface of his person, the Sun-father formed the seed-stuff of twain worlds, impregnating therewith the great waters, and lo! in the heat of his light these waters of the sea grew green and scums (*k'yanashótsiyallawe*) rose upon them, waxing wide and weighty until, behold! they became Áwitelin Tsíta, the "Four-fold Containing Mother-earth," and Ápoyan Tä'chu, the "All-covering Father-sky."

THE GENESIS OF MEN AND THE CREATURES

From the lying together of these twain upon the great world waters, so vitalizing, terrestrial life was conceived; whence began all beings of earth, men and the creatures, in the Four-fold womb of the World (Áwiten Téhu'hlnakwi).

Thereupon the Earth-mother repulsed the Sky-father, growing big and sinking deep into the embrace of the waters below, thus separating from the Sky-father in the embrace of the waters above. As a woman forebodes evil for her first-born ere born, even so did the Earth-mother forebode, long withholding from birth her myriad progeny and meantime seeking counsel with the Sky-father. "How," said they to one another, "shall our children, when brought forth, know one place from another, even by the white light of the Sun-father?"

Now like all the surpassing beings (*píkwaiyin áhâi*) the Earth-mother and the Sky-father were *'hlímna* (changeable), even as smoke in the wind; transmutable at thought, manifesting themselves in any form at will, like as dancers may by mask-making.

Thus, as a man and woman, spake they, one to the other. "Behold!" said the Earth-mother as a great terraced bowl appeared at hand and within it water, "this is as upon me the homes of my tiny children shall be. On the rim of each world-country they wander in, terraced mountains shall stand, making in one region many, whereby country shall be known from country, and within each, place from place. Behold, again!" said she as she spat on the water and rapidly smote and stirred it with her fingers. Foam formed, gathering about the terraced rim, mounting higher and higher. "Yea," said she, "and from my bosom they shall draw nourishment, for in such as this shall they find the substance of life whence we were ourselves sustained, for see!" Then with her warm breath she blew across the terraces; white flecks of the foam broke away, and, floating over above the water, were shattered by the cold breath of the Sky-father attending, and forthwith shed downward abundantly fine mist and spray! "Even so, shall white clouds float up from the great waters at the borders of the world, and clustering about the mountain terraces of the horizons be borne aloft and abroad by the breaths of the surpassing of soul-beings, and of the children, and shall hardened and broken be by thy cold, shedding downward, in rain-spray, the water of life, even into the hollow places of my lap! For therein chiefly shall nestle our children mankind and creaturekind, for warmth in thy coldness."

Lo! even the trees on high mountains near the clouds and the Sky-father crouch low toward the Earth-mother for warmth and protection! Warm is the Earth-mother, cold the Sky-father, even as woman is the warm, man the cold being!

"Even so!" said the Sky-father; "Yet not alone shalt *thou* helpful be unto our children, for behold!" and he spread his hand abroad with the palm downward and into all the wrinkles and crevices thereof he set the semblance of shining yellow corn-grains; in the dark of the early world-dawn they gleamed like sparks of fire, and moved as his hand was moved over the bowl, shining up from and also moving in the depths of the water therein. "See!" said he, pointing to the seven grains clasped by his thumb and four fingers, "by such shall our children be guided; for behold, when the Sun-father is not nigh, and thy terraces are as the dark itself (being all hidden therein), then shall our children be guided by lights—like to these lights of all the six regions turning round the midmost one—as in and around the midmost place, where these our children shall abide, lie all the other regions of space! Yea! and even as these grains gleam up from the water, so shall seed grains like to them, yet numberless, spring up from thy bosom when touched by my waters, to nourish our children." Thus and in other ways many devised they for their offspring.

THE GESTATION OF MEN AND
THE CREATURES

Anon in the nethermost of the four cave-wombs of the world, the seed of men and the creatures took form and increased; even as within eggs in warm places worms speedily appear, which growing, presently burst their shells and become as may happen, birds, tadpoles or serpents, so did men and all creatures grow manifoldly and multiply in many kinds. Thus the lowermost womb or cave-world, which was Ánosin téhuli (the womb of sooty depth or of growth-generation, because it was the place of first formation and black as a chimney at night time, foul too, as the internals of the belly), thus did it become overfilled with being. Everywhere were unfinished creatures, crawling like reptiles one over another in filth and black darkness, crowding thickly together and treading each other, one spitting on another or doing other indecency, insomuch that loud became their murmurings and lamentations, until many among them sought to escape, growing wiser and more manlike.

THE FORTHCOMING FROM EARTH OF
THE FOREMOST OF MEN

Then came among men and the beings, it is said, the wisest of wise men and the foremost, the all-sacred master, Póshaiyank‘ya, he who appeared in the waters below, even as did the Sun-father in the wastes above, and who arose from the nethermost sea, and pitying men still, won upward, gaining by virtue of his (innate) wisdom-knowledge issuance from that first world-womb through ways so dark and narrow that those who, seeing somewhat, crowded after, could not follow, so eager were they and so mightily did they strive with one another! Alone, then, he fared upward from one womb (cave) to another out into the great breadth of daylight. There, the earth lay, like a vast island in the midst of the great waters, wet and unstable. And alone fared he forth dayward, seeking the Sun-father and supplicating him to deliver mankind and the creatures there below.

THE BIRTH FROM THE SEA OF THE TWAIN DELIVERERS OF MEN

Then did the Sun-father take counsel within himself, and casting his glance downward espied, on the great waters, a Foam-cap near to the Earth-mother. With his beam he impregnated and with his heat incubated the Foam-cap, whereupon she gave birth to Úanam Achi Píahkoa, the Beloved Twain who descended; first, Úanam Éhkona, the Beloved Preceder, then Úanam Yáluna, the Beloved Follower, Twin brothers of Light, yet Elder and Younger, the Right and the Left, like to question and answer in deciding and doing. To them the Sun-father imparted, still retaining, control-thought and his own knowledge-wisdom, even as to the offspring of wise parents their knowingness is imparted and as to his right hand and his left hand a skillful man gives craft freely surrendering not his knowledge. He gave them, of himself and their mother the Foam-cap, the great cloud-bow, and for arrows the thunderbolts of the four quarters (twain to either), and for buckler the fog-making shield, which (spun of the floating clouds and spray and woven, as of cotton we spin and weave) supports as on wind, yet hides (as a shadow hides) its bearer, defending also. And of men and all creatures he gave them the fathership and dominion, also as a man gives over the control of his work to the management of his hands. Well instructed of the Sun-father, they lifted the Sky-father with their great cloud-bow into the vault of the high zenith, that the earth might become warm and thus fitter for their children, men and the creatures. Then along the trail of the sun-seeking Póshaiyank'ya, they sped backward swiftly on their floating fog-shield, westward to the Mountain of Generation. With their magic knives of the thunderbolt they spread open the uncleft depths of the mountain, and still on their cloud-shield—even as a spider in her web descendeth—so descended they unerringly, into the dark of the under-world. There they abode with men and the creatures, attending them, coming to know them, and becoming known of them as masters and fathers, thus seeking the ways for leading them forth.

THE BIRTH AND DELIVERY OF MEN AND THE CREATURES

Now there were growing things in the depths, like grasses and crawling vines. So now the Beloved Twain breathed on the stems of these grasses (growing tall, as grass is wont to do toward the light, under the opening they had cleft and whereby they had descended), causing them to increase vastly and rapidly by grasping and walking round and round them, twisting them upward until lo! they reach forth even into the light. And where successively they grasped the stems ridges were formed and thumb-marks whence sprang branching leaf-stems. Therewith the two formed a great ladder whereon men and the creatures might ascend to the second cave-floor, and thus not be violently ejected in after-time by the throes of the Earth-mother, and thereby be made demoniac and deformed.

Up this ladder, into the second cave-world, men and the beings crowded, following closely the Two Little but Mighty Ones. Yet many fell back and, lost in the darkness, peopled the under-world, whence they were delivered in after-time amid terrible earth shakings, becoming the monsters and fearfully strange beings of olden time. Lo! in this second womb it was dark as is the night of a stormy season, but larger of space and higher than had been the first, because it was nearer the navel of the Earth-mother, hence named K'ólin tehuli (the Umbilical-womb, or the Place of Gestation). Here again men and the beings increased and the clamor of their complainings grew loud and beseeching. Again the Two, augmenting the growth of the great ladder, guided them upward, this time not all at once, but in successive bands to become in time the fathers of the six kinds of men (the yellow, the tawny gray, the red, the white, the mingled, and the black races), and with them the gods and creatures of them all. Yet this time also, as before, multitudes were lost or left behind. The third great cave-world, whereunto men and the creatures had now ascended, being larger than the second and higher, was lighter, like a valley in starlight, and named Áwisho tehuli—the Vaginal-womb, or the Place of Sex-generation or Gestation. For here the various peoples and beings began to multiply apart in kind one from another; and as the nations and tribes of men and the creatures thus waxed numerous as before, here, too, it became overfilled. As before, generations of nations now were led out successively (yet many lost, also as hitherto) into the next and last world-cave, Tépahaian tehuli, the Ultimate-uncoverable, or the Womb or Parturition.

Here it was light like the dawning, and men began to perceive and to learn variously according to their natures, wherefore the Twain taught them to seek first of all our Sun-father, who would, they said, reveal to them wisdom and knowledge of the ways of life—wherein also they were instructing them as we do little children. Yet like the other cave-worlds, this too became, after long time, filled with progeny; and finally, at periods, the Two led forth the nations of men and the kinds of being, into this great upper world, which is called Ték'ohaian úlahnane, or the World of Disseminated Light and Knowledge or Seeing.

THE CONDITION OF MEN WHEN FIRST INTO THE WORLD OF DAYLIGHT BORN

Eight years made the span of four days and four nights when the world was new. It was while yet such days and nights continued that men were led forth, first in the night, that it might be well. For even when they saw the great star (*móyächun 'hlána*), which since then is spoken of as the lying star (*mókwanosona*), they thought it the Sun himself, so burned it their eyeballs! Men and the creatures were nearer alike then than now: black were our fathers the late born of creation, like the caves from which they came forth; cold and scaly their skins like those of mud-creatures; goggled their eyes like those of an owl; membranous their ears like those of cave-bats; webbed their feet like those of walkers in wet and soft places; and according as they were elder or younger, they had tails, longer or shorter. They crouched when they walked, often indeed, crawling along the ground like toads, lizards and newts; like infants who still fear to walk straight, they crouched, as before-time they had in their cave-worlds, that they might not stumble and fall, or come to hurt in the uncertain light thereof. And when the morning star rose they blinked excessively as they beheld its brightness and cried out with many mouth-motionings that surely now the Father was coming; but it was only the elder of the Bright Ones, gone before with elder nations and with his shield of flame, heralding from afar (as we herald with wet shell scales or crystals) the approach of the Sun-father! And when, low down in the east the Sun-father himself appeared, what though shrouded in the midst of the great world waters, they were so blinded and heated by his light and glory that they cried out to one another in anguish and fell down wallowing and covering their eyes with their bare hands and arms. Yet ever anew they looked afresh to the light and anew struggled toward the sun as moths and other night creatures seek the light of a camp fire; yea, and what though burned, seek ever anew that light!

Thus ere long they became used to the light, and to this high world they had entered. Wherefore, when they arose and no longer walked bended, lo! it was then that they first looked full upon one another and in horror of their filthier parts, strove to hide these, even from one another, with girdles of bark and rushes; and when by thus walking only upon their hinder feet the same became bruised and sore, they sought to protect them with plaited soles (sandals) of yucca fiber.

The Creation Account
of the Uitoto
of Colombia, South America

1.

In the beginning, the word gave origin to the Father. A phantasm, nothing else existed in the beginning; the Father touched an illusion, he grasped something mysterious. Nothing existed. Through the agency of a dream our Father Naimuena [he who is or has a phantasm] kept the mirage to his body, and he pondered long and thought deeply.

2.

Nothing existed, not even a stick to support the vision: our Father attached the illusion to the thread of a dream and kept it by the aid of his breath. He sounded to reach the bottom of the appearance, but there was nothing. Nothing existed indeed.

3.

Then the Father again investigated the bottom of the mystery. He tied the empty illusion to the dream thread and pressed the magical substance upon it. Thus by the aid of his dream he held it like a wisp of raw cotton.

4.

Then he seized the mirage bottom and stamped upon it repeatedly, sitting down at last on his dreamed earth.

5.

The earth-phantasm was now his, and he spat out saliva repeatedly so that the forests might grow. Then he lay down upon his earth and covered it with the roof of heaven. As he was the owner of the earth he placed above it the blue and the white sky.

6.

Thereupon, Rafuema, "the man who has the narratives," sitting at the base of the heavens, pondered, and he created this story so that we might listen to it here upon earth.

The Creation Account of the Luiseño, the Southernmost Division of the Shoshonean in California

In the beginning all was empty space. Ké-vish-a-tak-vish was the only being. This period was called *Om-ai-ya-mai*, signifying emptiness, nobody there. Then came the time called *Ha-ruh-rug*, upheaval, things coming into shape. Then a time called *Chu-tu-tai*, the falling of things downward, and after this, *Yu-vai-to-vai*, things working in darkness without the light of sun or moon. Then came the period *Tul-mul Pu-shim*, signifying that deep down in the heart of the earth things were working together.

Then came *Why-yai Pee-vai*, a gray glimmering like the whiteness of hoar frost; and then, *Mit'ai Kwai-rai*, the dimness of twilight. Then came a period of cessation, *Na-kai Ho-wai-yai*, meaning things at a standstill. Then Ké-vish-a-tak-vish made a man, Tuk-mit, the Sky, and a woman, To-mai-yo-vit, the Earth. There was no light, but in the darkness these two became conscious of each other.

"Who are you," asked the man.

"I am To-mai-yo-vit. I am stretched, I am extended. I shake, I resound. I am diminished, I am earthquake. I revolve, I roll, I disappear. And who are you?"

"I am Ké-vish-a-tak-vish. I am night. I am inverted. I cover, I rise. I devour, I drain [by death]. I seize, I send away the souls of men. I cut, I sever life."

"Then you are my brother."

"Then you are my sister."

And by her brother, the Sky, the Earth conceived and became the mother of all things.

Chapter 2

The Trickster, Heroes, and the Folk

The King James version of Genesis 6:1-4 recounts:

And it came to pass, when men began to multiply on the face of the earth, and daughters were born unto them, that the sons of God saw the daughters of men that they *were* fair; and they took them wives of all which they chose. And the LORD said, My spirit shall not always strive with man, for that he also *is* flesh: yet his days shall be a hundred and twenty years. There were giants in the earth in those days; and also after that, when the sons of God came in unto the daughters of men, and they bare *children* to them, the same *became* mighty men which *were* of old, men of renown.

The reader who is not compelled to be defensive about Judeo-Christianity recognizes the distinction between men and gods in this passage. Should he check the original language, he finds "sons of God" is itself euphemistic, the accurate rendition being "divine beings." Such reality is abhorrent to most Judeo-Christians because it poses an unresolvable question about the nature of monotheism.

Discussing the Iroquois in *Man's Rise to Civilization as Shown by the Indians of North America from Primeval Times to the Coming of the Industrial State*, Peter Farb observes:

The Iroquois represent the least complex social organization in North America in which monotheism existed. Monotheism, contrary to what most people believe, goes beyond simply a belief in one god. It signifies rather the belief in a supreme being who, himself uncreated, nevertheless is responsible for creating clusters of other supernatural and sacred beings, whether they be

63

angels, demons, or saints. Judaism, Christianity, and Mohammedanism are monotheistic beliefs not because Jehovah or God or Allah is the *only* supernatural being, but because each is the *first cause* and creator of the world. Our modern fundamentalists in religion often ignore the references in the Old Testament to immortals in addition to the supreme being Jehovah. In the King James Version the Hebrew words are often translated "sons of God"—but "divine beings" is more accurate. The Iroquois worshipped their Great Spirit for himself—and also for bringing the other gods into being.

The Iroquois raise an interesting question about the origins of monotheism. Many scholars have assumed that monotheism arises whenever people have experience with the powerful human rulers who hold sway over empires or kingdoms; a supreme god then becomes a celestial reflection of some supreme ruler on earth. That was probably true in Egypt, where the worship of the high god Aton lasted for a time under the fanatic Pharaoh Ikhnaton. Christianity increasingly came to reflect the political society of the Roman Empire in which it arose by developing a hierarchy of God, Jesus, the Pope and priesthood, angels, and saints. Eventually, there were nine orders of the celestial hierarchy, and they were supposed to number 26,613,336 angels. The Iroquois, on the contrary, lacked not only a single strong ruler but even any powerful government. The Council of Sachems, which limited itself mostly to external questions of war or peace, was unable even to control its own young Pine Tree warriors. The case of the Iroquois is in some ways similar to the ancient Israelites in the times of the Judges when a potent Jehovah controlled human affairs, yet the earthly government was that of a weak council of elders. These Israelite elders merely expressed the consensus of their communities and could not even enforce their views; they did not represent any strong, independent policies of their own.

The monotheistic societies of the Iroquois and other cultures, past and present and around the world, reveal one common characteristic: A hierarchy of numerous allegiances extends from the individual to the outermost boundaries of his society. Among the Iroquois, the individual was part of a nuclear family, which belonged to a household, which lived with other households in a longhouse, which constituted part of a clan which belonged to a moity, which made up a tribe, which in turn was part of the League of the Iroquois. The individual Iroquois was ensnared in a morass of allegiances; the only way to make sense out of it all was to postulate an orderly environment over which rules prevailed even at the ultimate, supernatural boundaries. The connection that has long been noted between monotheism and societies that practice agriculture now can be explained. Only under agriculture practice does a society become sufficiently complex for the hierarchy of groups and allegiances to appear that allows the birth of monotheism!

In Genesis 6:5-6 the *first cause* decided man had become excessively evil and must be destroyed. That evil had been the initial work of a trickster figure, Satan, who, with the aid of

---

[1]New York, 1968, pp. 107–08.

Lilith, infiltrated the garden and created the dissatisfaction that led to the creation of Eve and allowed death to become a reality.

Of those misty, early figures, it is difficult to be sure who is emulable as a hero. Adam is an innocent of sorts—but easily seduced. Satan is an undisciplined rebel who understands passion and the personal need to satisfy it.

Every cultural group has its heroic models—those emulable supra-humans who embody the most idealistically desirable aspects of the people even as they reveal the realistic behavior patterns that dominate in lives structured by geography and social need. Existing between the idealized and the realistic worlds, they are neither gods nor men—instead they are a curious combination of the two: immortals without allegiance to the limitations imposed by eternality; mortals reveling in the most conspicuous forms of personal anarchy. They are the link between man and his gods even as they are the link between man and his passion for self-indulgence.

Psychologists, theologians, and anthropologists spend an inordinate amount of time analyzing the origins of human conscious and unconscious activity in the creation of and belief in the accounts, their characters, and the meanings of both accounts and characters. The most ignorant, superstitious, terrified human of 10,000 years ago has his counterpart today—and in like degree. Only 10,000 years of technological creations stand between the two men. Remove the automobile, the machines of construction, electricity, and manufactured goods from that man today and he becomes as helpless in nature, as incapable of creating a hospitable environment, as anguished about the unseen around him as his 10,000-year-old counterpart. He sheds "civilization" as he loses the extensions of himself, for they have not changed him as an animal; they have merely served as a buffer between him and the inhospitable world, the night demons, and the chronic fear that somewhere, sometime, a better world does *not* exist.

That man of today will assure you he is superior to his distant ancestor, but he is ruthless about territorial rights which confine him more and more in smaller and smaller places so that he becomes antisocial and ulcer-ridden with all sorts of vague fears that he is as incapable of articulating as was his ancestor. He is as ritualistic in his religious beliefs and social conduct as any distant ancestor, perhaps because the intervening years haven't supplied any cosmic answers but have caused him to become arbitrary when he could not advance. He can express his technological needs, but he is no nearer an understanding of his emotional ones than his distant kinsman was. The basic difference in the two men is that the earlier one had too little time to worry about his emotions because physical survival was difficult; the later one has little problem with physical survival which gives him too much time to worry about his emotions —emotions he is as subject to and incapable of understanding and controlling as was his ancestor.

Technology has, indeed, advanced. Man has benefitted from it physically but remained relatively static within himself. He has become dependent on the machine, lost contact with nature, remained primitive in his basic human responses. Only technology can be called "civilized"; the man who uses the civilized implements is still primitive, for he cannot change himself even to the extent he can change cattle, horses, dogs. That primitive instinct prevails; he will not experiment with self—so he has remained "unimproved."

The trickster-hero is as much a personification of modern man's aspirations as he is of primitive man's. The technological skills modern man possesses merely keep him from finding the same satisfactions in the trickster that the primitive still does. Yet who can deny the veiled or open admiration we accord our most anarchistic elements: those men who refuse to observe moral or legal embargos, the Jesse Jameses, Al Capones, easy riders, and midnight cowboys of fact and fiction who claim our attention, enlist our loyalty, demand our admiration because, not liking the world as it is, they create a personal code without regard for others and manage to take advantage of the rewards of the world without paying the price demanded. They are, inevitably, people of limited physical or intellectual endowments who, in reality or fancy, are alienated from the group, who establish some sort of personal relationship with their concepts of the natural world and, within the concept, allow their passions to dominate their every act. (Whether their concepts be of a criminal ghetto, a gigantic motorcycle trail through backwoods country, or the sophisticated sexual jungles of large cities, they are the natural world to the alienated nonheroes.) Food, sex, sensual stimuli occupy them as they become rootless, always in flight, dissatisfied by each new anarchistic violation of the codes. Becoming the innocuous Tom Jones type created by Henry Fielding, the more despicable Sebastian Dangerfield created by J. P. Donleavy, or the dangerous Clyde Barrow created by social situation, they outrage the society they see inimical to their desires by flagrant social excess, deliberate violation, or violent act. Redeeming qualities usually surface at length: animals or children move them to acts of kindness, family ties draw them back, or the need for social approval causes them to attempt incognito respectability. Those whose sense of propriety has been outraged, those whose rights have been violated, those whose lives have been damaged by the now reformed rebels cannot be generously forgiving, however. Payment is demanded and the rebels must defend themselves against society's hostility. Eventually, they fall victim to society and die in some kind of prison or are killed outright.

Why do we empathize with such tricksters as they violate the codes that bind us? Why do we suffer with them as they seek reinclusion without regeneration? Why do we sympathize as they are restrained or eliminated? Because they represent that anarchy that resides in all of us but is restrained by personal timidity or social pressure so that we sublimate the egotistic impulse enough to live unexciting lives or utilize our redirected energies to attain a more satisfying existence within socially approved limits. But we can be defiantly anarchistic, supremely self-indulgent in vicarious association with those who lack our timidity or fear. They become our voyeuristic alteregos.

It takes no Freudian knowledge, no Jungian insight to see our own passions and desires at work in our responses. Nor does it take the ethnologist or anthropologist to analyze the trickster-hero accounts as primitive man's creations of the same escape hatches we employ daily. It does take a kind of honest appraisal of self, for the basic need is neither primitive nor civilized; it is timeless. Only the technological background changes; man remains constant.

The violent act, the self-serving episode, the antisocial life-style—these are the staples of much of the most popular television programs and movies. Occasionally a trickster-hero as obvious as Coyote, Hare, Raven, or Nanaboju is created in the person of an Amos Burke (*Burke's Law*), Kid Currey and Hannibal Hayes (*Smith and Jones*), or James Bond. Within the framework of acceptability for one reason or another, they are lawless, self-seeking, sybaritic, unrestrained, and enviable to the point of allowing us vicarious identification, therefore release of our own instinctive, irrational, antisocial urges. And our vicarious participation is socially acceptable for it is a sublimating process that protects the group from us.

Further, a didactic function is served by such accounts— for the primitive and the civilized man. No matter how desirable the unrestrained, untrammeled life may be, the price is always loneliness, unacceptability, ultimate unhappiness, or outright tragedy. It makes no difference whether the trickster figure is god or demi-god or hero, he is less than Wah'kon-tah but greater than the average mortal—his is a unique position. Coyote, Raven, and Hare are beyond restraint; so are James Bond and Sebastian Dangerfield.

Discussing the trickster figure, Carl Jung suggested that "the trickster is a collective shadow figure, an epitome of all the inferior traits of character in individuals."[2] Those traits may seem inferior to us (or at least we give lip service to their inferiority even as we envy their unabashed revelation in our trickster-heroes), but we seldom see Odysseus as an inferior representative in *The Odyssey*, Aeneas as reprehensible in *The Aeneid*, or the unchristianized aspects of Beowulf in the Anglo-Saxon epic-unemulable; yet each is a representative of the trickster figure in European literature. There he is the archetypal hero; clever, cunning, self-serving, self-indulgent, and powerful enough to effect his own grand designs. In a Prometheus or an Epimetheus he is the bestower of gifts (fire and woman respectively); in Satan he is the bestower of female sex object and cause of death; in an Oedipus he is a thoroughgoing self-server no matter how we attempt to elevate him with such pretentious words as "hubris" and "tragic flaw." All men are tragically flawed—some are just less apologetic about it than others; some need less to excuse the human behavior of their models and themselves. And, interestingly, it was not the Greeks who rationalized the behavior of Oedipus. They understood his relationship to the Odysseus and Achilles types so representative of their own needs.

Strangely, the ones who seem less in need of rationalizing the flaws function together more harmoniously than the ones who seek to veil the flaws in philosophical garb that fits uncomfortably.

The Native American, like his primitive counterpart in Greece, Rome, and northern Europe, established his models—epic in stature, undisciplined in conduct, noble in spite of ignoble features—to create his trickster-heroes, his heroes, and his representative average model. The following accounts reveal his success in structuring himself.

[2]Cited in Paul Radin, *The Trickster* (New York, 1956), p. 209.

Winabojo and the Medicine Man

(Ojibwa)

Winabojo lived after the earliest Indians. He was married, a fact which is not generally stated. He took an Indian wife and had three children, one a baby girl. His wife's parents lived with them and the family lived a long time in the Indian village.

There was an old custom that when two bands of Chippewa played a certain game together each band put up a person for a wager, this person being adopted by the winning band. Once Winabojo's band lost in such a game and refused to give up the wager. One morning Winabojo got up early and went into the woods. He saw a great many men with clubs and asked what they were doing. They replied, "We are going to get the boy that your people wagered in the game; you had better join us or you will be killed." Winabojo decided to do this in order to save his family. When they attacked the village he was so eager that he went right to his own lodge and began to kill his family. He killed the old people and the two boys and was about to kill the baby girl when some one stopped him. Then he was like some one waking from a dream and felt very sorry for what he had done. He took the baby and started to carry it to his grandmother. It was a long way but he reached there at last. The baby was crying, but he did not tell his grandmother what was the matter.

She said, "Why did you bring the baby here? Is its mother coming? I can not quiet this baby."

Winabojo said, "I made a terrible blunder. I joined an attacking party and killed all my family except this baby."

His grandmother said, "It is no use for us to stay here. The people will come and kill us. They will know that you joined an attacking party."

This was the worst thing that Winabojo ever did, and he took his final departure from the earth at this time.

He got some pods from the trees. They were shaped like little balls and he made them grow big. Then he put the baby in one and his grandmother in the other. He stood on the shore and tied them tight, then he put them in the water and asked the water to carry them all away. So they floated off and went clear across a great water toward the setting sun. There is another earth beyond this earth and Winabojo lives there now with his grandmother.

When the traders and the white people came among the Chippewa their manner of life changed, but they remembered Winabojo. Ten men decided to go and talk with Winabojo. They fasted and took a long time to prepare for the journey. They made a strong canoe and skirted along the edge of the great lake, camping at night. One man had a dream telling where Winabojo was living, and after they had traveled a long time they saw an island. They said, "That must be the place where he lives." They reached the island and went ashore. It was the home of Winabojo. They saw footprints on the shore and a trail leading inland. The men followed the trail and came to a large, firm lodge. They did not dare go near the lodge, but they stood around where they could see it.

Finally one man heard a voice say, "Well, well, my uncle; come in if you want to see me. Don't stand out there." (This was the voice of Winabojo.)

The man who heard the voice went and told the rest of the party. Each had a present for Winabojo. They went into the lodge and had the presents on their backs and in their arms and hands. Winabojo shook hands with them and they all sat down. There was absolute silence.

Beside the door was a stump overgrown with moss. After a while a voice came from this stump saying, "Why don't you speak to your uncle? When we were on earth we talked to our relations." (This was the voice of Winabojo's grandmother.)

Winabojo replied, "I am just thinking what to say. I will talk to our relations. If we are to follow the custom of the place they came from, we must give them food. They must be hungry."

In stories about Winabojo when he was on earth it is always said that he carried his lunch in a bag on his back. This bag still stood there, and in it were bones of bear, deer, and other animals. He had eaten the meat and put the bones back in the bag.

Winabojo got up on his knees, put his hand in the bag, and happened to take out the bone of a bear's foreleg. He threw it in front of them, and it became a bear. It was almost dead, and he told them to kill it and take it to their camp, saying they would find a big kettle there. The men killed the bear and dragged it to their camp. They cooked enough for one meal. It was greasy and there was a great deal of nice broth. When the meat was ready two men took the kettle on a stick and set it before Winabojo.

Winabojo lived with his grandmother. His daughter had grown up and lived in another lodge. He told his daughter to bring wooden dishes and spoons. She came bringing the dishes and spoons. She was very beautiful and wore a red sash. The men had their feast and took the kettle back to the camp. They had come to ask favors, but they decided to wait until the next day.

They went to Winabojo on the following day, and he said, "You have come to ask favors. I will do what I can for you."

One man said, "I have come to ask you to give me a life with no end." Winabojo twisted him around and threw him into a corner, and he turned into a black stone. Winabojo said, "You asked for a long life. You will last as long as the world stands."

Another man gave Winabojo a present and said, "I have come to ask for unfailing success and that I may never lack for anything." Winabojo turned him into a fox, saying, "Now you will always be cunning and successful."

The others saw what was happening to these men and they became frightened. They decided to ask for one thing together, so they asked that they might have healing power in their medicine.

Winabojo put some medicine in a little leather bag and gave it to each man. He said the others had asked so much that they had failed, but that he had given these eight men the real success. He said, "I have given you this medicine. Use it sparingly. When it is gone your power will also be gone." Then he said: "Ten men came to see me. Two made bad requests, and will never get home. The medicine I have given you will not last forever, but I will give my daughter to you. Do not approach her until you get home, then one of you may take her for his wife. She is to be the means of keeping up the power of medicine among men."

They started the next day, and Winabojo said, "I want my daughter to go back, for she is human. Protect her until you get home, then select one of your number to marry her, otherwise she will return here and you will lose the power of your medicine."

So they started; she sat in the middle of the canoe. They went across to the mainland and made a camp for the night. She cooked for them and had her camp at some distance from the rest of the party. It was necessary to camp three nights. All went well until the last night, when the men started a discussion as to which should be her husband. One said: "I suppose she knows which she wants. I will go quietly and ask her." All were watching as this man went and sat down a little distance from the girl's camp. He asked which one of them she would select for her husband if she had her choice. There was no reply. He came back and reported to the others. Then another man said he would go and would say a little more than the first had said. He thought he would say that she could have her choice. So he went toward the girl's camp, but she was gone. They had lost her.

The men felt very, very badly. They realized that a wrong had been done to the world, as her medicine would have been a benefit to the whole race.

Winabojo's Camping Around

(Ojibwa)

There was once an old man who had eight sons. They lived quietly in the deep woods and were very industrious. The old man kept the camp and his sons went hunting to secure food for them. One day a little boy came to the camp. He was a short, fat boy and was wandering in the woods. They took care of him and later he repaid them by guiding them and making them strong.

After a long time a girl came to the camp. The old man was alone. He asked the girl where she came from and she said that her parents had been killed by an enemy and that she was wandering around.

The old man said, "Come in, live here, and help me take care of the place." She proved to be a woman controlled by an evil spirit, but they got along.

At length one son said to another, "Do you notice that she never eats? She cooks the food for us but refuses to eat herself. We had better ask our father about her." The other son said that he also noticed it.

A third son said that he would pretend to be sick and would see if he could find out anything. He lay down in another part of the wigwam and pretended to be very sick indeed. His father went out and dug roots, but the medicine did him no good. Then his father went out and dug more roots, but still the son was very sick. The woman also went in and out of the wigwam and the boy noticed that she often brought in a bundle, hiding it behind her belongings. When she was outside the boy jumped up, opened the bundle, and found a human arm. Then he lay down as before.

That night he told his father and brothers when the woman was outside and they said, "We must leave here." The next evening when one of the boys came home he said, "I have killed a deer." According to the custom she went to get the deer, but the boy had hung it so high that it took her a long time to get it.

While she was away the father said, "An evil spirit is here. We must get away. Call on your dreams to help us, for she will follow us. You are young and can get away. I am old and she will probably overtake me. She probably knows by this time that we are going away." So they started in the night. They had the old man go ahead and did not go any faster than he could travel.

As they were going along they heard a voice say, "No matter how fast or how far you go, I will follow and overtake you. Even if you go to the ends of the earth you can not get away from me."

The old man said, "Her voice is getting nearer. Do something; have dreams given you anything that will help us?"

Finally the fat boy said, "I dreamed something that will help us. We will go to a certain river. She can not cross that, and if we can get across she can not reach us. This was my dream." This boy was a "wonder child." He said, "After we cross the river I will make a bog on her side of the river, and I will put prickles in her way before she gets to the bog." The man and the boys crossed the river, but soon they saw the woman coming through the bog.

The old man said, "Call on your dreams. Have you nothing that will help us?" They answered, "We have nothing."

The old man said, "In my youth I dreamed of a river with a waterfall. Below the waterfall there were rapids, and on a rock sat two pelicans. They said they would always help me. I am calling on them to help us."

The man and his sons came to the waterfall and the rapids, then to the smooth water below the rapids. There they saw a rock with two pelicans sitting on it. They could hear the woman approaching and saying that she would get them. The old man wished that the river would be very wide between them, and it was so. The woman raved and called on the pelicans to help her. One pelican said he would take her across on his back. They got halfway across and she beat him, saying, "Go faster, go faster." This made the pelican very angry. He called on the other pelican and they threw her into the water. She was drowned and floated away. She went over a waterfall and her body went into a whirlpool below the fall.

So the men were saved. The woman had called upon Winabojo, who heard her and hastened to see what was the matter. He was staying with his grandmother at the time. Winabojo followed the course of the river on the same side that the woman had traveled. The river was so mighty and terrible that even Winabojo could not cross it. As he stood on the shore he saw a little fish and said, "Little brother, can't you get me across this swift river?"

The fish said, "I am too small."

Winabojo said, "I will make you big." So he made the fish big and the fish took him across. In return for this he decorated the fish with spots and made his belly white. (This was a pickerel.) The fish told him that the woman's body was in a whirlpool below the falls, so Winabojo went there, guided by the fish. He saw the woman and tried to get her, but it was of no use. He got a long pole and finally dislodged the body and pulled it to the edge of the water. He snatched it and drew it ashore.

Then he began to talk to her as if she were alive and he had saved her. He said, "What shall we do?" And he answered for her, "Well, you had better think of something for us to do." He said, "If you are willing, I will put up a wigwam and hunt and get food for you." He answered for her, "Do whatever you think best."

He made lots of basswood-bark twine and carried her in a pack on his back. He would carry her until he was tired, then he would put her down, go on, and make a wigwam. He saw that she was in a trance and hoped that she would revive. He finished the lodge, went hunting, and brought food to her, as he would to a living person. So he camped in one place after another. When he went hunting he hid her in case anyone came to the camp. He was very successful with his hunting and lived in this way for a long time. When he had cooked the food he shook her, set her up, and tried to feed her; but it was of no use. He could get no sign of life.

Winabojo made three camps, carrying the woman's body from one camp to another on his back. Then he got tired of it and said, "If she is going to die she might as well die now." So he cut off her head and left her there. This story is called "Winabojo's camping around."

Winabojo's Diving for a Wager

(Ojibwa)

Winabojo was always wandering around through the woods. He walked many miles, following streams and gathering berries. Once as he was going along he saw a lot of loons at the other end of a lake. They had a wager as to which could start at the end of the lake, dive, swim the farthest, and come back again. They were playing in a wide, open space of water, but below this space the water was rapid and filled with rocks.

When Winabojo appeared suddenly to the loons they were frightened and started to fly away, but Winabojo said, "Don't go. We are all friends." He called them, and they came to him in flocks. He said, "We will have fun. I will dive, too. Let us put up a wager and see who can stay longest under the water. Your play is too easy for me. Let us make the space longer; go down with the current and come back again." The loons had put a stake under the water. The plan was that when a loon reached this stake he should move it farther down the stream; the one who followed him did the same, each proving that he could swim farther by moving the stake. Winabojo was the last to start, and the loons were all under the water when he was ready to dive. The loons swam with their eyes open, but Winabojo told the Indians that they must always close their eyes when they went into the water. Winabojo said, "Now I am ready," filled his lungs, threw himself into the water, and, as he supposed, swam toward the stake, but his eyes being closed, he lost the direction. Instead of swimming toward the stake he hit a great rock. It stunned him and cut a gash in his forehead. The loons saw him strike his head and float away. They said, "Winabojo can not be killed. He will come to life and do us some harm. He is so foolish that he will probably blame us."

75

Winabojo drifted down the stream until he came to some bushes. Then he revived and felt of his forehead. He took some clay and put it on his forehead to stop the bleeding. One of his teeth was gone. He stayed there until he felt better. After a while he got up and said he would go to his grandmother who could cure him. His grandmother scolded him well for his heedlessness but she healed him with an herb.

The story is called "Winabojo diving for a wager."

Manabozho's Flight

(Ojibwa)

At Lake St. Clair, Manabozho saw a number of ducks, and he thought to himself, "Just how am I going to kill them?" After a while, he took out one of his pails and started to drum and sing at the same time. The words of the song he sang were:

I am bringing new songs.

When the ducks saw Manabozho standing near the shore, they swam toward him and as soon as he saw this, he sent his grandmother ahead to build a little lodge, where they could live. In the meantime, he killed a few of the ducks, so, while his grandmother started out to build a shelter, Manabozho went towards the lake where the ducks and geese were floating around and around. Manabozho jumped into a sack and then dived into the water. The ducks and geese were quite surprised to see that he was such an excellent diver, and came closer and closer. Then Manabozho challenged them to a contest at diving. He said that he could beat them all. The ducks all accepted the challenge, but Manabozho beat them. Then he went after the geese and beat them too. For a time he was alternately diving and rising to the surface, all around. Finally he dived under the geese and started to tie their legs together with some basswood bark. When the geese noticed this, they tried to rise and fly away, but they were unable to do so, for Manabozho was hanging on to the other end of the string. The geese, nevertheless, managed to rise, gradually dragging Manabozho along with them. They finally emerged from the water and rose higher and higher into the air. Manabozho, however, hung on, and would not let go, until his hand was cut and the string broke.

Manabozho and the Berries

(Ojibwa)

While walking along the river he saw some berries in the water. He dived down for them, but was stunned when he unexpectedly struck the bottom. There he lay for quite a while, and when he recovered consciousness and looked up, he saw the berries hanging on a tree just above him.

Manabozho and the "Hell-Diver"

(Menomini)

While Manabozho was once walking along a lake shore, tired and hungry, he observed a long, narrow sandbar, which extended far out into the water, around which were myriads of waterfowl, so Manabozho decided to have a feast. He had with him only his medicine bag; so he entered the brush and hung it upon a tree, now called "Manabozho tree," and procured a quantity of bark, which he rolled into a bundle and placing it upon his back, returned to the shore, where he pretended to pass slowly by in sight of the birds. Some of the Swans and Ducks, however, recognizing Manabozho and becoming frightened, moved away from the shore.

One of the Swans called out, "Ho! Manabozho, where are you going?" To this Manabozho replied, "I am going to have a song. As you may see, I have all my songs with me." Manabozho then called out to the birds, "Come to me, my brothers, and let us sing and dance." The birds assented and returned to the shore, when all retreated a short distance away from the lake to an open space where they might dance. Manabozho removed the bundle of bark from his back and placed it on the ground, got out his singing-sticks, and said to the birds, "Now, all of you dance around me as I drum; sing as loudly as you can, and keep your eyes closed. The first one to open his eyes will forever have them red and sore."

Manabozho began to beat time upon his bundle of bark, while the birds, with eyes closed, circled around him singing as loudly as they could. Keeping time with one hand, Manabozho suddenly grasped the neck of a Swan, which he broke; but before he had killed the bird it screamed out, whereupon Manabozho said, "That's right, brothers, sing as loudly as you can." Soon another Swan fell a victim; then a Goose, and so on until the number of birds was greatly reduced. Then the "Hell-diver," opening his eyes to see why there was less sing- ing than at first, and beholding Manabozho and the heap of victims, cried out, "Manabozho is killing us! Manabozho is killing us!" and im- mediately ran to the water, followed by the remainder of the birds.

As the "Hell-diver" was a poor runner, Manabozho soon overtook him, and said, "I won't kill you, but you shall always have red eyes and be the laughing-stock of all the birds." With this he gave the bird a kick, sending him far out into the lake and knocking off his tail, so that the "Hell-diver" is red-eyed and tailless to this day.

Manabozho and the Winnebago

(Menomini)

Manabozho then gathered up his birds, and taking them out upon the sandbar buried them—some with their heads protruding, others with the feet sticking out of the sand. He then built a fire to cook the game, but as this would require some time, and as Manabozho was tired after his exertion, he stretched himself on the ground to sleep. In order to be informed if anyone approached, he slapped his thigh and said to it, "You watch the birds, and awaken me if anyone should come near them." Then, with his back to the fire, he fell asleep.

After awhile a party of Indians came along in their canoes, and seeing the feast in store, went to the sandbar and pulled out every bird which Manabozho had so carefully placed there, but put back the heads and feet in such a way that there was no indication that the bodies had been disturbed. When the Indians had finished eating they departed, taking with them all the food that remained from the feast.

Some time afterward, Manabozho awoke, and, being very hungry, bethought himself to enjoy the fruits of his strategem. In attempting to pull a baked swan from the sand he found nothing but the head and neck, which he held in his hand. Then he tried another, and found the body of that bird also gone. So he tried another, and then another, but each time met with disappointment. Who could have robbed him? he thought. He struck his thigh and asked, "Who has been here to rob me of my feast; did I not command you to watch while I slept?" His thigh responded, "I also fell asleep, as I was very tired; but I see some people moving rapidly away in their canoes; perhaps they were the thieves. I see also they are very dirty and poorly dressed." Then Manabozho ran out to the point of the sandbar, and beheld the people in their canoes, just disappearing around a point of land. Then he called to them and reviled them, calling them "Winnibe'go! Winnibe'go!" And by this term the Menomini have ever since designated their thievish neighbors.

Manabozho Changes Himself

(Timagami Ojibwa)

After this Manabozho began travelling again. One time he feasted a lot of animals. He had killed a big bear which was very fat and he began cooking it, having made a fire with his bow drill. When he was ready to spread his meat, he heard two trees scraping together, swayed by the wind. He didn't like this noise while he was having his feast and he thought he could stop it. He climbed up one of the trees and when he reached the spot where the two trees were scraping, his foot got caught in a crack between the trees and he could not free himself.

When the first animal guest came along and saw Manabozho in the tree, he, the Beaver, said "Come on to the feast, Manabozho is caught and can't stop us." And then the other animals came. The Beaver jumped into the grease and ate it, and the Otter did the same, and that is why they are so fat in the belly. The Beaver scooped up the grease and smeared it on himself, and that is the reason why he is so fat now. All the small animals came and got fat for themselves. Last of all the animals came the Rabbit, when nearly all the grease was gone and only a little left. So he put some on the nape of his neck and some on his groin and for this reason he has only a little fat in those places. So all the animals got their fat except Rabbit. Then they all went, and poor Manabozho got free at last. He looked around and found the bear's skull that was all cleaned except for the brain, and there was only a little of that left, but he couldn't get at it. Then he wished himself to be changed into an ant in order to get into the skull and get enough to eat, for there was only about an ant's meal left.

Manabozho Changes Himself Back

(Timagami Ojibwa)

Then he became an ant and entered the skull. When he had enough he
turned back into a man, but he had his head inside the skull; this
allowed him to walk but not to see. On account of this he had no idea
where he was. Then he felt the trees. He said to one, "What are you?"
It answered, "Cedar." He kept doing this with all the trees in order
to keep his course. When he got too near the shore, he knew it by the
kind of trees he met. So he kept on walking and the only tree that did
not answer promptly was the black spruce, and that said "I'm Se'se-
gandak" (black spruce). Then Manabozho knew he was on low ground.
He came to a lake, but he did not know how large it was, as he couldn't
see. He started to swim across. An Ojibwa was paddling on the lake with
his family and he heard someone calling, "Hey! There's a bear swimming across the lake." Manabozho became frightened at this and the
Ojibwa then said, "He's getting near the shore now." So Manabozho
swam faster, and as he could understand the Ojibwa language, he guided
himself by the cries. He landed on a smooth rock, slipped and broke the
bear's skull, which fell off his head. Then the Ojibwa cried out, "That's
no bear! That's Manabozho!" Manabozho was all right, now that he
could see, so he ran off, as he didn't want to stay with these people.

Ictinike and the Four Creators

(Omaha)

Ictinike married and dwelt in a lodge. One day he said to his wife, "Hand me that tobacco-pouch. I must go to visit your grandfather, the Beaver." So he departed. As he was entering the Beaver's lodge the latter person exclaimed, "Ho, pass around to one side." And they seated Ictinike on a pillow. The wife of the Beaver said, "We have been without food. How can we give your grandfather anything to eat?" Now, the Beaver had four young beavers. The youngest one said, "Father, let me be the one who shall serve as food." So the father killed him. After boiling her son, the Beaver's wife gave the meat to Ictinike, who ate it. But before Ictinike ate it the Beaver said to him, "Beware lest you break even a single bone by biting! Do not break a bone!" Yet Ictinike broke the bone of one of the toes. When Ictinike felt full, after eating, the Beaver gathered the bones and put them in a skin, which he plunged beneath the water. In a moment the youngest beaver came up alive out of the water. When the father said, "Is all right?" the son said, "Father, he broke one of my toes by biting." Therefore from that time every beaver has had one toe, that next to the little one, which has seemingly been split by biting. When Ictinike was about to go home, he pretended that he had forgotten about his tobacco-pouch, which he left behind. So the Beaver said to one of his children, "Take that to him! Do not go near him, but throw it to him when you are at a great distance from him, as he is always very talkative." Then the child took the tobacco-pouch and started after Ictinike. After getting in sight of the latter, the young beaver was about to throw the pouch to Ictinike when standing at a great distance from him; but Ictinike called to him, "Come closer! come closer!" And when the young beaver took the pouch closer Ictinike said, "Tell your father that he is to visit me." When the young beaver reached home he said, "O father, he said that you were to visit him." The Beaver replied, "As I apprehended that very thing, I said to you, 'Throw it to him while standing at a great distance from him.'" Then the Beaver went to see Ictinike. When he arrived there Ictinike wished to kill one of his own children (in imitation of what he had seen the Beaver do), and was making him cry by hitting him often. But the Beaver was un-willing for him to act thus, so he said, "Let him alone! You are making him suffer." And then the Beaver went to the stream where he found a young beaver that he took back to the lodge, and they ate it.

On another day Ictinike said to his wife, "Hand me that tobacco-pouch. I must go to call on your grandfather, the Muskrat." So he departed. As he was entering the Muskrat's lodge the latter ex-claimed, "Ho, pass around to one side." And Ictinike was seated on a pillow. The Muskrat's wife said, "We have been without food. How can we give your grandfather anything to eat?" Then, said the Muskrat, "Fetch some water." And the woman brought the water. He told her to put it in the kettle and hang the kettle over the fire. When the water was boiling very fast the husband upset the kettle, and instead of water out came wild rice! So Ictinike ate the wild rice. When Ictinike departed he left his tobacco-pouch, as before. Then the Muskrat called one of his children, to whom he said, "Take that to him! Do not go near him, but throw it to him when you are at a great distance from him, as he is always very talkative." So his child took the tobacco-pouch to return it to Ictinike. But when he was about to throw it to Ictinike the latter said, "Come closer! come closer." And when he took the pouch closer Ictinike said, "Tell your father that he is to visit me." When the young muskrat reached home he said, "O father, he said that you were to visit him." The Muskrat replied, "As I apprehended that very thing, I said to you, 'Throw it to him while standing at a great distance from him.'" Then the Muskrat went to see Ictinike. And Ictinike said to his wife, "Fetch water." Ictinike's wife went after water. She filled the kettle and hung it over the fire till it boiled. When Ictinike upset the kettle, only water came out. Ictinike wished to do just as the Muskrat had done, but he was unable. Then the Muskrat had the kettle refilled, and when the water boiled he upset it, and an abundance of wild rice was there, which he gave to Ictinike. And thereupon the Muskrat departed, leaving plenty of wild rice.

On another day Ictinike said to his wife, "I am going to see your grandfather, the Kingfisher." When he arrived there the King-fisher stepped on a bough of the large white willow, bending it down so far that it was horizontal; and he dived from it into the water. He came up with a fish, which he gave Ictinike to eat. And as Ictinike was start-ing home, he left one of his gloves, pretending that he had forgotten it. So the Kingfisher directed one of his boys to take the glove and restore it to the owner; but he charged him not to go near him, as Ictinike was very talkative and might detain him too long. Just as the boy was about to throw the glove to Ictinike the latter said, "Come closer! come closer!" So the boy carried the glove closer. And Ictinike said, "Tell your father that he is to visit me." And the boy said to his father, "O father, he said that you were to visit him." The Kingfisher replied, "As I apprehended that very thing, I said, 'Throw it to him while you stand at a great distance from him!'" Then the Kingfisher went to see Ictinike. When he arrived there Ictinike climbed upon a bough of a large white willow, bending it till it was horizontal; he leaped from it and plunged beneath the water. And it was with difficulty that the Kingfisher seized him and brought him to land. Ictinike had swallowed more of the water than he liked. Then the Kingfisher plunged into the stream, brought up a fish, which he gave to Ictinike. But the Kingfisher departed without eating any portion of it.

On another day Ictinike said to his wife, "I am going to see your grandfather, the Flying-squirrel." So he departed. When Ictinike arrived the Flying-squirrel said to his wife, "Hand me that awl." He took the awl and climbed up on his lodge. When he reached the very top *per testes subulam impulit*, causing a great many black walnuts to fall on the ground. Thus he provided black walnuts, which Ictinike ate. And when Ictinike departed he left one of his gloves, as before, pretending that he had forgotten it. In like manner did the Flying-squirrel send the glove to Ictinike by one of his sons. And Ictinike sent by the son an invitation to the Flying-squirrel to visit him. When the Flying-squirrel reached the lodge of Ictinike, the latter took an awl and climbed to the top of his lodge. He had barely reached the top of the lodge when *per testes subulam impulit*. And he forced out very dark blood. "Why," said the Flying-squirrel, "he has surely hurt himself severely!" So the Flying-squirrel took the awl and climbed up on the lodge. And the Flying-squirrel made a large quantity of black walnuts for Ictinike.

Ictinike, the Women, and Child

(Omaha)

Once upon a time Ictinike was going somewhere. Near the place was a lodge in which dwelt two women. Ictinike traveled till he reached the bank of a stream, and then he went along the bank. Beneath the water there appeared to be a great many plums, and they were red. "Oh!" said he, as he undressed; and, putting aside his miserable attire of raccoon skins, he dived down after the plums. But he seized a large handful of dirt. On returning to land and viewing what he had behold it was a lot of dirt! Again he looked at the water and there were the plums. So he dived again and with a similar result. Having returned the fourth time with nothing but dirt, he chanced to raise his eyes to a cliff above the stream, and there were many plum trees filled with fruit, which caused the branches to hang down over the stream. It was the reflection of these in the water that had deceived him. Then he put on his clothing, ascended the cliff, and gathered the plums, with which he filled one corner of his robe.

Then he went to the lodge. He rubbed semen over the plums, and threw them one by one down through the smoke-hole of the lodge. On seeing the first plum one of the women said, "Oh, sister-in-law! I have found a plum!" They scrambled for the plums. On entering the lodge, Ictinike observed, "Whew! my relations, my grand-child, and her sister-in-law have returned here! Why! those plums are very abundant, and yet you two have not picked any of them?" "Oh! grandfather, we have not gone anywhere. If they are near here, we may pick them for ourselves," exclaimed one of the women. "Ho, go and pick them," said he. The child of one of the women was still in the cradle, and the mother had set it up in the cradle against the side of the lodge. So Ictinike said, "When you go leave the child in the cradle with me, as it might get hurt if you took it among the plum trees." "Oh, grand-father! it shall be as you say," said the mother. Ictinike promised to watch over it as over a relation. So the women departed.

Presently Ictinike started to his feet in great haste, seized the kettle that had been placed there full of water, and hung it over the fire. Then he killed the child, and cut the flesh in narrow strips, which he boiled. But he put the head back in the cradle, wrapping it in the head covering, and arranged it just as if it was alive. He put wood on the fire without delay, and went out of the lodge from time to time to see whether the women were coming. At last the meat was cooked, and he sat eating it. Having devoured all of it before the women returned, he departed. When the women got home Ictinike was missing. "O sister-in-law," said one, "the old man is not here. Why! my child is still sleeping just as he was when I left him!" As she took up the cradle and was returning with it to the other woman the head of the child fell to the ground. "Oh! dear little child!" said she. Both the women wept.

And while they sat crying Ictinike, who had painted his face with clay, disguising himself, entered the lodge. "Strange! what cause have you for crying?" "Oh, grandfather! Ictinike came and told us about plums, and when we went to pick them we left the child here in the cradle; but he ate it and departed, after putting the head back in the cradle and wrapping the head-covering around it." "Really!" said he, "let me see; hand me the ax, I must pursue him." They gave him the ax and he departed, running very rapidly. He ran till he reached a very dense forest, where he sought for some wood mice. Passing the butt-end of the ax along a decayed log in which were some wood mice, he killed the mice and covered the ax with blood. He took the ax streaming with blood back to the lodge, and when he entered he said, "I killed him and I have now returned." "Oh! grandfather," said the women, "was not the place where you found him near here?" "Not at all! it is very far, but I overtook him by going very rapidly." This myth explains the cause of the gray down (?) on ripe plums: Ictinike was the cause of it.

Ictinike and the Turtle

(Omaha)

Ictinike was journeying. When he came in sight at a bend' of a stream, a Big Turtle was sitting there in a sheltered place warmed by the sun. Ictinike drew himself back out of sight, crouching at intervals as he retraced his steps, and ran down the hill to the place where the Big Turtle was. "Why! how is that you continue to pay no attention to what is going on? It has been said that yonder stream is to dry up, so all the quadrupeds that frequent the water have kept close to the (deep?) water," said Ictinike. And the Big Turtle said, "Why! I have been coming here regularly, but I have not heard anything at all. I usually come and sit in this place when the sun gets as high as it is at present." "Hurry!" said Ictinike, "for some of the young men died very soon for want of water. The young otters died, so did the young muskrats, the young beavers, and the young raccoons."

"Come, let us go," said the Big Turtle. So Ictinike departed with him. As he accompanied him, Ictinike sought for a dry bone. Having found one that would be good as a club, Ictinike said, "Friend, go on. *Mingam*." When he was alone, Ictinike seized the bone, and soon overtook the Big Turtle, walking beside him. "Friend," said he, "when a person walks, he stretches his neck often." So the Big Turtle began to stretch his neck very far, and he was walking with his legs bent exceedingly. As he was going thus, Ictinike gave him a hard blow on the neck, knocking him senseless, and he did not stop beating him until he killed him. "Ha! ha!" said Ictinike, as he carried the body away, "there are some days when I act thus for myself." He kindled a fire and began to roast the Big Turtle. Notwithstanding his desire to feast on the Big Turtle, he became sleepy, and said, "Ho! I will sleep, but you, O 'Ija^{n}xe,' must keep awake. When you are cooked, O, Big Turtle, you must say 'Puff!'" So he went to sleep. Then the Coyote was coming very cautiously. He seized the Turtle, pulled one of the legs out of the coals, and sat there biting off the meat. When he had devoured the meat on all the limbs, he pushed the bones back into their former places, arranged the fire over them, and departed after putting every thing just as he had found it. At length Ictinike awoke. He pushed into the ashes to find the Turtle, took hold of one limb and pulled it, when to his surprise only that limb came forth. "Pshaw!" said he. Then he tried another limb, with a like

87

result, and still another, but only the bones appeared. When he had pulled out the fourth leg he was astonished. "Surprising! O 'Ija^{n}xe,' I said to you, 'do not sleep,' but you have disobeyed me." Thereupon he scratched "Ija^{n}xe," but the latter fled often. "Do not flee," said Ictinike. All at once he exclaimed, "Surprising! I had eaten the Turtle, but I had forgotten it!"

The Coyote and the Snake

(Omaha)

The Coyote was going in a straight line across the prairie. While he was seeking something a person said very suddenly, "Stop!" The Coyote thought, "Who can it be?" He looked all around, but found no one. Then he went a few steps, when some one said, "Walk around me!" Then the Coyote saw that it was the Snake. "Fie!" said the Coyote, "when I walk here I do not wish to walk around any one at all. Do you go to one side. Get out of my way!" The Snake replied, "Though I am here, I have never thought for a moment of giving place to any one!" "Even if you think so," said the Coyote, "I will run over you." "If you do so, you shall die," said the Snake. "Why should I die? There is nothing that can kill me," said the Coyote. "Come! Step over me! Do it in spite of me," said the Snake. Then the Coyote stepped over him. And the Snake bit him. But the Coyote did not feel the slightest pain. "Where is it? You said that if I stepped over you I should die. Where have I received my death-blow?" said the Coyote. As the Snake made no reply, the Coyote departed. After some time he came to a creek. As he was about to take a drink he looked at the water, and he saw his reflection in the water. He appeared very fat. "Whew! I was never so before. I am very fat!" Saying this, he felt himself all over again and again; but that was all which he did. He departed after drinking the water. By and by he said, "I feel very sleepy." So he pushed his way into the thick grass and lay there. He died while sleeping, never awaking, and he was much swollen.

Adventures of the Orphan

(Omaha)

Once upon a time there was a village of Indians. And an old woman and her grandson, called the Orphan, dwelt in a lodge at a short distance from the village. The two were very poor, dwelling in a low tent made of grass. The grandson used to play games. One day he said, "Grandmother, make a small bow for me!" The grandmother made the bow and some arrows. The boy went to shoot birds. And after that he used to bring back many birds, putting them all around his belt. The boy became an excellent marksman, usually killing whatever game came in sight of him. About ten o'clock each morning all the people in the village used to make a great noise. At last the Orphan said, "Grandmother, why do they make such a noise?" The grandmother said, "There is a very red bird that goes there regularly, and when he alights on a very tall cottonwood tree he makes a very red glare over the whole village. So the chief has ordered the people to shoot at the bird, and whoever kills the bird can marry the chief's daughter." "Grandmother," said the Orphan, "I will go thither." "Of all places in the world that is the worst place for you to visit. They like to abuse strangers. They will abuse you. There is no reason why you should go." The boy paid no attention to her, but took his bow and went out of the lodge. "Beware lest you go," said his grandmother. "I am going away to play games," said the Orphan. But he went straight to the village. When he drew near the village, he noticed the red light all around. He also saw a great crowd of people, who were moving to and fro, shooting at the bird. The Orphan reached them. One man said, "Come, Orphan, you may shoot at it." But the Orphan continued to hesitate, as he feared the people. But the people continued to approach him, saying to the rest, "Stand off! Stand off! Let the Orphan shoot!" So the Orphan shot at the bird. And he barely missed it. Just then Ictinike shot, and sent a reed arrow beside that of the Orphan. The people said, "Oh! the Orphan came very near killing it!" But Ictinike said, "I am the one who came near killing it." When the bird flew away the people scattered, returning to their lodges. And the Orphan went home. Said he to his grandmother, "I came very near killing the bird." "Do not go again! They will abuse you. Did I not say, do not go?" said the old woman. On the morning of another day he went thither. And the people were making a great noise. And it hap-

pened as on the previous day; he was told to shoot at the bird, and he
barely missed it. On the third day he met with similar bad luck. But on
the fourth day he hit the bird, wounding it through and through. "Oho!
the Orphan has killed it," said the people. "Nonsense!" said Ictinike, "I
killed it! I killed it! You must not grumble! You must not grumble!" And
as Ictinike would not let the people do as they wished, he snatched the
honor of the occasion from the Orphan. And the people came in crowds
to view the spectacle, the body of the famous bird. And when the
Orphan approached the spot, he pulled out a feather, so the people
thought, but he really took the entire bird, and carried it home. And the
chief said, "Bring my son-in-law hither!" So the People took the bird,
as they imagined, that had been killed by Ictinike, and brought it and
Ictinike to the chief. And Ictinike married the elder daughter of the
chief, making his abode in the chief's lodge.

In the meantime the Orphan had reached home. "Grandmother," said he, "I have killed the bird." "Oh! my grandchild! Oh! my
grandchild!" said she. "Grandmother, make me a 'weҫitaⁿ-tegҫe' between
the fire-place and the seat at the back of the lodge," said the Orphan.
And after she made it (the Orphan hung the red bird upon it?). And the
Orphan and his grandmother had their lodge filled with a very red
light. By and by the young man said, "Grandmother, make me a hide
hoop." And his grandmother made the hoop for him, placing it aside
to dry. But the Orphan could hardly wait for it to dry. At last it was dry.
"Ho, grandmother, sit in the middle (between the fire-place and the
seat at the back of the lodge?)," said he. Then the Orphan went out of
the lodge and stood on the right side of the entrance. Said he, "Grandmother, you must say, O grandchild, one of the Buffalo people goes to
you." And the old woman obeyed. She rolled the hoop from the lodge
to the Orphan. When the hoop rolled out of the lodge, it changed suddenly into a buffalo, and the Orphan wounded it through and through,
killing it near the entrance. He and his grandmother cut up the body,
and his grandmother cut the entire carcass into slices for drying. At this
time the people in the village had nothing to eat. The grandmother
prepared a quantity of dried buffalo meat mixed with fat, and the
Orphan told her to take it to the lodge of the chief, and to say, to the
chief's (unmarried?) daughter, "O, daughter-in-law! your father may eat
that." The old woman threw the bundle into the lodge, turned around
suddenly, and went home. When the bundle was thrown into the lodge,
the chief said, "Look! Look! Look!" And when one of the daughters
went to look she could not see any one. (The Orphan, by his magic
power, had rendered his grandmother invisible; therefore on the fourth
day he said, "Grandmother, you shall be visible when you return.")
And Ictinike said, "Only one old woman dwells apart from us, and she
is the one." And it was so four times. When the fourth time came, the
old woman carried a sack of buffalo meat on her back, and on top of

the sack she carried the bird. Then said the Orphan, "Grandmother, now you shall be visible when you return." So the old woman departed. When she was very near the chief's tent, that tent began to shine with a red light. As she passed along by the lodges the people said, "Oho! we did think that the Orphan had killed the bird, but you said that Ictinike killed it. Now the Orphan's grandmother has brought it hither. To whom will she take it?" And the people stood looking. "Oho! she has carried it to the chief's lodge!" When she reached the entrance, she threw down the sack, letting it fall with a sudden thud. "Oh! daughter-in-law, your father and brothers may eat that," said she. "Look! Look! Look!" said the chief, "she has done that often!" And Ictinike said, "Only one old woman is left there, and she is the one. Who else could it be?" And they went to see. And behold it was the grandmother of the Orphan. "It is the Orphan's grandmother," said (one of the daughters). "Ho! bring my son-in-law to me," said the chief. And they took the pack which the old woman had brought and they hung it up with the bird. They placed it beside that which Ictinike had (seemingly) killed, and which had been hung up. And as they sat in the lodge it was filled with a very red glare. When they had returned with the Orphan, he married the younger daughter of the chief, making his abode in the chief's lodge. The Orphan's hair had not been combed for a long time, so it was tangled and matted. So Ictinike's wife said to her sister, "Sister, if he sits on the rug, he will make lice drop on it! Make him sit away from it! Is it possible that you do not loathe the sight of him?" The Orphan and his wife were displeased at this. When the wife wished to comb his hair, the Orphan was unwilling.

At length, one day, when the sun was approaching noon (*i.e.*, about 10 A.M.), he and his wife left the village and went to the shore of a lake. As they sat there the Orphan said, "I am going beneath this water, but do not return to your father's lodge! Be sure to remain here, even though I am absent for some time. I will return. Examine my forehead." Now, in the middle of his forehead was a depression. He had been a poor Orphan, and was brought up accordingly, so he had been hurt in some manner, causing a scar on his forehead. Then he started to wade into the lake. He waded until only his head was above the surface, then he turned and called to his wife, "Remember what I told you. That is all!" Having said this, he plunged under the surface. His wife sat weeping, and after awhile she walked along the lake shore, weeping because he did not return. At last her eyelids became weary, and she went to sleep at the very place where they had first reached the lake. When she was sleeping very soundly her husband returned. He took hold of her and roused her. "I have returned. Arise!" On arising suddenly and looking behold, he was a very handsome man, and his hair was combed very nicely, so the woman hesitated, thinking him a stranger, and she turned away from him. "Oh fie! you like to make sport of people! I married a very poor man, who plunged beneath this water, and I have been sitting weeping while awaiting his return," said she. "Why! I am he," said her husband. Still the woman paid no attention to his words. "Why! see that place about which I said, 'Examine it!'" When the woman turned around and saw it she no longer hesitated, but embraced him suddenly and kissed him. Then the husband went to the shore, drew together a quantity of the green scum that collects on the surface of water, and made of it a robe and skirt for his wife. The Orphan had birds resembling short-eared owls over his moccasins and robe, and he had some tied to his club. Whenever he laid down the club the birds used to cry out. Late in the afternoon he and his wife departed for the village. When they arrived the people exclaimed, "Why! The wife of the Orphan has returned with a very different man. I think that the Orphan has been killed. He went off in the morning. Why! this is a very handsome man." When the Orphan reached the chief's lodge all the birds made a great noise. Then said the wife of Ictinike, "Sister, let my sister's husband sit on part of the rug." "Why, elder sister! your sister's husband might drop lice on your rug," said the younger sister as she turned up one end of the rug and threw it towards the elder sister. Whereupon Ictinike's wife began to cry, and she cried incessantly. At last her father said to Ictinike, "This world is very large, but you are known everywhere as one who possesses various kinds of knowledge. Use one of these and make my daughter stop crying."

By and by Ictinike said to the Orphan, "Younger brother, let us go to cut arrow-shafts. Let us make arrows for your wife's brother." But the Orphan did not speak. So Ictinike addressed him again, "Younger brother, let us make arrows for your wife's brother. Let us go to cut arrow-shafts." Then the Orphan replied, "Come, elder brother, it shall be so." And Ictinike was highly delighted because the Orphan was about to go with him. When the Orphan spoke of laying aside his magic garments Ictinike objected. "Wear them at any rate! Why should you put them away?" So they departed together. When they reached the edge of a very dense forest, some wild turkeys flew off and alighted in a tree. "Oh! younger brother, shoot at them! I will eat a roasted one as I recline," said Ictinike. "No, elder brother," said the Orphan, "we are going in great haste." "Oh! younger brother, kill one for me," said Ictinike. "When my elder brother speaks about anything he has so much to say he does not stop talking!" said the Orphan, who then went towards the tree, taking his bow, in order to shoot at the turkeys. Just as he stood pulling the bow, Ictinike said in a whisper, "Let it lodge on a limb!" And when the Orphan shot he sent the arrow through the bird. "Let it lodge on a limb! Let it lodge on a limb," said Ictinike. And it fell and lodged on a limb. "Oho! younger brother! climb for me, get it and throw it down," said Ictinike. "No, elder brother, let us go on," said the Orphan. "Why! you ought not to leave your arrow as well as the bird," said Ictinike.

"Go up for it and throw it down!" "Why! when my elder brother speaks about anything he has so much to say he does not stop talking!" said the Orphan. He decided to go and climb the tree. So he went to the base of the tree. "Ho! lay your garments there! If you get caught in the branches the garments will be torn," said Ictinike, referring to the magic clothing. So the Orphan stripped off his garments, placing them at the foot of the tree. As he climbed, Ictinike said in a whisper, "Let this tree shoot up high very suddenly!" As the Orphan heard him whisper, he turned his head and questioned him: "Why! elder brother, what did you say?" "I said nothing of any consequence, younger brother. I was merely saying, 'When he brings that bird back I will eat it.'" So the Orphan continued climbing. When Ictinike whispered again, the Orphan repeated his question. "I said nothing of importance," said Ictinike. "I was merely saying, 'He has nearly reached it for me.'" Then the Orphan climbed higher. Ictinike whispered again, and made a similar reply to the query of the Orphan, who began to apprehend mischief. When Ictinike whispered the fourth time the Orphan said, "Fie! elder brother, but you have been saying something!" "I said nothing of importance," said Ictinike. "I said, 'Let this tree extend to the upper world.'" And as Ictinike went around the tree he hit it at short intervals, saying, "I say, 'Let this tree shoot up high very suddenly.'" And the tree extended to the upper world. And the Orphan stood in a very narrow place between the limb of the tree and the upper world. "Alas!" said he. And he wept incessantly. His hair, too, became exceedingly tangled. At length a young Eagle went to the weeping man. "O man, what are you saying," said he. "O grandfather! O grandfather! O grandfather!" said the Orphan to the young Eagle. "Come! do say it. Tell your story," said the Eagle. "Yes, grandfather, I am one of those who left at the timber at the foot of the bluff some parts of a young male elk for you all to fly over and eat." "That is right. One of your grandfathers shall come (to rescue you)," said the Eagle. So the Eagle departed. And the Orphan stood weeping, being very sorrowful. Presently the Buzzard went to him. And when the Orphan told him of another animal, which he had left for the buzzards, he was told, "That is right. One of your grandfathers shall come (to rescue you)." Then the Buzzard departed, leaving the Orphan weeping. By and by the Crow approached. And when the Orphan told him of an animal which he had left for the crows to eat he was told that another grandfather (a crow) should come to aid him. After the departure of the Crow the Magpie came. He made a like promise and departed. Then came the promised Eagle. "O grandfather! O grandfather! O grandfather!" said the Orphan, praying to him. "Ho! Catch hold of my wings at the shoulders, and lie on my back with your legs stretched out. Beware lest you open your eyes! Lie with closed eyes," said the Eagle. So he departed, flying with the Orphan on his back, flying round and round the tree till he became very tired. Then he alighted from time to time to rest himself, and when rested he resumed his flight. Finally he left the Orphan standing on a lower limb. Then came the Buzzard, who took the Orphan on his back, after giving him directions similar to those given by the Eagle. The Buzzard flew round and round the tree, going lower and lower, alighting from time to time to rest himself, and resuming his downward flight when rested. Finally he left the Orphan standing on a lower limb. Then came the Crow, who took the Orphan still lower. But while he was on the Crow's back he opened his eyes slightly and he saw the ground emitting a yellow light. So he lay down again on the Crow's back and begged him to continue to help him. But about this time came the Magpie very suddenly. And the Magpie carried the Orphan lower and lower till they reached the ground. When they reached there the Magpie lay insensible, as he was exhausted. When the Orphan went to get his garments he found that Ictinike had departed with them, leaving his own garments at the foot of the tree.

Now, when Ictinike returned home wearing the magic garments the birds on them did not cry out at all, so Ictinike pretended that they wanted to cry out, saying, "Keep quiet! You make a great noise in people's ears!" But when the Orphan returned on the Magpie's back to the foot of the tree the birds on the garments knew about it, and they cried out with a great noise for some time, as Ictinike had on the garments. Then Ictinike exclaimed, "Do keep quiet! You make a great noise in people's ears!"

When the Orphan hunted for his quiver he found that Ictinike had taken it, leaving instead his quiver with the reed arrows. When he looked at the arrows he found among them some wooden arrows having the points cut sharp with a knife. He also found that Ictinike had left there his robe of raccoon skins. The Orphan was highly displeased, but he seized the arrows, straightened the wooden ones, and with them he killed all the animals about which he had told his deliverers. Then he started back to the village wearing the robe of raccoon skins and taking the quiver. When he drew near the village the birds knew it, and they cried out and flew a little now and then. This made Ictinike feel very proud, and he commanded the birds to keep silent.

At length the Orphan returned and entered the lodge. He sat there a while, Ictinike still wearing the magic garments. At last the Orphan said to him, "Fie! you used to wear that thing, so wear it again!" throwing to him the raccoon skin robe. And the Orphan took back his own garments. But his hair was still in great disorder. After his return nothing special happened for some time. The Orphan caused a drum to be made. Said he to his wife, "I have returned after being in a very lonely situation! Tell the venerable man (your father) that I wish all the people to dance." And his wife told her father. And her father commanded an old man to go around among the people and proclaim all the words that the Orphan had told. So the old man went through the village as a crier or herald, saying, "He says indeed that you shall dance! He says indeed that all of you in the village, even the small children, are to dance!" The Orphan, his wife, and his grandmother, having the drum, went inside the circle (of lodges). The Orphan fastened his belt very tightly around his waist and then said to his wife, "Grasp my belt very hard. Beware lest you let it go!" Then he told his grandmother to grasp the other side (of the belt), saying, "Do not let go!"

When all the people assembled inside the circle of lodges the Orphan sat in the very middle (surrounded by the people). And when he beat the drum he made the people rise about a foot and then come to the ground again. The people were enjoying themselves when he beat the drum. When he beat it a second time he made them jump a little higher. Then said his grandmother, "Oh! grandchild! I usually dance very well." He made her jump and come down suddenly as he beat the drum, just as he had done to each of the others. When he gave the third beat he made the people jump still higher, and as they came down he beat the drum before they could touch the ground, making them leap up again. He beat the drum rapidly, sending all the people so high into the air that one could not get even a glimpse of them. And as they came down after a long time, he caused them to die one after another as they lay on the ground. He thus killed all the people by concussion, which resulted from his beating the drum.

Though the Orphan's wife and grandmother were taken up into the air at each beat of the drum, it happened that only their feet went up into the air and their heads and bodies were turned downward, because the women held him by the waist, as he had ordered them. Of all the people only three survived, Ictinike, the chief, and the chief's wife. As the chief was coming down he implored the Orphan to spare him. But the latter was inexorable, sending him up repeatedly until he grew tired of hearing the chief's entreaties. Then he let him fall to the earth and die. In like manner he caused the death of the chief's wife. Only Ictinike remained. "O younger brother! I go to you and my wife's sister! Pity ye me!" said Ictinike. But the Orphan beat the drum again and when Ictinike fell to the ground the concussion killed him.

A Yankton Story

(Yankton)

There was once a Yankton village in which was a young man who was
waiting for a chance to marry. The chief had two daughters, full sisters,
who were unmarried, and one son who was the youngest child. And
this man who, as I have said, was waiting for a chance to marry, wished
to court the sisters, and he was waiting on their account.

One night he went to their tent, which was a whitened
one, and he lay down outside at the rear of the tent in order to listen
to what the sisters might say. At length the sisters began a conversation.
One said, "Younger sister, we shall marry the person who takes our
little brother and enables him to insult our enemies." "Oho!" thought
the listener. As he lay there he matured a plan. Returning home he asked
his female kindred to sew moccasins. And they did it for him. The next
evening, when it was too dark for persons to distinguish one another's
faces, he started to seek the boy. The boy was playing, and the young
man found him. When he said, "Come, younger brother," the boy went
with him. The young man carried him on his back all night long, going
across the prairie in a straight line. When he carried him thus he was
going on the war path. He killed a buffalo bull, cut up the carcass,
and cooked the fresh meat that it might serve as rations for the journey.
He carried the provisions on his back, and besides them he carried
the boy. When he reached a stream he seated the boy among the undergrowth and gave him some dried meat to eat. Then said he, "Do not
depart! Remain here! Beware lest you peep outside of the undergrowth! I will return." Then he went as a scout. Not discovering any one
at all, he returned to the boy, and spoke to him as if he were a full-
grown man, "O war captain, there is no one at all. I did not find anything whatever." Then he took him on his back again, resuming his
march. Late in the evening he seated the boy amidst the undergrowth
and went off as a scout. At length there was some one shooting. It was
a man who killed an elk. The young man wished to fetch the boy, but it
was difficult, so he sat considering what to do. He crept up carefully
towards the man and killed him before his presence could be detected.

Then he fetched the boy. "O war captain, I have killed a
man. Hasten!" He carried the boy on his back, running to the place.

96

On arriving there he caused the boy to tread on the dead man. Then the two started home, taking part of the scalp of the slain man. As the man started back, he thought intently of the women. "I will take a wife," and he was very glad. On returning to the place where he had first met the boy and had overheard the sisters, behold, nothing remained but a single tent and the deserted village site. All the inhabitants had removed, leaving only the one tent standing. On reaching it he noticed that small pieces of sod had been piled up against the doorway, and that but a short time had elapsed since the departure of the other inhabitants. He followed close behind the villagers, and at length saw two persons sitting on a hill. Nearing them, he saw that they were the parents of the boy whom he was carrying.

They came towards him and kissed their son and also the young man. "You have done very well, but you have injured yourself," said they. When the young man carried off the boy he did not tell any one at all what he intended doing. And when the sisters did not find the boy, their brother, they killed themselves. The boy's father said to the young man, "You should have told about it when you carried him off. You have done well, but since his sisters had only him as their real brother they loved him, and, thinking that he was either lost or dead, they killed themselves." Then the young man related every occurrence to the boy's father, telling how he had killed the man.

The father said, "Come! Let us go. It is enough. You must eat." The young man said, "Depart ye! I will join you later." So he sat there and they departed. When they had gone out of sight he retraced his steps till he reached the place where the sisters had killed themselves. He pulled down the cubes of sod that had been piled up against the entrance, and then went into the tent. There were the two women, side by side, just as they had been laid there. He went to them, forced his way in between them, and lay down. Then he killed himself.

The Theft of Light

(Tsimshian)

Giant flew inland (toward the east). He went on for a long time, and finally he was very tired, so he dropped down on the sea the little round stone which his father had given to him. It became a large rock way out at sea. Giant rested on it and refreshed himself, and took off the raven skin.

At that time there was always darkness. There was no daylight then. Again Giant put on the raven skin and flew toward the east. Now, Giant reached the mainland and arrived at the mouth of Skeena River. There he stopped and scattered the salmon roe and trout roe. He said while he was scattering them, "Let every river and creek have all kinds of fish!" Then he took the dried sea lion bladder and scattered the fruits all over the land, saying, "Let every mountain, hill, valley, plain, the whole land, be full of fruits!"

The whole world was still covered with darkness. When the sky was clear, the people would have a little light from the stars; and when clouds were in the sky, it was very dark all over the land. The people were distressed by this. Then Giant thought that it would be hard for him to obtain his food if it were always dark. He remembered that there was light in heaven, whence he had come. Then he made up his mind to bring down the light to our world. On the following day Giant put on his raven skin, which his father the chief had given to him, and flew upward. Finally he found the hole in the sky, and he flew through it. Giant reached the inside of the sky. He took off the raven skin and put it down near the hole of the sky. He went on, and came to a spring near the house of the chief of heaven. There he sat down and waited.

Then the chief's daughter came out, carrying a small bucket in which she was about to fetch water. She went down to the big spring in front of her father's house. When Giant saw her coming along, he transformed himself into the leaf of a cedar and floated on the water. The chief's daughter dipped it up in her bucket and drank it. Then she returned to her father's house and entered.

After a short time she was with child, and not long after she gave birth to a boy. Then the chief and the chieftainess were very glad. They washed the boy regularly. He began to grow up. Now he was beginning to creep about. They washed him often, and the chief smoothed and cleaned the floor of the house. Now the child was strong and crept about every day. He began to cry, "Hama, hama!" He was crying all the time, and the great chief was troubled, and called in some of his slaves to carry about the boy. The slaves did so, but he would not sleep for several nights. He kept on crying, "Hama, hama!" Therefore the chief invited all his wise men, and said to them that he did not know what the boy wanted and why he was crying. He wanted the box that was hanging in the chief's house.

This box, in which the daylight was kept, was hanging in one corner of the house. Its name was Mā. Giant had known it before he descended to our world. The child cried for it. The chief was annoyed, and the wise men listened to what the chief told them. When the wise men heard the child crying aloud, they did not know what he was saying. He was crying all the time, "Hama, hama, hama!"

One of the wise men, who understood him, said to the chief, "He is crying for the mā." Therefore the chief ordered it to be taken down. The man put it down. They put it down near the fire, and the boy sat down near it and ceased crying. He stopped crying, for he was glad. Then he rolled the mā about inside the house. He did so for four days. Sometimes he would carry it to the door. Now the great chief did not think of it. He had quite forgotten it. Then the boy really took up the mā, put it on his shoulders, and ran out with it. While he was running, some one said, "Giant is running away with the mā!" He ran away, and the hosts of heaven pursued him. They shouted that Giant was running away with the mā. He came to the hole of the sky, put on the skin of the raven, and flew down, carrying the mā. Then the hosts of heaven returned to their houses, and he flew down with it to our world.

At that time the world was still dark. He arrived farther up the river, and went down river. Giant had come down near the mouth of Nass River. He went to the mouth of Nass River. It was always dark, and he carried the mā about with him. He went on, and went up the river in the dark. A little farther up he heard the noise of the people, who were catching olachen in bag nets in their canoes. There was much noise out on the river, because they were working hard. Giant, who was sitting on the shore, said, "Throw ashore one of the things that you are catching, my dear people!" After a while, Giant said again, "Throw ashore one of the things you are catching!" Then those on the water scolded him. "Where did you come from, great liar, whom they call Txä'msem?" The (animal) people knew that it was Giant. Therefore they made fun of him. Then Giant said again, "Throw ashore one of the things that you are catching, or I shall break the mā!" and all those who were on the water answered, "Where did you get what you are talking about, you liar?" Giant said once more, "Throw ashore one of the things that you are catching, my dear people, or I shall break the mā for you!" One person replied, scolding him.

Giant had repeated his request four times, but those on the water refused what he had asked for. Therefore Giant broke the mā. It broke, and it was daylight. The north wind began to blow hard; and all the fishermen, the Frogs, were driven away by the north wind. All the Frogs who had made fun of Giant were driven away down river until they arrived at one of the large mountainous islands. Here the Frogs tried to climb up the rock; but they stuck to the rock, being frozen by the north wind, and became stone. They are still on the rock. The fishing frogs named him Txä′msem, and all the world had the daylight.

The Theft of Fire

(Maidu)

At one time the people had found fire, and were going to use it; but Thunder wanted to take it away from them, as he desired to be the only one who should have fire. He thought that if he could do this, he would be able to kill all the people. After a time he succeeded, and carried the fire home with him, far to the south. He put Woswosim (a small bird) to guard the fire, and see that no one should steal it. Thunder thought that people would die after he had stolen their fire, for they would not be able to cook their food; but the people managed to get along. They ate most of their food raw, and sometimes got Toyeskom (another small bird) to look for a long time at a piece of meat; and as he had a red eye, this after a long time would cook the meat almost as well as a fire. Only the chiefs had their food cooked in this way. All the people lived together in a big sweat house. The house was as big as a mountain.

Among the people were Lizard and his brother; and they were always the first in the morning to go outside and sun themselves on the roof of the sweat house. One morning as they lay there sunning themselves, they looked west, toward the Coast Range, and saw smoke. They called to all the other people, saying that they had seen smoke far away to the west. The people, however, would not believe them, and Coyote came out, and threw a lot of dirt and dust over the two. One of the people did not like this. He said to Coyote, "Why do you trouble people? Why don't you let others alone? Why don't you behave? You are always the first to start a quarrel. You always want to kill people without any reason." Then the other people felt sorry. They asked the two Lizards about what they had seen, and asked them to point out the smoke. The Lizards did so, and all could see the thin column rising up far to the west. One person said, "How shall we get that fire back? How shall we get it away from Thunder? He is a bad man. I don't know whether we had better try to get it or not." Then the chief said, "The best one among you had better try to get it. Even if Thunder is a bad man, we must try to get the fire. When we get there, I don't know how we shall get in but the one who is the best, who thinks he can get in, let him try." Mouse, Deer, Dog, and Coyote were the ones who were to try but all the other people went too. They took a flute with them, for they meant to put the fire in it.

They travelled a long time, and finally reached the place where the fire was. They were within a little distance of Thunder's house, when they all stopped to see what they would do. Woswosim, who was supposed to guard the fire in the house, began to sing, "I am the man who never sleeps. I am the man who never sleeps." Thunder had paid him for his work in beads, and he wore them about his neck and around his waist. He sat on the top of the sweat-house, by the smoke-hole.

After a while Mouse was sent up to try and see if he could get in. He crept up slowly till he got close to Woswosim, and then saw that his eyes were shut. He was asleep, in spite of the song that he sang. When Mouse saw that the watcher was asleep, he crawled to the opening and went in. Thunder had several daughters, and they were lying there asleep. Mouse stole up quietly, and untied the waist-string of each one's apron, so that should the alarm be given, and they jump up, these aprons or skirts would fall off, and they would have to stop to fix them. This done, Mouse took the flute, filled it with fire, then crept out, and rejoined the other people who were waiting outside.

Some of the fire was taken out and put in the Dog's ear, the remainder in the flute being given to the swiftest runner to carry. Deer, however, took a little, which he carried on the hock of his leg, where today there is a reddish spot. For a while all went well, but when they were about half-way back, Thunder woke up, suspected that something was wrong, and asked, "What is the matter with my fire?" Then he jumped up with a roar of thunder, and his daughters were thus awakened, and also jumped up; but their aprons fell off as they did so, and they had to sit down again to put them on. After they were all ready, they went out with Thunder to give chase. They carried with them a heavy wind and a great rain and a hailstorm, so that they might put out any fire the people had. Thunder and his daughters hurried along, and soon caught up with the fugitives, and were about to catch them, when Skunk shot at Thunder and killed him. Then Skunk called out, "After this you must never try to follow and kill people. You must stay up in the sky, and be the thunder. That is what you will be." The daughters of Thunder did not follow any farther; so the people went on safely, and got home with their fire, and people have had it ever since.

The Origin of Corn

(Abanaki)

A long time ago, when Indians were first made, there lived one alone, far, far from any others. He knew not of fire, and subsisted on roots, barks, and nuts. This Indian became very lonesome for company. He grew tired of digging roots, lost his appetite, and for several days lay dreaming in the sunshine; when he awoke he saw something standing near, at which, at first, he was very much frightened. But when it spoke, his heart was glad, for it was a beautiful woman with long *light* hair, very unlike any Indian. He asked her to come to him, but she would not, and if he tried to approach her she seemed to go farther away; he sang to her of his loneliness and besought her not to leave him; at last she told him, if he would do just as she should say, he would always have her with him. He promised that he would.

She led him to where there was some very dry grass, told him to get two very dry sticks, rub them together quickly, holding them in the grass. Soon a spark flew out; the grass caught it, and quick as an arrow the ground was burned over. Then she said, "When the sun sets, take me by the hair and drag me over the burned ground." He did not like to do this, but she told him that wherever he dragged her something like grass would spring up, and he would see her hair coming from between the leaves; then the seeds would be ready for his use. He did as she said, and to this day, when they see the silk (hair) on the cornstalk, the Indians know she has not forgotten them.

Chapter 3

The Soul of the Indian: Pre-Columbian Poetry

If you would seek to know a people, look to their poetry. It is there in the most intense, controlled but emotionally honest statements that the natural eloquence of the group reveals itself in unguarded expression of unveiled needs and desires, passions, aspirations, and dreams. The rhythms of a people's poetry indicate the nature of their response to the rhythms of the world in which they live. The poetic devices of repetition, symbolism, imagery, onomatopoeia, alliteration, consonance and assonance reveal their capacity to hear with the third ear the voice of Wak'kon-tah, the spirit of place, and the relationship of self to self, to others, and to totality.

The measured line of *Beowulf*, for instance, is indicative of the musical response of the Norseman as he heard two balanced measures accompanied by the downward sweep of the bard's hand across the strings of his instrument, the pause, and the return stroke. The bold, unequivocal statement of the half lines resonate in the rich gutterals and sibilants to create a masculine, bold, adventuresome call to battle, to high passions, to honor, and to glorious death.

The rolling dactyllic hexameters of the epic Greek line capture the swell of the wine-dark sea luring Odysseus on to new adventures but soften and fall in their dying meter to capture the rosy-fingered dawn or touch the white arms of Hera. The hissing sibilants of Sophocles wind torturously through the eighteen syllables of each line to create coiled anger and imminent peril or drop on half lines of stichomythia to speed that direct, undiplomatic exchange of master and servant or foe and foe when diplomacy is irrelevant, the passion of the moment paramount.

The varieties of rhythm in English verse unroll rich skeins of sound that create the sensual response to Poe's "silken, sad, uncertain rustling of each purple curtain" yet allow the somber imperative of William Cullen Bryant's "Approach thy grave like one who wraps the drapery of his couch about him and lies down to pleasant dreams." The relationship of George Herbert and his God is made believable and understandable in the simplicity of "Methought I heard one calling, *Child;* and I replied, *My Lord*." The simplicity of the ballad with its narrative flow, the lyric that pines for lost love or asserts, "I am the master of my fate; I am the captain of my soul"—all couple the rhythms of the language with the harmonies of music integrated to reveal the anxieties and the aspirations of both poet and singer of the song. And all poetry is song, for it relies on that mathematical distillate of sound duration to create the sense of happiness, sadness, pathos, and so on, that prose can only approximate.

Pre-Columbian Native American poetry shares certain distinctive features with all poetry: it is richly evocative, succinct, revelatory of the spirit of the singer and the sharer. It differs less in method than in evoked response in non-American Indian sharers, for the language is, naturally, unfamiliar and, consequently, alien sounding—and the response to the alien is usually unpleasant. Because it is different in grammar, vocabulary, and syntax, the alien language seems cacaphonous, harsh, nasal. Because the accent pattern is more akin to that of oriental languages than to occidental ones, a sense of monotony results in the ears of hearers accustomed to accentual and cadencial verse.

The best translators of American Indian poetry have not ordinarily been poets themselves, and their translations lack that quality which more recent poets who have become interested in the literature manage to include—the flavor of the language coupled with an aesthetic rather than a scientific response to the people. In the earlier translations, the dominant Judeo-Christian beliefs of the translators were either deliberately intruded or subtly included despite the unquestioned good intentions of the translators. The problems encountered by the most dedicated of translators are readily apparent in the progress of the Ojibwa "Chant to the Fire-fly" from original through literal translation to literary translation in Henry Rowe Schoolcraft's pioneer work[1] that set the pattern for almost all his successors:

---

[1]*Historical and Statistical Information Respecting the History, Conditions, and Prospects of the Indian Tribes of the United States* (Philadelphia, 1851–1857).

Chant to the Fire-fly
(Chippewa Original)

Wau wau tay see!
Wau wau tay see!
E mow e shin
Tahe bwau ne baun-e wee!
Be eghaun—be eghaun—ewee!
Wau wau tay see!
Wau wau tay see!
Was sa koon ain je gun.
Was sa koon ain je gun.

LITERAL TRANSLATION

Flitting-white-fire-insect! waving-white-fire-bug! give me light before I go to bed! give me light before I go to sleep. Come, little dancing white-fire-bug! Come, little flitting white-fire-beast! Light me with your bright white-flame-instrument—your little candle.

LITERARY TRANSLATION

Fire-fly, fire-fly! bright little thing,
Light me to bed, and my song I will sing.
Give me your light, as you fly o'er my head,
That I may merrily go to my bed.
Give me your light o'er the grass as you creep,
That I may joyfully go to my sleep.
Come, little fire-fly, come, little beast—
Come! and I'll make you tomorrow a feast.
Come, little candle that flies as I sing,
Bright little fairy-bug—night's little king;
Come, and I'll dance as you guide me along,
Come, and I'll pay you, my bug, with a song.

MORE LITERAL LITERARY TRANSLATION

Fire-fly Song
(Ojibwa)

Flitting white-fire insects!
Wandering small-fire beasts!
Wave little stars about my bed!
Weave little stars into my sleep!
Come, little dancing white-fire bug,
Come, little flitting white-fire beast!
Light me with your white-flame magic,
Your little star-torch.

Such words as *insect* and *bug* in the literal translation serve the English version only nominally, for the connotative sense of the words reduces the "insect" in ways *"Wau wau tay see"* does not. The Ojibwa form recognizes the firefly's place in the grand scheme of things, that equality known to Mohandas K. Gandhi, for instance, and revealed in his refusal to step on an ant, squash a roach, or slap a mosquito. The western mind is imbued with the belief that a supreme being arbitrarily endowed man with superiority because he was molded in the form of his creator. Other forms are, then, inferior and therefore subject to man, his domination, and his disregard for their existence. Gandhi's pacificism could be understood only as opposition to war or violence in relation to man. Seated in an awareness of the equal importance of all living things in the Great Mystery, Gandhi's rejection of violence was a total rejection, one not reserved for man. His belief was no more understood by the western mind than is the harsh denigration involved in such words as *insect* and *bug*. But these words are far removed from the intellectual-emotional response of the Ojibwa to the winged fire-being he addresses.

The equal importance of Man, Coyote, Loon, Bear, and so on in the religious accounts readily testifies to the semantic inaccuracy of *white-fire-beast*, a concept the Ojibwa could not have held. *Bed* and *candle* are European concepts that cannot be equated with *pallet* or *couch* or *torch*, terms closer to the idea of the Ojibwa words. The literary translation further compounds the semantic difficulties as European poetic conventions are overlaid.

Rhyme, parallel ideas, measured sound duration (metrics), and repetition are all apparent in the original, but not as they are common to English versification. The rhyme is not deliberate in the slant *shin/gun*, for rhyme (either slant or pure) per se was not an aspect of Native American poetry. That it sometimes appears is incidental, a natural aspect of language. While language conventions preclude hard and fast statements about "American Indian Poetry"— a term which embraces works from hundreds of languages—some generalization is possible. In *Songs of the Tewa*,[2] Herbert J. Spinden makes one such useful and defeasible generalization:

The device of rhyme seems not to have been used by the most cultivated Americans of pre-Columbian times....Nor were there any certain stanza forms except such as were brought about by the repetition of phrases. The outstanding fea-

2New York, 1933, p. 58.

ture of American Indian verse constructions comes from parallel phrasing, or, let us say, repetition with an increment, which gives an effect not of rhyming sounds but of rhyming thoughts. Sometimes this ceremonial pattern demands a repetition for each world direction with formal changes involving the color, plant, animal, and so forth, associated with each station on the circuit.

The first literary translation of "Chant to the Fire-fly" suffers from such English conventions as pseudo-heroic couplets and ideas intruded in words used to flesh out the basic iambic pentameter lines. Exactly how the Ojibwa singer would make a feast for the firefly defies thought. The Native American's trip to the sleep area may have been weary, glad, grateful, or merely resigned, but he would no more turn sleepward "merrily" or "joyfully" than would his white counterpart. That the reality-defying convention is ubiquitous in English poetry does not justify its inclusion in the Ojibwa poem. And nothing (in English or Ojibwa versification) could justify the artificial inversions that create the rhyme.

The second, more literal version avoids the most objectionable features of the first but might be improved in some comparable fashion to:

Fire-fly Song
(Ojibwa)

Flitting, darting white-fire!
Air-borne, roving white-fire!
Shine your light about my lodging,
Light the way to where I sleep!
Tireless, darting white-fire!
Restless, roving white-fire!
Guide me with your gleaming.
Guide me with your torch.

An hypnotic formula is at work in such a poem. Designed to soothe the senses, lull the hearer to sleep, the poem assumes the proportion of incantation, psychologically sound and efficient. The repetitions are pleasingly monotonous, the incremental idea suggestive. Couple the words with the music that accompanies them and caressing, enveloping euphoria results; the lullaby works its magic.

Nor can the magic property of the song (which all Indian poems are) be understated. Any Indian song contains four interrelated elements: music, words, the body movements accompanying the words and music, and the belief of the singer-dancer. Music which lifts the words to Wah'kon-tah embodies the inexpressible soul of the Indian which is added to the expressible in words—words which have, in and of themselves, magical properties. Some Native Americans believed that the word existed prior to the existence of anything else—including the gods—because thought precedes creation. There was never nothingness entirely, for the thought existed; and thought is manifest only in words. If such a concept seems difficult, consider the same belief as it is stated in the New Testament, Chapter I of The Gospel according to Saint John:

In the beginning was the Word, and the Word was with God, and the Word was God. The same was in the beginning with God. All things were made by him; and without him was not any thing made that was made.

Belief in the magic of the word is apparent in the first century B.C. account from the Hebraic-Hellenic world that ultimately precipitated the Western European into the "new world." Compare it with the account of the genesis according to the Uitoto of Columbia:

In the beginning, the word gave origin to the Father.

The converted John conceived the word as existing simultaneously with the first cause; the word for the Uitoto was the thought that preceded the Great Mystery, allowing it existence. The Zuñi account begins:

Before the beginning of the new-making, Awonawilona (the maker and Container of All, the All-father) solely had being. There was nothing else whatsoever throughout the great space of the ages save everywhere black darkness in it, and everywhere void desolation. In the beginning of the new-made, Awonawilona conceived within himself and thought outward in space, whereby mists of increase, streams potent of growth, were evolved and uplifted.

Here, the first cause exists independently of the word, but before anything can be created, the word (thought) must be conceived within himself.

Whether it existed before Wah'kon-tah, simultaneously, or shortly after, the word is vital to the Great Mystery, being perhaps the greatest mystery, for it has power to cause medicine to work, to lure game into range, to cause plants to grow, to allow man to address, be heard by, and join with the Great Mystery. As such, language itself is sacred, not to be profaned by cavalier and casual usage or misused for the utterance of false statements or spiritual obscenities.

The attitude prevails today, prevails so firmly that white commentators are invariably aware of it. Whether or not they believe such assertions as Cherokee Jess Sixkiller's answers to Associate Editor Martha Lane of *Together* magazine, they find them worthy of print:

Are there Indians who do not speak English?

Yes, quite a number don't speak English. My grandmother doesn't, and my father doesn't very well.

Did you learn English as a second language?

Yes. English is the only foreign language I know. I spoke Cherokee first—and I wasn't able to swear or tell many lies till I learned English.[3]

Music and dance are an inseparable part of Indian poetry, so inseparable a part that an Indian may observe, "I can't sing that dance" or "I can't dance that song." Alice C. Fletcher, one of the earliest and most accurate recorders of Indian music, explains why this is true in *Indian Story and Song from North America*:[4]

Music enveloped the Indian's individual and social life like an atmosphere. There was no important personal experience where it did not bear a part, nor any ceremonial where it was not essential to the expression of religious feeling. The songs of a tribe were coextensive with the life of the people.

This universal use of music was because of the belief that it was a medium of communication between man and the unseen. The invisible voice could reach the invisible power that permeates all nature, animating all natural forms. As success depended upon help from this mysterious power, in every avocation, in every undertaking, and in every ceremonial, the Indian appealed to this power through song. When a man went forth to hunt, that he might secure food and clothing for his family, he sang songs to insure the assistance of the unseen power in capturing the game. In like manner, when he confronted danger and death, he sang that strength might be given him to meet his fate unflinchingly. In gathering the healing herbs and in administering them, song brought the required efficacy. When he planted, he sang, in order that the seed might fructify and the harvest follow. In his sports, in his games, when he wooed and when he mourned, song alike gave zest to pleasure and brought solace to his suffering. In fact, the Indian sang in every experience of life from his cradle to his grave.

It would be a mistake to fancy that songs floated indiscriminately about among the Indians, and could be picked up here and there by any chance observer. Every song had originally its owner. It belonged either to a society, secular or religious, to a certain clan or political organization, to a particular rite or ceremony, or to some individual.

Religious songs were known only to the priesthood; and, as music constituted a medium between man and the unseen powers which controlled his life, literal

---

[3] "An Urban Indian Says: We Want to Speak for Ourselves," January, 1970, p. 9.

[4] Boston, 1900, pp. 114–17.

accuracy was important, otherwise the path between the god and the man would not be straight, and the appeal would miscarry.

In every tribe there were societies having a definite membership, with initiatory rites and reciprocal duties. Each society had its peculiar songs; and there were officials chosen from among the members because of their good voices and retentive memories, to lead the singing and to transmit with accuracy the stories and songs of the society, which frequently preserved bits of tribal history. Fines were imposed upon any member who sang incorrectly, while ridicule always and everywhere followed a faulty rendering of a song.

The right to sing a song which belonged to an individual could be purchased, the person buying the song being taught it by its owner.

These beliefs and customs among the Indians have made it possible to preserve their songs without change from one generation to another. Many curious and interesting proofs of accuracy of transmittal have come to my knowledge during the past twenty years, while studying these primitive melodies.

Indian singing was always in unison; and, as the natural soprano, contralto, tenor, and bass moved along in octaves, the different qualities of tone in the voices brought out the overtones and produced harmonic effects. When listening to chorals sung by two or three hundred voices, as I have many times heard them in ceremonials, it has been difficult to realise that all were singing in unison.

Close and continued observation has revealed that the Indian, when he sings, is not concerned with the making of a musical presentation to his audience. He is simply pouring out his feelings, regardless of artistic effects. To him music is subjective: it is the vehicle of communication between him and the object of his desire.

Brevity characterizes most Native American poetry for the same reasons and in the same ways it characterizes Japanese haiku. Some basic truth or desire, a seasonal reference, the metaphorical compression of symbol, regard for the simple eloquence and magic of language—all are apparent in this haiku of parting by Buson:

> You must remain...I
> must depart: two autumns fall
> within our one heart.

And this Ojibwa maid's lament when she realizes her love is leaving:

> A loon I thought it was
> But it was
> My love's
> Splashing oar.[5]

[5]Frances Densmore, trans., *Chippewa Music, I. Bureau of American Ethnology Bulletin 45* (Washington, 1910), p. 89.

Emotional embellishment, verbal extensions beyond those needed to involve the sharer and his emotions through memory, poetic devices overlaid for aesthetic effect—all of the artful contrivances that intensify the intellectual response at the expense of personal involvement—are absent in the Japanese and the Ojibwa works. Without sentimentality, these works create a great sense of loss, of bittersweet memory of loss, and the gentle realization that such loss is a part of the human condition. And the human condition proceeds from the Great Mystery. It is the awareness wedded to minimal wordage and maximal reader response that allows the reader to understand the understated, unsentimental, acceptance of the closing lines of Ernest Hemingway's short story, "A Clean, Well-Lighted Place":

> Now, without thinking further,
> he would go home to his room.
> He would lie in the bed
> and finally,
> with daylight,
> he would go to sleep.
> After all, he said to himself,
> it is probably only insomnia.
> Many must have it.

The soul of the author resides somehow in such lines—perhaps because he addresses his concept of Wah'kon-tah in them. Shared with man they ascend to the Great Mystery and, with their magic, bridge the distances that seem to exist between earth and its mantle of enveloping air.

It is that sense of soul, that sense of Orenda that echoes from the very best literature of all men and sings in Native American poetry even when it must pass through a second language. The problems are explored and made manifest in *American Primitive Music*[6] by Frederick R. Burton.

TRANSLATION AND INTERPRETATION

A better example of compactness may be found in the following to which I have previously referred as the song that awakened my interest in Ojibway music and led me to this prolonged investigation. Short as it is, the Indian does not piece it out with "heyah." The entire poem is here given as sung by the Indians, with the meaning of the words under the Ojibway equivalent:

[6]New York, 1909, pp. 149–53.

Chekahbay tebik ondandeyan
Throughout night I keep awake

chekaybay tebik ondandeyan
throughout night I keep awake

ahgahmah-sibi ondandeyan
upon a river I keep awake.

I am quite sure that this literal transfer of meanings from one language to another would convey nothing to the English paleface who knew nothing by direct contact of Indian life. His poetic fancy might evolve a meaning from it, but it is hardly likely that it would be in consonance with the Indian's meaning. I venture to take the reader over the course that was necessarily mine when I undertook to translate the song. At that time I knew not one Ojibway word. The intelligent Indian whom I asked for a translation slowly dictated the following:

"I am out all night on the river seeking for my sweetheart."

This impressed me as poetic in feeling, but I wished to get closer to the words themselves which I had carefully spelled from dictation and written as above, leaving spaces beneath for the English equivalents. I could see that there were only four words. By dint of patient, detailed questioning I arrived approximately at the English equivalents above given. Then I was puzzled and disturbed.

"Where is the word for sweetheart?" I asked.

"It is not there," replied the Indian, tranquilly.

"Then," said I, "how do you make out that the song means 'I am seeking for my sweetheart'?"

Had he been a paleface he would have smiled pityingly at my lack of comprehension, but, as he had all the traditional courtesy and dignity of his race, he put my own patience to the blush by pointing to the word *ondandeyan* which occurs three times.

"That mean," said he, "'I keep awake.' I get tired, yes, and sleepy, but I no sleep. I keep awake. That word (*tebik*) is night. Now you see. Why does a man keep awake all night when he want to sleep?"

Like the true orator and debater, he paused for reply.

"Well," I suggested, half in weakness, and half in determination to make him work out the meaning, "he might be hunting for deer, or something else to eat."

"No, no!" he responded gravely, "not this time. See: I keep awake all night long on the river. Only one reason. I go to find my sweetheart. The word is not there but we understand it. We know what is meant. Perhaps mebbe her family has gone away. Perhaps mebbe she said she would meet me and something happened so she couldn't. I don't know; but we know that the man who made this song was looking for his sweetheart, and we do not need the word there."

With this bewildering light thrown on the subject, I retired to my own quarters and pondered. It was my eager desire to make the attractive melody available for paleface singers. To this end it was essential that there should be singable verses. Observe the use of the plural. One verse, or one stanza would not do for the demands of civilization. The Indian is content to sing his one line over and over again, but the paleface must have variety in his language even in so short a song as this. I confess that my first impulse was to string together some rhymed lines that would fit the tune, and let it go at that, as the easiest way out of the difficulty, but it seemed a shame to discard the suggestion offered in the Indian verse, and doubly wrong to put forth an Indian song that should not at least reflect the Indian thought; but so much was implied and so little expressed! And that despairing reflection was the key to the problem. So much implied! I set myself to studying how much more might be implied than the search for a sweetheart, and it occurred to me that if an Ojibway were on the river he would necessarily be in his canoe. Here was promise of singable results and of the verbal repetition without which no representation of the original could be regarded as satisfactory. It was with conscious excitement that I hurried to my Indian friend and asked the question—would not the singing lover be in his canoe?

"Of course," said he, and then a ghost of a smile lit up his dark features; "but you don't find the word *chemaun* there, do you?" he asked.

Chemaun means canoe. "No," I answered, "but it's understood, isn't it?"

"Yes," said he, "we understand it so," and he turned away as if that settled it, or as if a continuance of the conversation would lead him to inquire sarcastically if I supposed the lover would be swimming the river all night, or balancing on a perilous, uncomfortable log?

It did settle it, and before I arrived back at my table I was humming the first of the stanzas with which the song has been identified since its publication—

> In the still night, the long hours through,
>   I guide my bark canoe,
> My bark canoe, my love, to you.
>
> While the stars shine and falls the dew
>   I seek my love in bark canoe,
> In bark canoe I seek for you.
>
> It is I, love, your lover true,
>   Who glides the stream in bark canoe;
> It glides to you, my love, to you.

Probably the most consistent single observation of the men and women who have collected, translated, and recorded the music-poem-dances of the Native American concerns the personal revelation inherent in the poem. The reaction of self to the song is the only important thing; that reaction is the measure of success. What the hearer receives is only a fragment or a précis of the total poem which remains unsung, its magic at work in the silence of the inner song. And silence is a very large part of any Native American poem, for, as Ohiyesa says in Chapter 1 of *The Soul of the Indian*:[7]

[7]Eastman (Boston, 1911), pp. 3–15.

The original attitude of the American Indian toward the Eternal, the "Great Mystery" that surrounds and embraces us, was as simple as it was exalted. To him it was the supreme conception, bringing with it the fullest measure of joy and satisfaction possible in this life.

The worship of the "Great Mystery" was silent, solitary, free from all self-seeking. It was silent, because all speech is of necessity feeble and imperfect; therefore the souls of my ancestors ascended to God in wordless adoration. It was solitary, because they believed that He is nearer to us in solitude, and there were no priests authorized to come between a man and his Maker. None might exhort or confess or in any way meddle with the religious experience of another. Among us all men were created sons of God and stood erect, as conscious of their divinity. Our faith might not be formulated in creeds, nor forced upon any who were unwilling to receive it; hence there was no preaching, proselyting, nor persecution, neither were there any scoffers or atheists.

There were no temples or shrines among us save those of nature. Being a natural man, the Indian was intensely poetical. He would deem it sacrilege to build a house for Him who may be met face to face in the mysterious, shadowy aisles of the primeval forest, or on the sunlit bosom of virgin prairies, upon dizzy spires and pinnacles of naked rock, and yonder in the jeweled vault of the night sky! He who enrobes Himself in filmy veils of cloud, there on the rim of the visible world where our Great-Grandfather Sun kindles his evening camp-fire, He who rides upon the rigorous wind of the north, or breathes forth His spirit upon aromatic southern airs, whose war-canoe is launched upon majestic rivers and inland seas—He needs no lesser cathedral!

That solitary communion with the Unseen which was the highest expression of our religious life is partly described in the word *hambeday*, literally "mysterious feeling," which has been variously translated "fasting" and "dreaming." It may better be interpreted as "consciousness of the divine."

The first *hambeday*, or religious retreat, marked an epoch in the life of the youth, which may be compared to that of confirmation or conversion in Christian experience. Having first prepared himself by means of the purifying vapor-bath, and cast off as far as possible all human or fleshly influences, the young man sought out the noblest height, the most commanding summit in all the surrounding region. Knowing that God sets no value upon material things, he took with him no offerings or sacrifices other than symbolic objects, such as paints and tobacco. Wishing to appear before Him in all humility, he wore no clothing save his moccasins and breech-clout. At the solemn hour of sunrise or sunset he took up his position, overlooking the glories of earth and facing the "Great Mystery," and there he remained, naked, erect, silent, and motionless, exposed to the elements and forces of His arming, for a night and a day to two days and nights, but rarely longer. Sometimes he would chant a hymn without words, or offer the ceremonial "filled pipe." In this holy trance or ecstasy the Indian mystic found his highest happiness and the motive power of his existence.

When he returned to the camp, he must remain at a distance until he had again entered the vapor-bath and prepared himself for intercourse with his fellows. Of the vision or sign vouchsafed to him he did not speak, unless it had included some commission which must be publicly fulfilled. Sometimes an old man, standing upon the brink of eternity, might reveal to a chosen few the oracle of his long-past youth.

The Native American has been generally despised by his white conquerors for his poverty and simplicity. They forget, perhaps, that his religion forbade the accumulation of wealth and the enjoyment of luxury. To him, as to other single-minded men in every age and race, from Diogenes to the brothers of Saint Francis, from the Montanists to the Shakers, the love of possessions has appeared a snare, and the burdens of a complex society a source of needless peril and temptation. Furthermore, it was the rule of his life to share the fruits of his skill and success with his less fortunate brothers. Thus he kept his spirit free from the clog of pride, cupidity, or envy, and carried out, as he believed, the divine decree—a matter profoundly important to him.

It was not, then, wholly from ignorance or improvidence that he failed to establish permanent towns and to develop a material civilization. To the untutored sage, the concentration of population was the prolific mother of all evils, moral no less than physical. He argued that food is good, while surfeit kills; that love is good, but lust destroys; and not less dreaded than the pestilence following upon crowded and unsanitary dwellings was the loss of spiritual power inseparable from too close contact with one's fellow-men. All who have lived much out of doors know that there is a magnetic and nervous force that accumulates in solitude and that is quickly dissipated by life in a crowd; and even his enemies have recognized the fact that for a certain innate power and self-poise, wholly independent of circumstances, the American Indian is unsurpassed among men.

The red man divided mind into two parts—the spiritual mind and the physical mind. The first is pure spirit, concerned only with the essence of things, and it was this he sought to strengthen by spiritual prayer, during which the body is subdued by fasting and hardship. In this type of prayer there was no beseeching of favor or help. All matters of personal or selfish concern, as success in hunting or warfare, relief from sickness, or the sparing of a beloved life, were definitely relegated to the plane of the lower or material mind, and all ceremonies, charms, or incantations designed to secure a benefit or to avert a danger, were recognized as emanating from the physical self.

The rites of this physical worship, again, were wholly symbolic, and the Indian no more worshiped the Sun than the Christian adores the Cross. The Sun and the Earth, by an obvious parable, holding scarcely more of poetic metaphor than of scientific truth, were in his view the parents of all organic life. From the Sun, as the universal father, proceeds the quickening principle in nature, and in the patient and fruitful womb of our mother, the Earth, are hidden embryos of plants and men. Therefore our reverence and love for them was really an imaginative extension of our love for our immediate parents, and with this sentiment of filial piety was joined a willingness to appeal to them, as to a father, for such good gifts as we may desire. This is the material or physical prayer.

The elements and majestic forces in nature, Lightning, Wind, Water, Fire, and Frost, were regarded with awe as spiritual powers, but always secondary and intermediate in character. We believed that the spirit pervades all creation and that every creature possesses a soul in some degree, though not necessarily a soul conscious of itself. The tree, the waterfall, the grizzly bear, each is an embodied Force, and as such an object of reverence.

The Indian loved to come into sympathy and spiritual communion with his brothers of the animal kingdom, whose inarticulate souls had for him something of the sinless purity that we attribute to the innocent and irresponsible child. He had faith in their instincts, as in a mysterious wisdom given from above; and while he humbly accepted the supposedly voluntary sacrifice of their bodies to preserve his own, he paid homage to their spirits in prescribed prayers and offerings.

The most significant aspects of Native American thought that create problems for the non-Indian reader are indicated in Ohiyesa's statement:

1. The ceremonial pattern that includes the four world directions (east, west, south, north) which are analagous to the four planes of the human body (front, back, left, right) creates the repetitions and pairings in both song and story. (Reread Herbert J. Spinden's statement earlier in this introduction.)

2. The ceremonial pattern emphasizes pairings of words, colors, animals, expressions, stanzas. The sort of pairing obvious in light and dark, yellow and white, sun and rain, land and water rises out of the idea of duality most apparent in Father Sky and Mother Earth. Just as the closed couplet in English versification creates a sense of completion, so does this pairing in Native American poetry—as Spinden says, "an effect not of rhyming sounds but of rhyming thoughts."

3. The magic of words creates incantation in such a poem as this Crow war song:

> Whenever there is any trouble,
> I shall not die but get through.
> Though arrows are many, I shall arrive.
> My heart is manly.[8]

The poem is not an assertion that the singer will survive nor a declaration that he is brave. Through the magic of the words, he assumes command, he sings for power—and achieves it. Articulation will cause the formulated phrase to become reality. The poem is a prayer; the prayer becomes incantation; incantation creates granting.

---

[8]R. H. Lowie, *Crow Religion. Anthropological Papers of the American Museum of Natural History,* XXV, 1922, p. 410.

4. Visions come in dreams and are messages from those nonliving forms in Wah'kon-tah. Invested with power, they are made operative in the utterance. Dream songs are, ordinarily, brief.

5. Every living creature (man, rabbit, wolf, tree, bear) and every object (rock, river, mountain) as well as each physical force (wind, water, light) or abstract quality (death, disease, hunger, thirst) has spirit that personifies it. This is most easily seen in the religious accounts. It is not *the* Hare or *the* Raven which acts, it is Hare or Raven—the spirit of the creature.

6. Authorship of a poem is not possible. Though a man may own his poem or song, he does not create it himself. It becomes his through Wah'kon-tah, a lesser divinity, or an elder—alive or dead. We can, then, only attribute the poem to the poet's culture: Ojibwa (Chippewa), Cherokee, Navaho, etc.

The power of the word, whether it reside in the personal song or the ceremonial dance, may seem a superstitious, primitive belief in an age of science. Or does it? This April 22, 1972, Associated Press feature[9] may give those who think so cause to reconsider. The Native American reading this article would have good reason to emit a stereotyped "Ugh" and wonder at the backward ways of his Christian brother.

Sing a Song in Praise of Mother Earth
George W. Cornell
AP Religion Writer

Now that the churches have started stressing the urgency of taking care of Mother Earth, they want some songs to sing about it.

The lyrics are needed as part of the religious efforts to "rebuild man's attitudes about protecting the environment," says Anastasia Van Burkalow, of the Hymn Society of America. A geology professor and organist, she adds: "We need to be reminded that the good gifts of the earth come to us from God the Creator, to whom we should give thanks, and that we hold them in our possession not as outright owners but as stewards.

"We are responsible for their preservation and even for their enhancement because of the power he has given us to be co-creators with him."

However, the preachments about it need some musical reinforcement, in the view of the Hymn Society, which has issued an appeal to church people to submit hymns, hymn-prayers and hymn verses on the subject.

[9]*The Tampa Tribune*, Tampa, Florida, April 22, 1972, p. D1.

The interdenominational society, which seeks to improve standards of church hymnody and encourage production of contemporary hymns, asks that entries be sent to its New York headquarters at 475 Riverside Drive by the end of May.

The society, including both Protestant and Roman Catholic hymnologists, is observing its 50th anniversary this spring.

"While ecology is a relatively new emphasis for the preacher and the congregation, for the teacher and class, it is vital for the survival of mankind," the society says in starting its new hymn search.

Fundamentally, it is a "religious problem," the society adds, and appropriate hymns are needed that "will speak to God and will also move men to action."

The best offerings will be selected by a committee of judges. Composers then will be assigned to set them to tunes for later publication. Some of the society's new hymns eventually find their way into church hymnbooks.

Miss Van Burkalow, a geology professor at Hunter College and also a Methodist church organist who is on the society's executive board, initiated the new hunt for hymns as a result of her special knowledge in the earth sciences.

Noting that the earth not only provides the materials that sustain mankind physically but also the natural beauty that inspires his mind and spirit, she adds:

"And yet because of our greed and our ignorance and our rapidly growing numbers we are fast destroying these great resources on which we depend for our very existence."

Only by widespread recognition of humanity's duty to safeguard and enhance the earth, she says, "can we hope to turn back the forces of destruction that threaten us on all sides."

Stirring hymns on the subject, she says, can offer "inspiration and guidance" in that cause.

Meanwhile, another Catholic-Protestant group, the Consultation on Ecumenical Hymnody, released a list of 150 hymns and tunes recommended for ecumenical use.

The list grew out of a study of all hymnals now in use by the major Christian denominations in America to determine which hymns are common to the heritage of all.

The consultation expressed hope that denominational agencies which publish hymnbooks will include the hymns chosen in a special "common core" listing, as an aid to "development of a common hymnody among American Christians."

The ethnological custom of grouping Native American works by geographical location of the tribe (Eastern Woodlands, Horse Plains, Desert Dwellers, and so forth) is deliberately avoided in this chapter. Certainly the geography of a people shapes their thought to a great extent; certainly the individual tribes are unique in the same way that the British, the French, the Germans are unique in Europe; certainly each people's poetry is worthy of individual study. However, the collectivity that is apparent in the word *Indian* to identify these many peoples has attributed the worst features of some groups to the total group, ignored the best features of all groups, and assumed a general attitude that is far removed from the true generalizations that can be made.

Just as the collective soul of the European can be seen in the works of the Greeks, the Germans, the Italians, etc., as they are assembled in anthologies of European literature, the collective idea of the "Indian" might best be served by seeing his collective soul free of the generalizations that have unfairly accrued to certain tribes. For that reason, a thematic arrangement guides this chapter, the people's identity appended to each poem.

And, as poets speak best for themselves, critical comment or explanatory information is deliberately omitted except in those cases where it seems vital. In spite of our earlier statement that Native American poets did not identify their work by name, this chapter contains a few poems by poets of recorded identity—Aztec poets. That advanced technological culture had perfected paper and set down its works—works which were, in the main, destroyed by the invading barbarians. Advanced technology creates that sundering from the group identity which allows for the egocentricity of personal identification, so these poets are identified. Their attitude toward the poem, toward the word, toward the communication and the sharing is, generally, at the heart of all Native American poetry, so they serve their fellow poets of all tribes.

The book of flowers of Huezotzincos was as literal a book as is the one from which you are reading; it was also a collection, a bouquet of words. The gathering of the poems in this chapter, then, creates a book of flowers, the highly cultivated and exotic rose of the Aztec complementing the sweet naturalness of the Ojibwa field daisy. We feel it would be an impertinence to explain how you are to respond to a natural outpouring of sweetness or to the pungency of tansy in such a bouquet. Because the poems cannot be dated for certain, we have selected those which have the best claim to predating the transplant American historically or in temper. We have weeded out the flowers that seemed, to us, damaged by Euro-American gardeners.

The Person: The Poet

A Song of the Huezotzincos

(Aztec)

Raining down writings for thy mind, O Montezuma, I come
hither, I come raining them down, a very jester, a painted
butterfly; stringing together pretty objects, I seem to be
as one cementing together precious stones, as I chant my
song on my emerald flute, as I blow on my golden flute,
ya ho, ay la.

Yes, I shall cause thy flowers to rejoice the Giver of Life,
the first cause, as hither I come raining down my songs,
ya ho.

A sweet-voiced flower is my mind, a sweet-voiced flower
is my drum, and I sing the words of this flowery book.

Rejoice and be glad ye who live amid the flowers in the
house of my great lord Montezuma, we must finish with
this earth, we must finish with the sweet flowers, alas.

At the Mount of Battle we bring forth our sweet and glitter-
ing flowers before the first cause, plants having the luster
of the tiger, like the cry of the eagle, leaving glorious
memory, such are the plants of this house.

Alas! in a little while there is an end before the first cause to
all living; let me therefore string together beauteous and
yellow feathers, and mingling them with the dancing
butterflies rain them down before you, scattering the
words of my song like water dashed from flowers.

I would that I could go there where lies the great blue
water surging, and smoking and thundering, till after a
time it retires again: I shall sing as the quetzal, the blue
quechol, when I go back to Huezotzinco among the waters.

I shall follow them, I shall know them, my beloved Huezotzincos; the emerald *quechol* birds, the green *quechol*, the
golden butterflies, and yellow birds, guard Huezotzinco
among the waters.

Among the flowery waters, the golden waters, the emerald
waters, at the junction of the waters which the blue duck
rules, moving her spangled tail.

I the singer stand on high on the yellow rushes; let me go
forth with noble songs and laden with flowers.

A Modoc Singer

(Modoc)

I
the song
I walk here

My Music Reaches to the Sky

(Ojibwa)

My music
    Reaches
    To the sky.

Song of the Poet

(Tlingit)

It is only crying about myself
that comes to me in song.

An Otomi Song

(Aztec)

I, the singer, polished my noble new song like a shining emerald, I arranged it like the voice of the *tzinitzcan* bird, I called to mind the essence of poetry, I set it in order like the chant of the *zacuan* bird, I mingled it with the beauty of the emerald, that I might make it appear like a rose bursting its bud, so that I might rejoice the Cause of All.

I skillfully arranged my song like the lovely feathers of the *zacuan* bird, the *tzinitzcan* and the *quechol*; I shall speak forth my song like the tinkling of golden bells; my song is that which the *miaua* bird pours forth around him; I lifted my voice and rained down flowers of speech before the face of the Cause of All.

In the true spirit of song I lifted my voice through a trumpet of gold, I let fall from my lips a celestial song, I shall speak notes precious and brilliant as those of the *miaua* bird, I shall cause to blossom out a noble new song, I lifted my voice like the burning incense of flowers, so that I the singer might cause joy before the face of the Cause of All.

The divine *quechol* bird answers me as I, the singer, sing, like the *coyol* bird, a noble new song, polished like a jewel, a turquoise, a shining emerald, darting green rays, a flower song of spring, spreading a celestial fragrance, fresh with the dews of roses, thus have I the poet sung.

I colored with skill, I mingled choice roses in a noble new song, polished like a jewel, a turquoise, a shining emerald, darting green rays, a flower song of spring, spreading celestial fragrance, fresh with the dews of roses, thus have I the poet sung.

I was glorified, I was enriched, by the flower-sweet song as by the smoke of the *poyomatl*, my soul was contented, I trembled in spirit, I inhaled the sweetness, my soul was intoxicated, I inhaled the fragrance of delicious flowers in the place of riches, my soul was drunken with the flowers.

To the Great Mystery

Plaint Against the Fog

(Nootka)

Don't you ever,
You up in the sky,
Don't you ever get tired
Of having the clouds between you and us?

Prayer Spoken During the Sun Dance

(Teton Sioux)

Wakan'tanka
When I pray to him
Hears me.
Whatever is good he
Grants me.

Song to Bring Fair Weather

(Nootka)

You, whose day it is, make it beautiful.
Get out your rainbow colors,
So it will be beautiful.

The Creation of the Earth

(Pima)

Earth Magician shapes this world.
    Behold what he can do!
Round and smooth he molds it.
    Behold what he can do!
Earth Magician makes the mountains.
    Heed what he has to say!
He it is that makes the mesas.
    Heed what he has to say!
Earth Magician shapes this world;
    Earth Magician makes its mountains;
Makes all larger, larger, larger.
    Into the earth the Magician glances;
Into its mountains he may see.

Prayer of a Warrior

(Assiniboine)

O Wakonda, you see me a poor man.
Have pity on me.
I go to war to revenge the death of my brother.
Have pity upon me.
I smoke this tobacco taken from my medicine sack, where it has been enveloped with the remains of my dead brother [a lock of his hair]. I smoke it to my tutelary, to you; aid me in revenge.
On my path preserve me from mad wolves.
Let no enemies surprise me.
I have sacrificed, I have smoked, my heart is low, have pity upon me. Give me the bows and arrows of my enemies. Give me their guns. Give me their horses. Give me their bodies. Let me have my face blackened on my return. Let good weather come that I can see. Good dreams give that I can judge where they are. I have suffered. I wish to live. I wish to be revenged. I am poor. I want horses. I will sacrifice. I will smoke. I will remember. Have pity on me.

Belief in the Power of the Word

Prayer for Stalking Deer

(Zuñi)

This day
He who holds our roads,
Our sun father,
Has come out standing to his sacred place.
Now that he has passed us on our roads,
Here we pass you on your road.
Divine one,
The flesh of the white corn,
Prayer meal,
Shell,
Corn pollen,
Here I offer to you.
With your wisdom
Taking the prayer meal,
The shell,
The corn pollen,
This day,
My fathers,
My mothers,
In some little hollow,
In some low brush,
You will reveal yourselves to me.
Then with your flesh,
With your living waters,
May I sate myself. In order that this may be
Here I offer you prayer meal.

Charm to Cause Love

(Ojibwa)

I can charm the man.
He is completely fascinated by me.

From *The Rite of Vigil* *The Chant of the* *Symbolic Colors*

(Osage)

With what shall the little ones adorn their bodies, as they
    tread the path of life? it has been said, in this house.
The crimson color of the God of Day who sitteth in the
    heavens,
They shall make to be their sacred color, as they go forth
    upon life's journey.
Verily, the god who reddens the heavens as he approaches,
They shall make to be their sacred color, as they go forth
    upon life's journey.
When they adorn their bodies with the crimson hue shed
    by that God of day,
Then shall the little ones make themselves to be free from
    all causes of death, as they go forth upon life's journey.

What shall the people use for a symbolic plume? they said
    to one another, it has been said, in this house.
Verily, the God who always comes out at the beginning of
    day,
Has at his right side
A beam of light that stands upright like a plume.
That beam of light shall the people make to be their sacred
    plume.
When they make of that beam of light their sacred plume,
Then their sacred plume shall never droop for want of
    strength as they go forth upon life's journey.

What shall they place as a pendant upon his breast? they
    said to one another.
The shell of the mussel who sitteth upon the earth,
They shall place as a pendant upon his breast.
It is as the God of Day who in the heavens,
Close to their breast they shall verily press this god;
As a pendant upon his breast they shall place this god.
Then shall the little ones become free from all causes of
    death, as they go forth upon life's journey.

Verily, at that time and place, it has been said, in this house,
They said to one another: What shall the people place upon
   his wrists?
It is a bond spoken of as the captive's bond,
That they shall place upon his wrists.
Verily, it is not a captive's bond,
That is spoken of,
But it is a soul
That they shall place upon his wrists.

Verily at that time and place, it has been said, in this house,
They said to one another: What is he upon whom a girdle
   is to be placed?
Verily, it is not a captive that is spoken of,
It is a spirit upon whom they will place a girdle, they said,
   it has been said, in this house.
Verily at that time and place, it has been said, in this house,
They said to one another: What is he upon whose feet these
   moccasins are to be placed?
It is a captive
Upon whose feet these moccasins are to be placed.
Verily, it is not a captive that is spoken of,
It is a spirit
Upon whose feet these moccasins are to be placed, they
   said, it has been said, in this house.

A Charm Against Sickness

(Papago)

The sun is rising,
At either side a bow is lying,
Beside the bows are lion-babies,
The sky is pink,
   That is all.

The moon is setting,
At either side are bamboos for arrow-making,
Beside the bamboos are wild-cat babies,
They walk uncertainly,
   That is all.

Love-Incantation
(Ojibwa)

In the center of the earth
Wherever he may be
Or under the earth.

A Song of Healing
(Ojibwa)

You will recover; you will walk again.
It is I who say it; my power is great.
Through our white shell
I will enable you to walk again.

The Sky Clears
(Ojibwa)

Verily
The sky clears
When my Mide drum*
Sounds
For me.
Verily
The waters are smooth
When my Mide drum
Sounds
for me.

*medicine drum

A Spell to Destroy Life

(Cherokee)

Listen!
Now I have come to step over your soul
  (I know your clan)
  (I know your name)
  (I have stolen your spirit
    and buried it
    under earth)
I bury your soul under earth
I cover you over with black rock
I cover you over with black cloth
I cover you over with black slabs
You disappear forever
Your path leads to the black coffin
  in the hills
   of the DarkeningLand
   So let it be for you
The clay of the hills covers you
The black clay of the DarkeningLand
  Your soul fades away
  It becomes blue
When darkness comes your spirit shrivels
    and dwindles
    to disappear
     forever

Listen!

From the Houses of Magic

(Pima)

I

Down from the houses of magic,
Down from the houses of magic;
Blow the winds, and from my antlers
And my ears, they stronger gather.

Over there I ran trembling,
Over there I ran trembling,
For bows and arrows pursued me,
Many bows were on my trail.

II

I ran into the swamp confused,
There I heard the tadpoles singing.
I ran into the swamp confused,
Where the bark-clothed tadpoles sang.

In the west the dragonfly wanders,
Skimming the surfaces of the pools,
Touching only with his tail. He skims
With flapping and rustling wings.

Thence I ran as the darkness gathers,
Wearing cactus flowers in my hair.
Thence I ran as the darkness gathers,
In fluttering darkness to the singing-place.

III

At the time of the white dawning,
At the time of the white dawning,
I arose and went away,
At Blue Nightfall I went away.

IV

The evening glow yet lingers,
The evening glow yet lingers:
And I sit with my gourd rattle
Engaged in the sacred chant.
As I wave the eagle feathers
We hear the magic sounding.

The strong night is shaking me,
Just as once before he did
When in spirit I was taken
To the great magician's house.

V

Pitiable harlot though I am,
My heart glows with the singing
While the evening yet is young.
My heart glows with the singing.

VI

Now the swallow begins his singing;
Now the swallow begins his singing;
And the women who are with me,
The poor women commence to sing.

The swallows met in the standing cliff;
The swallows met in the standing cliff;
And the rainbows arched above me,
There the blue rainbow-arches met.

VII

In the reddish glow of the nightfall,
In the reddish glow of the nightfall.
I return to my burrow
About which the flowers bloom.

With the four eagle feathers,
With the four eagle feathers,
I stir the air. When I turn
My magic power is crossed.

The calumet is the sacred pipe of the Native American. It is the word in physical form. Père Marquette, the Catholic priest, was protected by its pledge, for, carrying it in his canoe, he passed with impunity from tribe to tribe on his trip down the Mississippi River. Nor did the "man of God" understand the word made physical. He said the "calumet is the most mysterious thing in the world. The sceptres of our kings are not so much respected...for one with this calumet may venture among his enemies, and in the hottest battles they lay down their arms before this sacred pipe." The presentation of the calumet is the most binding rite between men. They may not be of any blood relationship, and the presentation creates a tie that is stronger than blood. The one who brings and presents the calumet is called "the father"; the one who receives it is called "the child," for the bond cemented by the passing of the pipe is more sacred than even the bond of blood. The calumets are of Wah'kon-tah; so the ceremony of presentation is the most holy of ceremonies. And the chorals that are sung by the people are mighty hymns. The power of the "Hallelujah Chorus" of Handel's The Messiah is the nearest analogy in non-Native American music. The peace of the calumet is sacred in the same sense that an oath taken on the Bible is sacred. It is, simply, not broken.

Chorals of the Calumet

I

Down through the ages vast,
On wings strong and true,
From great Wa-kon'-da comes
Good will unto you, —
Peace that shall here remain.

(Omaha)

II

Far above the earth he soars,
Circling the clear sky,
Flying over forests dim,
Peering in shadows,
Seeking far and wide his child,
To give him peace.

(Otoe)

If children cried during the ceremony, special lullabies were sung as the calumets were passed over the infants. The symbolism is too obvious to suffer explanation. "Kawas" is a form of the word "Ti-ra'-wa," or "the animating power of Wah'kon-tah in all things.

I

Kawas, thy baby is crying!
Grieving sore, wailing, and weeping.
Aye, forsooth! wailing and weeping.
Kawas, thy baby is crying!

(Pawnee)

II

Thy father is coming,
E'en now he is near thee;
Cry no more: the mighty one,
Thy father, is coming!

(Pawnee)

III

Lift thine eyes, 'tis the gods who come near,
Bringing thee joy, release from all pain.
Sending sorrow and sighing
Far from the child, Ti-ra'-wa makes fain.

Ah, you look! Surely, you know who comes,
Claiming you his and bidding you rise,
Blithely smiling and happy,
Child of Ti-ra'-wa, Lord of the skies!

(Pawnee)

The Children, Always the Children
—Their Lullabies, Training Songs,
Prayers—Always the Children

Cradle Song
(Ojibwa)

Who is this?
Who is this?
Eyes aglow
On the top of my lodge.

It is I—the little owl,
    Coming,
It is I—the little owl,
    Coming,
Down! Down!

Lullaby

(Kiowa)

Hush thee, child—
Mother bringeth an antelope,
And the tid-bit shall be thine.

Cradle-Song for a Boy

(Tlingit)

Let me shoot a small bird for my younger brother.
Let me spear a small trout for my sister.

Introduction of the Child
to the Cosmos

(Omaha)

Ho! Ye Sun, Moon, Stars, all ye that move in the heavens,
    I bid you hear me!
Into your midst has come a new life.
    Consent ye, I implore!
Make its path smooth, that it may reach the brow of the
    first hill!

Ho! Ye Winds, Clouds, Rain, Mist, all ye that move in
    the air,
    I bid you hear me!
Into your midst has come a new life.
    Consent ye, I implore!
Make its path smooth, that it may reach the brow of the
    second hill!

Ho! Ye Hills, Valleys, Rivers, Lakes, Trees, Grasses, all
   ye of the earth,
     I bid you hear me!
Into your midst has come a new life.
     Consent ye, I implore!
Make its path smooth, that it may reach the brow of the
   third hill!

Ho! Ye Birds, great and small, that fly in the air,
Ho! Ye Animals, great and small, that dwell in the forest,
Ho! Ye Insects that creep among the grasses and burrow
   in the ground—
     I bid you hear me!
Into your midst has come a new life.
     Consent ye, I implore!
Make its path smooth, that it may reach the brow of the
   fourth hill!

Ho! All ye of the heavens, all ye of the air, all ye of the
   earth;
     I bid you all to hear me!
Into your midst has come a new life.
     Consent ye, consent ye all, I implore!
Make its path smooth—then shall it travel beyond the
   four hills!

Cradle Song

(Creek)

Down the stream
You hear the noise of her going
That is what they say
Up the stream
Running unseen
Running unseen
Up the stream
You hear the noise of her going
That is what they say
To the top of the bald peak
Running unseen
Running unseen.

Prayer Spoken While Presenting an Infant to the Sun

(Zuñi)

Now this is the day.
Our child,
Into the daylight
You will go out standing.
Preparing for your day,
We have passed our days.
When all your days were at an end,
When eight days were past,
Our sun father
Went in to sit down at his sacred place.
And our night fathers,
Having come out standing to their sacred place,
Passing a blessed night.
Now this day,
Our fathers, Dawn priests,
Have come out standing to their sacred place,
Our sun father,
Having come out standing to his sacred place,
Our child, it is your day.
This day,
The flesh of the white corn, prayer meal,
To our sun father
This prayer meal we offer.

May your road be fulfilled.
Reaching to the road of your sun father,
When your road is fulfilled,
In your thoughts may we live,
May we be the ones whom your thoughts will embrace,
For this, on this day
To our sun father,
We offer prayer meal.
To this end:
May you help us all to finish our roads.

Song of Parents Who Want Their Son to Awaken

(Kwakiutl)

Don't sleep! for your paddle fell into the water, and
    your spear.
Don't sleep! for the ravens and crows are flying about.

Lullaby

(Ojibwa)

It is hanging
In the edge of the sunshine.
It is a pig, I see,
With its cloven hoofs;
It is a very fat pig.
The people who live in a hollow tree
Are fighting,
They are fighting bloodily.
He is rich.
He will carry a pack toward the great water.

Rabbit speaks:

At the end of the point of land,
I eat the bark off the tree;
I see the track of a lynx.
I don't care; I can get away from him.
It is a jumping trail—
Sep!

Lullaby

(Kiowa)

Baby swimming down the river,
Driftwood leggies, rabbit leggies,
   Little rabbit leggies.

Makah Lullaby

(Makah)

My little son,
You will put a whale harpoon and a sealing spear into
   your canoe,
Not knowing what use you will make of them.

Song of Parents
Who Want to Wake Up
Their Daughter

(Kwakiutl)

Don't sleep too much! Your digging-stick fell into the
   water, and your basket.
Wake up! It is nearly low water. You will be late down on
   the beach.

In the Voice of the Thunder, the Rush of the Rain

Song of the Rain Chant
(Navaho)

Far as man can see,
    Comes the rain,
    Comes the rain with me.

From the Rain-Mount,
Rain-Mount far away,
    Comes the rain,
    Comes the rain with me.

O'er the corn,
O'er the corn, tall corn,
    Comes the rain,
    Comes the rain with me.

'Mid the lightnings,
'Mid the lightning zigzag,
'Mid the lightning flashing,
    Comes the rain,
    Comes the rain with me.

'Mid the swallows,
'Mid the swallows blue
Chirping glad together,
    Comes the rain,
    Comes the rain with me.

Through the pollen,
Through the pollen blest,
All in pollen hidden
    Comes the rain,
    Comes the rain with me.

Far as man can see
    Comes the rain,
    Comes the rain with me.

Song of the Thunders
(Ojibwa)

Sometimes I,
    I go about pitying
    Myself
    While I am carried by the wind
    Across the sky.

The Approach of the Storm
(Ojibwa)

From the half
Of the sky
That which lives there
Is coming, and makes a noise.

Rain Song
(Papago)

Close to the west the great ocean is singing.
The waves are rolling toward me, covered with many
    clouds.
Even here I catch the sound.
The earth is shaking beneath me and I hear the deep
    rumbling.

Corn-Grinding Song
(Zuñi)

Lovely! See the cloud, the cloud appear!
Lovely! See the rain, the rain draw near!
    Who spoke?
Twas the little corn-ear
High on the tip of the stalk
Saying while it looked at me
    Talking aloft there—
"Ah, perchance the floods
    Hither moving—
Ah, may the floods come this way!"

Mocking Bird Song
(Tigua)

Rain, people, rain!
The rain is all around us.
It is going to come pouring down,
And the summer will be fair to see,
The mocking bird has said so.

Song of the Trees
(Ojibwa)

The wind
    Only
    I am afraid of.

The Sky Will Resound
(Ojibwa)

It will resound finely,
    The sky,
    When I come making a noise.

The Rhythms of Life

Corn-Grinding Song
(Laguna)

Butterflies, butterflies,
Now fly away to the blossoms,
    Fly, blue-wing,
    Fly, yellow-wing,
Now fly away to the blossoms,
    Fly, red-wing,
    Fly, white-wing,
Now fly away to the blossoms,
    Butterflies, away!
Butterflies, butterflies,
Now fly away to the blossoms,
    Butterflies, away!

Spring Song
(Ojibwa)

As my eyes search the prairie
I feel the summer in the spring.

The Bright Dawn Appears in the Heavens
(Pima)

The bright dawn appears in the heavens,
The bright dawn appears in the heavens;
And the paling pleiades grow dim,
The moon is lost in the rising sun.

With the women bluebird came running,
With the women bluebird came running.
All came carrying clouds on their heads
And these were seen shaking as they danced.

See there the gray spider magician,
See there the gray spider magician;
Who ties the sun while the moon rolls on.
Turn back, the green staff raising higher.

Prayer at Sunrise
(Zuñi)

Now this day,
My sun father,
Now that you have come out standing to your sacred
    place,
That from which we draw the water of life,
Prayer meal,
Here I give to you.
Your long life,
Your old age,
Your waters,
Your seeds,
Your riches,
Your power,
Your strong spirit,
All these to me may you grant.

The Land Is Parched and Burning

(Pima)

The land is parched and burning,
The land is parched and burning;
Going and looking about me
A narrow strip of green I see

Yet I do not know surely,
Yet I do not know surely:
The harlot is here among us—
I go away toward the west.

The shadow of crooked mountain,
The curved and pointed shadow,
'Twas there that I heard the singing,
Heard the songs that harmed my heart.

The light glow of the evening,
The light glow of the evening
Comes, as the quails fly slowly,
And it settles on the young.

It Is My Form and Person

(Ojibwa)

It is my form and person that makes me great.
Hear the voice of my song—it is my voice.
I shield myself with secret coverings.
All your thoughts are known to me—blush!
I could draw you hence, were you on a distant island;
Though you were on the other hemisphere.
I speak to your naked heart.

Yaqui Song
(Yaqui)

In summer the rains come and the grass comes up.
That is the time that the deer has new horns.

Daylight
(Pawnee)

Day is here! Day is here, is here!
Arise, my son, lift thine eyes. Day is here! Day is here,
   is here!
Day is here! Day is here, is here!
Look up, my son, and see the day. Day is here! Day is
   here, is here!
Day is here! Day is here, is here!

Lo, the deer! Lo, the deer, the deer
Comes from her covert of the night! Day is here! Day is
   here, is here!
Lo, the deer! Lo, the deer, the deer!
All creatures wake and see the light. Day is here! Day is
   here, is here!
Day is here! Day is here, is here!

The Noise of the Village
(Ojibwa)

Whenever I pause—
   The noise
   Of the village.

Mount Koonak: A Song of Arsut

(Eskimo)

I look toward the south, to great Mount Koonak,
To great Mount Koonak, there to the south;
I watch the clouds that gather round him;
I contemplate their shining brightness;
They spread abroad upon great Koonak;
They climb up his seaward flanks;
See how they shift and change;
Watch them there to the south;
How one makes beautiful the other;
How they mount his southern slopes,
Hiding him from the stormy sea,
Each lending beauty to the other.

The Song of the Stars

(Algonquin)

We are the stars which sing,
We sing with our light;
We are the birds of fire,
We fly over the sky.
Our light is a voice;
We make a road for spirits,
For the spirits to pass over.
Among us are three hunters
Who chase a bear;
There never was a time
When they were not hunting.
We look down on the mountains.
This is the Song of the Stars.

From *The Rite of Vigil*
The Song of the Maize
Sung by the
Spirits of the Dead

(Osage)

Amid the earth, renewed in verdure,
Amid rising smoke, my grandfather's footprints
I see, as from place to place I wander,
The rising smoke I see as I wander.
Amid all forms visible, the rising smoke
I see, as I move from place to place.

Amid all forms visible, the little hills in rows
I see, as I move from place to place.

Amid all forms visible, the spreading blades
I see as I move from place to place.

Amid all forms visible, the light day
I see as I move from place to place.

The Shooting-Star

(Eskimo)

You star up yonder,
You who gaze up yonder,
Your fingers up yonder,
Didn't hold very fast,
Didn't knit very tight.
It fell down without touching,
Without entirely touching against—
It didn't touch.

As Summer Comes
(Tlingit)

How will the coming July morning be,
I wonder?
My mind is very weak at the thought
Of being unable to see my sweetheart.

Present or Absent or
Absent Yet Present: Love Songs
and Incantations

The Song of Kuk-Ook,
the Bad Boy
(Eskimo)

This is the song of Kuk-Ook, the bad boy.
    Imakayah—hayah,
    Imakayah—hah—hayah.
I am going to run away from home, *hayah,*
In a great big boat, *hayah,*
To hunt for a sweet little girl, *hayah;*
I shall get her some beads, *hayah;*
The kind that look like boiled ones, *hayah;*
Then after a while, *hayah,*
I shall come back home, *hayah,*
I shall call all my relations together, *hayah,*
And shall give them all a good thrashing, *hayah;*
I shall marry two girls at once, *hayah;*
One of the sweet little darlings, *hayah,*
I shall dress in spotted seal-skins, *hayah,*
And the other dear little pet, *hayah,*
Shall wear skins of the hooded seal only, *hayah.*

Tule Love Song
(Yaqui)

Many pretty flowers, red, blue, and yellow.
We say to the girls, "Let us go and walk among the
    flowers."
The wind comes and sways the flowers.
The girls are like that when they dance.
Some are wide-open, large flowers and some are tiny
    little flowers.
The birds love the sunshine and the starlight.
The flowers smell sweet.
The girls are sweeter than the flowers.

We Must Part
(Oglala Sioux)

Many are the youths indeed,
But thou alone art pleasing to me;
You, O chief, I love.
But we must part
And long will be the time!

Wind Song
(Kiowa)

Idlers and cowards are here at home now
Whenever they wish, they see their beloved ones.
Oh, idlers and cowards are here at home now,
Idlers and cowards are here at home now,
But the youth I love is gone to war, far hence.
Weary, lonely, for me he longs.

Later

(Menominee)

At some future time
you will think of me
and cry.

The last line of this next song is a self-satisfied, irresponsible sigh.

Song of the Young Man Girls Cannot Resist

(Omaha)

It was the gods that made me as I am:
blame them,
if you will!
Hiiiiiiiiiiiiiiiiiiiii....

An Omaha Love Song

(Omaha)

As the day comes forth from night
   So I come forth to seek thee.
Lift thine eyes and behold him.
   Who comes with the day to thee.

Love-Charm

(Ojibwa)

What are you saying to me?
I am arrayed like the roses
And beautiful as they.

Suggestion

(Menominee)

You had better go home,
Your mother
loves you so much.

When I Think of Him

(Ojibwa)

Although he said it
Still
I am filled with longing
When I think of him.

Truth

(Ojibwa)

I do not care
for you any more;
Someone else
is in my thoughts.

The Lover Who Did Not Come

(Ojibwa)

A loon I thought it was,
But it was
My love's
Splashing oar.

To Sault Ste. Marie
He has departed.
My love
Has gone on before me.
Never again
Can I see him.

Love Song

(Nootka)

No matter how hard I try
to forget you,
you always
come back to my mind,
and when you hear me singing
you may know
I am weeping for you.

Sharing

(Ojibwa)

Come,
let us
drink.

Parting
(Ojibwa)

Come,
I am going away.
I pray you
Let me go.
I will return again.
Do not weep for me.

Behold,
We will be very glad
To meet each other
When I return.
Do not weep for me.

Why?
(Ojibwa)

Come,
I beseech you,
let us sing.
Why are you offended?

The Truth Is...
(Ojibwa)

You desire vainly
that I seek you;
The reason is,
I come to see
Your younger sister.

I Will Walk

(Ojibwa)

I will walk into somebody's dwelling,
Into somebody's dwelling will I walk.

To thy dwelling, my dearly beloved,
Some night will I walk, will I walk.

Some night in the winter, my beloved,
To thy dwelling will I walk, will I walk.

This very night, my beloved,
To thy dwelling will I walk, will I walk.

Song Written by a Man Who Was Jilted by a Young Woman

(Kwakiutl)

Oh, how, my ladylove, can my thoughts be conveyed to
   you, my ladylove, on account of your deed, my ladylove?
In vain, my ladylove, did I wish to advise you, my
   ladylove, on account of your deed, my ladylove.
It is the object of laughter, my ladylove, it is the object
   of laughter, your deed, my ladylove.
It is the object of contempt, my ladylove, it is the object
   of contempt, your deed, my ladylove.
Oh, if poor me could go, my ladylove! How can I go to
   you, my ladylove, on account of your deed, my ladylove!
Now, I will go, my ladylove, go to make you happy, my
   ladylove, on account of your deed, my ladylove.
Farewell to you, my ladylove! Farewell, mistress, on
   account of your deed, my ladylove!

Retort to the Preceding Song

O friends! I will now ask you about my love.
Where has my love gone, my love who is singing
    against me?
I ask you, who walks with my love?
Oh, where is my love, where is the love that I had for
    my love?
For I feel, really feel, foolish, because I acted foolishly
    against my love.
For what I did, caused people to laugh at me on account
    of what I did to you, my love.
For I am despised on account of my love for you, my true
    love, for you, my love.
For you have said that you will live in Knight Inlet.
Oh, Knight Inlet is far away, for that is the name of the
    place where my love is going.
O Rivers Inlet is far away, for that is the name of the
    place where my love is going.
For he forgot of my love, my true love.
For in vain he goes about trying to find some one who
    will love him as I did, my love.
Don't try to leave me without turning back to my love,
    my love.
Oh, my love, turn back to your slave, who preserved
    your life.
I am downcast, and I cry for the love of my love.
But my life is killed by the words of my love.
Good-by, my love, my past true love!

Satisfaction

(Menominee)

O my!
How that girl loves me—
The one I am secretly courting.

Alone

(Ojibwa)

I sit here
thinking of her.
I am sad
as I think
of her.

Love Song

(Ojibwa)

Oh
I am thinking
Oh
I am thinking
I have found my lover
Oh
I think it is so!

Love Song

(Aztec)

I know not whether thou hast been absent:
I lie down with thee, I rise up with thee,
In my dreams thou art with me.
If my eardrops tremble in my ears,
I know it is thou moving within my heart.

A Woman's Song

(Ojibwa)

You are walking around
Trying to remember
What you promised,
But you can't remember.

Wolf Woman

(Tlingit)

If one had control of death,
it would be very easy to die
with a Wolf woman.
It would be very pleasant.

Identity: In My People's Eyes

Friendship

(Oglala Sioux)

Friend, whatever hardships threaten
If thou call me,
I'll befriend thee;
All-enduring, fearlessly,
I'll befriend thee.

War Song of Encouragement
(Teton Sioux)

Soldiers,
You fled.
Even the eagle dies.

Mourning Song
for a Father and Uncle
(Tlingit)

The nation's drum has fallen down, my mother.
Take the drum out from among the nations
so that they can hear my mother.

I Sing for the Animals
(Teton Sioux)

Out of the earth
I sing for them,
A Horse nation
I sing for them.
Out of the earth
I sing for them,
The animals
I sing for them.

When I Come to Be a Man

(Kwakiutl)

You were given by good fortune to your slave,
You were given by good fortune to your slave,
To come and take the place of your slave!
O tribes, now hide yourselves!
I have come to be a man and my name is Hellebore!
The cedar withes are twisted even now, that I shall pass
Through the mouths, through the heads that I obtain
    in war,
For I am true Hellebore!
Princes' heads in war I'll take when I come to be a man,
And then I shall have your names, as my father he
    has done,
He who now has your names for his own!

Prayer of the Traveler Placing Memorial Rocks on Wayside Cairn

(Navaho)

I place this rock—a male one.
I place this rock—female one.
Wherever I go, myself may go,
May I have luck.
Wherever they go, close relatives go,
May they have luck.

Insight and Vision: The Self

First Song of Dawn Boy
(Navaho)

Where my kindred dwell,
    There I wander.
The Red Rock house,
    There I wander.
Where dark *kethawns* [sacred sticks]
      are at the doorway,
    There I wander.
At the *yuni* [seat of honor] the striped
      cotton hangs with pollen.
    There I wander.
Going around with it.
    There I wander.
Taking another, I depart with it.
    With it I wander.
In the house of long life,
    There I wander.
In the house of happiness,
    There I wander.
Beauty before me,
    With it I wander.
Beauty behind me,
    With it I wander.
Beauty below me,
    With it I wander.
Beauty above me,
    With it I wander.
Beauty all around me,
    With it I wander.
In old age traveling,
    With it I wander.
On the beautiful trail I am,
    With it I wander.

Mourning Song for Modana
(Kwakiutl)

Ye he he ya! It deprived me of my mind, when the moon
went down at the edge of the waters. *Ye he he ya!*
Ye he he ya! It deprived me of my breath, when the
mouse-dancer began to gnaw on the water. *Ye he he ya!*
Ye he he ya! It deprived me of my mind when Modana
began to utter the cannibal-cry on the water. *Ye he he ya!*

Prayer to the Sun
(Blackfeet)

Okōhe! okōhe! natosi! iyo!
Sun, take pity on me; take pity on me.
Old age, old age,
We are praying to your old age,
For that I have chosen.
Your children, morningstar, seven stars, the bunched stars,
  these and all stars,
We can call upon them for help.
I have called upon all of them.
Take pity on me;
Take pity on me that I may lead a good life.
My children, now I have led them to old age.
That which is above, now I choose, take pity on me.
Iyo!
Old age, let me lead my children to it.
Let me get a stock of many horses...
Take pity on me that I get the full pay for all my work.
Iyo!
Take pity on me; take pity on me; take heed.

Morning Song

(Cheyenne)

He, our Father,
He hath shown His mercy unto me.
In peace I walk the straight road.

The Old Warrior

(Oglala Sioux)

Mighty, mighty, great in war,
So was I honored;
Now behold me old and wretched!

Dream Song

(Ojibwa)

In the Sky
I am walking,
A Bird
I accompany.

Song of Failure

(Teton Sioux)

A wolf
I considered myself,
But the owls are hooting
And the night
I fear.

A Prayer

(Havasupai)

Sun, my relative
Be good coming out
Do something good for us.

Make me work,
So I can do anything in the garden
I hoe, I plant corn, I irrigate.

You, sun, be good going down at sunset
We lay down to sleep I want to feel good.

While I sleep you come up.
Go on your course many times.
Make good things for us men.

Make me always the same as I am now.

Dream Song of a Woman

(Papago)

Where the mountain crosses,
On top of the mountain,
    I do not myself know where.
I wandered where my mind and my heart
    seemed to be lost.
I wandered away.

Carrying My Mind Around

(Tlingit)

My own mind is very hard to me.
It is just as if I were carrying my mind around.
What is the matter with you?

Homesickness for the Land I Stand On

(Navaho)

That flowing water! That flowing water!
My mind wanders across it.
That broad water! That flowing water!
My mind wanders across it.
That old age water! That flowing water!
My mind wanders across it.

Let Us See

(Pawnee)

Let us see, is this real,
Let us see, is this real,
Let us see, is this real,
This life I am living?
Ye gods, who dwell everywhere,
Let us see, is this real,
This life I am living?

Incantations for Bravery

I Am Rising

(Ojibwa)

I am rising to seek the warpath.
The earth and the sky are before me.
I walk by day and by night,
And the evening star is my guide.

Song of the Buffalo, A War Song

(Ojibwa)

Strike ye
    Our land
    With curved horns.

Here on My Breast

(Ojibwa)

Here on my breast have I bled!
See—see! My battle scars!
Ye mountains, tremble at my yell!

I strike for life.

Men Must Die

(Crow)

Sky and earth are everlasting,
Men must die.
Old age is a thing of evil,
Charge, and die!

Arrow Song

(Ojibwa)

Scarlet
    Is its head.

The We'-ton song is an incantation sung by women to give strength to men in battle miles away.

The We'-ton Song
(Dakota)

All the tribes shall hear of you!
Put forth your strength.
Truly this shall come to pass.

Warrior Song of the Hethushka Society
(Omaha)

I shall vanish and be no more,
But the land over which I now roam
Shall remain
And change not.

The War Song of Butterfly, A Warrior
(Ojibwa)

In the coming heat
    Of the day
    I stood there.

A Warrior's Song of Defiance

(Osage)

You speak to me of dangers that I may fear,
But I have willed to go, my friends.
Waxada-in's crying stirs my wrath,
I go forth to strike, even Wa-kon-da, should
     He oppose me.
You speak to me of dangers that I may fear.
But I have willed to go, my friends.

From *The Rite of Vigil* The Rising of the Buffalo Men

(Osage)

I rise, I rise,
I, whose tread makes the earth to rumble.

I rise, I rise,
I, in whose thighs there is strength.

I rise, I rise,
I, who whips his back with his tail when in rage.

I rise, I rise,
I, in whose humped shoulder there is power.

I rise, I rise,
I, who shakes his mane when angered.

I rise, I rise,
I, whose horns are sharp and curved.

On the Bank of a Stream
(Ojibwa)

Across the river
They speak of me as being.

The War Song

Passamaquoddy War Song
(Passamaquoddy)

I will arise with my tomahawk in my hand, and I must have
    revenge on that nation which has slain my poor people.
I arise with war club in my hand, and follow the bloody
    track of that nation which killed my people.
I will sacrifice my own life and the lives of my warriors.
I arise with war club in my hand, and follow the track of
    my enemy.
When I overtake him I will take his scalp and string it on a
    long pole, and I will stick it in the ground, and my war-
    riors will dance around it for many days; then I will sing
    my song for the victory over my enemy.

A Song of Nayenzgani
(Navaho)

I am the Slayer of the Alien Gods.
Where'er I roam,
Before me
Forests white are strewn around.
The lightning scatters;
But 'tis I who cause it.

I am the Child of the Water.
Where'er I roam,
Behind me
Waters white are strewn around.
The tempest scatters;
But 'tis I who cause it.

Hear My Voice
(Ojibwa)

Hear my voice, Birds of War!
I prepare a feast for you to feed on;
I see you cross the enemy's lines;
Like you I shall go.
I wish the swiftness of your wings;
I wish the vengeance of your claws;
I muster my friends;
I follow your flight.
Ho, you young men warriors,
Bear your angers to the place of fighting!

From the South
(Ojibwa)

From the south they come,
The birds, the warlike birds,
    With sounding wings.

I wish to change myself
To the body of that swift bird.

I throw away my body in the strife.

The Battle-Birds
(Ojibwa)

The battle-birds swoop from the sky,
They thirst for the warrior's heart;
They look from their circles on high,
And scorn every flesh but the brave.

Cherokee War Song
(Cherokee)

Hayi! Yu! Listen!
Now instantly we have lifted up the red war club.
Quickly his soul shall be without motion.
There under the earth, where the black war clubs shall
    be moving about like ball sticks in the game, there his
    soul shall be, never to reappear.
We cause it to be so.
He shall never go and lift up the war club.
We cause it to be so.
There under the earth the black war club and the black
    fog have come together as one for their covering.
It shall never move about [i.e., the black fog shall never be
    lifted from them].
We cause it to be so.

Instantly shall their souls be moving about there in the
    seventh heaven.
Their souls shall never break in two.
So shall it be.

Quickly we have moved them [their souls] on high for
    them, where they shall be going about in peace.
 You have shielded yourselves with the red war clubs.
Their souls shall never be knocked about.
Cause it to be so.
There on high their souls shall be going about.
Let them shield themselves with the white war-whoop.
Instantly grant that they shall never become blue.
Yu!

And to the Victor...

In the Victors' Camp
(Ojibwa)

The Sioux women
Pass to and fro wailing.
As they gather
Their wounded men,
The voice of their wailing comes to us.

Hunting-Song
(Navaho)

Comes the deer to my singing,
Comes the deer to my song,
Comes the deer to my singing.

He, the blackbird, he am I,
Bird beloved of the wild deer.
Comes the deer to my singing.

From the Mountain Black,
From the summit,
Down the trail, coming, coming now,
Comes the deer to my singing.

Through the blossoms,
Through the flowers, coming, coming now,
Comes the deer to my singing.

Through the flower dew-drops,
Coming, coming now,
Comes the deer to my singing.

Through the pollen, flower pollen,
Coming, coming now,
Comes the deer to my singing.

Starting with his left fore-foot,
Stamping, turns the frightened deer,
   Comes the deer to my singing.

Quarry mine, blessed am I
In the luck of the chase.
   Comes the deer to my singing.

   Comes the deer to my singing,
   Comes the deer to my song,
   Comes the deer to my singing.

I Do Wonder
(Ojibwa)

I do wonder
If she truly is humiliated—
The Sioux woman—
Whose head I have cut off?

Prophecy and Vision: The People

A Song of Huezotzinco
(Aztec)

Only sad flowers, sad songs, are here in Mexico, in Tlatilolco, in this place these alone are known, alas.

It is well to know these, if only we may please the Giver of
Life, lest we be destroyed, we his subjects, alas.

We have angered him, we are only wretched beings, slaves,
by flood; we have seen and known affliction, alas.

We are disturbed, we are embittered, thy servants here in
Tlatilolco, deprived of food, made acquainted with affliction, we are fatigued by labor, O Giver of Life, alas.

Weeping is with us, tears fall like rain, here in Tlatilolco; as the Mexican women go down to the water, we beg of them for ourselves and our friends, alas.

Even as the smoke, rising, lies in a cloud over Mount Atloyan, in Mexico, so does it happen unto us, O Giver of Life, alas.

And you Mexicans, may you remember concerning us when you descend and suffer before the majesty of God, when there you shall howl like wolves.

There, there will be only weeping as your greeting when you come, there you will be accursed, all of you, workers in filth, slaves, rulers or warriors, and thus Tenochtitlan will be deserted.

O friends, do not weep, but know that sometime we shall have left behind us the things of Mexico, and then their water shall be made bitter and their food shall be made bitter, here in Tlatilolco, as never before, by the Giver of Life.

The disdained and the slaves shall go forth with song; but in a little while their oppressors shall be seen in the fire, amid the howling of wolves.

Opening Prayer of the Sun Dance

(Teton Sioux)

Grandfather!
A voice I am going to send,
Hear me!
All over the universe
A voice I am going to send,
Hear me,
Grandfather!
I will live!
I have said it.

Song to the Pleiades
(Pawnee)

Look as they rise, rise
Over the line where sky meets the earth;
Pleiades!
Lo! They ascending, come to guide us,
Leading us safely, keeping us one;
Pleiades,
Teach us to be, like you, united.

These prophecies are from the books of Chilan Balan, *the Mayan chronicles set down in the fifteenth century before the arrival of the gold-seeking Europeans.*

Recital of the Priest Chilan
(Maya)

Eat, eat, while there is bread,
Drink, drink, while there is water;
A day comes when dust shall darken the air,
When a blight shall wither the land,
When a cloud shall arise,
When a mountain shall be lifted up,
When a strong man shall seize the city,
When ruin shall fall upon all things,
When the tender leaf shall be destroyed,
When eyes shall be closed in death;
When there shall be three signs on a tree,
Father, son and grandson hanging dead on the same tree;
When the battle flag shall be raised,
And the people scattered abroad in the forests.

Prophecy of Pech, Priest of Chichen-Itzá

(Maya)

Ye men of Itzá, hearken to the tidings,
Listen to the forecast of this cycle's end;
Four have been the ages of the world's progressing,
Now the fourth is ending, and its end is near.
A mighty lord is coming, see you give him honor;
A potent lord approaches, to whom all must bow;
I, the prophet, warn you, keep in mind my boding,
Men of Itzá, mark it, and await your lord.

Thoughts on Death

By a Certain Ruler in Memory of Former Rulers

(Aztec)

Weeping, I, the singer, weave my song of flowers of sadness;
  I call to memory the youths, the shards, the fragments,
  gone to the land of the dead; once noble and powerful
  here on earth, the youths were dried up like feathers,
  were split into fragments like an emerald, before the face
  and in sight of those who saw them on earth, and with
  the knowledge of the Cause of All.

Alas! alas! I sing in grief as I recall the children.
Would that I could turn back again; would that I could
grasp their hands once more; would that I could call
them forth from the land of the dead; would that we
could bring them again on earth, that they might rejoice
and we rejoice, and that they might rejoice and delight

the Giver of Life; is it possible that we his servants should
reject him or should be ungrateful?

Thus I weep in my heart as I, the singer, review my memories, recalling things sad and grievous.

Would only that I knew they could hear me, there in the
land of the dead, were I to sing some worthy song.

Would that I could gladden them, that I could console the
suffering and the torment of the children.

How can it be learned?

Whence can I draw the inspiration?

They are not where I may follow them; neither can I reach
them with my calling as one here on earth.

Love-Song of the Dead
(Kwakiutl)

You are hard-hearted against me, you are hard-hearted
against me, my dear, *ha ha ye ha ha ha!*

You are cruel against me, you are cruel against me, my dear,
ha ha ye ha ha ha!

For I am tired waiting for you to come here, my dear, *ha ha
ye ha ha ha!*

Now I shall cry differently on your account, my dear, *ha ha
ye ha ha ha!*

Ah, I shall go down to the lower world, there I shall cry for
you, my dear, *ha ha ye ha ha ha!*

Battle Thought
(Ojibwa)

They are talking about me
Saying, "Come with us."

Is there anyone
Who would weep for me?
My wife would weep for me.

Death Song
(Papago)

In the great night my heart will go out.
Toward me the darkness comes rattling.
In the great night my heart will go out.

Song of the Deathless Voice
(Dakota)

This was a warrior,
who died the death of a warrior.
There was joy in his voice!

Song of a Man About to Die in a Strange Land
(Ojibwa)

If I die here in a strange land,
If I die in a land not my own,
Nevertheless, the thunder,
The rolling thunder,
Will take me home.

If I die here, the wind,
The wind rushing over the prairie,
The wind will take me home.

The wind and the thunder,
They are the same everywhere,
What does it matter, then,
If I die here in a strange land?

Now I Am Left

(Wabanaki)

Now I am left on this lonely island to die—
No one to hear the sound of my voice.
Who will bury me when I die?
Who will sing my death-song for me?
My false friends leave me here to die alone;
Like a wild beast, I am left on this island to die.
I wish the wind spirit would carry my cry to my love!
My love is as swift as the deer; he would speed through
    the forest to find me;
Now I am left on this lonely island to die.
I wish the spirit of air would carry my breath to my love.
My love's canoe, like the sunlight, would shoot through
    the water to my side;
But I am left on this lonely island to die, with no one to
    pity me but the little birds.
My love is brave and strong; but, when he hears my fate,
    his stout heart will break;
And I am on this lonely island to die.
Now the night comes on, and all is silent but the owl.
He sings a mournful song to his mate, in pity for me.
I will try to sleep.
I wish the night spirit to hear my song; he will tell my
    love of my fate; and when I awake, I shall see the one
    I love.
I am on this lonely island to die.

Song Sung Over a Dying Person

(Ojibwa)

You are a spirit,
I am making you a spirit,
In the place where I sit
I am making you a spirit.

Song of the Spirit

(Luiseño)

At the time of death,
When I found there was to be death,
I was very much surprised.
All was failing.
My home,
I was sad to leave it.

I have been looking far,
Sending my spirit north, south, east, and west,
Trying to escape from death,
But could find nothing,
No way of escape.

Set into print at least two centuries before the transplant American William Cullen Bryant was born, "The Song of Nezahualcoyotl" has been called "The Indian Thanatopsis." It would be more accurate to call "Thanatopsis" "The Transplant American Song of Nezahualcoyotl."

Song of Nezahualcoyotl

(Aztec)

The fleeting pomps of the world are like the green willow trees, which, aspiring to permanence, are consumed by a fire, fall before the ax, are upturned by the wind, or are scarred and saddened by age.

The grandeurs of life are like the flowers in color and in fate; the beauty of these remains so long as their chaste buds gather and store the rich pearls of the dawn and saving it, drop it in liquid dew; but scarcely has the Cause of All directed upon them the full rays of the sun, when their beauty and glory fail, and the brilliant gay colors which decked forth their pride wither and fade.

The delicious realms of flowers count their dynasties by short periods; those which in the morning revel proudly in beauty and strength, by evening weep for the sad destruction of their thrones, and for the mishaps which drive them to loss, to poverty, to death and to the grave.

All things of earth have an end, and in the midst of the most joyous lives, the breath falters, they fall, they sink into the ground.

All the earth is a grave, and naught escapes it; nothing is so perfect that it does not fall and disappear.

The rivers, brooks, fountains and waters flow on, and never return to their joyous beginnings; they hasten on to the vast realms of Tlaloc, and the wider they spread between their marges the more rapidly do they mold their own sepulchral urns.

That which was yesterday is not today; and let not that which is today trust to live tomorrow.

The caverns of the earth are filled with pestilential dust which once was the bones, the flesh, the bodies of great ones who sat upon thrones, deciding causes, ruling assemblies, governing armies, conquering provinces, possessing treasures, tearing down temples, flattering themselves with pride, majesty, fortune, praise and dominion.

These glories have passed like the dark smoke thrown out by the fires of Popocatepetl, leaving no monuments but the rude skins on which they are written.

Ha! ha! Were I to introduce you into the obscure bowels of this temple, and were to ask you which of these bones were those of the powerful Achalchiuhtlanextin, first chief of the ancient Toltecs; of Necazecmitl, devout worshiper of the gods; if I inquire where is the peerless beauty of the glorious empress Xiuhtzal, where the peaceable Topiltzin, last monarch of the hapless land of Tulan; if I ask you where are the sacred ashes of our first father Xolotl; those of the bounteous Nopal; those of the generous Tlotzin; or even the still warm cinders of my glorious and immortal, though unhappy and luckless father Ixtlilxochitl; if I continued thus questioning about all our august ancestors, what would you reply?

The same that I reply—I know not, I know not; for first and last are confounded in the common clay.

What was their fate shall be ours, and of all who follow us.

Unconquered princes, warlike chieftains, let us seek, let us
sigh for the heaven, for there all is eternal, and nothing is
corruptible.

The darkness of the sepulchre is but the strengthening
couch for the glorious sun, and the obscurity of the night
but serves to reveal the brilliancy of the stars.

No one has power to alter these heavenly lights, for they
serve to display the greatness of their Creator, and as our
eyes see them now, so saw them our earliest ancestors,
and so shall see them our latest posterity.

Prophecy of Destruction
(Aztec)

The sweet voiced *quechol* there, ruling the earth, has
intoxicated my soul.

I am like the quetzal bird, I am created in the house of
the one only God; I sing sweet songs among the
flowers; I chant songs and rejoice in my heart.

The fuming dewdrops from the flowers in the field
intoxicate my soul.

I grieve to myself that ever this dwelling on earth
should end.

I foresaw, being a Mexican, that our rule began to be
destroyed; I went forth weeping that it was to bow
down and be destroyed.

Let me not be angry that the grandeur of Mexico is to
be destroyed.

The smoking stars gather together against it; the one
who cares for flowers is about to be destroyed.

He who cared for books wept, he wept for the beginning of
the destruction.

Death-Song of Namebines
(Ojibwa)

The odor of death,
    I discern the odor of death
    In the front of my body.

I Feel No Fear
(Ojibwa)

I feel no fear
When the Great River Man
Death speaks of.

Chapter 4

The Liberated and the League: The Law of the Great Peace and the American Epic

When Henry David Thoreau "heartily accepted" the motto, "That government governs best which governs least,"[1] he was expressing (as he so often did) an idea held by primitive people because they ascribe to a group responsibility that transcends personal desires. Ambition becomes such men because any personal glory accrues to the group rather than to the individual, and he governs his own conduct more rigidly than any codified statutes could demand. If he fails to exercise proper self-control, he fails to exhibit due consideration for the group. And his punishment is immediate and fair, for it is known to all and it is beyond extenuation. He is immediately expelled from the group by group accord (that is, he is not punished as an individual by individual dictate) and, cut away from his source of identity, he pays the greatest of all penalties: he exists henceforth alone.

The "authority" of a sachem, massassoit, or chief was, then, utterly removed from the "old world" concept of absolute power, unquestioned authority, and despotism. In short, no one could "speak for the group" in any sense—a fact that was to cause untold difficulties for Native Americans in the signing of treaties

---

[1]The opening sentence of "Civil Disobedience."

and in land cessions. The power to sign such treaties was not vested in the signers nor was the concept of land ownership understood by the American Indian as it was by those European representatives whose lives had been conditioned and enthralled by the loss of group identity and the acceptance of executive authority.

In *The World of Primitive Man*, Paul Radin explains the idea anthropologically:

Obedience, among aboriginal peoples, be it remembered, was never enforced by a single well-defined agency or institution. This was due to a variety of causes, but, fundamentally it is to be ascribed to the fact that law was not thought of as an individualized *fiat*-command emanating from a particular source and which had then to be carried out at a particular time and in a specified manner. On the contrary, law was conceived of as if it were a traditional non-individualized order, diffused, as it were, over the whole group. It was obligatory to obey it but, then again, it was also obligatory for the "command" to be made. In this way, the more personal aspects of force and coercion never came into play and punishment never took on the form of a coercion exercised by one particular individual upon another. Such a conception was naturally fatal to the development of an executive with well-defined authority.[2]

The Hollywood-television version of the absolute, unquestioned, and arbitrary leader disguised as Cochise or Geronimo or some fanciful "Indian-sounding" fictional unreality is too ridiculous to merit attention but too widely believed to be ignored. That kind of power would have offended the group, alienated the individual, and destroyed the capacity for leadership in any Native American aberrational enough to conceive it for himself. Further, the women of the group would not have permitted it even momentarily—neither among the agrarian peoples where the female was very powerful nor among the hunters where she was less powerful but still so formidable that her displeasure would not have been encouraged.

That curious concept of "squaw," the enslaved, demeaned, voiceless childbearer, existed and exists only in the mind of the non-Native American and is probably a French corruption of the Iroquois word *otsiskwa* meaning "female sexual parts," a word almost clinical both denotatively and connotatively. The corruption suggests nothing about the Native American's attitude toward women; it does indicate the wasichu's view of Native American women in particular if not all women in general. In reality, Native American males and females were, generally speaking, equals in

2New York, 1971, pp. 202–03.

the group. Whether descent was reckoned matrilineally or patri-lineally, whether status rested on the food-gathering role or food-producing role, the equality of sexes was obvious, varying only in small degree from group to group. As Radin observes of primitive woman generally:

Where fishing and hunting exist, associated with a clan organization, her position is still that of a complete equal, in spite of the fact that fishing and hunting are predominantly male occupations. Marriage, in those societies, never affects the status of either of the contracting parties. It is, thus, the clan, plus the role woman plays in agriculture there, which gives her her favored position.

Where her role is only that of food-producer there is a tendency for her status to be lower than that of man. This is, however, not marked, since the economic and political structure of these societies is quite unfavorable to the development of a division of labor that would accentuate great inequalities of this kind.[3]

Nor is Radin's observation restricted to some anthro-political past. Any number of commentators have been impressed by the male-female relationship in various Indian tribes today. One such observer is John Major Hurdy who has spent considerable time among various peoples of the Southwest. The first chapter of his *American Indian Religions*[4] is devoted to the Hopi way of life—a way of life that leads Hurdy to conclude, "The Hopis are not trying to find God; they live there." Perhaps the best reason for his belief lies in the male-female relationship he summarizes this way:

Women are not exploited among the Hopis. The male and female principles in the creation and maintenance of life are equally honored. This attitude is reflected, not denied, in the daily pattern of living. Their system of inheritance insures woman's economic independence. Their system of marriage and divorce respects her person. And the Hopi emphasis on nurture rather than aggression as a life style contributes to the recognition of her crucial part in the struggle for existence.

The amount and type of work a Hopi woman does are similar to that done by a pioneer white woman a century ago. However, the difference in social attitude toward their work is great.

The male pioneer was given credit for "supporting his wife and family by the sweat of his brow," while it was considered to be the woman's duty to perform the menial tasks of cooking and cleaning the house—which with rare exceptions belonged to her husband, along with the rest of the family possessions. And to a large extent marriage gave a man the right to his wife's sexuality, her person, and the fruits of her person, her children.

[3]Ibid., p. 208.
[4]Los Angeles, 1970.

The Hopis feel that a woman earns her living by cooking, grinding grain, and keeping house. If she provides cooked food for men, it is fair exchange for the heavy labor which they do for her. The relationship of a married man and woman is that of equals specializing in different professions.[5]

It is easy enough to understand that a people who hold Father Sky and Mother Earth as equal principals in the creation would automatically hold males and females to be "equals specializing in different professions." At least it is easy for the primitive mind to understand. And because it was both understood and lived, the relationship is not singled out for discussion in Native American literature, though it is obvious in the religious writings and poetry through implication and very apparent in the political document of the Iroquois League.

This document is an historically neglected work utterly unknown to the great majority of present-day Americans; yet it is one of the most important statements in the history of the democratic concept. Without recorded ancestor, it is the ancestor of the Constitution of the United States. This debt is not only unacknowledged in history books, it is usually rationalized away by those few authors who are aware of its existence. Attempting to trace the origins of the Constitution of the United States to Europe, historians have cited the *Constitution of Athens* (lost from the seventh century A.D. to its rediscovery in 1890), the *Magna Carta* and the general body of English law as a kind of en masse intellectual attitude that, like the head of Zeus giving birth to Aphrodite, produced a structurally refined, politically sophisticated concept spontaneously.

Certain historical facts cannot be disputed; they can only be ignored. Those facts are:

1. According to the Mohawk chiefs, when Cartier landed at Hochelega (Montreal) in the early sixteenth century, the Atataho (head chief of the Iroquois) was the thirty-third such man named to that lifetime position. This means the League would have been founded about 950 A.D.

2. In 1390 A.D. (according to the Council of Chiefs and the Six Nations Council of Grand River, Canada, July 3, 1900), the League of the Five Nations was formed. It included the Mohawk, Oneida, Onondaga, Cayuga, and Seneca. The Tuscarora came under the protection of the League in 1712, after which time the British called it the League of Six Nations though the Iroquois never changed the name. This league composed the Iroquois Constitu-

[5]Ibid., p. 31.

tion which was passed down in time in oral form by certain lords of the confederacy with the aid of wampum belts and strings which serve as the memory device for each law or regulation. Since 1898 the wampum collection has been housed in the State Museum of New York at Albany. Although the Great Binding Law or the Great Immutable Law was not translated and set down in English until the twentieth century, extracts exist in many of the sachems' speeches recorded by early American historians. Various non-Indian historians date Dekanawidah's vision of the pine tree at "about 1570" or "in the middle of the sixteenth century," dates preceded by the word *probably*, the date never being given any more historical authenticity than the dates ascribed by the Iroquois. The accuracy of Indian oral material disposes us to accept the Indian dates until white historians provide substantial evidence to support their supposition. It is historically probable that the white man did not learn of the League's existence until about 1640. It and his ignorance of it had existed simultaneously.

3. Some historians concede the League Constitution may have served as "one of the models on which the Constitution of the United States was based." What the other "models" may have been is studiously omitted. Peter Farb considers the matter in his *Man's Rise to Civilization...*, noted in Chapter 2.

The League deeply impressed the White settlers, and some historians believe that it was one of the models on which the Constitution of the new United States of America was based. The League did somewhat resemble the union of the Thirteen Colonies in organization, but it could more accurately be compared to the United Nations. It did not deal with the internal problems of the member tribes but solely with external affairs of war and peace. The League had a constitution, orally transmitted, but it could not levy taxes, and it lacked a police force to carry out its decisions. The hereditary leaders, the Council of Sachems, could not interfere in the affairs of the individual tribes, a situation similar to the small influence the United States federal government once had over the internal affairs of the thirteen states. Each tribe had its own sachems, but they also were limited in their powers; they dealt with the tribe's relations with other tribes and not with clan matters.

There were inequities in the tribal representation in the Council of Sachems, but these were more apparent than real, for the Iroquois worked out their primitive democracy in a way that modern Americans are not used to. Of the fifty hereditary sachems, the Onondaga had fourteen; Cayuga, ten; Mohawk and Oneida, nine each; and Seneca, even though the most numerous, only eight. Before any vote was taken, the sachems of each tribe met in private so that each tribe could speak with one voice, just as in a presidential election in the United States each state casts its entire electoral vote for one candidate. The major difference in the Iroquois system was that all decisions reached by the Council of Sachems had to be unanimous. If four of the tribes were in favor of a motion, but the fifth against it, then they would argue until the fifth gave in — or until the single recalcitrant tribe won over the other four. So any inequality in representation between the numerically superior Seneca, with only eight sachems, and the Onondaga, with fourteen, was meaningless.

Democratic as the Iroquois system might have appeared to the early settlers, after the Iroquois were more scientifically studied it was learned that such was not the case at all. The fifty sachem titles were rigidly controlled. Only males belonging to certain matrilineages within each tribe could hold the sachem titles. When a sachem died, his successor could be selected from only the matriliny holding that title, and the women were the ones who did the choosing. The headwoman of the lineage assembled all the women of her household and her clan and discussed with them her choice for a successor sachem. Then she went to both moieties and got their approval. The women's control over the sachem did not end with his selection. If he failed to perform his duties as they liked, the headwoman gave him three stern warnings, after which he was removed and his badge of office given to a new candidate. So even though the women did not themselves rule, they had the sole power to appoint and to remove from office.

All of which only emphasizes the control exerted by women among the Iroquois. All property and goods were inherited through the female line. The women owned the longhouse, the garden plots (even though they were cleared by the men), and the tools used to cultivate the land. Peace and order in the longhouse were maintained by the women. Husbands came and went, either through losses in warfare or the simple process of divorce, and the children of these unions belonged to the mother's lineage. In the political sphere, women appointed the sachems, named their successors when they died, and might even act as a regent for a sachem too young to rule. For all these reasons the Iroquois are usually regarded as having come as close to being a matriarchate as any society in the world.[6]

Rarihokwats of the Mohawk observes of Farb's statement, "It is basically correct, but some clarifications should be noted. Of tax levying: In a free, sharing society taxes create a repressive atmosphere so they were simply not considered. Of sachems: The sachems of the council and the national sachems were one and the same. Of matrilineage sachem titles: If this sounds undemocratic, remember that every person belonged to a clan and, therefore, participated in the choice of his chief. Of the headwoman's successor sachem discussions: Between the conference among women of the clan and the moities conference, the clan women's representative gained approval of their choice from the males of the clan. Of the three warnings: The third warning was an-

[6]New York, 1968, pp. 98–99.

swered on the spot, a negative response automatically relieving the sachem."

4. In 1744, Canasatego, Chief of the Iroquois, advised the colonial governors meeting in Lancaster:

Our Wise Forefathers established Union and Amity between the Five Nations. This has made us formidable; this has given us great Weight and Authority with our neighboring Nations. We are a powerful Confederacy; and by your observing our same Methods, our Wise Forefathers have taken, you will acquire such Strength and Power. Therefore, whatever befalls you, never fall out with one another.[7]

5. Benjamin Franklin (a man who could admire the Indian for his manliness, self-restraint to the point of needing no law enforcement agencies, and disdain of personal possessions on the one hand, yet, on the other, who could suggest that rum was an agent of Providence which should be used "to extirpate these savages in order to make room for the cultivators of the earth") was not without awareness of the existence and excellence of the Constitution of the League. As Alvin M. Josephy, Jr., observes in *The Indian Heritage of America*:

The League of the Iroquois was particularly influential on the thinking of some of the leaders of the American Colonies. Benjamin Franklin had great respect for the organization of the League and, when making his proposals for a union of the Colonies at Albany in 1754, wrote: "It would be a strange thing if Six Nations of ignorant savages should be capable of forming a scheme for such an union, and be able to execute it in such a manner as that it has subsisted ages and appears indissoluble; and yet that a like union should be impracticable for ten or a dozen English colonies, to whom it is more necessary and must be more advantageous, and who cannot be supposed to want an equal understanding of their interests." In time, the structure of the League had an indirect influence not only on the union of the Colonies, but on the government of the United States as it was constituted in 1789. In such forms as the methods by which congressional Senate and House conferees work out bills in compromise sessions, for instance, one may recognize similarities to the ways in which the Iroquois League functioned.[8]

6. Even the League symbols (pine tree, eagle, bound arrows which equal the number of nations and symbolize their union) were to be "borrowed" by the transplant Americans.

[7]See Warren H. Cohen and Philip L. Manle, "The Indian, the Forgotten American," *Harvard Law Review*, June, 1968, p. 1820.

[8]New York, 1969, p. 33.

7. Marxist theory has been strangely influenced by the Great Law. The curious route of that influence lay through two pioneering anthropological works of Lewis Henry Morgan (1818-1881), a Rochester, New York, lawyer often called "the father of American anthropology." His association with the Iroquois in general and with Seneca Ely S. Parker in particular led to the publication of *The League of the Ho-de-no-sau-nee, or Iroquois* in 1851 and *Ancient Society* in 1877. At that time Karl Marx was completing *Das Kapital* and taking copious notes on Morgan's study. Before he could incorporate them into his works, Marx died, but his successor, Friedrich Engels, relied on the notes of Marx and the theories of Morgan which became the core ideas of *The Origin of the Family, Private Property and the State* in 1884. Engels waxed eloquent about The Law of the Great Peace, assessing, "And a wonderful constitution it is... in all its childlike simplicity! No soldiers, no gendarmes or police, no nobles, kings, regents, prefects or judges, no prisons, no lawsuits."[9] Franklin's statement in *Poor Richard's Almanac* (1775) noted the "great order and decency among the Indians" and added that "the Savages" had developed a society where "There is no force, there are no prisons, no officers to compel obedience or inflict punishment." Engels found the Iroquois exemplary of the Communist ideal: "There cannot be any poor or needy—the communal household and the gens know their responsibilities towards the old, the sick, and those disabled in war. All are equal and free—the women included."

8. American literary students, teachers, and critics have lamented the lack and even the probable impossibility of an "American epic" in the tradition of *The Iliad, The Aeneid,* or even *Paradise Lost.* They have attempted to elevate Mark Twain's *Adventures of Huckleberry Finn* to that position—unsuccessfully. They have made extravagant claims for the incredible mishmash entitled *The Song of Hiawatha* (1855) by Henry Wadsworth Longfellow who appropriated the plot and characters from Henry Rowe Schoolcraft's 1839 *Algic Researches,* the unrhymed trochaic dimeter from the Finnish national epic *Kalevala.* Erroneously making the Mohawk Hiawatha an Ojibwa, confusing the geography completely, and never knowing that Hiawatha and Manabozho the trickster figure were two separate entities, he anguished over a title, settling for "Manabozho" on June 25, 1854, but, on June 28, decided on "Hiawatha—that being another name for the same personage."[10]

[9]Cited in Farb, p. 100.
[10]See Samuel Longfellow, *Life of Henry Wadsworth Longfellow* (Boston, 1891).

By every European literary traditional definition, the Iroquois account of Dekanawidah and Hiawatha *is* an American epic. National culture heroes (one of divine origin, one a redeemed man) create functional political order and a sense of cohesion in culturally similar but nationally divers peoples. Dekanawidah is flawed: Native American leaders generally were noted for their oratorical powers; the Iroquois particularly were preempt in the eloquent art. Hiawatha is verbally superior and it is he (in the company of Dekanawidah) who spreads the unifying philosophy among the groups. In conflict with an almost supernaturally evil opponent, Hiawatha and Dekanawidah exert great spiritual and physical strength to overcome the evil man and create the binding sense of identity in the people that lifts them above provincially political concepts and makes them politically potent. The accounts, orally transmitted, vary in satisfying degree until they are codified in a written form.

The beauty of the Native American accounts sharply contrasts with the sentimental effort of the transplant American poet. That Longfellow's trivial product was so ardently received while the vigorous original—the most "American" American literature—was virtually unknown suggests something about the literary vagaries of the transplant American, for until recent years, almost every school child memorized portions of the Longfellow verses and could recite them by rote, his voice lurching along on the monotonous rhythms as he mouthed the artificial

> By the shores of Gitche Gumee,
> By the shining Big-Sea-Water,
> Stood the wigwam of Nokomis,
> Daughter of the moon, Nokomis.

The strained effects of the opening lines so irritated the authors of this complaint that, even now, they remain, like an odious television commercial, in memory. And we were forced to learn them while the great original work languished so unnoticed by the American school system that we did not even know of its existence until recently, our educations having been received in the public systems of Rhode Island and Oklahoma where, along with white and other Indian students, we were denied access to this most "American" American literature while we were forced to memorize the ersatz lines of Longfellow.

Even the Christianizing process that scholars note, decry, and study endlessly in the Anglo-Saxon *Beowulf* are evident in the account presented in this chapter. The intellectual, scholarly neglect would be indefeasible even if the greater inequity of denying both transplant and Native Americans their cultural heritage were excusable.

Of course it is not. And, of course, it will continue.

But among the Native American Iroquois, the epic not only survives, it is epically alive. Like all nations, the Iroquois knows times of stress and division. When national unity needs reinforcement, when the people need to strengthen a flagging sense of national cohesion and identity, a special reading is called. If the nation is free of crisis for extended periods, the reading takes place every five years automatically. The people assemble and, in a five-day ceremony, the epic is recited by an honored speaker, his version always slightly different from other versions because the epic is still a live form—perhaps the only live form of the epic in existence. At the conclusion of the recital, the law is read. It is a set, unchanging law, the reading being a recital from memory in the traditional fashion, the reader being monitored by two elders who correct any mispronunciation, incorrect word, or deviation from the authorized text. At the end of the reading, the people have relived their past and reminded themselves that it extends into and shapes their present. Orenda has been made manifest—Orenda, that spiritual power that summarizes the past of the people and makes them cohesive in the present—that force has created a sense of "happening now," a sense that works mystically and actually. It is, in short, the collective unconscious sensitized into the collective conscious. The force it generates among the people has the power to ward off evil, make good possible, and keep the nation strong. Such was always the purpose of the epic and the law among all peoples; but, among the Iroquois, it is a *living* tradition.

The form of the epic here presented is the Seth Newhouse version, the version Rarihokwats says is most in favor among the Iroquois. The translation and codification of the epic and The Law of the Great Peace is a story of some historical and scholarly interest which may be found in summary in William N. Fenton's introduction to the Syracuse University Press collection of Arthur C. Parker Bulletins titled Parker on the Iroquois *(Syracuse, 1968). It is sufficient here to note that all work was done by Indians (Parker was probably one-fourth Seneca), their judgments having been validated by the passing years. Seth Newhouse, an Onondaga of the Six Nations Reserve, gave invaluable assistance to Parker and to the League itself. Dayodakane (Newhouse) so irritated the Council of Chiefs of the League with his own persistent efforts at codification that it appointed itself a committee to set down the version it approved in 1900. The committee of chiefs also set down "The Traditional Narrative of the Origin of the Confederation of the Five Nations" and approved it also. Epics are seldom approved in such fashion because the people who give birth to epics seldom survive into a period that could approve a version of its epic. Nor, in this one case, is the approved version the one favored by the people. This is just one more unique facet of this living American epic.*

The Epic of Dekanawida

DEKANAWIDA'S BIRTH AND JOURNEY

North of the beautiful lake (Ontario) in the land of the Crooked Tongues, was a long winding bay and at a certain spot was the Huron town, Ka-ha-nah-yenh. Near by was the great hill, Ti-ro-nat-ha-ra-da-donh. In the village lived a good woman who had a virgin daughter. Now strangely this virgin conceived and her mother knew that she was about to bear a child. The daughter about this time went into a long sleep and dreamed that her child should be a son whom she should name Dekanawida. The messenger in the dream told her that he should become a great man and that he should go among the Flint people to live and that he should also go to the Many Hill Nation and there raise up the Great Tree of Peace. It was true as had been said the virgin gave birth to a boy and the grandmother greatly disliked him and she rebuked her daughter.

"You refuse to tell me the father of the child," she said, "and now how do you know that great calamity will not befall us, and our nation? You must drown the child."

So then the mother took the child to the bay and chopped a hole in the ice where she customarily drew water and thrust him in, but when night came the child was found at his mother's bosom. So then the mother took the child again and threw him in the bay but at night the child returned. Then the third time the grandmother herself took the child and drowned him but in the morning the child nestled as before on its mother's own bosom.

So the grandmother marveled that the child, her grandson, could not be drowned. Then she said to her daughter:

"Mother, now nurse your child for he may become an important man. He can not be drowned, we know, and you have borne him without having marriage with any man. Now I have never heard of such an occurrence nor has the world known of it before."

Beginning with that time the mother took great care of her child and nursed him. She named him Dekanawida in accord with the instruction of her dream.

The child rapidly grew and was remarkably strong and healthy. His appearance was noticed for its good aspect and his face was most handsome.

When Dekanawida had grown to manhood he was greatly abused by the Huron people because of his handsome face and his good mind. He was always honest and always told what he believed was right. Nevertheless he was a peculiar man and his people did not understand him.

Many things conspired to drive him away for the Crooked Tongues had no love for such a man. Their hearts were bitter against a man who loved not war better than all things.

After a journey by canoe across the lake he came into the hunting territory of the Flint Nation. He journeyed on to the lower fall of the river of the Flint Nation and made a camp a short way from the fall on the flat land above it. He sat beneath a tall tree and smoked his pipe in quiet meditation.

A man of the Flints passed by and seeing the fire and the stranger approached him cautiously to discover what weapon he bore, if any. Carefully the man of the Flint reconnoitered but saw no weapon, but only the stranger quietly smoking. Returning to the town a short distance away the presence of the odd stranger was reported. Then the chiefs and their men went out and assembled about the man who smoked. One of the head men was delegated to question the stranger and so he asked "From whence came you?"

"I am from Ka-ha-na-yenh," the stranger replied.

"I am of the Wyandots, whom you call the Crooked Tongues because our speech is slightly different," answered the stranger. "My mother is a virgin woman."

"Then," said the speaker, "by what name are you known?"

"I am Dekanawida, so named because my virgin mother dreamed that it should be so and no one else shall ever be named by this name."

"What brought you here to us," asked the speaker.

So then Dekanawida answered, "The Great Creator from whom we all are descended sent me to establish the Great Peace among you. No longer shall you kill one another and nations shall cease warring upon each other. Such things are entirely evil and he, your Maker, forbids it. Peace and comfort are better than war and misery for a nation's welfare."

Then answered the speaker of the Flints, "All that you say is surely true and we are not able to contradict it. We must have proof, however, before we submit ourselves to you whereby we may know that you indeed possess rightful power to establish the Great Peace."

So answered Dekanawida, "I am able to demonstrate my power for I am the messenger of the Creator and he truly has given me my choice of the manner of my death."

"Choose then," said the speaker, "a manner of destruction for we are ready to destroy you." Dekanawida replied, "By the side of the falls at the edge of a precipice stands a tall tree. I will climb the tree and seat myself in the topmost branches. Then shall you cut down the tree and I shall fall into the depths below. Will not that destroy me?"

Then said the speaker, "Let us proceed at once."

Dekanawida ascended the tree and it was chopped down. A multitude of people saw him fall into the chasm and plunge into the water. So they were satisfied that he was surely drowned. Night came but Dekanawida did not appear and thus were the people sure of his death, and then were they satisfied.

The next morning the warriors saw strange smoke arising from the smoke hole of an empty cabin. They approached cautiously and peering in the side of the wall where the bark was loosened they saw Dekanawida. He was alive and was not a ghost and he was cooking his morning meal.

So the watchers reported their discovery and then were the chiefs and people truly convinced that indeed Dekanawida might establish the Great Peace.

THE TROUBLED NATIONS

The Ongwe-oweh had fought long and bravely. So long had they fought that they became lustful for war and many times Endeka-Gakwa, the

Sun, came out of the east to find them fighting. It was thus because the Ongwe-oweh were so successful that they said the Sun loved war and gave them power.

All the Ongwe-oweh fought other nations sometimes together and sometimes singly and, ah-gi! ofttimes they fought among themselves. The Nation of the Flint had little sympathy for the Nation of the Great Hill, and sometimes they raided one another's settlements. Thus did brothers and Ongwe-oweh fight. The nation of the Sunken Pole fought the Nation of the Flint and hated them, and the Nation of the Sunken Pole was Ongwe.

Because of bitter jealousy and love of bloodshed sometimes towns would send their young men against the young men of another town to practise them in fighting.

Even in his own town a warrior's own neighbor might be his enemy and it was not safe to roam about at night when Soi-ka-Gakwa, our Grandmother, the Moon, was hidden.

Everywhere there was peril and everywhere mourning. Men were ragged with sacrifice and the women scarred with the flints, so everywhere there was misery. Feuds with outer nations, feuds with brother nations, feuds of sister towns and feuds of families and of clans made every warrior a stealthy man who liked to kill.

Then in those days there was no Great Law. Our founder had not yet come to create peace and give united strength to the Real Men, the Ongwe-oweh.

In those same days the Onondagas had no peace. A man's life was valued as nothing. For any slight offence a man or woman was killed by his enemy and in this manner feuds started between families and clans. At night none dared leave their doorways lest they be struck down by an enemy's war club. Such was the condition when there was no Great Law.

South of the Onondaga town lived an evil-minded man. His lodge was in a swale and his nest was made of bulrushes. His body was distorted by seven crooks and his long tangled locks were adorned by writhing living serpents. Moreover, this monster was a devourer of raw meat, even of human flesh. He was also a master of wizardry and by his magic he destroyed men but he could not be destroyed. Adodarhoh was the name of the evil man.

Notwithstanding the evil character of Adodarhoh the people of Onondaga, the Nation of Many Hills, obeyed his commands and though it cost many lives they satisfied his insane whims, so much did they fear him for his sorcery.

The time came, however, when the Onondaga people could endure him no longer. A council was called to devise a way to pacify him and to entreat him to cease his evil ways. Hayonhwatha called the council for he had many times sought to clear the mind of

Adodarhoh and straighten his crooked body. So then the council was held in the house of Hayonhwatha. It was decided that half the people should go by boat across the creek where it widens and that others should skirt the shore. Adodarhoh was not in his nest in the swale but in a new spot across the wide place in the creek.

The boats started and the people walked. From the bushes that overhung the shore a loud voice sounded. "Stand quickly and look behind you for a storm will overwhelm you."

In dismay the people arose in their canoes and turned about. As they did so the canoes overturned and the men were plunged into the water and many were drowned. A few escaped and then all survivors returned to the village. So had Adodarhoh frustrated the attempt to meet with him.

Again the people prepared to conciliate Adodarhoh. Three times they agreed to attempt the undertaking. So on the second occasion they go by canoe and by land, those who go by canoe follow the shore and those who go by land walk on the pebbles close to the water's edge.

Again the cunning Adodarhoh sees them and calling down Hagoks he shook him, and the people in a wild rush scramble for the feathers, for the plumes of Hagoks are most beautiful and men are proud when their heads are adorned with them. There is a tumult and blows are struck. Evil feelings arise and in anger the people return to the village still contending. The mission of conciliation is forgotten.

The next day Hayonhwatha called the people to their promise and for the third time to attempt a council with Adodarhoh. Moreover, they promised to obey every instruction and listen neither to a voice outside nor an omen nor any commotion.

Another council was held in the lodge of a certain great dreamer. He said, "I have dreamed that another shall prevail. He shall come from the north and pass to the east. Hayonhwatha shall meet him there in the Mohawk country and the two together shall prevail. Hayonhwatha must not remain with us but must go from us to the Flint land people."

So when the journey across the lake was attempted there was a division and the dreamer's council prevailed.

Then the dreamer held two councils and those who believed in him conspired to employ Osinoh, a famous shaman.

Hayonhwatha had seven daughters whom he loved and in whom he took great pride. While they lived the conspirators knew he would not depart. With the daughters dead they knew the crushing sorrow would sever every tie that bound him to Onondaga. Then would he be free to leave and in thinking of the welfare of the people forget his own sorrow.

Hayonhwatha could not call the people together for they refused further to listen to his voice. The dreamer's council had prevailed.

At night Osinoh climbed a tree overlooking his lodge and sat on a large limb. Filling his mouth with clay he imitated the sound of a screech owl. Calling the name of the youngest daughter he sang:

> Unless you marry Osinoh
> You will surely die, -whoo-hoo!

Then he came down and went to his own home.

In three days the maiden strangely died. Hayonhwatha was disconsolate and sat sitting with his head bowed in his hands. He mourned, but none came to comfort him.

In like manner five other daughters passed away and the grief of Hayonhwatha was extreme.

Clansmen of the daughters then went to the lodge of Hayonhwatha to watch, for they knew nothing of Osinoh's sorcery. They gathered close against the large trees and in the shadows of bushes. The clansmen suspected some evil treachery and were there to discover it.

There was no moon in the sky when Osinoh came. Cautiously he came from habit but he was not afraid. He drove his staff in the ground, he breathed loud like a magic totem animal snorting and then he climbed the tree. He spat the clay about the tree to imitate the screech owl and as he did he said: "Si-twit, si-twit, si-twit." Then he sang:

> Unless you marry Osinoh
> You shall surely die, whoo-hoo!

The morning came and Osinoh descended. As he touched the ground a clansman shot an arrow and transfixed him. Prostrate fell Osinoh and the clansman rushed at him with a club.

Osinoh looked up. "You are unable to club me," he said. "Your arm has no power at all. It weakens. Today I shall recover from this wound. It is of no purpose to injure me."

It was true indeed; the clansman could not lift the club to kill Osinoh. Then Osinoh arose and went home and in three days the daughter died. So perished all by the evil magic arts of Osinoh.

The grief of Hayonhwatha was terrible. He threw himself about as if tortured and yielding to the pain. No one came near him so awful was his sorrow. Nothing would console him and his mind was shadowed with the thoughts of his heavy sorrow.

"I shall cast myself away, I shall bury myself in the forest, I shall become a woodland wanderer," he said. Thus he expressed his desire to depart. Then it was known that he would go to another nation.

Hayonhwatha "split the heavens," Watanwhakacia, when he departed and his skies were rent asunder.

Toward the south he went and at night he camped on the mountain. This was the first day of his journey. On the second day he descended and camped at the base of the hill. On the third day he journeyed onward and when evening came he camped in a hickory grove. This he named O-nea-no-ka-res-geh, and it was on the morning he came to a place where round jointed rushes grew. He paused as he saw them and made three strings of them and when he had built a fire he said: "This would I do if I found anyone burdened with grief even as I am. I would console them for they would be covered with night and wrapped in darkness. This would I lift with words of condolence and these strands of beads would become words with which I would address them."

So at this place he stayed that night and he called the spot O-hon-do-gon-wa, meaning Rush-land.

When daylight came he wandered on again and altering the course of his journey turned to the east. At night he came to a group of small lakes and upon one he saw a flock of ducks. So many were there and so closely together did they swim that they seemed like a raft.

"If I am to be truly royaneh (noble)," he said aloud to himself, "I shall here discover my power." So then he spoke aloud and said: "Oh you who are 'floats' lift up the water and permit me to pass over the bottom of the lake dryshod."

In a compact body the ducks flew upward suddenly and swiftly, lifting the water with them. Thus did he walk down the shore and upon the bottom of the lake. There he noticed lying in layers the empty shells of the water snail, some shells white, and others purple. Stooping down he filled a pouch of deer skin with them, and then passed on to the other shore. Then did the ducks descend and replace the water.

It was here that Hayonhwatha desired for the first time to eat. He then killed three ducks and roasted them. This was the evening of the fifth day.

In the morning he ate the cold meat of the roasted ducks and resumed his journey. This was the sixth day and on that day he hunted for small game and slept.

On the morning of the seventh day he ate again and turned his way to the south. Late in the evening he came to a clearing and found a bark field hut. There he found a shelter and there he erected two poles, placed another across the tops and suspended three shell strings. Looking at them he said: "Men boast what they would do in extremity but they do not do what they say. If I should see anyone in deep grief I would remove these shell strings from the pole and console them. The strings would become words and lift away the darkness with which they are covered. Moreover what I say I would surely do." This he repeated.

A little girl discovered smoke arising from the field lodge and she crept up and listened. She advanced and peered in a chink in the bark. Then she ran homeward and told her father of the strange man.

"The stranger must be Hayonhwatha," said the father, "I have heard that he has departed from Onondaga. Return, my daughter, and invite him to our house."

The girl-child obeyed and Hayonhwatha went to her house. "We are about to hold a council," the father said. "Sit in that place on one side of the fire and I will acquaint you with our decisions."

The council was convened and there was a great discussion. Before darkness every evening the council dissolved and at no time was Hayonhwatha called upon for advice nor was anything officially reported to him.

On the tenth day of his journey during the debate in the council Hayonhwatha quietly left and resumed his wandering. Nothing had been asked of him and he felt himself not needed by the people. Late in the evening he came to the edge of another settlement and as was his custom he kindled a fire and erected a horizontal pole on two upright poles. On this he place three strings of the wampum shells. Then he sat down and repeated his saying: "Men boast what they would do in extremity but they do not do what they promise. If I should see any one in deep grief I would remove these shells from this pole and console him. The shells would become words and lift away the darkness with which they are covered. Moreover, I truly would do as I say." This he repeated.

The chief man of the village saw the smoke at the edge of the forest and sent a messenger to discover who the stranger might be. Now when the messenger reached the spot he saw a man seated before a fire and a horizontal pole from which three strings of small shells were suspended. He also heard the words spoken as the stranger looked at the strings. So then when he had seen all he returned and reported what he had seen and heard.

Then said the chief man, "The person whom you describe must truly be Hayonhwatha whom we have heard left his home at Onondaga. He it is who shall meet the great man foretold by the dreamer. We have heard that this man should work with the man who talks of the establishment of peace."

So then the chiefs sent a messenger who should say, "Our principal chief sent me to greet you. Now then I wish you would come into our village with me."

Hayonhwatha heard the messenger and gathered up his goods and went into the village and when he had entered the chief's house the chief said, "Seat yourself on the opposite side of the fire so that you may have an understanding of all that we do here in this place."

Then Hayonhwatha sat there for seven days and the

chiefs and people talked without arriving at any decision. No word was asked Hayonhwatha and he was not consulted. No report was made officially to him. So he did not hear what they talked about.

On the eighteenth night a runner came from the south. He was from the nation residing on the seashore. He told the chiefs of the eminent man who had now come to the town on the Mohawk river at the lower falls. Then the messenger said: "We have heard of the dream of Onondaga which told of the great man who came from the north. Now another great man who shall now go forward in haste to meet him shall change his course and go eastward to meet in the Flinty land village (Kanyakahake), the great man. There shall the two council together and establish the Great Peace." So said the messenger from the salt water seashore, who came to tell Hayonhwatha to journey east.

So the chiefs of the town where Hayonhwatha was staying chose five men as an escort for Hayonhwatha. They must go with him until he reached the house where Dekanawida was present. So then on the next day the chief himself went with the party and watched carefully the health of Hayonhwatha. The journey lasted five days and on the fifth day the party stopped on the outskirts of the town where Dekanawida was staying and then they built a fire. This was the custom, to make a smoke so that the town might know that visitors were approaching and send word that they might enter without danger to their lives. The smoke was the signal of friends approaching. The Mohawks (People of the Flinty Country) knew the meaning of the signal so they sent messengers and invited the party into the village.

When Hayonhwatha had entered the house where the people had gathered the chief asked him whom he would like to see most. Then Hayonhwatha answered, "I came to see a very great man who lately came from the north." The chief said, "I have with you two men who shall escort you to the house where Dekanawida is present." Then the people went out and the two men escorted Hayonhwatha to Dekanawida. This was on the twenty-third day. Then Dekanawida arose when Hayonhwatha had entered and he said: "My younger brother I perceive that you have suffered from some deep grief. You are a chief among your people and yet you are wandering about."

Hayonhwatha answered, "That person skilled in sorcery, Osinoh, has destroyed my family of seven daughters. It was truly a great calamity and I am now very miserable. My sorrow and my rage have been bitter. I can only rove about since now I have cast myself away from my people. I am only a wanderer. I split the heavens when I went away from my house and my nation."

Dekanawida replied, "Dwell here with me. I will represent your sorrow to the people here dwelling."

So Hayonhwatha had found some one who considered

his distress and he did stay. Then Dekanawida told of his suffering and the people listened.

The five escorts were then dismissed and Hayonhwatha gave thanks to them and told them to return to their own region again. Then the escorts said, "Now today it has happened as was foretold in a dream. The two are now together. Let them now arrange the Great Peace." Then they returned home.

When Dekanawida laid the trouble before the council he promised to let Hayonhwatha know their decision. The chiefs deliberated over the sad events and then decided to do as Dekanawida should say. He then should remedy the trouble. Then Dekanawida went in perplexity to his lodge and as he came to it he heard Hayonhwatha say, "It is useless, for the people only boast what they will do, saying 'I would do this way,' but they do nothing at all. If what has befallen me should happen to them I would take down the three shell strings from the upright pole and I would address them and I would console them because they would be covered by heavy darkness." Dekanawida stood outside the door and heard all these words. So then Dekanawida went forward into the house and he went up to the pole, then he said: "My younger brother, it has now become very plain to my eyes that your sorrow must be removed. Your griefs and your rage have been great. I shall now undertake to remove your sorrow so that your mind may be rested. Have you no more shell strings on your pole?"

Hayonhwatha replied, "I have no more strings but I have many shells in a tanned deer's skin." So he opened his bundle and a great quantity of shells fell out. So then Dekanawida said, "My younger brother, I shall string eight more strands because there must be eight parts to my address to you." So then Hayonhwatha permitted the stringing of the shells and Dekanawida made the strings so that in all there were thirteen strings and bound them in four bunches. These must be used to console the one who has lost by death a near relative. "My younger brother, the thirteen strings are now ready on this horizontal pole. I shall use them. I shall address you. This is all that is necessary in your case."

So then he took one bunch off the pole and held it in his hand while he talked. While he talked one after another he took them down and gave one to Hayonhwatha after each part of his address.

The words that he spoke when he addressed Hayonhwatha were eight of the thirteen condolences.

When the eight ceremonial addresses had been made by Dekanawida the mind of Hayonhwatha was made clear. He was then satisfied and once more saw things rightly.

Dekanawida then said, "My younger brother, these thirteen strings of shell are now completed. In the future they shall be used in this way: They shall be held in the hand to remind the speaker of each part of his address, and as each part is finished a string shall be given to the bereaved chief (Royaneh) on the other side of the fire. Then shall the Royaneh hand them back one by one as he addresses a reply; it then can be said, 'I have now become even with you.'"

Dekanawida then said, "My junior brother, your mind being cleared and you being competent to judge, we now shall make our laws and when all are made we shall call the organization we have formed the Great Peace. It shall be the power to abolish war and robbery between brothers and bring peace and quietness.

"As emblems of our Royaneh titles we shall wear deer antlers and place them on the heads of Royaneh men."

Hayonhwatha then said, "What you have said is good, I do agree."

Dekanawida said, "My younger brother, since you have agreed I now propose that we compose our Peace song. We shall use it on our journey to pacify Adodarhoh. When he hears it his mind shall be made straight. His mind shall then be like that of other men. This will be true if the singer remembers and makes no error in his singing from the beginning to the end, as he walks before Adodarhoh."

Hayonhwatha said, "I do agree, I truly believe the truth of what you say."

Then Dekanawida said, "My younger brother, we shall now propose to the Mohawk council the plan we have made. We shall tell our plan for a confederation and the building of a house of peace. It will be necessary for us to know its opinion and have its consent to proceed."

The plan was talked about in the council and Dekanawida spoke of establishing a union of all the nations. He told them that all the chiefs must be virtuous men and be very patient. These should wear deer horns as emblems of their position, because as he told them their strength came from the meat of the deer. Then Hayonhwatha confirmed all that Dekanawida had said.

Then the speaker of the Mohawk council said, "You two, Dekanawida and Hayonhwatha, shall send messengers to the Oneida (People of the Stone) and they shall ask Odatshedeh if he will consider the plan."

When Odatshedeh had been asked he replied, "I will consider this plan and answer you tomorrow."

When the tomorrow of the next year had come, there came the answer of the Oneida council, "We will join the confederation."

So then the Mohawks (Kanyenga) sent two messengers to Onondaga asking that the nation consider the proposals of Dekanawida. It was a midsummer day when the message went forth and the Onondaga council answered, "Return tomorrow at high sun." So the two great men returned home and waited until the next midsummer.

Then the midday came and the Onondaga council sent messengers who said, "We have decided that it would be a good plan to build the fire and set about it with you." Dekanawida and Hayonhwatha heard this answer.

So then at the same time Dekanawida and Hayonhwatha sent messengers to the Cayuga nation and the answer was sent back. The Cayugas said they would send word of their decision tomorrow, upon the midsummer day. The next year at midsummer the Cayugas sent their answer and they said, "We do agree with Dekanawida and Hayonhwatha."

Now the People of the Great Hill were divided and were not agreed because there had been trouble between their war chiefs, but messengers were sent to them but the Senecas could not agree to listen and requested the messengers to return the next year. So when the messengers returned the councils did listen and considered the proposals. After a year had passed they sent messengers to say that they had agreed to enter into the confederacy.

Then Dekanawida said, "I now will report to the Mohawk council the result of my work of five years." Hayonhwatha then said, "I do agree to the report."

THE ESTABLISHMENT OF THE GREAT PEACE

Dekanawida requested some of the Mohawk chiefs to call a council, so messengers were sent out among the people and the council was convened.

Dekanawida said, "I, with my co-worker, have a desire to now report what we have done on five successive midsummer days, of five successive years. We have obtained the consent of five nations. These are the Mohawks, the Oneidas, the Onondagas, the Cayugas and the Senecas. Our desire is to form a compact for a union of our nations. Our next step is to seek out Adodarhoh. It is he who has always set at naught all plans for the establishment of the Great Peace. We must seek his fire and look for his smoke."

The chief speaker of the council then said, "We do agree and confirm all you have said and we wish to appoint two spies who shall volunteer to seek out the smoke of Adodarhoh."

Two men then eagerly volunteered and Dekanawida asked them if they were able to transform themselves into birds or animals, for such must be the ability of the messengers who approached Adodarhoh. The two men replied, "We are able to transform ourselves into herons and cranes."

"Then you will not do for you will pause at the first creek or swamp and look for frogs and fish."

Two men then said, "We have magic that will transform us into humming birds. They fly very swiftly."

"Then you will not do because you are always hungry and are looking for flowers."

Two other men then said, "We can become the Dare, the white crane."

"Then you will not do because you are very wild and easily frightened. You would be afraid when the clouds move. You would become hungry and fly to the ground looking about for ground nuts."

Then two men who were crows by magic volunteered but they were told that crows talked too loudly, boasted and were full of mischief.

So then in the end two men who were powerful by the magic of the deer and the bear stepped before the council and were chosen. The speaker for the council then reported to Dekanawida that the spies were ready to go. Then they went.

Now Dekanawida addressed the council and he said, "I am Dekanawida and with me is my younger brother. We two now lay before you the laws by which to frame the Ka-ya-neh-renh-ko-wa. The emblems of the chief rulers shall be the antlers of deer. The titles shall be vested in certain women and the names shall be held in their maternal families forever." All the laws were then recited and Hayonhwatha confirmed them.

Dekanawida then sang the song to be used when conferring titles. So in this way all the work and the plans were reported to the Mohawk council and Hayonhwatha confirmed it all. Therefore the council adopted the plan.

When the spies returned the speaker of the council said, "Ska-non-donh, our ears are erected." Then the spies spoke and they said, "At great danger to ourselves we have seen Adodarhoh. We have returned and tell you that the body of Adodarhoh has seven crooked parts, his hair is infested with snakes and he is a cannibal."

The council heard the message and decided to go to Onondaga at midsummer.

Then Dekanawida taught the people the Hymn of Peace and the other songs. He stood before the door of the longhouse and walked before it singing the new songs. Many came and learned them so that many were strong by the magic of them when it was time to carry the Great Peace to Onondaga.

When the time had come, Dekanawida summoned the chiefs and people together and chose one man to sing the songs before Adodarhoh. Soon then this singer led the company through the forest and he preceded all, singing the Peace songs as he walked. Many old villages and camping places were passed as they went and the names were lifted to give the clan name holders. Now the party passed through these places:

Old Clearing
Overgrown with bushes
A temporary place
Protruding rocks
Between two places
Parties opposite at the council fire
In the Valley
Drooping Wing
On the Hillside
Man Standing
I have daubed it
Lake Bridge
Between two side hills
Lake Outlet
At the forks
Long Hill
Broken Branches Lying
The Spring
White
Corn Stalks on both sides
Two Hillsides
The Old Beast

All these places were in the Mohawk country.

Now they entered the Oneida country and the great chief Odatshedeh with his chiefs met them. Then all of them marched onward to Onondaga, the singer of the Peace Hymn going on ahead.

The frontier of the Onondaga country was reached and the expedition halted to kindle a fire, as was customary. Then the chiefs of the Onondagas with their head men welcomed them and a great throng marched to the fireside of Adodarhoh, the singer of the Peace Hymn leading the multitude.

The lodge of Adodarhoh was reached and a new singer was appointed to sing the Peace Hymn. So he walked before the door of the house singing to cure the mind of Adodarhoh. He knew that if he made a single error or hesitated his power would be weakened and the crooked body of Adodarhoh remain misshapen. Then he hesitated and made an error. So another singer was appointed and he too made an error by hesitating.

Then Dekanawida himself sang and walked before the door of Adodarhoh's house. When he finished his song he walked toward Adodarhoh and held out his hand to rub it on his body and to know its inherent strength and life. Then Adodarhoh was made straight and his mind became healthy.

When Adodarhoh was made strong in rightful powers and his body had been healed, Dekanawida addressed the three nations.

He said, "We have now overcome a great obstacle. It has long stood in the way of peace. The mind of Adodarhoh is now made right and his crooked parts are made straight. Now indeed may we establish the Great Peace.

"Before we do firmly establish our union each nation must appoint a certain number of its wisest and purest men who shall be rulers, Rodiyaner. They shall be the advisers of the people and make the new rules that may be needful. These men shall be selected and confirmed by their female relations in whose lines the titles shall be hereditary. When these are named they shall be crowned, emblematically, with deer antlers."

So then the women of the Mohawks brought forward nine chiefs who should become Rodiyaner and one man, Ayenwaehs, as war chief.

So then the women of the Oneidas brought forward nine chiefs who should become Rodiyaner, and one man, Kahonwadironh, who should be war chief.

So then the Onondaga women brought forward fourteen chiefs who should become Rodiyaner, and one man, Ayendes, who should be war chief.

Each chief then delivered to Dekanawida a string of lake shell wampum a span in length as a pledge of truth.

Dekanawida then said: "Now, today in the presence of this great multitude I disrobe you and you are not now covered by your old names. I now give you names much greater." Then calling each chief to him he said: "I now place antlers on your head as an emblem of your power. Your old garments are torn off and better robes are given you. Now you are Rodiyaner, each of you. You will receive many scratches and the thickness of your skins shall be seven spans. You must be patient and henceforth work in unity. Never consider your own interests but work to benefit the people and for the generations not yet born. You have pledged yourselves to govern yourselves by the laws of the Great Peace. All your authority shall come from it.

"I do now order that Skanawateh shall in one-half of his being be a Royaneh of the Great Peace, and in his other half a war chief, for the Rodiyaner must have an ear to hear and a hand to feel the coming of wars."

Then did Dekanawida repeat all the rules which he with Hayonhwatha had devised for the establishment of the Great Peace.

Then in the councils of all the Five Nations he repeated them and the Confederacy was established.

The Law of the Great Peace of the People of the Longhouse (1390 A.D.) is *the world's oldest continuously observed agreement between peoples of honor and good faith. It is also the world's oldest living constitution, its Council Fire never having been covered since it was first kindled. In addition to the wisdom and fairness of its articles, it is possessed of a beauty of language that lifts it into the realm of literature. With the exception of The Declaration of Independence, no national document of a people is as stylistically perfected. The major difference between the two documents lies in the sincerity of The Law of the Great Peace. Its framers stated their beliefs, agreed to live by them, did live by them, do live by them.*

The version printed here is set from the document published by White Roots of Peace, the Mohawk Nation at Akwesasne, New York, the document authorized by the League of Six Nations.

The Law of the Great Peace of the People of the Longhouse

(Iroquois)
(League of Six Nations)

1

With the statesmen of the League of Five Nations, I plant the Tree of Great Peace.

I plant it in your territory, Atotarho, and the Onondaga Nation: in the territory of you who are Firekeepers.

I name the tree *Tsioneratasekowa*, the Great White Pine.

Under the shade of this Tree of Great Peace, we spread the soft, white, feathery down of the Globe Thistle as seats for you, Atotarho, and your cousin statesmen.

We place you upon those seats, spread soft with the feathery down of the Globe Thistle, there beneath the shade of the spreading branches of the Tree of Great Peace. There shall you sit and watch the Fire of the League of Five Nations. All the affairs of the League shall be transacted at this place before you, Atotarho and your cousin statesmen, by the statesmen of the League of Five Nations.

2

Roots have spread out from the Tree of Great Peace, one to the north, one to the east, one to the south, and one to the west. These are the Great White Roots, and their nature is Peace and Strength.

If any man or any nation of the Five Nations shall obey the laws of the Great Peace (Kaianerekowa), and shall make this known to the statesmen of the League, they may trace back the roots to the Tree. If their minds are clean, and if they are obedient and promise to obey the wishes of the Council of the League, they shall be welcomed to take shelter beneath the Great Evergreen Tree.

We place at the top of the Tree of Great Peace an eagle, who is able to see afar. If he sees in the distance any danger threatening, he will at once warn the people of the League.

3

To you, Atotarho and the Onondaga statesmen, I and the other statesmen of the League have entrusted the caretaking and watching of the Five Nations Council Fire.

When there is any business to be transacted and the Council of the League is not in session, a messenger shall be sent either to Atotarho, Hononwirehton, or Skanawate, firekeepers, or to their War Chiefs, with a full statement of the business to be considered. Then Atotarho shall call his cousin chiefs together and consider whether the business is of sufficient importance to call the attention of the Council of the League. If so, Atotarho shall send messengers to summon all the chiefs of the League and to assemble beneath the Tree of the Great Peace.

When the statesmen are assembled, the Council Fire shall be kindled, but not with chestnut wood, and Atotarho shall formally open the Council. Then shall Atotarho and his cousin statesmen, the Firekeepers, announce the subject for discussion.

The smoke of the Council Fire of the League shall ever ascend and pierce the sky so that other nations who may be allies may see the Council Fire of The Great Peace.

4

You, Atotarho and your thirteen cousin statesmen shall faithfully keep the space about the Council Fire clean, and you shall allow neither dust nor dirt to accumulate. I lay a long seagull wing (Tsiowatstekawe Onerahontsha) before you as a broom.

As a weapon against a crawling creature, I lay a stick with you so that you may thrust it away from the Council Fire. If you fail to cast it out, then call all the rest of the united statesmen to your aid.

5

The Council of the Mohawks shall be divided into three parties:
Tehanakarine, Ostawenserentha and Soskoharowane are the first.
Tekarihoken, Ayonwatha and Satekariwate are the second.
Sarenhowane, Teyonhekwen and Orenrekowa are the third.
The first party is to listen only to the discussion of the second and third parties and if an error is made, or the proceeding irregular, they are to call attention to it and when the case is right and properly decided by the two parties, they shall confirm the decision of the two parties and refer the case to the Seneca statesmen for their decision. When the Seneca statesmen have decided, in accord with the Mohawk statesmen, the case or question shall be referred to the Cayuga and Oneida statesmen on the opposite side of the house.

6

I, Tekanawita, appoint the Mohawk statesmen the head and the Leaders of the Five Nations League. The Mohawk statesmen are the foundation of the Great Peace, and it shall therefore be against the Great Binding Law to pass measures in the Council of the League after the Mohawk statesmen have protested against them.

No Council of the League shall be legal unless all of the statesmen of the Mohawks are present.

THANKSGIVING

7

Whenever the statesmen of the League shall assemble for the purpose of holding a council, the Onondaga statesmen shall open it by expressing their gratitude to their cousin statesmen, and greeting them, and they shall make an address and offer thanks to the earth where men dwell, to the streams of water, the pools and the lakes, to the maise and the fruits, to the medicinal herbs and trees, to the forest trees for their usefulness, and to the animals that serve as food and give their pelts for clothing, to the great winds and the lesser winds, to the Thunderers; to the Sun, the mighty warrior; to the moon, to the messengers of the Creator who reveals his wishes, and to the Great Creator who dwells in the heavens above who gives all the things useful to men, and who is the source and the ruler of health and life.

Then shall the Onondaga statesmen declare the Council open.

The Council shall not sit after darkness has set in.

8

The Firekeepers shall formally open and close all councils of the statesmen of the League, they shall pass upon all matters deliberated upon by the two sides, and render their decision.

Every Onondaga statesman (or his deputy) must be present at every Council of the League, and must agree with the majority without unwarrantable dissent, so that a unanimous decision may be rendered.

If Atotarho or any of his cousin statesmen are absent from a Council of the League, any other Firekeeper may open and close the Council, but the Firekeepers present may not give any decisions, unless the matter is of small importance.

9

All the business of the Five Nations League Council shall be conducted by the two combined bodies of Confederate statesmen. First the question shall be passed upon by the Mohawk and Seneca statesmen, then it shall be discussed and passed by the Oneida and Cayuga statesmen. Their decision shall then be referred to the Onondaga statesmen, the Firekeepers, for final judgment.

The same process shall be followed when a question is brought before the Council by an individual or a War Chief.

10

In all cases, the procedure must be as follows: when the Mohawk and Seneca statesmen have unanimously agreed upon a question, they shall report their decision to the Cayuga and Oneida statesmen, who shall deliberate upon the question and report a unanimous decision to the Mohawk statesmen. The Mohawk statesmen will then report the standing of the case to the Firekeepers, who shall render a decision as they see fit in case of a disagreement by the two bodies, or confirm the decisions of the two bodies if they are identical. The Firekeepers shall then report their decision to the Mohawk statesmen who shall announce it to the open Council.

11

If through any misunderstanding or obstinacy on the part of the Fire-keepers, they reach a decision at variance with that of the Two Sides, the Two Sides shall reconsider the matter and if their decisions are jointly the same as before, they shall report to the Firekeepers, who are then compelled to confirm their joint decision.

12

When a case comes before the Onondaga statesmen, the Firekeepers, for discussion and decision, Atotarho shall introduce the matter to his comrade statesmen, who shall then discuss it in their two bodies. Every Onondaga statesmen except Hononwireton shall deliberate and he shall listen only. When a unanimous decision shall have been reached by the two bodies of Firekeepers, Atotarho shall notify Hononwireton of the fact, then he shall confirm it. He shall refuse to confirm a decision if it is not unanimously agreed upon by both sides of the Firekeepers.

13

No chief shall ask a question of the body of chiefs of the League when they are discussing a case, question, or proposition. He may only delib-erate in a low tone with the separate body of which he is a member.

14

When the Council of the Five Nation chiefs shall convene, they shall appoint a speaker for the day. He shall be a chief of either the Mohawk, Onondaga, or Seneca.

The next day, the Council shall appoint another, but the first speaker may be reappointed if there is no objection, but a speaker's term shall not be regarded more than for the day.

15

No individual or foreign nation interested in a case, question, or propo-sition shall have any voice in the Council of the League except to answer a question put to him or them by the speaker for the chiefs.

16

If the conditions which shall arise at any future time call for an addition to or change of this law, the case shall be carefully considered and if a new beam seems necessary or beneficial, the proposed change shall be decided upon, and if adopted, shall be called, "Added to the Rafters."

RIGHTS, DUTIES, QUALIFICATIONS
OF THE STATESMEN

17

A bunch of certain shell (wampum) strings each two spans in length shall be given to each of the female families in which the chieftain titles are vested. The right of bestowing the titles shall be hereditary in the family of females legally possessing the bunch of shell strings, and the strings shall be the token that the females of the family have the ownership to the chieftainship title for all time to come, subject to certain restrictions mentioned here.

18

If any chief of the League neglects or refuses to attend the Council of the League, the other chiefs of the nation of which he is a member shall require their War Chief to request the female sponsors of the chief so guilty of neglecting his duties to demand his attendance at the Council. If he refuses, the women holding the title shall immediately select another candidate for the title.

No chief shall be asked more than once to attend the Council of the League.

19

If at any time it shall be apparent that a chief of the League has not in mind the welfare of the people, or disobeys the rules of the Great Law, the men or the women of the League, or both jointly, shall come to the Council and scold the erring chief through his war chief. If the complaint of the people through the war chief is not heeded, on the first occasion, it shall be uttered again, and then if no attention is given, a third complaint and a warning shall be given. If the chief is still disobedient, the matter shall go to the Council of War Chiefs. The War Chiefs shall then take away the title of the erring chief by order of the women in whom the title is vested. When the chief is deposed, the women shall notify the chiefs of the League through their war chief and the chiefs of the League shall sanction the act. The women will then select another of their sons as a candidate and the chiefs shall elect him. Then the chosen one shall be installed by the Installation Ceremony.

When a chief is deposed, his war chief shall address him as follows:
"So you, ..., *disregard and set at naught the warnings of your women relatives. You fling the warnings over your shoulder to cast them behind. Behold the brightness of the Sun, and in the brightness of the Sun's light, I depose you of your title and remove the sacred*

emblem of your chieftainship title. I remove from your brow the deer's antlers which was the emblem of your position and token of your nobility. I now depose you, and return the antlers to the women whose heritage they are."

The war chief shall now address the women of the deposed chief and say:
"Mothers, as I have deposed your chief, I now return to you the emblem and the title of chieftainship; therefore, repossess them."

Again addressing the deposed chief, he shall say:
"As I have deposed and discharged you so you are no longer chief. You shall go your way alone. The rest of the people of the League shall not go with you, for we know not the kind of mind you possess. As the Creator has nothing to do with wrong, so he will not come to rescue you from the precipice of destruction in which you have cast yourself. You shall never be restored to the position which you once occupied."

Then shall the war chief address himself to the chiefs of the nation to which the deposed chief belongs and say:
"Know you, my chiefs, that I have taken the deer's antlers from the brow of ...., the emblem of his position, and the token of his greatness."

The chiefs of the League shall have no other alternative then except to sanction the discharge of the offending chief.

20

If a chief of the League of Five Nations should commit murder the other chiefs of the nation shall assemble at the place where the corpse lies and prepare to depose the criminal chief. If it is impossible to meet at the scene of the crime the chiefs shall discuss the matter at the next Council of their nation and request their war chief to depose the chief guilty of the crime, to "bury his women relatives and to transfer the chieftainship title to a sister family."

The war chief shall address the chief guilty of murder and say:
"So you, ..., did kill ...., with your own hands! You have committed a grave crime in the eyes of the Creator. Behold the bright light of the Sun, and in the brightness of the Sun's light, I depose you of your title and remove the horns, the sacred emblem of your chieftainship title. I remove from your brow the deer's antlers which was the emblem of your position and token of your nobility. I now

*depose you and expel you and you shall depart at once from the
territory of the League of Five Nations and nevermore return again.
We, the League of Five Nations, moreover, bury your women relatives
because the ancient chieftainship title was never intended to have
any union with bloodshed. Henceforth, it shall not be their heritage.
By the evil deed that you have done they have forfeited it forever."*

The war chief shall then hand the title to a sister family, and he shall
address it and say:

*"Our mothers, ..., listen attentively while I address you on a
solemn and important subject. I hereby transfer to you an ancient
chieftainship title for a great calamity has befallen it in the hands
of the family of a former chief. We trust that you, our mothers, will
always guard it and that you will warn your chief always to be dutiful
and to advise his people to ever live in love, peace and harmony that
a great calamity may never happen again."*

21

Certain physical defects in a statesman of the League make him ineligible to sit in the League Council. Such defects are infancy, idiocy,
blindness, deafness, dumbness and impotency. When a statesman of
the League is restricted by any of these conditions, a deputy shall be
appointed by his sponsors to act for him, but in cases of extreme necessity, the restricted statesman may exercise his rights.

22

If a statesman of the League desires to resign his title, he shall notify
the statesmen of the nation of which he is a member of his intentions.
If his co-active statesmen refuse to accept his resignation, he may not
resign his title.

A statesman in proposing to resign may recommend any proper candidate which recommendation shall be received by the statesmen but
unless confirmed and nominated by the women who hold the title,
the candidate shall not be considered.

23

Any chief of the League of Five Nations may construct shell strings or
wampum belts of any size or length as pledges or records of matters of
national or international importance.

When it is necessary to dispatch a shell string by a war chief or other
messenger as a token of a summons, the messenger shall recite the

contents of the string to the party to whom it is sent. That party shall repeat the message and return the shell string, and if there has been a summons, he shall make ready for his journey.

Any of the people of the Five Nations may use shells or wampum as the record of a pledge, contract, or an agreement entered into and the same shall be binding as soon as shell strings shall have been exchanged by both parties.

24

The chiefs of the League of Five Nations shall be mentors of the people for all time. The thickness of their skin shall be seven spans (tsiataniio-ronkarake), which is to say that they shall be proof against anger, offensive action, and criticism. Their hearts shall be full of peace and good will, and their minds filled with a yearning for the welfare of the people of the League. With endless patience, they shall carry out their duty. Their firmness shall be tempered with a tenderness for their people. Neither anger nor fury shall find lodging in their minds and all their words and actions shall be marked by calm deliberation.

25

If a chief of the League should seek to establish any authority independent of the jurisdiction of the League of the Great Peace, which is the Five Nations, he shall be warned three times in open Council, first by the women relatives, second by the men relatives, and finally by the chiefs of the Nation to which he belongs.

If the offending chief is still persistent, he shall be dismissed by the war chief of his nation for refusing to conform to the laws of the Great Peace. His Nation shall then install the candidate nominated by the female name holders of his family.

26

It shall be the duty of all the chiefs of the League of Five Nations, from time to time as occasion demands, to act as teachers and spiritual guides of their people, and remind them of their Creator's will and words. They shall say:

"Listen, that peace may continue unto future days!

"Always listen to the words of the Great Creator, for he has spoken.

"United People, let not evil find lodging in your minds.

"For the Great Creator has spoken and the Cause of Peace shall not become old.

"The cause of peace shall not die if you remember the Great Creator."

27

All chiefs of the League of Five Nations must be honest in all things. They must not idle nor gossip, but be men possessing those honorable qualities that make true leaders. It shall be a serious wrong for anyone to lead a chief into trivial affairs, for the people must ever hold their chiefs high in estimation out of respect to their honorable positions.

A NEW CHIEF

28

When a candidate chief is to be installed, he shall furnish four strings of shells or wampum one span in length bound together at one end. Such will constitute the evidence of his pledge to the chiefs of the League that he will live according to the Constitution of the Great Peace and exercise justice in all affairs.

When the pledge is furnished, the Speaker of the Council must hold the shell strings in his hand and address the opposite side of the Council Fire, and he shall begin his address saying:

"Now behold him. He has now become a chief of the League. See how splendid he looks."

An address may then follow. At the end of it he shall send the bunch of shell strings to the opposite side, and they shall be received as evidence of the pledge. Then shall the opposite side say:

"We now do crown you with the sacred emblem of the deer's antlers, the emblem of your chieftainship. You shall now become a mentor of the people of the Five Nations. The thickness of your skin shall be seven spans, which is to say that you shall be proof against anger, offensive actions, and criticism. Your heart shall be filled with peace and good will. Your mind shall be filled with a yearning for the welfare of the people of the League. With endless patience you shall carry out your duty and your firmness shall be tempered with tenderness for your people. Neither anger nor fury shall find lodging in your mind. All your words and actions shall be marked with calm deliberation. In all your deliberations in the Council of the League, in all your efforts at law-making, in all your official acts, self-interest shall be cast away. Do not cast over your shoulder behind you the warnings of your nephews and nieces should they chide you for any error or wrong you may do, but return to the way of the Great Law which is right and just. Look and listen for the welfare of the whole people, and have always in view not only the present, but also the coming generations, even those whose faces are yet beneath the surface of the ground — the unborn of the future Nation."

29

When a chieftainship title is to be conferred, the candidate chief shall furnish the cooked venison, the corn bread and the corn soup, together with other necessary things and the labor for the Conferring of Titles Festival.

30

The chiefs of the League may confer the chieftainship title upon a candidate whenever the Great Law is recited, if there is a candidate, for the Great Law speaks all the rules.

31

If a chief of the League should become seriously ill and be thought near death, the women who are heirs of his title shall go to his house and lift his crown of deer antlers, the emblem of his chieftainship, and place them at one side. If the Creator spares him and he rises from his bed of sickness, he may rise with antlers on his brow.

The following words shall be used to temporarily remove the antlers: *"Now our comrade chief, the time has come when we must approach you in your illness. We remove for a time the deer's antlers from your brow. We remove the emblem of your chieftainship title. The Great Law has decreed that no chief should end his life with the antlers on his brow. We therefore lay them aside in the room. If the Creator spares you and you recover from your illness you shall rise from your bed with the antlers on your brow as before and you shall resume your duties as chief of the League and you may again labor for the people of the League."*

32

If a chief of the League should die while the Council of the Five Nations is in session, the Council shall adjourn for ten days. No Council of the League shall sit within ten days of the death of a chief of the League.

If the Three Brothers (ahsennihontatekenah) (the Mohawk, the Onondaga, and the Seneca) should lose one of their chiefs by death, the Younger Brothers (iatatekanah) (the Cayuga and the Oneida) shall come to the surviving chiefs of the Three Brothers on the tenth day and console them. If the Younger Brothers lose one of their chiefs, then the Three Brothers shall come to them and console them. And the consolation shall be the reading of the contents of the thirteenth shell (wampum) strings of Ayonwatha. At the termination of this rite, a successor shall be appointed, to be appointed by the women heirs of the Chieftainship title. If the women are not ready to place their nominee before the chiefs, the Speaker shall say, "Come let us go out." All shall then leave the Council or place of gathering. The Speaker shall lead the way from the house by saying, "Let us depart to the edge of the woods and lie in wait on our bellies." (Tenshakonatioswentarhese).

When the women title holders shall have chosen one of their sons, the chiefs of the League will assemble in two places, the Younger Brothers in one place and the Three Older Brothers in another. The chiefs who are to console the mourning chiefs shall choose one of their number to sing the Song of Peace as they journey to the sorrowing chiefs. The singer shall lead the way, and the chiefs and the people shall follow. When they reach the sorrowing chiefs, they shall hail the candidate chief and perform the rite of Conferring the Chieftainship title. (Oh-keiontentshera)

33

When a chief of the League dies, the surviving relatives shall immediately dispatch a messenger, a member of another clan, to the chiefs in another locality. When the runner comes within hailing distance of the locality, he shall utter a sad wail, thusly: "Kwa-ah! Kwa-ah!" The sound shall be repeated three times, and then again and again at intervals as many times as the distance may require. When the runner arrives at the settlement, the people shall assemble and one must ask him the nature of his sad message. He shall then say, "Let us consider." (rak-wennikonriak). Then he shall tell them of the death of the chief. He shall deliver to them a string of shells or wampum and say, "Here is the testimony, you have heard the message." He may return home.

It now becomes the duty of the chiefs of the locality to send runners to other localities and each locality shall send messengers until all chiefs are notified. Runners shall travel day and night.

34

If a chief dies and there is no candidate qualified for the office in the family of the women title holders, the chiefs of the Nation shall give the title into the hands of a sister family (Kentennonteron) in the clan until such time as the original family produces a candidate, when the title shall be restored to the rightful owners.

No chieftainship title may be carried into the grave. The chiefs of the League may dispossess a dead chief of his title even at the grave.

35

Should any man of the Nation assist with special ability or show great interest in the affairs of the Nation, if he proves himself wise and honest and worthy of confidence, the chiefs of the League may elect him to a seat among them, and he may sit in the Council of the League. He shall be proclaimed a Pine Tree, sprung up for the Nation, and be installed as such at the next assembly for the installation of chiefs. Should he ever do anything contrary to the rules of the Great Peace, he may not be deposed from office—no one shall cut him down—but thereafter everyone shall be deaf to his voice and his advice. Should he resign from his seat and title, no one shall prevent him. A Pine Tree Chief has no authority to name a successor nor is his title hereditary.

THE WAR CHIEFS

36

The title names of the war chiefs of the League shall be:
  Ayonwehs, war chief under chief Takarihoken (Mohawk)
  Kahonwaitiron, war chief under chief Otatsheteh (Oneida)
  Ayentes, war chief under chief Atotarho (Onondaga)
  Wenens, war chief under chief Dekaenyon (Cayuga)
  Shoneratowaneh, war chief under chief Skanyatariio (Seneca)

The women heirs of each head chief's title shall be the heirs of the war chief's title of their respective chief.

The war chiefs shall be selected from the eligible sons of the female families holding the head chieftainship title.

37

There shall be one war chief from each nation, and their duties shall be to carry messages for their chiefs, and to take up arms in case of emergency. They shall not participate in the proceedings of the Council of the League, but shall watch its progress and in case of an erroneous action by a chief, they shall receive the complaints of the people and convey the warnings of the women to him. The people who wish to convey messages to the chiefs of the League shall do so through the war chief of their nation. It shall always be his duty to lay the cases, questions, and propositions of the people before the council of the League.

38

When a war chief dies, another shall be installed by the same rite as that by which a chief is installed.

39

If a war chief acts contrary to instructions, or against the provisions of the Laws of the Great Peace, doing so in the capacity of his office, he shall be deposed by his women relatives and by his men relatives. Either the women or the men alone or jointly may act in such a case. The women title holders shall then choose another candidate.

40

When the chiefs of the League take occasion to dispatch a messenger in behalf of the Council of the League, they shall wrap up any matter they may send, and instruct the messenger to remember his errand, to turn not aside, but to proceed faithfully to his destination and deliver his message according to every instruction.

41

If a message borne by a runner is the warning of an invasion, he shall whoop, "Kwa-ah, Kwa-ah!" twice and repeat at short intervals, then again at a longer interval.

If a human is found dead, the finder shall not touch the body, but return home immediately shouting at short intervals, "Koo-weh!"

THE CLANS

42

Among the Five Nations and their descendants there shall be the following Clans: Great Name Bearer, Ancient Name Bearer, Great Bear, Ancient Bear, Turtle, Painted Turtle, Standing Rock, Large Plover, Little Plover (or Snipe), Deer, Wolf, Pigeon, Hawk, Eel, Ball, "Opposite-Side of the Hand" and Wild Potatoes. These clans distributed through their respective nations shall be the sole owners and holders of the soil of the country and in them is vested, as a birthright.

43

People of the Five Nations who are members of a certain clan shall recognize every member of the Clan, no matter what Nation, as relatives. Men and women, therefore, who are members of the same Clan are forbidden to marry.

44

The lineal descent of the people of the Five Nations shall run in the female line. Women shall be considered the progenitors of the Nation. They shall own the land, and the soil. Men and women shall follow the status of their mothers.

45

The women heirs of the chieftainship titles of the League shall be called Oianer or Otiianer (Noble) for all time to come.

46

The women of the 48 (now 50) noble families shall be the heirs of the Authorized Names for all time to come.

When an infant of the Five Nations is given an Authorized Name at the Midwinter Festival or at the Green Corn and Strawberry and Harvest Festival, one in the cousinhood of which the infant is a member shall be appointed a speaker. He shall then announce to the opposite cousin-hood the names of the father and mother of the child, together with the clan of the mother. Then the speaker shall announce the child's name twice. The uncle of the child shall then take the child in his arms and walking up and down the room shall sing, "My head is firm; I am of the League." As he sings the opposite cousinhood shall respond by chanting, "Hyen, Hyen, Hyen, Hyen" until the song is ended.

47

If the female heirs of a title of a chief of the League become extinct, the title shall be given by the chiefs of the League to a sister family whom they shall elect, and that family shall hold the name and transmit it to their female heirs, but they shall not appoint any of their sons as a candidate for a title until all the eligible men of the former family shall have died, or otherwise have become ineligible.

48

If all the heirs of a chieftainship become extinct, and so all the families in the Clan, then the title shall be given by the chiefs of the League to a family of a sister Clan whom they shall elect.

49

If any of the Otiianer women, heirs of a titleship, shall willfully with-hold a chieftainship or other title and refuse to bestow it, or if such heirs abandon, forsake, or despise their heritage, then shall such women be deemed buried, and their family extinct. The titleship shall then revert to a sister family, or Clan, upon application and complaint. The chiefs of the League shall elect the family or Clan which shall in future hold the title.

50

The Otiianer women of the League heirs of the chieftainship titles shall elect two women of their family as cooks for the chief when the people shall assemble at his house for business or other purposes.

It is not good nor honorable for a chief of the League to allow his people whom he has called to go hungry.

51

When a chief holds a conference in his home, his wife, if she wishes, may prepare the food for the union chiefs who assemble with him. This is an honorable right which she may exercise, and an expression of her esteem.

52

The Otiianer women, heirs of the chieftainship titles, shall, should it be necessary, correct and admonish the holders of the titles. Those only who attend the Council may do this, and those who do not shall not object to what has been said nor strive to undo the action.

53

When the Otiianer women, holders of a chieftainship title, select one of their sons as a candidate, they shall select one who is trustworthy, of good character, of honest disposition, one who manages his own affairs, and supports his own family, if any, and who has proven a faithful man to his Nation.

54

When a chieftainship title becomes vacant through death or other cause, the Otiianer women of the Clan in which the title is hereditary shall hold a council, and shall choose one of their sons to fill the office made vacant. Such a candidate shall not be the father of any chief of the League. If the choice is unanimous, the name is referred to the men relatives of the Clan. If they should disapprove, it shall be their duty to select a candidate from among their own number. If then the men and women are unable to decide which of the two candidates shall be named, then the matter shall be referred to the chiefs of the League in the Clan. They shall decide which candidate shall be named. If the men and women agree to a candidate, then his name shall be referred to the sister clans for confirmation. If the sister clans confirm the choice, they shall refer their action to the chiefs of the League who shall ratify the choice and present it to their cousin chiefs, and if the cousin chiefs confirm the name, then the candidate shall be installed by the proper ceremony for the conferring of chieftainship titles.

THE SYMBOLS

55

A large bunch of shell strings, in the making of which the Five Nations League chiefs have equally contributed, shall symbolize the completeness of the union, and certify the pledge of the Nations represented by the chiefs of the League of the Mohawk, the Oneida, the Onondaga, the Cayuga, and the Seneca, that all are united and formed into one body, or union, called the Union of the Great Law which they have established.

A bunch of shell strings is to be the symbol of the Council Fire of the League of Five Nations. And the chief whom the Council of Firekeepers shall appoint to speak for them in opening the Council shall hold the strands of shells in his hands when speaking. When he finishes speaking, he shall place the strings on an elevated place or pole so that all the assembled chiefs and the people may see it and know that the Council is open and in progress.

56

Five strings of shell tied together as one shall represent the Five Nations. Each string shall represent one territory, and the whole a completely united territory known as the Five Nations Territory.

57

Five arrows shall be bound together very strong and shall represent one Nation each. As the five arrows are strongly bound, this shall symbolize the complete union of the nations. Thus are the Five Nations completely united and enfolded together, united into one head, one body, and one mind. They therefore shall labor, legislate, and council together for the interest of future generations.

The chiefs of the League shall eat together from one bowl the feast of cooked beaver's tail. While they are eating, they are to use no sharp utensils, for if they should, they might accidentally cut one another, and bloodshed would follow. All measures must be taken to prevent the spilling of blood in any way.

58

There are now the Five Nations League chiefs standing with joined hands in a circle. This signifies and provides that should any one of the chiefs of the League leave the Council and the League, his crown of deer's antlers, the emblems of his chieftainship title, together with his birthright, shall lodge on the arms of the union chiefs whose hands are so joined. He forfeits his title, and the crown falls from his brow, but it shall remain in the League.

A further meaning of this is that if any time any one of the chiefs of the League chooses to submit to the law of a foreign people, he is no longer in but out of the League, and persons of this class shall be called "They have alienated themselves." (Tehonatonkoton). Likewise, such persons who submit to laws of foreign nations shall forfeit all birthrights and claims on the League of Five Nations and territory.

You, the League of Five Nations chiefs, be firm so that if a tree should fall upon your joined hands, it shall not separate you or weaken your hold. So shall the strength of union be preserved.

59

A bunch of wampum strings, three spans of the hand in length, the upper half of the bunch being white and the lower half black, and formed from equal contributions of the men of the Five Nations, shall be the token that the men have combined themselves into one head, one body, and one thought, and it shall symbolize their ratification of the peace pact of the League, whereby the chiefs of the Five Nations have established the Great Peace. The white portion of the shell strings represent the women, and the black portion the men. The black portion, furthermore, is a token of power and authority vested in the men of the Five Nations.

This string of wampum vests the people with the right to correct their erring Chiefs. In case a part of the chiefs or all of them pursue a course not vouched for by the people and heed not the third warning of their women relatives (Wasenensawenrate), then the matter shall be taken to the General Council of the Women of the Five Nations. If the chiefs notified and warned three times fail to heed, then the case falls into the hands of the men of the Five Nations. The War Chiefs shall then, by right of such power and authority, enter the open Council to warn the chief or chiefs to return from their wrong course. If the chiefs heed the warning, they shall say, "We shall reply tomorrow." If then an answer is returned in favor of justice and in accord with this Great Law, then the Chiefs shall individually pledge themselves again, by again furnishing the necessary shells for the pledge. Then the War Chief or chiefs exhort the chiefs, urging them to be just and true.

Should it happen that the chiefs refuse to heed the third warning, then two courses are open: either the men may decide in their council to depose the chief or chiefs, or to club them to death with war clubs. Should they in their council decide to take the first course, the War Chief shall address the chief or chiefs, saying,

> "Since you the chiefs of the Five Nations have refused to return to the procedure of the Constitution, we now declare your seats vacant, and we take off your horns, the token of your chieftainship, and others shall be chosen and installed in your seats. Therefore, vacate your seats."

Should the men in their council adopt the second course, the War Chief shall order his men to enter the council, to take positions beside the errant chiefs sitting between them wherever possible. When this is accomplished, the war chief holding in his outstretched hand a bunch of black wampum strings shall say to the erring chiefs,

"So now, chiefs of the Five Nations, harken to these last words from your men. You have not heeded the warnings of the General Council of Women, and you have not heeded the warning of the Men of the Nations, all urging you to the right course of action. Since you are determined to resist and to withhold justice from your people, there is only one course for us to adopt."

At this point, the War Chief shall drop the bunch of black wampum, and the men shall spring to their feet and club the erring chiefs to death. Any erring chief may become submissive before the War Chief lets fall the Black Wampum. Then his execution is withheld.

The Black Wampum here used symbolizes that the power to execute is buried, but it may be raised up again by the men. It is buried, but when the occasion arises, they may pull it up and derive their power and authority to act as here described.

60

A broad belt of wampum of thirty-eight rows, having a white heart in the center, on either side of which are two white squares all connected with the heart by white rows of beads shall be the emblem of unity of the Five Nations.

The first of the squares on the left represents the Mohawk Nation and its territory, the second square on the left and near the heart represents the Oneida Nation and its territory, and the white heart in the middle represents the Onondaga Nation and its territory. It also means that the heart of the Five Nations is single in its loyalty to the Great Peace, and that the Great Peace is lodged in the heart (meaning with Onondaga League chiefs) and that the Council Fire is to burn there for the Five Nations. Further it means that the authority is given to advance the cause of peace whereby hostile nations out of the League shall cease warfare. The white square to the right of the heart represents the Cayuga Nation and its territory and the fourth and last square represents the Seneca Nation and its territory.

White here symbolizes that no evil nor jealous thought shall creep into the minds of the chiefs while in Council under the Great Peace. White, the emblem of peace, love, charity, and equity surrounds and guards the Five Nations.

61

Should a great calamity threaten the generations rising and living of the Five United Nations, then he who is able to climb to the top of the Tree of the Great Long Leaves may do so. When he reaches the top of the Tree, he shall look about it in all directions and should he see evil things indeed approaching, then he shall call to the people of the Five United Nations assembled beneath the Tree of the Great Peace and say, "A Calamity threatens your happiness."

Then shall the Chiefs convene in Council and discuss the impending evil. When all the truths relating to the trouble shall be fully known and found to be truths, then shall the people seek a Tree of Kahon-kaahkona, the great swamp elm tree, and when they shall find it they shall assemble their heads together and lodge for a time between its roots. Then, their labors being finished, they may hope for happiness for many days after.

62

When the League of the Five Nations Council declares for a reading of the belts of shell calling to mind these laws, they shall provide for the reader a specially made mat woven of the fibers of wild hemp. The mat shall not be used again for such formality is called "honoring the importance of the law."

63

Should two sons of opposite sides of the Council Fire (iatawa) agree in a desire to hear the reciting of the laws of the Great Peace and so refresh their memories in a way specified by the Founder of the League, they shall notify Atotarho. He shall consult with five of his cousin chiefs and they in turn shall consult their eight brethren. Then should they decide to accede to the request of the two sons from the opposite sides of the Council Fire, Atotarho shall send messengers to notify the chiefs of each of the Five Nations. Then they shall despatch their War Chief to notify their brother and cousin chiefs of the meeting and its time and place.

When all have come and have assembled, Atotarho, in conjunction with his cousin chiefs, shall appoint one chief who shall repeat the laws of the Great Peace to the two sons. Then the chosen one shall repeat the laws of the Great Peace.

64

At the ceremony of the installation of chiefs, if there is only one expert speaker and singer of the Law and the Song of Peace to stand at the Council Fire, then when this speaker and singer has finished addressing one side of the Fire, he shall go to the opposite side and reply to his own speech and song. He shall thus act for both sides of the Fire until the entire ceremony has been completed. Such a speaker and singer shall be termed "Two-faced" because he speaks and sings for both sides of the Fire.

65

I, Tekanawita, and the United Chiefs, now uproot the tallest tree (skaren-hesekowa) and into the hole thereby made we cast all weapons of war. Into the depths of the earth, down into the deep underneath currents of water (Tionawatetsien) flowing to unknown regions we cast all the weapons of strife. We bury them from sight and we plant again the tree. Thus shall the Great Peace be established and hostilities shall no longer be known between the Five Nations, but peace to the United People.

ADOPTIONS

66

The father of a child of great comeliness, learning, ability or specially loved because of some circumstances may, at the will of the child's Clan, select a name from his own (the father's) Clan and bestow it by ceremony, such as is provided. This naming shall be only temporary, and shall be called, "A name hung about the neck."

67

Should any person, a member of the League of Five Nations, especially esteem a man or a woman of another Clan or of a foreign nation, he may choose a name, bestow it upon that person so esteemed. The naming shall be in accord with the ceremony of bestowing names. Such a name is only temporary and shall be called, "A name hung about the neck." A short string of shells shall be delivered with the name as a record and a pledge.

68

Should any member of the Five Nations, a family, or a person belonging to a foreign nation submit a proposal for adoption into a Clan of one of the Five Nations, he or they shall furnish a string of shells, a span in length, as a pledge to the Clan into which he or they wish to be adopted. The Chiefs of the Nation shall then consider the proposal and submit a decision.

69

Any member of the Five Nations, who through esteem or other feelings, wishes to adopt an individual, a family, or a number of families, may offer adoption to him or them, and if accepted, the matter shall be brought to the attention of the Chiefs for confirmation and the chiefs must confirm the adoption.

70

When the adoption of anyone shall have been confirmed by the chiefs of the Nation the chiefs shall address the people of the Nation and say:

"Now you of our Nation, be informed that .... (such a person, such a family, or such families) have ceased forever to bear their birth nation's name and have buried it in the depth of the earth. Henceforth let no one of our nation ever mention the original name or nation of their birth. To do so will hasten the end of our peace."

EMIGRATION

71

When a person or family belonging to the Five Nations desires to abandon their Nation and the territory of the Five Nations they shall inform the chiefs of their Nation and the Council of the League of Five Nations shall take notice of it.

When any person or any of the people of the Five Nations emigrate and reside in a distant region away from the territory of the League of Five Nations, the chiefs of the Five Nations at will may send a messenger carrying a broad belt of black shells and when the messenger arrives he shall call the people together or address them personally, displaying the belt of black shell and they shall know that this is an order for them to return to their original homes and to their Council Fires.

FOREIGN NATIONS

72

The soil of the earth from one end to the other is the property of the people who inhabit it. By birthright, the Onkwehonwe, the original beings, are the owners of the soil which they own and occupy and none other may hold it. The same law has been held from the oldest times.

73

The Great Creator has made us of one blood, and of the same soil he made us, and as only different tongues constitute different nations, he established different hunting grounds and territories and made boundary lines between them.

74

When any alien nation or individual is admitted into the League the admission shall be understood only to be a temporary one. Should the person or nation create loss, do wrong, or cause suffering of any kind to endanger the peace of the League, the League statesmen shall order one of their War Chiefs to reprimand him or them. If a similar offense is committed, the offending party or parties shall be expelled from the territory of the League.

75

When a member of an alien nation comes to the territory of the League and seeks refuge and permanent residence, the statesmen of the Nation to which he comes shall extend hospitality and make him a member of the Nation. Then shall he be accorded equal rights and privileges in all matters except as mentioned here.

76

No body of alien people who have been adopted temporarily shall have a vote in the Council of the chiefs of the League, for only they who have been invested with chieftainship titles may vote in the Council. Aliens have nothing by blood to make claim to a vote and should they have it, not knowing all the traditions of the League, might go against the Great Peace. In this manner, the Great Peace would be endangered and perhaps be destroyed.

77

When the chiefs of the League decide to admit a foreign nation and an adoption is made, the chiefs shall inform the adopted nation that its admission is only temporary. They shall also say to the nation that it must never try to control, to interfere with or to injure the Five Nations, nor disregard the Great Peace or any of its rules or customs. In no way should they cause disturbance or injury. Then shall the adopted nation disregard these injunctions, their adoption will be annulled and they will be expelled.

The expulsion shall be in the following manner: The council shall appoint one of their War Chiefs to convey the message of annulment and he shall say:

"You, ... (naming the nation), listen to me while I speak. I am here to inform you again of the will of the Five Nations Council. It was clearly made known to you at a former time. Now the chiefs of the Five Nations have decided to expel you and cast you out. We disown you now and annul your adoption. Therefore you must look for a path in which to go and lead away all your people. It was you, not we, who committed wrong and caused this sentence of annul-

ment. So then go your way and depart from the territory of the Five Nations and away from the League."

78

Whenever a foreign nation enters the League or accepts the Great Peace, the Five Nations and the foreign nation shall enter into an agreement and compact by which the foreign nation shall endeavor to persuade the other nations to accept the Great Peace.

WAR

79

Skanawati shall be vested with a double office, duty and with double authority. One half of his being shall hold the statesman title, and the other half shall hold the title of War Chief. In the event of war he shall notify the five War Chiefs of the League and command them to prepare for war and have the men ready at the appointed time and place for engagement with the enemy of the Great Peace.

80

When the council of the League has for its object the establishment of the Great Peace among the people of an outside nation and that nation refuses to accept the Great Peace, then by such refusal they bring a declaration of war upon themselves from the Five Nations. Then shall the Five Nations seek to establish the Great Peace by a conquest of the rebellious nation.

81

When the men of the League, now called forth to become warriors, are ready for battle with an obstinate opposing nation that has refused to accept the Great Peace, then one of the five War Chiefs shall be chosen by the warriors of the League to lead the army into battle. It shall be the duty of the War Chief so chosen to come before his warriors and address them. His aim shall be to impress upon them the necessity of good behavior and strict obedience to the commands of the War Chiefs.

He shall deliver an oration exhorting them with great zeal to be brave and courageous and never to be guilty of cowardice. At the conclusion of his oration he shall march forward and commence a War Song, and he shall sing:

Onenhonkenenrenne	*Now I am greatly surprised*
Nekati enkatieratakwe	*And therefore I shall use it,*
Tsiniwakerennotenne	*The power of my War Song.*

Wiskniwakonwentsiake	*I am of the Five Nations,*
Ehtokatiienker ihwaneke	*And I shall make an appeal*
Raohane Rohshatstenserewane	*To the Mighty Creator.*
Nerakwawi, nekati neakitiokwa	*He has furnished this army.*
Rotiskenrakete, nekati ese	*My warriors shall be mighty*
	In the strength of the Creator.
Sashatstenserowane	*Between him and my song they are,*
Tiokenshen, nishonne	*For it was he who gave the song,*
Ne kati ne takwawi	*This war song that I sing.*
Ne karenna enkaterennoten	

82

When the warriors of the Five Nations are on an expedition against the enemy, the War Chief shall sing the War Song as he approaches the country of the enemy and not cease until his scouts have reported that the army is near the enemy's lines when the War Chief shall approach with great caution and prepare for the attack.

83

When peace shall have been established by the termination of the war against a foreign nation, then the War Chief shall cause all the weapons of war to be taken from the nation. Then shall the Great Peace be established and that nation shall observe all the rules of the Great Peace for all time to come.

84

Whenever a foreign nation is conquered or has by their own will accepted the Great Peace, their own system of internal government may continue, but they must cease all warfare against other nations.

85

Whenever a war against a foreign nation is pushed until that nation is about exterminated because of its refusal to accept the Great Peace and if that nation shall by its obstinacy become exterminated, all their rights, property, and territory shall become the property of the Five Nations.

86

Whenever a foreign nation is conquered and the survivors are brought into the territory of the League of Five Nations and placed under the Great Peace, the two shall be known as the Conqueror and the Conquered. A symbolic relationship shall be devised, and be placed in some symbolic position. The conquered nation shall have no voice in the councils of the League in the body of chiefs.

87

When the War of the Five Nations on a foreign rebellious nation is ended, peace shall be restored to that nation by a withdrawal of all their weapons of war by the War Chief of the Five Nations. When all the terms of peace shall have been agreed upon, a state of friendship shall be established.

88

When the proposition to establish the Great Peace is made to a foreign nation, it shall be done in mutual council. The foreign nation is to be persuaded by reason, and urged to come into the Great Peace. If the Five Nations fail to obtain the consent of the nation at the first council, a second council shall be held and upon a second failure, a third council shall be held and this third council shall end the peaceful methods of persuasion. At the third council, the War Chief of the Five Nations shall address the chief of the foreign nation and request him three times to accept the Great Peace. If refusal steadfastly follows, the War Chief shall let the bunch of white lake shells drop from his outstretched hand to the ground, and shall bound quickly forward and club the offending chief to death. War shall thereby be declared, and the War Chief shall have his warriors to back any emergency. War must continue until the contest is won by the Five Nations.

89

When the chiefs of the Five Nations propose to meet in conference with a foreign nation with proposals for an acceptance of the Great Peace, a large band of Warriors shall conceal themselves in a secure place safe from the espionage of the foreign nation but as near at hand as possible. Two warriors shall accompany the Union Chief who carries the proposals, and these warriors shall be especially cunning. Should the chief be attacked, these warriors shall hasten back to the army of warriors with the news of the calamity which fell through the treachery of the foreign nation.

90

When the Five Nations Council declares war, any chief of the League may enlist with the warriors by temporarily renouncing his sacred chieftainship title which he holds through the nomination of his women relatives. The title then reverts to them and they may bestow it upon another temporarily until the war is over, when the chief, if living, may resume his title and seat in the council.

91

A certain wampum belt of black beads shall be the emblem of the authority of the Five War Chiefs to take up the weapons of war and with

their men to resist invasion. This shall be called a War in Defense of
the Territory.

92

If a nation, part of a nation, or more than one nation within the Five
Nations should in any way endeavor to destroy the Great Peace by
neglect or violating its laws and resolve to dissolve the League, such
a nation or such nations shall be deemed guilty of treason and called
enemies of the League and the Great Peace.

It shall then be the duty of the chiefs of the League who remain faithful
to resolve to warn the offending people. They shall be warned once,
and if a second warning is necessary, they shall be driven from the
territory of the League by the War Chief and his men.

RIGHTS OF THE PEOPLE

93

Whenever an especially important matter or a great emergency is presented before the League Council and the nature of the matter effects
the entire body of Five Nations, threatening their utter ruin, then the
chiefs of the League must submit the matter to the decision of their
people and the decision of the people shall affect the decision of the
League Council. This decision shall be a confirmation of the voice of
the people.

94

The men of every Clan of the Five Nations shall have a Council Fire
ever burning in readiness for a Council of the Clan. When it seems
necessary for the interest of the people, for a council to be held to discuss the welfare of the Clan, then the men may gather about the fire.
This council shall have the same rights as the Council of Women.

95

The women of every clan of the Five Nations shall have a Council Fire
ever burning in readiness for a council of the Clan. When in their opinion it seems necessary for the interest of the people, they shall hold a
council, and their decision and recommendation shall be introduced
before the Council of Chiefs by the War Chief for its consideration.

96

All the Clan Council Fires of a Nation or of the Five Nations may unite
into one general Council Fire, or delegates from all the Council Fires
may be appointed to unite in a general Council for discussing the interest
of the people. The people shall have the right to make appointments,

and to delegate their power to others of their number. When their council shall have come to a conclusion on any matter, their decision shall be reported to the Council of the Nation or the League Council (as the case may require) by the War Chief or the War Chiefs.

97

Before the real people united their nations, each Nation had its own Council Fires. Before the Great Peace their councils were held. The Five Council Fires shall continue to burn as before and they are not quenched. The chiefs of each Nation in the future shall settle their Nation's affairs at this Council Fire governed always by the laws and rules of the Council of the League and the Great Peace.

98

If either a nephew or a niece see an irregularity in the performance of the functions of the Great Peace and its laws, in the League Council or in the conferring of chief titles in an improper way, through their War Chief they may demand that such actions become subject to correction, and that the matter conform to the ways prescribed by the law of the Great Peace.

CEREMONIES

99

The rites and festivals of each nation shall remain undisturbed and shall continue as before, because they were given by the people of old times as useful and necessary for the good of men.

100

It shall be the duty of the chiefs of each brotherhood to confer at the approach of the time of the Midwinter Thanksgiving and to notify the people of the approaching festival. They shall hold a council over the matter, and arrange its details and begin the Thanksgiving five days after the moon of Tiskonah is new. The people shall assemble at the appointed place and the nephews shall notify the people of the time and place. From the beginning to the end, the chiefs shall preside over the Thanksgiving and address the people from time to time.

101

It shall be the duty of the appointed managers of the Thanksgiving festivals to do all that is needful for carrying out the duties of the occasions.

The recognized festivals of Thanksgiving shall be the Midwinter Thanksgiving, the Maple or Sugar Making Thanksgiving, the Raspberry Thanksgiving, the Strawberry Thanksgiving, the Cornplanting Thanksgiving, the Corn Hoeing Thanksgiving, The Little Festival of Green Corn, the Great Festival of Ripe Corn, and the Complete Thanksgiving for the Harvest. Each nation's festivals shall be held in their Longhouses.

102

When the Thanksgiving for the Green Corn comes, the special managers, both the men and women, shall give it careful attention and do their duties properly.

103

When the Ripe Corn Thanksgiving is celebrated, the chiefs of the Nation must give it the same attention as they give to the Midwinter Thanksgiving.

104

Whenever any man proves himself by his good life and his knowledge of good things, he shall be recognized by the chiefs as a Teacher of Peace and Kariwiio and the people shall hear him.

INSTALLATION SONG
105

The song used in installing the new chief of the League shall be sung by Atotarho and it shall be:

Haii, haii Akwa wiio	*(It is good indeed*
Haii, haii Akonhewawatha	*That a broom*
Haii, haii Skaweiesekowa	*A great wing*
Haii, haii Yonkwawi	*Is given me*
Haii, haii Iakonhewatha	*For a sweeping instrument.)*

106

Whenever a person properly entitled desires to learn the Song of Peace, he is privileged to do so, but he must prepare a feast at which his teachers may sit with him and sing. The feast is provided that no misfortune may befall them for singing the song when no Chief is installed.

PROTECTION OF THE HOUSE
107

A certain sign shall be known to all the people of the Five Nations which shall denote that the owner or occupant of a house is absent. A stick or pole in a slanting or leaning position shall indicate this and be the sign.

Every person not entitled to enter the house by right of living within upon seeing such a sign shall not enter the house by day or by night, but shall keep as far away as his business will permit.

FUNERALS

108

At the funeral of a chief of the League, these words are said:

"Now we become reconciled as you start away. You were once a chief of the League of Five Nations, and the united people trusted you. Now we release you, for it is true that it is no longer possible for us to walk about together on the earth. Now, therefore, we lay it (the body) here. Here we lay it away. Now then we say to you, 'Persevere onward to the place where the Creator dwells in peace. Let not the things of the earth hinder you. Let nothing that transpired while you lived hinder you. In hunting, you once delighted; in the game of lacrosse, you once took delight, and in the feast and pleasant occasions your mind was amused, but now do not allow thoughts of these things to give you trouble.

'Let not your relatives hinder you and also let not your friends and associates trouble your mind. Regard none of these things.'

"Now then, in turn, you here present who are related to the man, and you who were his friends and associates, behold the path that is yours also! Soon we ourselves will be left in that place. For this reason, hold yourselves in restraint as you go from place to place. In your actions and in your conversation do no idle thing. Speak not idle talk, neither gossip. Be careful of this, and speak not and do not give away to evil behaviour. One year is the time that you must abstain from unseemingly levity, but if you can not do this for ceremony, ten days is the time to regard these things for respect."

109

At the funeral of a War Chief, say:

"Now we become reconciled as you start away. Once you were a War Chief of the Five Nations League, and the United People trusted you as their guard from the enemy. (The remainder is the same as the address at the funeral of a chief.)

110

At the funeral of a warrior say:

"Now we become reconciled as you start away. Once you were a devoted provider and protector of your family, and you were ready to take part in battles for the Five Nations. The United People trusted..." (The remainder is the same as the address at the funeral of a chief.)

111

At the funeral of a young man say:

"Now we become reconciled as you start away. In the beginning of your career you are taken away, and the flower of your life is withered away."
(The remainder is the same as the address at the funeral of a chief.)

112

At the funeral of a chief woman say:

"Now we become reconciled as you start away. You were once a chief woman in the League of Five Nations. You once were a Mother of the Nations. Now we release you for it is true that it is no longer possible for us to walk about together on the earth. Now, therefore, we lay it (the body) here. Here we lay it away. Now then we say to you, 'Persevere onward to the place where the Creator dwells in peace. Let not the things of the earth hinder you. Let nothing that transpired while you lived hinder you. Looking after your family was a sacred duty, and you were faithful. You were one of the many joint heirs of the chieftainship titles. Feastings were yours and you had pleasant occasions...'"
(The remainder is the same as the address at the funeral of a chief.)

113

At the funeral of a woman of the people say:

"Now we become reconciled as you start away. You were once a woman in the flower of life and the bloom is now withered away. You once held a sacred position as mother of the Nation. (etc.) Looking after your family was a sacred duty and you were faithful. Feastings..."
(The remainder is the same as the funeral of a chief.)

114

At the funeral of an infant or young woman say:

"Now we become reconciled as you start away. You were a tender bud and gladdened our hearts for only a few days. Now the bloom has withered away...(etc.) Let none of these things that transpired on earth hinder. Let nothing that happened while you lived hinder you."
(The remainder is the same as at the funeral of a chief.)

115

When an infant dies within three days, mourning shall continue only five days. Then shall you gather the little boys and girls at the house of mourning and at the funeral feast, a speaker shall address the children and bid them to be happy once more, though by death, gloom has been cast over them. Then shall the children be again in the sunshine.

116

When a dead person is brought to the burial place, the speaker on the opposite side of the Council Fire shall bid the bereaved family cheer their minds once more and rekindle their hearth fires in peace, to put their house in order and once again be in brightness for darkness has covered them. He shall say that the black clouds shall roll away and that the bright blue sky is visible once more. Therefore they shall be at peace in the sunshine again.

117

Three strings of shell one span in length shall be employed in addressing the assemblage at the burial of the dead. The speaker shall say:

"Hearken you who are here, this body is to be covered. Assemble in this place again in ten days hence, for it is the decree of the Creator that mourning shall cease when ten days have expired. Then a feast shall be made."

Then at the expiration of ten days, the Speaker shall say:

"Continue to listen you who are here. The ten days of mourning have expired and your mind must now be freed of sorrow as before the loss of your relative. The relatives have decided to make a little compensation to those who have assisted at the funeral. It is a mere expression of thanks. This is to the one who did the cooking while the body was lying in the house. Let her come forward and receive this gift and be dismissed from the task." (In substance, this will be repeated for everyone who assisted in any way until all have been remembered.)

Chapter 5

The Golden Word

Unheard: Oratory

Because the word is magic, possessing the power of incantation and being as one with Wah'kon-tah, the Native American sang for power in his songs. He spoke for power around the council fire, in speeches to his people, and in negotiations with the conquering white man. His great respect for the word, an inherent love and need of ritual, a memory shaped and sharpened by necessity (in the absence of writing)—these elements combined to make the American Indian an artist with words.

The oratorical skills had been developed long before the arrival of the European, speeches and debate being the media of idea exchange among peoples without print. The organizational powers, the retentive memories, the capacity for maximum communication in a minimum of words is not unique among Native Americans, however. The eloquence of Homeric Greek heroes and the historical accounts of Greek warriors who could repeat the plays of Sophocles, Euripides, and Aristophanes after only one hearing attest to the obvious fact that memory is a reliable, adequate tool when man needs it. Print causes him to need it less and less, so it naturally becomes less and less reliable as his technological aids minimize the need. The obvious problems accompanying his loss probably account for the fascination of the transplant Americans in treaty negotiations when the Indians recalled minor points with absolute accuracy, a feat the white negotiators checked again and again, always finding the memory of the Native American reliable as it was verified by the written record.

The oratorical arts of the Indian so impressed the European-American that he used the speeches as compositional models in the schools that trained his children even as he disregarded the organization, logic, and presentation he so admired. That ambivalence is not intellectually understandable, but reason, intellectual discipline, and honesty do not characterize the white man's behavior when possession and material benefit are at issue. And they were always at issue in one way or another in all exchanges between representatives of the two cultural groups.

Before the arrival of the white man, the oral traditions of the people of this hemisphere had shaped the oratorical skills as, around the council fires, the eloquent and the respected of the tribe presented the seriously reasoned argument, delivered the scathing and witty charge, or enthralled the audience with reports of courageous conduct and valorous deeds. Nor were those audiences easy to mislead with spurious reasoning, to move with unfair, emotionally charged arguments, or to deceive with hyperbole or falsification. Listening attentively with their own developed powers of reasoning, remarkable memories, love of truth, and suspicion of ambiguity, they were quick to challenge, repudiate, and dismiss as unworthy any but the most considered presentation.

Training of the young men of the tribe included their attendance at the presentations, for by observation and analysis they learned the art of oratory as they absorbed past history and current events. They were, in reality, the blank sheets of the next generation's records, the new editions that would come into their own custodial care. Such sessions were audio-visual presentations of the highest order, the technical elements being the human body that projected nuance with every gesture, the human voice that supplied its own musical background, the intellectual process that organized, edited, revised, and delivered the finished speech without notes or prompters.

In some cases, memory aids were employed. These aids included knotted strings, thongs with evenly spaced shells or beads (serving the same function as the beads on a rosary), or wampum strings and belts whose colors and patterns served as mnemonic devices in the fashion of acronyms. The efficiency of these memory aids is unquestioned if one considers the fact that the Great Law of Peace survived the centuries, its preservation depending on the undeviating accuracy of its oral transmitters aided only by the wampum belts now housed in the State Museum of New York at Albany. The ceremonial prayers of many tribes extended over a period of hours and allowed for no deviation whatsoever in the wording on pain of displeasing the gods who would then withhold rain or game or whatever boon was sought.

Only among the Sioux and the Kiowa were historical accounts "recorded." They too were mnemonic, however, as they were pictures—symbols and figures drawn or painted on dressed hides. These calendar pictures are sometimes called the "winter-count" because, created in the winter, they depicted the most important event of the preceding twelve months and, collectively, served as an historical record for those instructed in their meaning.

Whether or not the orator used memory aids, he did follow a ritual formula or presentation: unhurried delivery compounded of ritually acceptable phrases at given intervals and stylized gestures; deliberate pauses for audience approval after each important point or stylistically polished phrase the speaker deemed meritorious; and, in some tribes, the bestowal of gifts of wampum or horses after each particularly important point—a ritual giving that attested to the honor, integrity, or sincerity of the speaker. Such gift-giving consumed a great deal of time (often impoverishing the speaker in the process), so words were carefully chosen for maximum communication because the delivery ritual was so lengthy.

In areas where gift-giving did not accompany the speeches, oratory suffered in the mouths of the loquacious bores who constitute a part of every society, primitive or technological. Since good manners precluded rude curtailment of their earned rights to be heard, the garrulous were manipulated into speaking positions near the end of session, their own respect for courteous conduct imposing brevity upon them.

The dignity and impressiveness of Native American oratory was noted by no less an artist with English words than Thomas Jefferson:

Before the revolution, the Indians were in the habit of coming often and in great numbers to the seat of government where I was very much with them. I knew much the Great Outacite, the warrior and orator of the Cherokees; he was always the guest of my father, on his journeys to and from Williamsburg. I was in his camp when he made his great farewell oration to his people the evening before his departure for England...; his sounding voice, distinct articulation, animated action, and the solemn silence of his people at their several fires, filled me with awe and veneration, although I did not understand a word he uttered.[1]

It is not unreasonable to assume the white men as a group did not understand a word the Native American uttered

[1]Letter from Thomas Jefferson to John Adams, March, 1812. In John P. Foley, ed., *The Jefferson Cyclopedia* (New York, 1900), pp. 422–23.

even though translators acceptable to the Indian were on hand to render services that can only be considered respectable, for the Native American would have otherwise rejected the services. The white man had, unfortunately, already decided on the outcome of treaty sessions, the exchange being a necessary concession to that myth of fairness perpetuated by the invading, conquering, dispossessing horde of men with insatiable appetites for land.

The extant Native American orations and speeches are a matter of record because they are a part of either concession assemblies or capitulation ceremonies which the transplant Americans wished recorded for future proof of legal or moral good faith.

The position of the translator in such cases is by no means enviable. Clyde Kluckhorn and Dorothea Leighton summarize the problem in *The Navaho*, a book so objectively sound that the fairness of the authors is above question.

The interpreter's lot is not a happy one. He is under pressure from both the Navaho and the English-speaker to translate quickly, and so does not have time to think out the full implications of what he is saying in either language. Old Navahos are exasperated when the interpreter asks them to repeat or re-phrase some verb form that has baffled him. Whites become impatient at the amount of time consumed. Both sides blame the interpreter if they sense that effective communication is not being established. At the same time they too frequently trust the translations, believing that their own meanings have been transmitted intact and without essential distortion. Most Navahos and whites alike assume naïvely that an interpreter can or ought to be able to work with the precision of a machine. The interpreter deserves sympathy for his almost impossible job, for it is too much to expect one man to take the whole responsibility for bridging the gulf between worlds that are as different as their languages.

To turn a sentence from English into Navaho or from Navaho into English involves a great deal more than choosing the proper word for word equivalents from a dictionary. Bewildered by the lack of structural correspondences between the two tongues, most interpreters succumb to one or both of two temptations: either they leave out a great deal in passing from Navaho to English (or vice versa); or they translate all too freely, projecting their own meanings into the sentences they "translate." Sometimes difficulties arise because the interpreter tries to stick too closely to the literal text of the English. For example, at a Navaho Council meeting within the last few years there was a discussion of how to develop mineral and gas resources on the Reservation. The white speaker from Washington who introduced the matter used the phrase "hidden beneath the ground." When translated literally into Navaho this had the sense of "secreted beneath the ground." The Council got the sense that there was some skulduggery in the whole business and got so worked up that certain measures which should have been passed in the interests of the war had to be held over until the next meeting.

A Navaho Service interpreter may take a speech that an official has couched in conciliatory and expository English, and by his compression and by the Navaho forms he selects, may give the Navaho audience the impression that a brusque order has been issued. The official meant to present a policy for discussion, or to explain and win the assent of the Navaho group to a policy that had been decided upon. But the English nuances which imply courtesy and interest in Navaho opinion are too difficult to get over (at least without long thought in advance), so The People get the sense that they are being told to do thus and so without any if's, and's, or but's. On the basis of detailed examination of certain cases that are probably all too typical, it can be asserted without any doubt whatsoever that the resentment and resistance that occurred at certain points during the stock reduction program might have been avoided, or at least much mitigated, if communication had not been so faulty from inaccurate interpreting.

One should not expect too much from interpreters, but one should expect the right things.[2]

Although the problem here is in the translation of English-Navaho, the basic problem would be applicable to any transplant American-Native American exchange. By way of further elaboration, this comparison from the same work reveals the problem in all its complexity.

Further, the fluid and ambiguous English sentence makes all white men seem liars to Navahos, whose language is so literal and precise. All these feelings and the conflict between old ways and new ways, between the school generation and nonschool generation, come out vividly in the following excerpt from the report turned in by a Navaho government employee who had been sent to a Navaho ceremonial to show motion pictures as part of the prewar educational program in connection with soil conservation and livestock management.

Original	*Translation*
We get to dance late in the evening and we went to call of that dance to talk to him instead he pointed to the Navaho policemen of that dance and we told them right from begin to end of our work and what we are trying to do to the people. He said there no just such thing the land sick or die we leaving just found we leave on our sheep and goats what do we about show we no white	We got to the dance late in the evening. We went to call on the leader of that dance to talk to him. Instead he pointed to the Navaho policemen of that section. We told them everything about our work, from the beginning to the end, and what we were trying to do for the people. They said, "There is just no such thing as that the land can get sick or die. We are living just fine. We

[2]Cambridge, Mass., 1946, pp. 210–11.

Original

men. The white told us lie so many time now and we don't care to believe now. I said him what the lie about. He told us he was going to have Navaho the work and money if they only reduce the sheep and goats now then the goats has gone and no work no money don't you think we will try again and then if we let white man work around our reservation and on they say it they land because they worked on and soon they will try to ran the land all over so we don't want anything now we living good rite now.

I told them we were not a white man but one and we not asking to save land for someone else for the money this is to tell you save by you own hand and head and that it will be your land and to tell you that you could have a better wool and sheep in peace and all way as it is they is many sheep and goats right now and that the land is about to go to pieces now if we don't care make we lose our land some day.

Well they said if you are going to tell us we will hear you at big dance tonight but we don't want the show. They were four big head men there and three men wanted show and one not.

The head medicine man of that dance came up after we get the show wagon was set up. He ask what's all the things was have and what's all about we going to do there.

Translation

live on our sheep and goats. What do we know about a show? We are no white men. The whites have told us lies so many times that we don't care to believe them now."

I said to them, "What lie are you talking about?" They said, "They told us Navahos would have work and money if they would only reduce the sheep and goats. Now then the goats have gone, but no work, no money. Don't think we will try it again. If we let white men work around our Reservation and on it, they will say it is their land because they worked on it, and soon they will run all over the land. So we don't want anything now. We are living well right now."

I told them we were not white men, except one of us, and we were not asking them to save the land for somebody else or for money. We wanted to show them how to save it by their own hands and heads, and it would be their own land. We wanted to tell them how they could have better wool and sheep, in peace and for always. As it is now there are too many sheep and goats, and the land is about to go to pieces. If we don't take care of it, we won't have any land someday.

"Well," they said, "if you are going to talk to us, you can do it at the big dance tonight, but we don't want any show." There were four big head-men there. Three men wanted the show and one did not.

The head medicine man of the dance came up after we got the show wagon all set up. He asked about all the things we had there and what we were going to do.

Original

I told him we going to give a picture show if they can let us. He said to go on and show to white men and not come around to their ceremonial place and try to take picture and make money on it.

I told him this was the Soil Conservation Service work with Indian to understand just what it mean to save the land from Erosion and over grazing land by too many goats and sheep that just running around over the land.

Why your coming back again with the white man idea trying to do away the goats and sheep from our poor people as you might think your helping your people but you not for you helping the white or the people of Erosion are trying to run the Navaho land and when they do we the poor one are going to be the end and you young men that are trying to be like a white man are going to get what you wanted and not the poor one.

I tell him that I was Navaho myself that we were working for Navaho not against them and that if we can show let our old man Police talk to them.

He told me that if we was going to have show and teaching why don't we go to school and not come around or ceremonial place for that was no place for it.

One woman beside us objected but I didn't ask the reason but soon learned that it was for the fox pictures we show at first dance and she afraid we show again but we didn't

Translation

I told him we were going to give a picture show if they would let us. He said to go on and show it to the white men, but not to come around the Navahos' ceremonial place and try to take pictures and make money on it.

I told him this was Soil Conservation Service work, trying to make the Indians understand just what it means to save the land from erosion, and how the land was being overgrazed by too many goats and sheep that were just running around over it.

"Why are you coming back again with the white man's idea of trying to do away with the sheep and goats of our poor people? You might think you are helping your people, but you are not. You are helping the whites, or the Soil Erosion people. They are trying to run the Navaho land, and when they do it is going to be the end for us poor ones. You young men that are trying to be like white men are going to get what you want, but not the poor ones."

I told him I was a Navaho myself, and that we were all working for the Navahos, not against them and to let our old policeman ask the people if we can have the show.

He said to me, "If you are going to have a show and some teaching, why don't you go to a school instead of coming around our ceremonial, which is no place for it?"

One woman beside us objected. I didn't ask her the reason, but I soon learned that it was because of the coyote pictures we showed at the first dance. She was afraid we were

Original	*Translation*
for it was strong up against religious ceremonial.	going to show that one again, but we didn't because it is a very bad thing to have around a religious ceremonial.

Finally some Indian want to see and they all started talking about it and it was OK. After the show we heard nothing bad about the talk but just a little about the picture. That was a picture about snake which part of the great ceremonial and they didn't want to see in first place but they like the show and talk.	Finally some Indians said they wanted to see the picture, and they all started talking about it and decided it was OK. After the show we heard nothing bad about the talk, just a little they didn't like about the picture. There was a picture of a snake, which is a part of the great ceremonial, and they didn't want to see it. But they liked the show and the talk.[3]

One additional note of explanation is worth mentioning before you begin to hear these voices from a ghostly past. "Brother," as indicated earlier, was a stylized form of address designed to reveal the honesty that would characterize the words because it signifies regard for an unequivocal equal. Variations on the form suggest the response desired by the speaker. These forms are, in themselves, indicative of the subtlety of the speaker.

When Osamekun, Massassoit of the Wampanoag Nation, died, rule passed to his two sons, Wamsutta and Metacomet. The conservative Osamekun had generously given land to the Plymouth colonists with the words, "Englishmen, take that land (parts of Massachusetts and Rhode Island) for none is left to occupy it. Manito has swept its people from the face of the earth." His brother Quadequina and two Wampanoag leaders, Samoset and Squanto, approved the gift, and the colonists began their tenure under the auspices of the kindly massassoit of Pokanoket (known today as Mount Hope, near Bristol, Rhode Island). By the time of his death, the colonists had set the Narragansetts and the Mohicans against the Pequots, defeated that culturally advanced people, and sold all survivors into slavery in the Bermudas, Massachusetts, and Connecticut. With the passing of the Pequot, genocide had been deliberately accomplished by the Christian colonists. Nor did the colonists encounter further difficulty with the Native Americans until Massassoit Osamekun's death in 1660. Sensing the sons of the massassoit would not be so easily mollified, the English conferred the

---

[3]Ibid., pp. 117–20.

title of Prince Alexander on Wamsutta, Prince Philip on Metacomet. When the colonists observed a change in the Wampanoag temper, they called Wamsutta to Duxbury and he died under mysterious circumstances in the home of a friend in Marshfield. Philip became King on the Wampanoag throne and attempted to continue the peace of his father. Between the impatience of the Narragansetts (who saw the smug superiority and greed of the colonists as the threat they were) and the humiliations he suffered in being forced to sign two treaties with the now strong colonists, King Philip was forced to involve himself and his nation in the war that bears his name. When it ended on August 12, 1676, with Metacomet's death, organized Native American resistance also ended in New England. It is sad indeed that the present Prince Metacomet (Walter Peek, co-editor of this collection) is greeted with blank stares when he is asked to identify his tribe. The transplant American, as a general rule, has so little concept of his own history that he has never heard of King Philip's War. One hundred and fifty years after King Philip's death, William Apes, an Indian, delivered a "Eulogy on King Philip" at the Odeon Club in Boston. Included was this speech of Osamekun's son, Metacomet.

The Prophecy of Metacomet

Brothers,—You see this vast country before us, which the Great Spirit gave to our fathers and us; you see the buffalo and deer that now are our support.—Brothers, you see these little ones, our wives and children, who are looking to us for food and raiment; and you now see the foe before you, that they have grown insolent and bold; that all our ancient customs are disregarded; the treaties made by our fathers and us are broken, and all of us insulted; our council fires disregarded, and all the ancient customs of our fathers; our brothers murdered before our eyes, and their spirits cry to us for revenge. Brothers, these people from the unknown world will cut down our groves, spoil our hunting and planting grounds, and drive us and our children from the graves of our fathers, and our council fires, and enslave our women and children.

Competitors and enemies in Europe, the British and the French vied for the rich fur country of the Canadian and American Northeast, home of the Huron and the Five Nations. At Fort Cadarqui in 1684, the French threatened representatives of the Five Nations with an alliance between the European powers that would "burn the castles of the Five Nations, and destroy you." Answering the Canadian governor, the Onondaga orator Garangula responded with a statement indicating the independent spirit and the ecological awareness of the Native American.

They Left None
of the Beavers Alive

Yonondio! [the title always given to the Canadian governor by the Five Nations]—I honor you, and the warriors that are with me all likewise honor you. Your interpreter has finished your speech; I now begin mine. My words make haste to reach your ears. Hearken to them.

Yonondio!—You must have believed when you left Quebec, that the sun had burnt up all the forests, which render our country inaccessible to the French, or that the lakes had so far overflown the banks, that they had surrounded our castles, and that it was impossible for us to get out of them. Yes, surely you must have dreamed so, and the curiosity of seeing so great a wonder, has brought you so far. *Now* you are undeceived. I and the warriors here present, are come to assure you, that the Senecas, Cayugas, Onondagas, Oneidas and Mohawks are yet alive. I thank you in their name, for bringing back into their country the calumet, which your predecessor received from their hands. It was happy for you, that you left under ground that murdering hatchet, so often dyed in the blood of the French.

Hear, Yonondio!—I do not sleep. I have my eyes open. The sun, which enlightens me, discovers to me a great captain at the head of a company of soldiers, who speaks as if he were dreaming. He says, that he only came to the lake to smoke on the great calumet with the Onondagas. But *Garangula* says, that he sees the contrary; that it was to knock them on the head, if sickness had not weakened the arms of the French. I see Yonondio raving in a camp of sick men, whose lives the Great Spirit has saved by inflicting this sickness on them.

Hear, Yonondio!—Our women had taken their clubs, our children and old men had carried their bows and arrows into the heart of your camp, if our warriors had not disarmed them, and kept them back, when your messenger came to our castles. It is done and I have said it.

Hear, Yonondio!—We plundered none of the French, but those that carried guns, powder and balls to the Twightwies and Chictaghicks, because those arms might have cost us our lives. Herein we follow the example of the Jesuits, who break all the kegs of rum brought to our castles, lest the drunken Indians should knock them on the head. Our warriors have not beaver enough to pay for all the arms they have taken, and our old men are not afraid of the war. This belt preserves my words.

We carried the English into our lakes, to trade there with the Utawawas and Quatoghies, as the Adirondacks brought the French to our castles, to carry on a trade, which the English say is theirs. We are born free. We neither depend on Yonondio nor Corlear. [The name given the governors of New York.] We may go where we please, and carry with us whom we please, and buy and sell what we please. If your allies be your slaves, use them as such, command them to receive no other but your people. This belt preserves my words.

We knock the Twightwies and Chictaghicks on the head, because they had cut down the trees of peace, which were the limits of our country. They have hunted beaver on our lands. They have acted contrary to the customs of all Indians, for they left none of the beavers alive,—they killed both male and female. They brought the Satanas into their country, to take part with them, after they had concerted ill designs against us. We have done less than either the English or French, that have usurped the lands of so many Indian nations, and chased them from their own country. This belt preserves my words.

Hear, Yonondio!—What I say is the voice of all the Five Nations. Hear what they answer. Open your ears to what they speak. The Senecas, Cayugas, Onondagas, Oneidas and Mohawks say, that when they buried the hatchet at Cadarackui, in the presence of your predecessor, in the middle of the fort, they planted the tree of peace in the same place, to be there carefully preserved: That in the place of a retreat for soldiers, that fort might be a rendezvous for merchants: that in place of arms and ammunition of war, beavers and merchandise should only enter there.

Hear, Yonondio!—Take care for the future that so great a number of soldiers as appear there, do not choke the tree of peace planted in so small a fort. It will be a great loss, if, after it had so easily taken root, you should stop its growth, and prevent its covering your country and ours with its branches. I assure you, in the name of the Five Nations, that our warriors shall dance to the calumet of peace under its leaves. They shall remain quiet on their mats, and shall never dig up the hatchet, till their brother Yonondio, or Corlear, shall either jointly or separately endeavor to attack the country, which the Great Spirit has given to our ancestors. This belt preserves my words, and this other the authority which the Five Nations have given me.

[Here the orator paused for a moment, and then addressed himself to Monsieur Le Maine, who stood near him, acting as interpreter.]

Take courage, Ohguesse! You have spirit—Speak! Explain my words. Forget nothing. Tell all that your brethren and friends say to Yonondio, your Governor, by the mouth of Garangula, who loves you, and desires you to accept of this present of beaver, and take part with me in my feast, to which I invite you. This present of beaver is sent to Yonondio, on the part of the Five Nations.

The white men who were to become Pennsylvanians and their leader, William Penn, were, in the main, more honorable in their dealings with the Native American than any other group. Still, their obsessive need to prove to themselves that their Elohim was the "one true god" caused chronic confrontation between the religious philosophies that could have coexisted peacefully had the Christian missionaries been less insecure about their religion. About 1710, a Swedish missionary attempted to persuade the Susquehanna (Conestoga) that they were damned eternally as a result of "original sin" unless they converted to Christianity. A Conestoga chief so logically refuted the contention that the missionary sent the refutation to his theological superiors with a plea for argumentative aid.

We Find the Christians Depraved

Our forefathers were under a strong persuasion (as we are) that those who act well in this life will be rewarded in the next according to the degrees of their virtues, and, on the other hand, that those who behave wickedly here will undergo such punishments hereafter as were proportionate to the crimes they were guilty of. This has been constantly and invariably received and ackowledged for a truth through every successive generation of our ancestors. It could not, then, have taken its rise from fable; for human fiction, however artfully and plausibly contrived, can never gain credit long among people where free inquiry is allowed, which was never denied by our ancestors....Now we desire to propose some questions. Does he believe that our forefathers, men eminent for their piety, constant and warm in their pursuit of virtue, hoping thereby to merit eternal happiness, were all damned? Does he think that we who are zealous imitators in good works, and influenced by the same motives as we are, earnestly endeavoring with the greatest circumspection to tread the path of integrity, are in a state of damnation? If that be his sentiment, it is surely as impious as it is bold and daring....Let us suppose that some heinous crimes were committed by some of our ancestors, like to that we are told of another race of people. In such a case God would certainly punish the criminal, but would never involve us that are innocent in the guilt. Those who think otherwise must make the Almighty a very whimsical, evil-natured being....Once more: are the Christians more virtuous, or, rather, are they not more vicious than we are? If so, how came it to pass that they are the objects of God's beneficence, while we are neglected? Does he daily confer his favors without reason and with so much partiality? In a word, we find the Christians much more depraved in their morals than we are; and we judge from their doctrine by the badness of their lives.

The Ottawa orator and leader, Pontiac, possessed all of those qualities that, among the transplant Americans, are the mark of a messiah or a general or a president. The objective historian of some distant future may assess his conduct indicative of greatness. "Conspiracy," as used by Francis Parkman and other white historians to designate Pontiac's strategy, is a denigratory word the future historian may change to "diplomatic and religious leadership." The quality of that leadership is revealed in Pontiac's summary of grievances against the British. The date of the speech: 1763.

The Words of the Master of Life to the Wolf

It is important for us, my brothers, that we exterminate from our land this nation which only seeks to kill us. You see, as well as I do, that we cannot longer get our supplies as we had them from our brothers, the French. The English sell us the merchandise twice dearer than the French sold them to us, and their wares [are worth] nothing. Hardly have we bought a blanket, or something else to cover us, than we must think of having another of the kind. When we want to start for our winter quarters they will give us no credit, as our brothers, the French, did. When I go to the English chief to tell him that some of our comrades are dead, instead of weeping for the dead, as our brothers, the

French, used to do, he makes fun of me and of you. When I ask him for something for our sick, he refuses, and tells me that he has no need of us. You can well see by that that he seeks our ruin. Well, my brothers, we must all swear to ruin them! Nor will we wait any longer, nothing impedes us. There are very few of them, and we can easily overcome them. All the nations who are our brothers strike a blow at them; why should we not do the same? Are we not men like them? Have I not shown you the war-belts which I have received from our great father, the Frenchman? He tells us to strike; why should we not listen to his words? Whom fear we? It is time. Are we afraid that our brothers, the French, who are here amongst us, would hinder us? They know not our designs, and could not if they wanted to. You know as well as I do, that when the English came to our country to drive out our father, Belleestre, they have taken away all the guns of the Frenchmen, and that they have no weapons to defend themselves. Thus it is. Let us strike all together! If there are any French who take up for them, we shall strike them as we do the English. Remember what the Master of Life has said to our brother, the Wolf. That regards us all as well as them. I have sent war-belts and word to our brothers, the Sauteux, of the Saginaw, and to our brothers, the Ottawas, of Michelimakinak, and to those of the river's mouth to join them with us, and they will not tarry to come. While waiting for them, let us commence the attack. There is no more time to lose, and when the English shall be defeated, we shall see what to do, and we shall cut off the passage so that they cannot come back to our country.

Tah-ha-yu-ta (His Eyelashes Stick Out) was an Iroquois who befriended Philadelphia mayor James Logan and took his name as a mark of friendship. Long an advocate of peaceful accommodation with the whites, Logan was forced to take arms after the Earl of Dunmore laid territorial claim to the southern portion of the Northwest Territory, land that had been "guaranteed" the Native American in the Proclamation of 1763. During Lord Dunmore's War, a white settler named Daniel Greathouse moved a party of men against an unarmed party of Indian women and children accompanied by one man. In the encounter, Greathouse killed Logan's wife and children and only brother, the one male in the party. Logan did not turn the other cheek this time. He allied himself with those Iroquois, Delaware, Shawnee, and Wyandotte who had banded under the Shawnee leader Cornstalk. Their defeat at Point Pleasant, Ohio, forced them to surrender the Kentucky hunting grounds and all lands south of the Ohio River. Logan refused to attend the peace council, his refusal being delivered to Lord Dunmore by a white emissary in 1774. Ultimately killed by a party of whites, Logan was memorialized in the eclectic readers used in white schools. His speech served as a compositional model for the children, a model Thomas Jefferson assessed: "I challenge the whole orations of Demosthenes and Cicero, and of any more eminent, to produce a single passage superior to the speech of Logan."

Logan's Speech

I appeal to any white man to say, if ever he entered Logan's cabin hungry, and he gave him not meat; if ever he came cold and naked, and he clothed him not. During the course of the last long and bloody war, Logan remained idle in his cabin, an advocate of peace. Such was my love for the whites, that my countrymen pointed as they passed, and said, "Logan is the friend of white man." I had even thought to have lived with you but for the injuries of one man. Colonel Cresap,* the last spring, in cold blood and unprovoked, murdered all the relations of Logan,† not even sparing my women and children. There

---

*Logan never learned his people had been killed by Greathouse. He died thinking this colonel in Dunmore's army had led the attack.

†Historians argue endlessly over the identity of "all the relations of Logan." Some say he had no wife, no children. Others say he had a wife who was not killed in the massacre.

runs not a drop of my blood in the veins of any living creature. This called on me for revenge. I have sought it; I have killed many; I have fully glutted my vengeance. For my country, I rejoice at the beams of peace. But do not harbor a thought that this is the joy of *fear.* Logan never felt fear. He will not turn on his heel to save his life. Who is there to mourn for Logan?—Not one!

The Delaware Pachgantschilas saw the struggle between the transplant American and the British as an internecine war whose ultimate outcome would destroy the Native American. The transplant American was the most imperative evil only because of his propinquity. In 1781 Pachgantschilas made that position clear to his people. "Father" refers to the British, "sons" and "children" to the colonists, "Long Knives" to the transplant Americans.

A Powerful Nation Divided

Friends and kinsmen!—Listen to what I say to you! You see a great and powerful nation divided! You see the father fighting against the son, and the son against the father!—The father has called on his Indian children, to assist him in punishing his children, the Americans, who have become refractory!—I took time to consider what I should do— whether or not I should receive the hatchet of my father, to assist him!—At first I looked upon it as a family quarrel, in which I was not interested—However, at length it appeared to me, that the father was in the right; and his children deserved to be punished a little!—That this must be the case, I concluded from the many cruel acts his off-spring had committed from time to time, on his Indian children; in encroaching on our land, stealing their men, women and children— Yes! even murdering those, who at times had been friendly to them, and were placed for protection under the roof of their father's house! —The father himself standing sentry at the door, at the time.

Friends! Often has the father been obliged to settle, and make amends for the wrongs and mischiefs done to us, by his refractory children, yet these do not grow better! No! they remain the same, and will continue to be so, as long as we have any land left us! Look back at the murders committed by the Long Knives on many of our relations, who lived peaceable neighbors to them on the Ohio! Did they not kill them without the least provocation?—Are they, do you think, better now than they were then?—No, indeed not; and many days are not elapsed since you had a number of these very men at your doors, who panted to kill you, but fortunately were prevented from doing so by the *Great Sun*, [the name the Indians had given to Col. Daniel Broadhead] who, at that time, had been ordained by the Great Spirit to protect you!

Friends and relatives!—Now listen to me, and hear what I have to say to you. —I am myself come to bid you rise and go with me to the secure place! Do not, my friends, covet the land you now hold under cultivation. I will conduct you to a country [the Miami country] equally good, where your cattle shall find sufficient pasture; where there is plenty of game; where your women and children, together with yourselves, will live in peace and safety; where no Long Knife shall ever molest you!—Nay, I will live between you and them, and not even suffer them to frighten you!—There, you can worship your God without fear!—Here, where you are, you cannot do this!—Think on what I have said to you, and believe, that if you stay where you now are, one day or another the Long Knives will, in their usual way, speak fine words to you, and at the same time murder you!

Contemporary and rival of the great Seneca Orator Red Jacket, Ki-on-twog-ky or Cornplanter was the son of a Seneca mother and (probably) an Irishman named O'Bail or O'Beale. Cornplanter is often referred to as John O'Beale or O'Bail as a result. He became a respected chief of the Seneca and worked tirelessly for peacefully arrived at, improved conditions for his people. The following speech was delivered in Philadelphia in 1790. The form "Father" was used deferentially in preference to "Brother" which implied equality.

You Have Now Got the Most of Our Lands

The Fathers of the Quaker State, Obeale or Cornplanter, returns thanks to God for the pleasure he has in meeting you this day with six of his people.

Fathers: Six years ago I had the pleasure of making peace with you, and at that time a hole was dug in the earth, and all contentions between my nation and you ceased and were buried there.

At a treaty then held at Fort Stanwix between the six nations of Indians and the Thirteen Fires, three friends from the Quaker State came to me and treated with me for the purchase of a large tract of land upon the northern boundary of Pennsylvania, extending from Tioga to Lake Erie for the use of their warriors. I agreed to sale of the same, and sold it to them for four thousand dollars. I begged of them to take pity on my nation and not buy it forever. They said they would purchase it forever, but that they would give me further one thousand dollars in goods when the leaves were ready to fall, and when I found that they were determined to have it, I agreed that they should have it. I then requested, as they were determined to have the land to permit my people to have the game and hunt upon the same, which request they complied with, and promised me to have it put upon record, that I and my people should have that privilege.

Fathers: The six nations then requested that another talk might be held with the Thirteen Fires, which was agreed to, and a talk afterwards held between them at Muskingum. Myself with three of my chiefs attended punctually, and were much fatigued in endeavoring to procure the attendance of the other nations, but none of them came to the council fire except the Delawares and the Wyandots.

Fathers: At the same treaty the Thirteen Fires asked me on which side I would die, whether on their side, or the side of those nations who did not attend the council fire. I replied, listen to me fathers of the Thirteen Fires, I hope you will consider how kind your fathers were treated by our fathers, the six nations, when they first came into this country, since which time you have become strong, insomuch, that I now call you fathers.

In former days when you were young and weak, I used to call you brother, but now I call you father. Father, I hope you will take pity on your children, for now I inform you that I'll die on your side. Now, father, I hope you will make my bed strong.

Fathers of the Quaker State: I speak but little now, but will speak more when the Thirteen Fires meet, I will only inform you further, that when I had finished my talk with the Thirteen Fires, General Gibson, who was sent by the Quaker State, came to the fire, and said that the Quaker State had bought of the Thirteen Fires a tract of land extending from the northern boundary of Pennsylvania at Connewango River to Buffaloe Creek on Lake Erie, and thence along the said lake to the northern boundary of Pennsylvania aforesaid. Hearing this I run to my father, and said to him, father have you sold this land to the Quaker State, and he said he did not know, it might have been done since he came there. I then disputed with Gibson and Butler, who was with him about the same, and told them I would be satisfied if the line was run from Connewango River through Chatochque Lake to Lake Erie, for Gibson and Butler had told me that the Quaker State had purchased the land from the Thirteen Fires, but that notwithstanding the Quaker State had given to me one thousand dollars in fine prime goods which were ready for me and my people at Fort Pitt, we then agreed that the line should be run from Connewango River through Chatochque Lake into Lake Erie, and that one-half of the fish in Chatochque Lake should be mine and one-half theirs.

They then said as the Quaker State had purchased the whole from the Thirteen Fires, that the Thirteen Fires must pay back to the Quaker State the value of the remaining land. When I heard this my mind was at ease, and I was satisfied.

I then proposed to give a half mile square of land upon the line so agreed upon to a Mr. Hartzhorn who was an ensign in General Harmar's army out to a Mr. Britt, a cadet who acted as a clerk upon occasion, and who I well know by the name of Half-Town, for the purpose of their settling there to prevent any mischief being committed in future upon my people's lands, and I hoped that the Quaker State would in addition thereto give them another half mile square on their side of the line so agreed upon for the same purpose, expecting thereby that the line so agreed upon would be known with sufficient certainty and that no disputes would thereafter arise between my people and the Quaker State concerning it. I then went to my father of the Thirteen Fires and told him I was satisfied, and the coals being covered up I said to my children you must take your course right through the woods to Fort Pitt. When I was leaving Muskingum my own son who remained a little behind to warm himself at the fire was robbed of a rifle by one of the white men, who I believe to have been a Yankee. Myself with Mr. Joseph Nicholson and a Mr. Morgan then travelled three days together through the wilderness, but the weather being very severe they were obliged to separate from me, and I sent some of my own people along with Mr. Nicholson and Mr. Morgan as guides to conduct them on to Wheelen.

After I had separated from Mr. Nicholson and Mr. Morgan, I had under my charge one hundred and seventy persons of my own nation, consisting of men, women and children to conduct through the wilderness through heaps of briars, and having lost our way, we, with great difficulty reached Wheelen. When arrived there being out of provision I requested of a Mr. Zanes to furnish me and my people with bacon and flour to the amount of seventeen dollars, to be paid for out of goods belonging to me and my people at Fort Pitt. Having obtained my request, I proceeded on my journey for Pittsburg, and about ten miles from Wheelen my party were fired upon by three white people, and one of my people in the rear of my party received two shot through his blanket.

Fathers: It was a constant practice with me throughout the whole journey to take great care of my people, and not suffer them to commit any outrages or drink more than their necessities required. During the whole of my journey only one accident happened which was owing to the kindness of the people of the town called Catfish, in the Quaker State, who, while I was talking with the head men of the town, gave to my people more liquor than was proper, and some of them got drunk, which obliged me to continue there with my people all night, and in the night my people were robbed of three rifles and one shot gun; and though every endeavor was used by the head men of the town upon complaint made to them to discover the perpetrators of the robbery, they could not be found; and on my people's complaining to me I told them it was their own fault by getting drunk.

Fathers: Upon my arrival at Fort Pitt I saw the goods which I had been informed of at Muskingum, and one hundred of the blankets were all moth eaten and good for nothing, I was advised not to take the blankets, but the blankets which I and my people then had being all torn by the briars in our passage through the wilderness, we were under the necessity of taking them to keep ourselves warm; and what most surprised me, was that after I had received the goods they extinguished the fire and swept away the ashes, and having no interpreter there I could talk with no one upon the subject. Feeling myself much hurt upon the occasion, I wrote a letter to you Fathers of the Quaker State, complaining of the injury, but never received any answer. Having waited a considerable time, and having heard that my letter got lost, I wrote a second time to you Fathers of the Quaker State and then I received an answer.

I am very thankful to have received that answer, and as the answer intreated me to come and speak for myself, I thank God that I have this opportunity, I therefore speak to you as follows. I hope that you, the Fathers of the Quaker State, will fix some person at Fort Pitt to take care of me and my people. I wish, and it is the wish of my people if agreeable to you that my present interpreter, Joseph Nicholson, may be the person, as I and my people have a confidence in him, and are satisfied that he will always exert himself to preserve peace and harmony between you and us. My reasons for wishing an interpreter to be placed there, are that often times when my hunters and people come there, their canoes and other things are stolen, and they can obtain no redress, not having any person there on whom they can rely to interpret for them and see justice done to them.

Fathers of the Quaker State: About a year ago a young man, one of my tribe who lived among the Shawnee, was one of a party who had committed some outrages and stolen a quantity of skins the property of David Duncan, being at Fort Pitt, was seized by the white people there who would have put him into confinement and perhaps to death had not some of the chiefs of the Seneca Nation interfered and bound themselves to the said David Duncan, who insisted upon satisfaction, for payment of the sum of five hundred and thirty dollars for the said skins so stolen, upon which the young man aforesaid was released and delivered up to them.

Fathers of the Quaker State: I wish now to acquaint you with what happened to one of my people about four years ago, four miles above Fort Pitt: A young man who was married to my wife's sister, when he was hunting, was murdered by a white man. There were three reasons for his being killed: In the first place he had a very fine riding horse; secondly, he was very richly dressed, and had about him a good deal of silver; and thirdly, he had with him a very fine rifle. The white man invited him to his house, to light from his horse, and as he was getting off his horse, his head being rather down, the white man struck him with a tomahawk on the head and killed him, and having plundered him dragged him into the river. Upon discovery of the murder, my people, with Mr. Nicholson and Mr. Duncan, had a great deal of trouble, and took a great deal of pains to find out the person who had committed the murder, and after three days' searching, they discovered him.

Fathers of the Quaker State: About five years ago, one of my chiefs, name Half-Town, was sent to Fort Pitt to deliver up into your hands your own flesh and blood who were taken in the war, and before he returned two horses were stolen from him by the white people. Now, Fathers, I will inform you of another accident which happened to my people last winter, fifteen miles below Fort Pitt. My nephew, with a hunting party, being there, was shot through the head in Mr. Nicholson's camp, the particulars of which Mr. Nicholson, who is here present, can inform you.

Well, Fathers, I beg of you once more not to let such bad people be 'longside of me. And, Fathers, you must not think I or any of my people are bad or wish evil to you and yours, nor must you blame us for mischiefs that have been committed by the other nations. Fathers, consider me and my people, and the many injuries we have sustained by the repeated robberies, and in the murders and depredations committed by the whites against us.

It is my wish and the wishes of my people to live peaceably and quietly with you and yours, but the losses we have sustained require some compensation. I have, with the consent of my people, agreed to receive from you eight hundred and thirty dollars, as a satisfaction for all losses and injuries I and my people have sustained, and this being paid me by you, to enable me to satisfy such of my people as have sustained those losses and suffered those injuries, we shall, I hope, in future live peaceable together, and bury in the earth all ill will and enmity to each other.

Fathers of the Quaker State: I have now had the pleasure to meet you with six of my people. We have come a great way, by your desire, to talk with you and to show to you the many injuries my nation has sustained. It now remains with you to do with me and my people what you please, on account of the present trouble which I and my people have taken for your satisfaction, and in compliance with your request.

Fathers, having come this great way at your request, and as it is necessary for some of us to remain here to talk with the Thirteen Fires when they meet, I have concluded to send back four of my people, and to remain here myself with Half-Town and my interpreter, Mr. Nicholson, until that time, which I hope you will approve of. But should you not approve of it, I must be under the necessity of returning with the whole of my people, which will be attended with a considerable expense.

Fathers of the Quaker State: You have now got the most of our lands, and have taken the game upon the same. We have only the privilege of hunting and fishing thereon. I, therefore, would make this further request, that a store be established at Fort Pitt for the accommodation of my people and the other nations when they go out to hunt; and where they may purchase goods at a reasonable price. For, believe me, Fathers, you yourselves would be frightened were you to know the extravagant prices we are obliged to pay for the goods we purchase.

There is a man (Esquire Wilkie) in Pittsburg, who has taken a great deal of pains to serve my people, and has pitied them; my people, when there, are very kindly treated by him, and give him a great deal of trouble, but he thinks nothing of it; he is the man my people wish should have charge of the store.

Fathers of the Quaker State: I have heard that you have been pleased to present to me a tract of land, but as yet I have not seen no writings for the same; well, Fathers, if it is true that you have given me this tract of land, I can only thank you for the same, but I hope you will also give me tools and materials for working the same.

Fathers of the Quaker State: Five years ago, when I used to be with my present interpreter, Joseph Nicholson, he took care of me and my people. Considering his services and the difficulties he underwent in his journey from Muskingum to Fort Pitt, the Six Nations wished to have him seated upon a tract of land of six miles square, lying in the forks of Allegheny River, and Broken Straw creek, and accordingly patented the same to him, this being the place where the battle was fought between my people and yours, and where about thirty of my people were beaten by him and twenty-five of your people, and where he was shot through the thigh. Now, Fathers, it is my wish, and I tell you it is the wish of the whole Six Nations, in behalf of whom and myself, I request that you would grant and confirm to our brother and friend, the before named Joseph Nicholson, the aforesaid tract of land, as described in our patent or grant to him.

This, Fathers, is all I have to say to the Quaker State, and I hope you will consider well all I have mentioned.

*After the British had been defeated in the American Revolution, the
Continental Congress declared the Indians a defeated enemy who had
forfeited all rights to expect earlier territorial treaties to be recognized
or honored. As some states had promised Indian lands to veterans if
the rebellion were successful, they did not welcome Secretary of War
Henry Knox's statement on June 15, 1789, that included the observation,
"The Indians being the prior occupants, possess the right of the soil.
It cannot be taken from them unless by their free consent, or by the right
of conquest in case of a just war." The Demarcation Line between the
Wabash Indians and the whites had been repeatedly violated, however,
and finally the United States insisted the Wabash recognize the white's
rightful occupancy of the breached Ohio and Kentucky territory. The
Council of Indians at Miami Rapids (August 13, 1793) composed the
following argument and sent it to the Commissioners appointed by the
President of the United States.*

The Line Between Us

Brothers: Money to us is of no value, and to most of us unknown; and
as no consideration whatever can induce us to sell the lands on which
we get sustenance for our women and children, we hope we may be
allowed to point out a mode by which your settlers may be easily removed, and peace thereby obtained.

　　　　We know that these settlers are poor, or they would never
have ventured to live in a country which has been in continual trouble
ever since they crossed the Ohio. Divide, therefore, this large sum of
money which you have offered us among these people; give to each,
also, a proportion of what you say you would give to us annually, over
and above this very large sum of money, and we are persuaded they
would most readily accept it in lieu of the lands you sold them. If you
add, also, the great sums you must expend in raising and paying armies
with a view to force us to yield you our country, you will certainly have
more than sufficient for the purpose of repaying these settlers for all
their labor and their improvements.

　　　　You have talked to us about concessions. It appears strange
that you should expect any from us, who have only been defending
our just rights against your invasions. We want peace. Restore to us our
country, and we shall be enemies no longer.

Brothers: You make one concession by offering to us your money, and another by having agreed to do us justice, after having long and injuriously withheld it; we mean, in the acknowledgement you have now made that the King of England never did, nor ever had a right to give you our country by the treaty of peace. And you want to make this act of common justice a great part of your concession, and seem to expect, that because you have at last acknowledged our independence, we should for such a favor surrender to you our country.

Brothers: You have also talked a great deal about preemption, and your exclusive right to purchase the Indian lands, as ceded to you by the King at the treaty of peace.

Brothers: We never made any agreement with the King, nor with any other nation, that we would give to either the exclusive right to purchase our lands; and we declare to you, that we consider ourselves free to make any bargain or cession of lands whenever and to whomsoever we please. If the white people, as you say, made a treaty that none of them but the King should purchase of us, and he has given that right to the United States, it is an affair that concerns you and him, and not us. We have never parted with such a power.

Brothers: At our general council held at the Glaize last Fall, we agreed to meet Commissioners from the United States, for the purpose of restoring peace, provided they consented to acknowledge and confirm our boundary line to be the Ohio; and we determined not to meet you until you gave us satisfaction on that point. That is the reason we have never met.

Brothers: We desire you to consider that your only demand is the peaceable possession of a small part of our once great country. Look back and view the lands from whence we have been driven to this spot. We can retreat no farther, because the country behind hardly affords food for its present inhabitants; and we have therefore resolved to leave our bones in this small space, to which we are now consigned.

Brothers: We shall be persuaded that you mean to do us justice, if you agree that the Ohio shall remain the boundary line between us. If you will not consent thereto, our meeting will be altogether unnecessary. This is the great point, which we hoped would have been explained before you left your houses; as our message last Autumn was principally directed to obtain that information.

Done in General Council at the foot of the Miami Rapids, on the 13th day of August, 1793.

Had the war chief of the Miamis been born in Europe, he would have been considered a true Renaissance Man, for, like Francis Bacon, he considered all knowledge his province and he was superior in every endeavor. He even managed to irritate the United States government so thoroughly that it behaved with the whimsical irrationality of the Renaissance's Queen Elizabeth. The circumstances were these: President George Washington so admired Little Turtle that he commissioned Gilbert Charles Stuart to paint the Miami's portrait—a singular honor. After Little Turtle defeated the United States in a continuing series of battles, Washington ordered the portrait destroyed. Elizabeth I would have understood that kind of thinking! The keen mind of Little Turtle is evident in the following speech delivered on July 29, 1795, during the discussions which culminated in the Treaty of Greenville (Ohio).

These People Never Told Us They Wished to Purchase Our Lands from Us

Elder Brother, and all you present: I am going to say a few words, in the name of the Pottawatamies, Weas and Kickapoos. It is well known to you all, that people are appointed on those occasions, to speak the sentiments of others; therefore am I appointed for those three nations.

       Elder Brother: You told your younger brothers, when we first assembled, that peace was your object; you swore your interpreters before us, to the faithful discharge of their duty, and told them the Great Spirit would punish them, did they not perform it. You told us, that it was not you, but the President of the Fifteen Fires of the United States, who spoke to us; that, whatever he should say, should be firm and lasting; that it was impossible he should say what was not true. Rest assured, that your younger brothers, the Miamis, Ottawas, Chippewas, Pottawatamies, Shawnees, Weas, Kickapoos, Piankeshaws, and Kaskaskias, are well pleased with your words, and are persuaded of their sincerity. You have told us to consider of the boundaries you showed us; your younger brothers have done so, and now proceed to give you their answer.

Elder Brother: Your younger brothers do not wish to hide their sentiments from you. I wish to be the same with those of the Wyandottes and Delawares; you have told us that most of the reservations you proposed to us belonged to our fathers, the French and the British. Permit your younger brothers to make a few observations on this subject.

Elder Brother: We wish you to listen with attention to our words. You have told your younger brothers that the British imposed falsehoods on us when they said the United States wished to take our lands from us, and that the United States had no such designs. You pointed out to us the boundary line, which crossed a little below Loromie's Store and struck Fort Recovery and run from thence to the Ohio, opposite the mouth of the Kentucky river.

Elder Brother: You have told us to speak our minds freely, and we now do it. This line takes in the greater and best part of your brothers' hunting ground. Therefore, your younger brothers are of opinion you take too much of their lands away and confine the hunting of our young men within the limits too contracted. Your brothers, the Miamis, the proprietors of those lands, and all your younger brothers present, wish you to run the lines as you mentioned to Fort Recovery and to continue it along the road; from thence to Fort Hamilton, on the great Miami River. This is what your brothers request you to do, and you may rest assured of the free navigation of that river, from thence to its mouth, forever.

Brother: Here is the road we wish to be the boundary between us. What lies to the east we wish to be yours; that to the west, we would desire to be ours.

Elder Brother: In speaking of the reservations, you say they are designed for the same purpose as those for which our fathers, the French and English, occupied them. Your younger brothers now wish to make some observations on them.

Elder Brother: Listen to me with attention. You told us you discovered on the Great Miami traces of an old fort. It was not a French fort, brother; it was a fort built by me. You perceived another at Loromies. 'Tis true a Frenchman once lived there for a year or two. The Miami villages were occupied as you remarked, but it was unknown to your younger brothers until you told them that we had sold the land there to the French or English. I was much surprised to hear you say that it was my forefathers had set the example to other Indians in selling their lands. I will inform you in what manner the French and English occupied those places.

Elder Brother: These people were seen by our forefathers first at Detroit. Afterwards we saw them at the Miami village — that glorious gate, which your younger brothers had the happiness to own, and through which all the good words of our chiefs had to pass, from the north to the south, and from the east to the west. Brothers, these people never told us they wished to purchase our lands from us.

Elder Brothers: I now give you the true sentiment of your younger brothers the Miamis, with respect to the reservation at the Miami villages. We thank you for kindly contracting the limits you at first proposed. We wish you to take this six miles square on the side of the river where your fort now stands, as your younger brothers wish to inhabit that beloved spot again. You shall cut hay for your cattle wherever you please, and you shall never require in vain the assistance of your younger brothers at that place.

Elder Brother: The next place you pointed to was the Little River, and said you wanted two miles square at that place. This is a request that our fathers, the French or British, never made us. It was always ours. This carrying place has heretofore proved in a great degree the subsistence of your younger brothers. That place has brought us in the course of one day the amount of one hundred dollars. Let us both own this place and enjoy in common the advantages it affords. You told us at Chicago the French possessed a fort. We have never heard of it. We thank you for the trade you promised to open in our country, and permit us to remark that we wish our former traders may be continued and mixed with yours.

Elder Brother: On the subject of hostages, I have only to observe that I trust all my brothers present are of my opinion with regard to peace and our future happiness. I expect to be with you every day when you settle on your reservations, and it will be impossible for me or my people to withhold from you a single prisoner. Therefore, we don't know why any of us should remain here. These are the sentiments of your younger brothers present, on these particulars.

Sagu-yu-what-hah (Keeper Awake) of the Seneca is commonly known as Red Jacket, an appellation from the period of captivity when he served the British as a runner and they clothed him in that garb to cover his nakedness. An orator of the front ranks among a people who created great orators, Red Jacket was always ordered and logical in his presentations. And he was capable of penetrating analysis, brilliant riposte. It is reported he once listened to a missionary who spoke at length in the religious cliches of missionaries on the folly of paganism. When the missionary had concluded, Red Jacket responded: "If you white people murdered 'the Savior,' make it up among yourselves. We had nothing to do with it. If he had come among us we should have treated him better." The underlying truth of the statement doubtless made it even less palatable to the missionary. In the following speech, Red Jacket responds to a missionary by the name of Cram who represented the Boston Missionary Society in council called by that august body in 1805. The Reverend Mr. Cram assured the Indians that he and his society were interested only in the souls of the Native Americans, that the lands and monies of the Indian were of no interest. The Indians withdrew to consider the presentation (as was their custom) and to formulate a reasoned response (as was their custom), a response they empowered Red Jacket to make. As you read the final commendation of Red Jacket, reflect on the recorded response of the Reverend Mr. Cram. Refusing to shake the proffered Indian hands, he observed there could be "no fellowship between the religion of God and the devil." It is further reported the Indians turned away with enigmatic smiles. Enigmatic? Not to the religiously secure!

Red Jacket to the Missionary

Friend and Brother! It was the will of the Great Spirit that we should meet together this day. He orders all things, and he has given us a fine day for our council. He has taken his garment from before the sun, and caused it to shine with brightness upon us. Our eyes are opened that we see clearly. Our ears are unstopped that we have been able to hear distinctly the words you have spoken. For all these favors we thank the Great Spirit, and him only.

Brother! This council fire was kindled by you. It was at your request that we came together at this time. We have listened with attention to what you have said. You requested us to speak our minds freely. This gives us great joy, for we now consider we stand upright before you, and can speak what we think. All have heard your voice, and all speak to you as one man. Our minds are agreed.

Brother! You say you want an answer to your talk before you leave this place. It is right you should have one, for you are a great distance from home, and we do not wish to detain you. But we will first look back a little, and tell you what our fathers have told us, and what we have heard from the white people.

Brother, listen to what we say. There was a time when our forefathers owned this great land. Their seats extended from the rising to the setting sun. The Great Spirit had made it for the use of the Indians. He had created the buffalo, the deer, and other animals for food. He made the bear and the beaver, and their skins served us for clothing. He had scattered them over the country, and taught us how to take them. He had caused the earth to produce corn for bread. All this he had done for his red children because he loved them. If we had any disputes about hunting grounds, they were generally settled without the shedding of much blood: but an evil day came upon us; your forefathers crossed the great waters and landed on this island. Their numbers were small; they found friends, not enemies; they told us they had fled from their own country for fear of wicked men, and come here to enjoy their religion. They asked for a small seat; we took pity on them, granted their request, and they sat down among us; we gave them corn and meat; they gave us poison in return. The white people had now found our country, tidings were carried back, and more came among us; yet we did not fear them, we took them to be friends; they called us brothers; we believed them and gave them a larger seat. At length their number had greatly increased; they wanted more land; they wanted our country. Our eyes were opened, and our minds became uneasy. Wars took place; Indians were hired to fight against Indians, and many of our people were destroyed. They also brought strong liquors among us: it was strong and powerful, and has slain thousands.

Brother, our seats were once large, and yours were very small; you have now become a great people, and we have scarcely left a place to spread our blankets; you have got our country, but are not satisfied; you want to force your religion upon us.

Brother, continue to listen. You say that you are sent to instruct us how to worship the Great Spirit agreeably to his mind, and if we do not take hold of the religion which you white people teach, we shall be unhappy hereafter; you say that you are right, and we are lost; how do we know this to be true? We understand that your religion is written in a book; if it was intended for us as well as you, why has not the Great Spirit given it to us, and not only to us, but why did he not give to our forefathers the knowledge of that book, with the means of understanding it rightly? We only know what you tell us about it; how shall we know when to believe, being so often deceived by the white people?

Brother, you say there is but one way to worship and serve the Great Spirit; if there is but one religion, why do you white people differ so much about it? Why do not all agree, as you can all read the book?

Brother, we do not understand these things; we are told that your religion was given to your forefathers, and has been handed down from father to son. We also have a religion which was given to our forefathers, and has been handed down to us their children. We worship that way. It teacheth us to be thankful for all the favors we receive; to love each other, and to be united. We never quarrel about religion.

Brother, the Great Spirit has made us all; but he has made a great difference between his white and red children; he has given us a different complexion, and different customs. To you he has given the arts; to these he has not opened our eyes. We know these things to be true. Since he has made so great a difference between us in other things, why may we not conclude that he has given us a different religion, according to our understanding? The Great Spirit does right. He knows what is best for his children. We are satisfied.

Brother! We do not wish to destroy your religion, or take it from you. We only want to enjoy our own.

Brother! You say you have not come to get our land or our money, but to enlighten our minds. I will now tell you that I have been at your meetings and saw you collecting money from the meeting. I cannot tell what this money was intended for, but suppose it was for your minister; and if we should conform to your way of thinking, perhaps you may want some from us.

Brother! We are told that you have been preaching to white people in this place. These people are our neighbors. We are acquainted with them. We will wait a little while, and see what effect your preaching has upon them. If we find that it does them good and makes them honest and less disposed to cheat Indians, we will then consider again what you have said.

Brother! You have now heard our answer to your talk, and this is all we have to say at present. As we are going to part, we will come and take you by the hand, and hope the Great Spirit will protect you on your journey, and return you safe to your friends.

Most Native Americans consider themselves members of their tribes first, Indians second. Tecumtha (or Tecumseh meaning "Cougar crouching for his prey") considered himself a Native American first, a Shawnee second. His one desire was to see the tribes united into a single, cohesive, powerful force capable of defending itself against the white man. With his brother Elkswatawa, the Prophet, Tecumtha established Prophet Town at Tippecanoe and attempted to unify all of the tribes. The follies of Elkswatawa, the deviousness of General William Henry Harrison, the absence of Tecumtha on alliance travels—all led to the destruction of Prophet Town, the uncoordinated border warfare Tecumtha feared, and the eventual election of Harrison to the presidency on the slogan "Tippecanoe and Tyler too." The year after Tippecanoe, the War of 1812 gave Tecumtha his last chance to oppose the transplant Americans and, allying himself with the British, he distinguished himself again. The following speech was delivered to the Osage in 1811 before the fall of Prophet Town.

We Must Smoke the Same Pipe

Brothers,—We all belong to one family; we are all children of the Great Spirit; we walk in the same path; slake our thirst at the same spring; and now affairs of the greatest concern lead us to smoke the pipe around the same council fire!

Brothers,—We are friends; we must assist each other to bear our burdens. The blood of many of our fathers and brothers has run like water on the ground, to satisfy the avarice of the white men. We, ourselves, are threatened with a great evil; nothing will pacify them but the destruction of all the red men.

Brothers,—When the white men first set foot on our grounds, they were hungry; they had no place on which to spread their blankets, or to kindle their fires. They were feeble; they could do nothing for themselves. Our fathers commiserated their distress, and shared freely with them whatever the Great Spirit had given his red children. They gave them food when hungry, medicine when sick, spread skins for them to sleep on, and gave them grounds, that they might hunt and raise corn.

Brothers—the white people are like poisonous serpents: when chilled, they are feeble, and harmless, but invigorate them with warmth, and they sting their benefactors to death.

The white people came among us feeble; and now we have made them strong, they wish to kill us, or drive us back, as they would wolves and panthers.

Brothers,—The white men are not friends to the Indians: at first, they only asked for land sufficient for a wigwam; now, nothing will satisfy them but the whole of our hunting grounds, from the rising to the setting sun.

Brothers,—The white men want more than our hunting grounds; they wish to kill our warriors; they would even kill our old men, women and little ones.

Brothers,—Many winters ago, there was no land; the sun did not rise and set: all was darkness. The Great Spirit made all things. He gave the white people a home beyond the great waters. He supplied these grounds with game, and gave them to his red children; and he gave them strength and courage to defend them.

Brothers,—My people wish for peace; the red men all wish for peace; but where the white people are, there is no peace for them, except it be on the bosom of our mother.

Brothers,—The white men despise and cheat the Indians; they abuse and insult them; they do not think the red men sufficiently good to live.

The red men have borne many and great injuries; they ought to suffer them no longer. My people will not; they are determined on vengeance; they have taken up the tomahawk; they will make it fat with blood; they will drink the blood of the white people.

Brothers,—My people are brave and numerous; but the white people are too strong for them alone. I wish you to take up the tomahawk with them. If we all unite, we will cause the rivers to stain the great waters with their blood.

Brothers,—If you do not unite with us, they will first destroy us, and then you will fall an easy prey to them. They have destroyed many nations of red men because they were not united, because they were not friends to each other.

Brothers,—The white people send runners amongst us; they wish to make us enemies, that they may sweep over and desolate our hunting grounds, like devastating winds, or rushing waters.

Brothers,—Our Great Father, over the great waters, is angry with the white people, our enemies. He will send his brave warriors against them; he will send us rifles, and whatever else we want— he is our friend, and we are his children.

Brothers,—Who are the white people that we should fear them? They cannot run fast, and are good marks to shoot at: they are only men; our fathers have killed many of them; we are not squaws, and we will stain the earth red with their blood.

Brothers,—The Great Spirit is angry with our enemies; he speaks in thunder, and the earth swallows up villages, and drinks up the Mississippi. The great waters will cover their lowlands; their corn cannot grow; and the Great Spirit will sweep those who escape to the hills from the earth with his terrible breath.

Brothers,—We must be united; we must smoke the same pipe; we must fight each other's battles; and more than all, we must love the Great Spirit; he is for us; he will destroy our enemies, and make his red children happy.

Of indeterminate origin, Pushmataha was born in Mississippi and became the leader without peer among the Choctaw. A familiar figure to several presidents, he served his tribe well—at times to the detriment of the Native Americans as a whole. When Tecumtha spoke to the Choctaw in 1811, Pushmataha listened carefully and responded with the following reasoned speech. The Choctaws and Chickasaws supported Pushmataha almost to a man.

We Do Not Take Up the Warpath Without a Just Cause

Attention, my good red warriors! Hear ye my brief remarks.

The great Shawnee orator has portrayed in vivid picture the wrongs inflicted on his and other tribes by the ravages of the pale-face. The candor and fervor of his eloquent appeal breathe the conviction of truth and sincerity, and, as kindred tribes, naturally we sympathize with the misfortunes of his people. I do not come before you in any disputation either for or against these charges. It is not my purpose to contradict any of these allegations against the white man, but neither am I here to indulge in any indiscreet denunciation of him which might bring down upon my people unnecessary difficulty and embarrassment.

The distinguished Shawnee sums up his eloquent appeal to us with this direct question:

"Will you sit idly by, supinely awaiting complete and abject submission, or will you die fighting beside your brethren, the Shawnees, rather than submit to such ignominy?"

These are plain words and it is well they have been spoken, for they bring the issue squarely before us. Mistake not, this language means war. And war with whom, pray? War with some band of marauders who have committed there depredations against the Shawnees? War with some alien host seeking the destruction of the Choctaws and Chickasaws? Nay, my fellow tribesmen. None of these are the enemy we will be called on to meet. If we take up arms against the Americans we must of necessity meet in deadly combat our daily neighbors and associates in this part of the country near our homes.

If Tecumseh's words be true, and we doubt them not, then the Shawnee's experience with the whites has not been the same as that of the Choctaws. These white Americans buy our skins, our corn, our cotton, our surplus game, our baskets, and other wares, and they give us in fair exchange their cloth, their guns, their tools, implements, and other things which the Choctaws need but do not make. It is true we have befriended them, but who will deny that these acts of friendship have been abundantly reciprocated? They have given us cotton gins, which simplify the spinning and sale of our cotton; they have encouraged and helped us in the production of our crops; they have taken many of our wives into their homes to teach them useful things, and pay them for their work while learning; they teach our children to read and write from their books. You all remember the dreadful epidemic visited upon us last winter. During its darkest hours these neighbors whom we are now urged to attack responded generously to our needs. They doctored our sick; they clothed our suffering; they fed our hungry; and where is the Choctaw or Chickasaw delegation who has ever gone to St. Stephens with a worthy cause and been sent away empty handed? So, in marked contrast with the experiences of the Shawnees, it will be seen that the whites and Indians in this section are living on friendly and mutually beneficial terms.

Forget not, O Choctaws and Chickasaws, that we are bound in peace to the Great White Father at Washington by a sacred treaty and the Great Spirit will punish those who break their word. The Great White Father has never violated that treaty and the Choctaws have never been driven to the necessity of taking up the tomahawk against him or his children. Therefore the question before us tonight is not the avenging of any wrongs perpetrated against us by the whites, for the Choctaws and Chickasaws have no such cause, either real or imaginary, but rather it is a question of carrying on that record of fidelity and justice for which our forefathers ever proudly stood, and doing that which is best calculated to promote the welfare of our own people. Yea, my fellow tribesmen, we are a just people. We do not take up the warpath without a just cause and honest purpose. Have we that just cause against our white neighbors, who have taken nothing from us except by fair bargain and exchange? Is this a just recompense for their assistance to us in our agricultural and other pursuits? Is this to be their gracious reward for teaching our children from their books? Shall this be considered the Choctaws' compensation for feeding our hungry, clothing our needy, and administering to our sick? Have we, O Choctaws and Chickasaws, descended to the low estate of ruthlessly breaking the faith of a sacred treaty? Shall our forefathers look back from the happy hunting grounds only to see their unbroken record for justice, gratitude, and fidelity thus rudely repudiated and abruptly abandoned by an unworthy offspring?

We Choctaws and Chickasaws are a peaceful people, making our subsistence by honest toil; but mistake not, my Shawnee brethren, we are not afraid of war. Neither are we strangers to war, as those who have undertaken to encroach upon our rights in the past may abundantly testify. We are thoroughly familiar with war in all its details and we know full well all its horrible consequences. It is unnecessary for me to remind you, O Choctaws and Chickasaws, veteran braves of many fierce conflicts in the past, that war is an awful thing. If we go into this war against the Americans, we must be prepared to accept its inevitable results. Not only will it foretoken deadly conflict with neighbors and death to warriors, but it will mean suffering for our women, hunger and starvation for our children, grief for our loved ones, and devastation of our beloved homes. Notwithstanding these difficulties, if the cause be just, we should not hesitate to defend our rights to the last man, but before that fatal step is irrevocably taken, it is well that we fully understand and seriously consider the full portent and consequences of the act.

Hear me, O Choctaws and Chickasaws, for I speak truly for your welfare. It is not the province of your chiefs to settle these important questions. As a people, it is your prerogative to have either peace or war, and as one of your chiefs, it is mine simply to counsel and advise. Therefore, let me admonish you that this critical period is no time to cast aside your wits and let blind impulse sway; be not driven like dumb brutes by the frenzied harangue of this wonderful Shawnee orator; let your good judgment rule and ponder seriously before breaking bonds that have served you well and ere you change conditions which have brought peace and happiness to your wives, your sisters, and your children. I would not undertake to dictate the course of one single Choctaw warrior. Permit me to speak for the moment, not as your chief but as a Choctaw warrior, weighing this question beside you. As such I shall exercise my calm, deliberate judgment in behalf of those most dear to me and dependent on me, and I shall not suffer my reason to be swept away by this eloquent recital of alleged wrongs which I know naught of. I deplore this war, I earnestly hope it may be averted, but if it be forced upon us I shall take my stand with those who have stood by my people in the past and will be found fighting beside our good friends of St. Stephens and surrounding country. I have finished. I call on all Choctaws and Chickasaws endorsing my sentiments to cast their tomahawks on this side of the council fire with me.

Perhaps the greatest mark of the oratorical skill of a man is his capacity to articulate his thoughts when he knows death is imminent. The death song of Red Bird of the Winnebago, judged by those standards, must be one of the greatest oratorical offerings in the history of mankind. It was composed as a result of a series of incidents both bizarre and bitter. In 1827 the Winnebago discovered a group of transplant Americans surreptitiously tapping sugar maples on the Winnebago reservation in Illinois. In the ensuing altercation, several of the whites were killed. In reprisal, the whites invaded the reservation and "executed" several of Red Bird's people. They retaliated with a raid on Prairie du Chien. United States troops besieged the reservation, and Red Bird surrendered himself in agreement that his people would suffer no further deaths. In immaculate white buckskins decorated with two small stuffed cardinals on his shoulders, he walked out to meet the government troops. As he walked, he sang his death song.

The Deathsong of Red Bird

I am ready.
I do not want to be put in chains.
Let me be free.
I have given away my life—

(*Stooping, he picked up a pinch
of dust and blew it away.*)

—it is gone like that!
I would not take it back.
It is gone.

Black Hawk of the Sauk was a valiant foe. When he was only seventeen, he led a war party against the transplant Americans. He fought on the side of the British in the War of 1812. He fomented Black Hawk's War in 1832, and, after his surrender, he was imprisoned for a time, then sent on an elaborate tour that included a scolding from President Andrew Jackson (Black Hawk's realism and dignity are apparent in his response: "Your people are stronger than mine. You can dictate your terms."); views of Norfolk, Baltimore, and Philadelphia; a tour of New York City. "Black Hawk's Farewell" is his surrender speech at the close of Black Hawk's War.

Black Hawk's Farewell

You have taken me prisoner with all my warriors. I am much grieved, for I expected, if I did not defeat you, to hold out much longer, and give you more trouble before I surrendered. I tried hard to bring you into ambush, but your last general understands Indian fighting. The first one was not so wise. When I saw that I could not beat you by Indian fighting, I determined to rush on you, and fight you face to face. I fought hard. But your guns were well aimed. The bullets flew like birds in the air, and whizzed by our ears like the wind through the trees in winter. My warriors fell around me; it began to look dismal. I saw my evil day at hand. The sun rose dim on us in the morning, and at night it sank in a dark cloud, and looked like a ball of fire. That was the last sun that shone on Black Hawk. His heart is dead, and no longer beats quick in his bosom. He is now a prisoner to the white men; they will do with him as they wish. But he can stand torture, and is not afraid of death. He is no coward. Black Hawk is an Indian.

He has done nothing for which an Indian ought to be ashamed. He has fought for his countrymen, the squaws and papooses, against white men, who came, year after year, to cheat them and take away their lands. You know the cause of our making war. It is known to all white men. They ought to be ashamed of it. The white men despise the Indians, and drive them from their homes. But the Indians are not deceitful. The white men speak bad of the Indian, and look at him spitefully. But the Indian does not tell lies; Indians do not steal.

An Indian who is as bad as the white men, could not live in our nation; he would be put to death, and eaten up by the wolves. The white men are bad schoolmasters; they carry false looks and deal in false actions; they smile in the face of the poor Indian to cheat him; they shake them by the hand to gain their confidence, to make them drunk, to deceive them, and ruin our wives. We told them to let us alone, and keep away from us; but they followed on and beset our paths, and they coiled themselves among us like the snake. They poisoned us by their touch. We were not safe. We lived in danger. We were becoming like them, hypocrites and liars, adulterers, lazy drones, all talkers, and no workers.

We looked up to the Great Spirit. We went to our great father. We were encouraged. His great council gave us fair words and big promises; but we got no satisfaction. Things were growing worse. There were no deer in the forest. The opossum and beaver were fled; the springs were drying up, and our squaws and papooses without victuals to keep them from starving; we called a great council and built a large fire. The spirit of our fathers arose and spoke to us to avenge our wrongs or die. We all spoke before the council fire. It was warm and pleasant. We set up the war-whoop, and dug up the tomahawk; our knives were ready, and the heart of Black Hawk swelled high in his bosom when he led his warriors to battle. He is satisfied. He will go to the world of spirits contented. He has done his duty. His father will meet him there, and commend him.

Black Hawk is a true Indian, and disdains to cry like a woman. He feels for his wife, his children and friends. But he does not care for himself. He cares for his nation and the Indians. They will suffer. He laments their fate. The white men do scalp the head; but they do worse—they poison the heart; it is not pure with them. His countrymen will not be scalped, but they will, in a few years, become like white men, so that you can't trust them, and there must be, as in the white settlements, nearly as many officers as men, to take care of them and keep them in order.

Farewell, my nation! Black Hawk tried to save you, and avenge your wrongs. He drank the blood of some of the whites. He has been taken prisoner, and his plans are stopped. He can do no more. He is near his end. His sun is setting, and he will rise no more. Farewell to Black Hawk.

The "Blackbird Hills" are named "On'pontonga xaithon" ("Where Big Elk is buried") by the Omaha. The third leader to carry the name, Big Elk died in 1853. About 1850, Big Elk visited Washington, and, on his return, he called the tribe together. He knew he had not long to live; he had seen his only son die so his line would end with him. With those realizations, he delivered the following prophecy.

The Prophecy of
Big Elk

My chiefs, braves, and young men, I have just returned from a visit to a far-off country toward the rising sun, and have seen many strange things. I bring to you news which it saddens my heart to think of. There is a coming flood which will soon reach us, and I advise you to prepare for it. Soon the animals which Wako^{n}'da has given us for sustenance will disappear beneath this flood to return no more, and it will be very hard for you. Look at me; you see I am advanced in age; I am near the grave. I can no longer think for you and lead you as in my younger days. You must think for yourselves what will be best for your welfare. I tell you this that you may be prepared for the coming change. You may not know my meaning. Many of you are old, as I am, and by the time the change comes we may be lying peacefully in our graves; but these young men will remain to suffer. Speak kindly to one another; do what you can to help each other, even in the troubles with the coming tide. Now, my people, this is all I have to say. Bear these words in mind, and when the time comes think of what I have said.

Chief of the Suquamish and Duwamish tribes, Sealth (Seattle) converted to Catholicism in the 1830s and lived by the ideal Christian precepts in such a way that neither Native nor transplant Americans can but admire him. After the Washington Territory was organized in 1853, the town of Seattle was named after Sealth, and Governor Stevens of the territory addressed its residents. Sealth delivered the response, a poignant, flawless response in the richest oratorical tradition.

The White Man Will Never Be Alone

Yonder sky that has wept tears of compassion upon my people for centuries untold, and which to us appears changeless and eternal, may change. Today is fair. Tomorrow it may be overcast with clouds. My words are like the stars that never change. Whatever Seattle says the great chief at Washington can rely upon with as much certainty as he can upon the return of the sun or the seasons. The White Chief says that Big Chief at Washington sends us greetings of friendship and goodwill. This is kind of him for we know he has little need of our friendship in return. His people are many. They are like the grass that covers vast prairies. My people are few. They resemble the scattering trees of a storm-swept plain. The great—and I presume—good White Chief sends us word that he wishes to buy our lands but is willing to allow us enough to live comfortably. This indeed appears just, even generous, for the Red Man no longer has rights that he need respect, and the offer may be wise also, as we are no longer in need of an extensive country.

There was a time when our people covered the land as the waves of a wind-ruffled sea cover its shell-paved floor, but that time long since passed away with the greatness of tribes that are now but a mournful memory. I will not dwell on, nor mourn over, our untimely decay, nor reproach my paleface brothers with hastening it as we too may have been somewhat to blame.

Youth is impulsive. When our young men grow angry at some real or imaginary wrong, and disfigure their faces with black paint, it denotes that their hearts are black, and that they are often cruel and relentless, and our old men and old women are unable to restrain them. Thus it has ever been. Thus it was when the white man first began to push our forefathers westward. But let us hope that the hostilities between us may never return. We would have everything to lose and nothing to gain. Revenge by young men is considered gain, even at the cost of their own lives, but old men who stay at home in times of war, and mothers who have sons to lose, know better.

Our good father at Washington—for I presume he is now our father as well as yours, since King George has moved his boundaries further north—our great and good father, I say, sends us word that if we do as he desires he will protect us. His brave warriors will be to us a bristling wall of strength, and his wonderful ships of war will fill our harbors so that our ancient enemies far to the northward—the Hydas and Tsimpsians—will cease to frighten our women, children and old men. Then in reality will he be our father and we his children. But can that ever be? Your God is not our God! Your God loves your people and hates mine. He folds his strong protecting arms lovingly about the paleface and leads him by the hand as a father leads his infant son—but He has forsaken His red children—if they really are His. Our God, the Great Spirit, seems also to have forsaken us. Your God makes your people wax strong every day. Soon they will fill all the land. Our people are ebbing away like a rapidly receding tide that will never return. The white man's God cannot love our people or He would protect them. They seem to be orphans who can look nowhere for help. How then can we be brothers? How can your God become our God and renew our prosperity and awaken in us dreams of returning greatness? If we have a common heavenly father He must be partial—for He came to His paleface children. We never saw Him. He gave you laws but had no word for his red children whose teeming multitudes once filled this vast continent as stars fill the firmament. No; we are two distinct races with separate origins and separate destinies. There is little in common between us.

To us the ashes of our ancestors are sacred and their resting place is hallowed ground. You wander far from the graves of your ancestors and seemingly without regret. Your religion was written upon tables of stone by the iron finger of your God so that you could not forget. The Red Man could never comprehend nor remember it. Our religion is the traditions of our ancestors—the dreams of our old men, given them in the solemn hours of night by the Great Spirit; and the visions of our sachems, and is written in the hearts of our people.

Your dead cease to love you and the land of their nativity as soon as they pass the portals of the tomb and wander way beyond the stars. They are soon forgotten and never return. Our dead never forget the beautiful world that gave them being. They still love its verdant valleys, its murmuring rivers, its magnificent mountains, sequestered vales and verdant lined lakes and bays, and ever yearn in tender, fond affection over the lonely hearted living, and often return from the Happy Hunting Ground to visit, guide, console and comfort them.

Day and night cannot dwell together. The Red Man has ever fled the approach of the White Man, as the morning mist flees before the morning sun.

However, your proposition seems fair and I think that my people will accept it and will retire to the reservation you offer them. Then we will dwell in peace, for the words of the Great White Chief seem to be the words of nature speaking to my people out of dense darkness.

It matters little where we pass the remnant of our days. They will not be many. The Indians' night promises to be dark. Not a single star of hope hovers above his horizon. Sad-voiced winds moan in the distance. Grim fate seems to be on the Red Man's trail, and wherever he goes he will hear the approaching footsteps of his fell destroyer and prepare stolidly to meet his doom, as does the wounded doe that hears the approaching footsteps of the hunter.

A few more moons. A few more winters—and not one of the descendants of the mighty hosts that once moved over this broad land or lived in happy homes, protected by the Great Spirit, will remain to mourn over the graves of a people—once more powerful and hopeful than yours. But why should I mourn at the untimely fate of my people? Tribe follows tribe, and nation follows nation, like the waves of the sea. It is the order of nature, and regret is useless. Your time of decay may be distant, but it will surely come, for even the White Man whose God walked and talked with him as friend with friend, cannot be exempt from the common destiny. We may be brothers after all. We will see.

We will ponder your proposition and when we decide we will let you know. But should we accept it, I here and now make this condition that we will not be denied the privilege without molestation of visiting at any time the tombs of our ancestors, friends and children. Every part of this soil is sacred in the estimation of my people. Every hillside, every valley, every plain and grove, has been hallowed by some sad or happy event in days long vanished. Even the rocks, which seem to be dumb and dead as they swelter in the sun along the silent shore, thrill with memories of stirring events connected with the lives of my people, and the very dust upon which you now stand responds more lovingly to their footsteps than to yours, because it is rich with the blood of our ancestors and our bare feet are conscious of the sympathetic touch. Our departed braves, fond mothers, glad, happy-hearted maidens, and even our little children who lived here and rejoiced here for a brief season, will love these somber solitudes and at eventide they greet shadowy returning spirits. And when the last Red Man shall have perished, and the memory of my tribe shall have become a myth among the White Men, these shores will swarm with the invisible dead of my tribe, and when your children's children think themselves alone in the field, the store, the shop, upon the highway, or in the silence of the pathless woods, they will not be alone. In all the earth there is no place dedicated to solitude. At night when the streets of your cities and villages are silent and you think them deserted, they will throng with the returning hosts that once filled them and still love this beautiful land. The White Man will never be alone.

Let him be just and deal kindly with my people, for the dead are not powerless. Dead, did I say? There is no death, only a change of worlds.

At the Sand Creek Massacre of 1864, White Antelope of the Cheyenne died with the dignity expected of and befitting a war captain of some fifty years. With folded arms, he stood singing his death song as he was killed.

The Deathsong of
White Antelope

Nothing lives long
except the earth
and the mountains.

On October 20, 1867, the venerable Yamperethka Comanche leader, Ten Bears, spoke for the Comanche at the Medicine Lodge council. His prefatory statement, "What I say is law for the Comanches," was correct—with one exception: Quanah Parker and his band of warriors continued their intermittent raids.

Do Not Ask Us to Give Up the Buffalo for the Sheep

My heart is filled with joy, when I see you here, as the brooks fill with water, when the snows melt in the spring, and I feel glad, as the ponies do when the fresh grass starts in the beginning of the year. I heard of your coming, when I was many sleeps away, and I made but few camps before I met you. I knew that you had come to do good to me and to my people. I looked for the benefits, which would last forever, and so my face shines with joy, as I look upon you. My people have never first drawn a bow or fired a gun against the whites. There has been trouble on the line between us, and my young men have danced the war dance. But it was not begun by us.

It was you who sent out the first soldier, and it was we who sent out the second. Two years ago, I came up upon this road, following the buffalo, that my wives and children might have their cheeks plump, and their bodies warm. But the soldiers fired on us, and since that time there has been a noise, like that of a thunderstorm, and we have not known which way to go. So it was upon the Canadian. Nor have we been made to cry once alone. The blue-dressed soldiers and the Utes came from out of the night, when it was dark and still, and for campfires, they lit our lodges. Instead of hunting game, they killed my braves and the warriors of the tribe cut short their hair for the dead. So it was in Texas. They made sorrow come into our camps, and we went out like the buffalo bulls, when the cows are attacked. When we found them we killed them, and their scalps hang in our lodges.

The Comanches are not weak and blind, like the pups of a dog when seven sleeps old. They are strong and farsighted, like grown horses. We took their road and we went on it. The white women cried, and our women laughed. But there are things which you have said to me which I do not like. They were not sweet like sugar, but bitter like gourds. You said that you wanted to put us upon a reservation, to build us houses and to make us Medicine lodges. I do not want them.

I was born upon the prairie, where the wind blew free, and there was nothing to break the light of the sun. I was born where there were no enclosures, and where everything drew a free breath. I want to die there, and not within walls. I know every stream and every wood between the Rio Grande and the Arkansas. I have hunted and lived over that country. I lived like my fathers before me, and like them, I lived happily.

When I was at Washington, the Great Father told me that all the Comanche land was ours, and that no one should hinder us in living upon it. So why do you ask us to leave the rivers, and the sun, and the wind, and live in houses? Do not ask us to give up the buffalo for the sheep. The young men have heard talk of this, and it has made them sad and angry. Do not speak of it more. I love to carry out the talk I get from the Great Father. When I get goods and presents, I and my people feel glad since it shows that he holds us in his eye. If the Texans had kept out of my country, there might have been peace. But that which you now say we must live on is too small.

The Texans have taken away the places where the grass grew the thickest and the timber was the best. Had we kept that, we might have done the thing you ask. But it is too late. The white man has the country which we loved and we only wish to wander on the prairie until we die. Any good thing you say to me shall not be forgotten. I shall carry it as near to my heart as my children, and it shall be as often on my tongue as the name of the Great Spirit. I want no blood upon my land to stain the grass. I want it all clear and pure, and I wish it so, that all who go through among my people may find peace when they come in, and leave it when they go out.

On June 16, 1870, Red Cloud of the Teton Sioux was the guest of honor at a Cooper Union reception in New York. At that time, he addressed those who had come to honor the war leader who had commanded the Sioux at the Fetterman Massacre in 1866 and the Wagon Box Fight in 1867 before making the trip to Washington in 1870 that was called "Red Cloud's Peace Crusade" because he had buried the war hatchet forever. The New York Times, *that most "objective" of American newspapers, gave the story front-page coverage the next day. Its account included the following statement:*

His earnest manner, his impassioned gestures, the eloquence of his hands, and the magnetism which he evidently exercises over his audience, produced a vast effect on the dense throng which listened to him yesterday. "You have children, and so have we. We want to rear our children well, and ask you to help us in doing so." It seems to us that this is not an unreasonable request even though it does come from a "savage."

No rationalization or explanation of "intent" can remove the barbaric tastelessness of the last line. Red Cloud's magnetism is apparent even in the printed words of his speech.

Indian Rights

My brethren and my friends who are here before me this day, God Almighty has made us all, and He is here to bless what I have to say to you today. The Good Spirit made us both. He gave you lands and He gave us lands; He gave us these lands; you came in here, and we respected you as brothers. God Almighty made you but made you all white and clothed you; when He made us He made us with red skins and poor; now you have come.

When you first came we were very many, and you were few; now you are many, and we are getting very few, and we are poor. You do not know who appears before you today to speak. I am a representative of the original American race, the first people of this continent. We are good and not bad. The reports that you hear concerning us are all on one side. We are always well-disposed to them. You are here told that we are traders and thieves, and it is not so. We have given you nearly all our lands, and if we had any more land to give we would be very glad to give it. We have nothing more. We are driven into a very little land, and we want you now, as our dear friends, to help us with the government of the United States.

The Great Father made us poor and ignorant—made you rich and wise and more skillful in these things that we know nothing about. The Great Father, the Good Father in Heaven, made you all to eat tame food—made us to eat wild food—gives us the wild food. You ask anybody who has gone through our country to California; ask those who have settled there and in Utah, and you will find that we have treated them always well. You have children; we have children. You want to raise your children and make them happy and prosperous; we want to raise and make them happy and prosperous. We ask you to help us to do it.

At the mouth of the Horse Creek, in 1852, the Great Father made a treaty with us by which we agreed to let all that country open for fifty-five years for the transit of those who were going through. We kept this treaty; we never treated any man wrong; we never committed any murder or depredation until afterward the troops were sent into that country, and the troops killed our people and ill-treated them, and thus war and trouble arose; but before the troops were sent there we were quiet and peaceable, and there was no disturbance. Since that time there have been various goods sent from time to time to us, the only ones that ever reached us, and then after they reached us (very soon after) the government took them away. You, as good men, ought to help us to these goods.

Colonel Fitzpatrick of the government said we must all go to farm, and some of the people went to Fort Laramie and were badly treated. I only want to do that which is peaceful, and the Great Fathers know it, and also the Great Father who made us both. I came to Washington to see the Great Father in order to have peace and in order to have peace continue. That is all we want, and that is the reason why we are here now.

In 1868 men came out and brought papers. We are ignorant and do not read papers, and they did not tell us right what was in these papers. We wanted them to take away their forts, leave our country, would not make war, and give our traders something. They said we had bound ourselves to trade on the Missouri, and we said, no, we did not want that. The interpreters deceived us. When I went to Washington I saw the Great Father. The Great Father showed me what the treaties were; he showed me all these points and showed me that the interpreters had deceived me and did not let me know what the right side of the treaty was. All I want is right and justice...I represent the Sioux Nation; they will be governed by what I say and what I represent....

Look at me. I am poor and naked, but I am the Chief of the Nation. We do not want riches, we do not ask for riches, but we want our children properly trained and brought up. We look to you for your sympathy. Our riches will...do us no good; we cannot take away into the other world anything we have—we want to have love and peace....We would like to know why commissioners are sent out there to do nothing but rob [us] and get the riches of this world away from us?

I was brought up among the traders and those who came out there in those early times. I had a good time for they treated us nicely and well. They taught me how to wear clothes and use tobacco, and to use firearms and ammunition, and all went on very well until the Great Father sent out another kind of men—men who drank whisky. He sent out whiskymen, men who drank and quarreled, men who were so bad that he could not keep them at home, and so he sent them out there.

I have sent a great many words to the Great Father, but I don't know that they ever reach the Great Father. They were drowned on the way, therefore I was a little offended with it. The words I told the Great Father lately would never come to him, so I thought I would come and tell you myself.

And I am going to leave you today, and I am going back to my home. I want to tell the people that we cannot trust his agents and superintendents. I don't want strange people that we know nothing about. I am very glad that you belong to us. I am very glad that we have come here and found you and that we can understand one another. I don't want any more such men sent out there, who are so poor that when they come out there their first thoughts are how they can fill their own pockets.

We want preserves in our reserves. We want honest men, and we want you to help to keep us in the lands that belong to us so that we may not be a prey to those who are viciously disposed. I am going back home. I am very glad that you have listened to me, and I wish you good-bye and give you an affectionate farewell.

The Apache are a people determined to endure. And they have had a great deal of practice in the art of enduring. They managed to outlast the might of the Spanish conquest for two centuries. They outlasted the depredations of the Mexican government that sent soldiers against them, settlers into their lands, slavers among their people, and scalp hunters everywhere looking for Apache scalps worth $250 each. Then the transplant Americans assumed "the white man's burden" of extirpating the Apache. But with such leaders as Mangas Coloradas, Geronimo, and Cochise, a determined people perfected the art of enduring. Movies and television were more formidable opponents, and the integrity of Cochise has had difficulty surviving their assaults. Still, it survives. And it is readily apparent in the Chiricahua Apache leader's 1871 pledge to remain at peace.

Why Has the Virgin Mary Never Entered the Wigwams of the Apache?

The sun had been very hot on my head and made me as in a fire; my blood was on fire, but now I have come into this valley and drunk of these waters and washed myself in them and they have cooled me. Now that I am cool I have come with my hands open to you to live in peace with you. I speak straight and do not wish to deceive or be deceived. I want a good, strong and lasting peace. When God made the world he gave one part to the white man and another to the Apache. Why was it? Why did they come together? Now that I am to speak, the sun, the moon, the earth, the air, the waters, the birds and beasts, even the children unborn shall rejoice at my words. The white people have looked for me long. I am here! What do they want? They have looked for me long; why am I worth so much? If I am worth so much why not mark when I set my foot and look when I spit; the coyotes go about at night to rob and kill; I cannot see them; I am not God. I am no longer chief of all the Apaches. I am no longer rich; I am but a poor man. The world was not always this way. I cannot command the animals; if I would they would not obey me. God made us not as you; we were born like the animals, in the dry grass, not on beds like you. This is why we do as the animals, go about of a night and rob and steal. If I had such things as you have, I would not do as I do, for then I would not need to do so. There are Indians who go about killing and robbing. I do not command them. If I did, they would not do so. My warriors have been killed in Sonora. I came in here because God told me to do so. He said it was good to be at peace—so I came! I was going around the world with the clouds, and the air, when God spoke to my thought and told me to come in here and be at peace with all. He said the world was for us all; how was it? When I was young I walked all over this country, east and west, and saw no other people than the Apaches. After many summers I walked again and found another race of people had come to take it. How is it? Why is it that the Apaches wait to die— that they carry their lives on their finger nails? They roam over the hills and plains and want the heavens to fall on them. The Apaches were once a great nation; they are now but few, and because of this they want to die and so carry their lives on their finger nails. Many have been killed in battle. You must speak straight so that your words may go as sunlight to our hearts. *Tell me, if the Virgin Mary has walked throughout all the land, why has she never entered the wigwam of the Apache? Why have we never seen or heard her?*

I have no father nor mother; I am alone in the world. No one cares for Cochise; that is why I do not care to live, and wish the rocks to fall on me and cover me up. If I had a father and a mother like you, I would be with them and they with me. When I was going around the world, all were asking for Cochise. Now he is here—you see him and hear him—are you glad? If so, say so. Speak, Americans and Mexicans, I do not wish to hide anything from you nor have you hide anything from me; I will not lie to you; do not lie to me. I want to live in these mountains; I do not want to go to Tularosa. That is a long ways off. The flies on those mountains eat out the eyes of the horses. The bad spirits live there. I have drunk of these waters and they have cooled me; I do not want to leave here.

The Sioux warrior Sitting Bull has suffered as many indignities as Cochise, and fact and fiction have become incredibly mixed. Some few incontrovertible facts do exist: He was an extraordinarily clever leader who might have changed the history of Western America had he been able to secure adequate arms for his warriors. He was murdered by Indian police in the hire of transplant Americans. They must have been afraid he would rise like Lazarus, for they opened his crude coffin and poured chloride of lime and muriatic acid on his corpse. His last song was sung after he had surrendered to the United States authorities after the defeat of Custer. He sang this song in 1876.

The Last Song of Sitting Bull, the Teton Sioux

A warrior
I have been.
Now
It is all over.
A hard time
I have.

Crazy Horse of the Sioux insisted he could not be killed by a bullet. He obviously believed he could not, for he was indifferent, even cavalier, about gunfire. Others shared his belief. Afraid he might be planning an uprising, those who feared him most sent forty-three policemen to arrest him. One ran a bayonet into his stomach. A few hours later, after speaking with Indian Agent Jesse M. Lee, he died. His last speech:

We Preferred Our Own Way

My friend, I do not blame you for this. Had I listened to you this trouble would not have happened to me. I was not hostile to the white men. Sometimes my young men would attack the Indians who were their enemies and took their ponies. They did it in return.

We had buffalo for food, and their hides for clothing and for our teepees. We preferred hunting to a life of idleness on the reservation, where we were driven against our will. At times we did not get enough to eat, and we were not allowed to leave the reservation to hunt.

We preferred our own way of living. We were no expense to the government. All we wanted was peace and to be left alone. Soldiers were sent out in the winter, who destroyed our villages.

Then "Long Hair" (Custer) came in the same way. They say we massacred him, but he would have done the same thing to us had we not defended ourselves and fought to the last. Our first impulse was to escape with our squaws and papooses, but we were so hemmed in that we had to fight.

After that I went up on the Tongue River with a few of my people and lived in peace. But the government would not let me alone. Finally, I came back to the Red Cloud Agency. Yet I was not allowed to remain quiet.

I was tired of fighting. I went to the Spotted Tail Agency and asked that chief and his agent to let me live there in peace. I came here with the agent (Lee) to talk with the Big White Chief but was not given a chance. They tried to confine me. I tried to escape, and a soldier ran his bayonet into me.

I have spoken.

Chief Joseph of the Nez Percé has probably been quoted more often than any other Native American. His dignity, his determination, and his dedication to all he considered honorable make him one of the exemplary models for all Native Americans. He speaks best for himself in "An Indian's Views of Indian Affairs" which appeared in the North American Review *of April, 1879.*

An Indian's Views of Indian Affairs

My friends, I have been asked to show you my heart. I am glad to have a chance to do so. I want the white people to understand my people. Some of you think an Indian is like a wild animal. This is a great mistake. I will tell you all about our people, and then you can judge whether an Indian is a man or not. I believe much trouble and blood would be saved if we opened our hearts more. I will tell you in my way how the Indian sees things. The white man has more words to tell you how they look to him, but it does not require many words to speak the truth. What I have to say will come from my heart, and I will speak with a straight tongue. Ah-cum-kin-i-ma-me-hut (the Great Spirit) is looking at me, and will hear me.

My name is In-mut-too-yah-lat-lat (Thunder traveling over the Mountains). I am chief of the Wal-lam-wat-kin band of Chute-pa-lu, or Nez Percés (nose-pierced Indians). I was born in eastern Oregon, thirty-eight winters ago. My father was chief before me. When a young man, he was called Joseph by Mr. Spaulding, a missionary. He died a few years ago. He left a good name on earth. He advised me well for my people.

Our fathers gave us many laws, which they had learned from their fathers. These laws were good. They told us to treat all men as they treated us; that we should never be the first to break a bargain; that it was a disgrace to tell a lie; that we should speak only the truth; that it was a shame for one man to take from another his wife or his property without paying for it. We were taught to believe that the Great

Spirit sees and hears everything, and that he never forgets; that hereafter he will give every man a spirit-home according to his desserts:
if he has been a good man, he will have a good home; if he has been a
bad man, he will have a bad home. This I believe, and all my people
believe the same.

We did not know there were other people besides the Indian until about one hundred winters ago, when some men with white
faces came to our country. They brought many things with them to
trade for furs and skins. They brought tobacco, which was new to us.
They brought guns with flint stones on them, which frightened our
women and children. Our people could not talk with these white-faced
men, but they used signs which all people understand. These men were
Frenchmen, and they called our people "Nez Percés," because they
wore rings in their noses for ornaments. Although very few of our
people wear them now, we are still called by the same name. These
French trappers said a great many things to our fathers, which have
been planted in our hearts. Some were good for us, but some were bad.
Our people were divided in opinion about these men. Some thought
they taught more bad than good. An Indian respects a brave man, but
he despises a coward. He loves a straight tongue, but he hates a forked
tongue. The French trappers told us some truths and some lies.

The first white men of your people who came to our country were named Lewis and Clarke. They also brought many things that
our people had never seen. They talked straight, and our people gave
them a great feast, as a proof that their hearts were friendly. These men
were very kind. They made presents to our chiefs and our people made
presents to them. We had a great many horses, of which we gave them
what they needed, and they gave us guns and tobacco in return. All the
Nez Percés made friends with Lewis and Clarke, and agreed to let them
pass through their country, and never to make war on white men. This
promise the Nez Percés have never broken. No white man can accuse
them of bad faith, and speak with a straight tongue. It has always been
the pride of the Nez Percés that they were the friends of the white men.
When my father was a young man there came to our country a white man
(Rev. Mr. Spaulding) who talked spirit law. He won the affections of our
people because he spoke good things to them. At first he did not say anything about white men wanting to settle on our lands. Nothing was said
about that until about twenty winters ago, when a number of white
people came into our country and built houses and made farms. At first
our people made no complaint. They thought there was room enough
for all to live in peace, and they were learning many things from the
white men that seemed to be good. But we soon found that the white
men were growing rich very fast, and were greedy to possess everything
the Indian had. My father was the first to see through the schemes of the
white men, and he warned his tribe to be careful about trading with

them. He had suspicion of men who seemed anxious to make money. I was a boy then, but I remember well my father's caution. He had sharper eyes than the rest of our people.

Next there came a white officer (Governor Stevens), who invited all the Nez Percés to a treaty council. After the council was opened he made known his heart. He said there were a great many white people in our country, and many more would come; that he wanted the land marked out so that the Indians and white men could be separated. If they were to live in peace it was necessary, he said, that the Indians should have a country set apart for them, and in that country they must stay. My father, who represented his band, refused to have anything to do with the council, because he wished to be a free man. He claimed that no man owned any part of the earth, and a man could not sell what he did not own.

Mr. Spaulding took hold of my father's arm and said, "Come and sign the treaty." My father pushed him away, and said: "Why do you ask me to sign away my country? It is your business to talk to us about spirit matters and not to talk to us about parting with our land." Governor Stevens urged my father to sign his treaty, but he refused. "I will not sign your paper," he said; "you go where you please, so do I; you are not a child, I am no child; I can think for myself. No man can think for me. I have no other home than this. I will not give it up to any man. My people would have no home. Take away your paper. I will not touch it with my hand."

My father left the council. Some of the chiefs of the other bands of the Nez Percés signed the treaty, and then Governor Stevens gave them presents of blankets. My father cautioned his people to take no presents, for "after a while," he said, "they will claim that you have accepted pay for your country." Since that time four bands of the Nez Percés have received annuities from the United States. My father was invited to many councils, and they tried hard to make him sign the treaty, but he was firm as the rock, and would not sign away his home. His refusal caused a difference among the Nez Percés.

Eight years later (1863) was the next treaty council. A chief called Lawyer, because he was a great talker, took the lead in this council, and sold nearly all the Nez Percés country. My father was not there. He said to me: "When you go into council with the white man, always remember your country. Do not give it away. The white man will cheat you out of your home. I have taken no pay from the United States. I have never sold our land." In this treaty Lawyer acted without authority from our band. He had no right to sell the Wallowa (winding water) country. That had always belonged to my father's own people, and the other bands had never disputed our right to it. No other Indians ever claimed Wallowa.

In order to have all people understand how much land we owned, my father planted poles around it and said:

"Inside is the home of my people — the white man may take the land outside. Inside this boundary all our people were born. It circles around the graves of our fathers, and we will never give up these graves to any man."

The United States claimed they had bought all the Nez Percés country outside the Lapwai Reservation, from Lawyer and other chiefs, but we continued to live on this land in peace until eight years ago, when white men began to come inside the bounds my father had set. We warned them against this great wrong, but they would not leave our land, and some bad blood was raised. The white men represented that we were going upon the warpath. They reported many things that were false.

The United States Government again asked for a treaty council. My father had become blind and feeble. He could no longer speak for his people. It was then that I took my father's place as chief. In this council I made my first speech to white men. I said to the agent who held the council:

"I did not want to come to this council, but I came hoping that we could save blood. The white man has no right to come here and take our country. We have never accepted any presents from the Government. Neither Lawyer nor any other chief had authority to sell this land. It has always belonged to my people. It came unclouded to them from our fathers, and we will defend this land as long as a drop of Indian blood warms the hearts of our men."

The agent said he had orders, from the Great White Chief at Washington, for us to go upon the Lapwai Reservation, and that if we obeyed he would help us in many ways. "You must move to the agency," he said. I answered him: "I will not. I do not need your help; we have plenty, and we are contented and happy if the white man will let us alone. The reservation is too small for so many people with all their stock. You can keep your presents; we can go to your towns and pay for all we need; we have plenty of horses and cattle to sell, and we won't have any help from you; we are free now; we can go where we please. Our fathers were born here. Here they lived, here they died, here are their graves. We will never leave them." The agent went away, and we had peace for a little while.

Soon after this my father sent for me. I saw he was dying. I took his hand in mine. He said: "My son, my body is returning to my mother earth, and my spirit is going very soon to see the Great Spirit Chief. When I am gone, think of your country. You are the chief of these people. They look to you to guide them. Always remember that your father never sold this country. You must stop your ears whenever you are asked to sign a treaty selling your home. A few years more, and white men will be all around you. They have their eyes on this land. My son, never forget my dying words. This country holds your father's body. Never sell the bones of your father and your mother." I pressed my father's hand and told him I would protect his grave with my life. My father smiled and passed away to the spirit land.

I buried him in that beautiful valley of winding waters. I love that land more than all the rest of the world. A man who would not love his father's grave is worse than a wild animal.

For a short time we lived quietly. But this could not last. White men had found gold in the mountains around the land of winding water. They stole many horses from us, and we could not get them back because we were Indians. The white men told lies for each other. They drove off a great many of our cattle. Some white men branded our young cattle so they could claim them. We had no friend who would plead our cause before the law councils. It seemed to me that some of the white men in Wallowa were doing these things on purpose to get up a war. They knew that we were not strong enough to fight them. I labored hard to avoid trouble and bloodshed. We gave up some of our country to the white men, thinking that then we could have peace. We were mistaken. The white man would not let us alone. We could have avenged our wrongs many times, but we did not. Whenever the Government has asked us to help them against other Indians, we have never refused. When the white men were few and we were strong we could have killed them all off, but the Nez Percés wished to live at peace.

If we have not done so, we have not been to blame. I believe that the old treaty has never been correctly reported. If we ever owned the land we own it still, for we never sold it. In the treaty councils the commissioners have claimed that our country had been sold to the Government. Suppose a white man should come to me and say, "Joseph, I like your horses, and I want to buy them." I say to him, "No, my horses suit me, I will not sell them." Then he goes to my neighbor, and says to him: "Joseph has some good horses. I want to buy them, but he refuses to sell." My neighbor answers, "Pay me the money, and I will sell you Joseph's horses." The white man returns to me, and says, "Joseph, I have bought your horses, and you must let me have them." If we sold our lands to the Government, this is the way they were bought.

On account of the treaty made by the other bands of the Nez Percés, the white men claimed my lands. We were troubled greatly by white men crowding over the line. Some of these were good men, and we lived on peaceful terms with them, but they were not all good.

Nearly every year the agent came over from Lapwai and ordered us on to the reservation. We always replied that we were satisfied to live in Wallowa. We were careful to refuse presents or annuities which he offered.

Through all the years since the white men came to Wallowa we have been threatened and taunted by them and the treaty Nez Percés. They have given us no rest. We have had a few good friends among white men, and they have always advised my people to bear these taunts without fighting. Our young men were quick-tempered, and I have had great trouble in keeping them from doing rash things. I have carried a heavy load on my back ever since I was a boy. I learned then that we were but few, while the white men were many, and that we could not hold our own with them. We were like deer. They were like grizzly bears. We had a small country. Their country was large. We were contented to let things remain as the Great Spirit Chief made them. They were not; and would change the rivers and mountains if they did not suit them.

Year after year we have been threatened, but no war was made upon my people until General Howard came to our country two years ago and told us he was the white war-chief of all that country. He said: "I have a great many soldiers at my back. I am going to bring them up here, and then I will talk to you again. I will not let white men laugh at me the next time I come. The country belongs to the Government, and I intend to make you go upon the reservation."

I remonstrated with him against bringing more soldiers to the Nez Percés country. He had one house full of troops all the time at Fort Lapwai.

The next spring the agent at Umatilla agency sent an Indian runner to tell me to meet General Howard at Walla Walla. I could not go myself, but I sent my brother and five other head men to meet him, and they had a long talk.

General Howard said: "You have talked straight, and it is all right. You can stay in Wallowa." He insisted that my brother should go with him to Fort Lapwai. When the party arrived there General Howard sent runners and called all the Indians in to a grand council. I was in that council. I said to General Howard, "We are ready to listen." He answered that he would not talk then, but would hold a council next day, when he would talk plainly. I said to General Howard: "I am ready to talk today. I have been in a great many councils, but I am no wiser. We are all sprung from a woman, although we are unlike in many things. We can not be made over again. You are as you were made, and as you were made you can remain. We are just as we were made by the Great Spirit, and you can not change us; then why should children of one mother and one father quarrel—why should one try to cheat the other? I do not believe that the Great Spirit Chief gave one kind of men the right to tell another kind of men what they must do."

General Howard replied: "You deny my authority, do you? You want to dictate to me, do you?"

Then one of my chiefs—Too-hool-hool-suit—rose in the council and said to General Howard: "The Great Spirit Chief made the world as it is, and as he wanted it, and he made a part of it for us to live upon. I do not see where you get authority to say that we shall not live where he placed us."

General Howard lost his temper and said: "Shut up! I don't want to hear any more of such talk. The law says you shall go upon the reservation to live, and I want you to do so, but you persist in disobeying the law" (meaning the treaty). "If you do not move, I will take the matter into my own hand, and make you suffer for your disobedience."

Too-hool-hool-suit answered: "Who are you, that you ask us to talk, and then tell me I shan't talk? Are you the Great Spirit? Did you make the world? Did you make the sun? Did you make the rivers to run for us to drink? Did you make the grass to grow? Did you make all these things, that you talk to us as though we were boys? If you did, then you have the right to talk as you do."

General Howard replied, "You are an impudent fellow, and I will put you in the guard house," and then ordered a soldier to arrest him.

Too-hool-hool-suit made no resistance. He asked General Howard: "Is that your order? I don't care. I have expressed my heart to you. I have nothing to take back. I have spoken for my country. You can arrest me, but you can not change me or make me take back what I have said."

The soldiers came forward and seized my friend and took him to the guard house. My men whispered among themselves whether they should let this thing be done. I counseled them to submit. I knew if we resisted that all the white men present, including General Howard, would be killed in a moment, and we would be blamed. If I had said nothing, General Howard would never have given another unjust order against my men. I saw the danger, and, while they dragged Too-hool-hool-suit to prison, I arose and said: "I am going to talk now. I don't care whether you arrest me or not." I turned to my people and said: "The arrest of Too-hool-hool-suit was wrong, but we will not resent the insult. We were invited to this council to express our hearts, and we have done so." Too-hool-hool-suit was prisoner for five days before he was released.

The council broke up for that day. On the next morning General Howard came to my lodge, and invited me to go with him and White-Bird and Looking-Glass, to look for land for my people. As we rode along we came to some good land that was already occupied by Indians and white people. General Howard, pointing to this land, said: "If you will come on to the reservation, I will give you these lands and move these people off."

I replied: "No. It would be wrong to disturb these people. I have no right to take their homes. I have never taken what did not belong to me. I will not now."

We rode all day upon the reservation, and found no good land unoccupied. I have been informed by men who do not lie that General Howard sent a letter that night, telling the soldiers at Walla Walla to go to Wallowa Valley, and drive us out upon our return home.

In the council, next day, General Howard informed me, in a haughty spirit, that he would give my people thirty days to go back home, collect all their stock, and move on to the reservation, saying,

"If you are not here in that time, I shall consider that you want to fight, and will send my soldiers to drive you on."

I said: "War can be avoided, and it ought to be avoided. I want no war. My people have always been the friends of the white man. Why are you in such a hurry? I can not get ready to move in thirty days. Our stock is scattered, and Snake River is very high. Let us wait until fall, then the river will be low. We want time to hunt up our stock and gather supplies for winter."

General Howard replied: "If you let the time run over one day, the soldiers will be there to drive you on to the reservation, and all your cattle and horses outside of the reservation at that time will fall into the hands of the white men."

I knew I had never sold my country, and that I had no land in Lapwai; but I did not want bloodshed. I did not want my people killed. I did not want anybody killed. Some of my people had been murdered by white men, and the white murderers were never punished for it. I told General Howard about this, and again said I wanted no war. I wanted the people who lived upon the lands I was to occupy at Lapwai to have time to gather their harvest.

I said in my heart that, rather than have war, I would give up my country. I would give up my father's grave. I would give up everything rather than have the blood of white men upon the hands of my people.

General Howard refused to allow me more than thirty days to move my people and their stock. I am sure that he began to prepare for war at once.

When I returned to Wallowa I found my people very much excited upon discovering that the soldiers were already in the Wallowa Valley. We held a council and decided to move immediately, to avoid bloodshed.

Tool-hool-hool-suit, who felt outraged by his imprisonment, talked for war, and made many of my young men willing to fight rather than be driven like dogs from the land where they were born. He declared that blood alone would wash out the disgrace General Howard had put upon him. It required a strong heart to stand up against such talk, but I urged my people to be quiet, and not to begin a war.

We gathered all the stock we could find, and made an attempt to move. We left many of our horses and cattle in Wallowa, and we lost several hundred in crossing the river. All of my people succeeded in getting across in safety. Many of the Nez Percés came together in Rocky Cañon to hold a grand council. I went with all my people. This council lasted ten days. There was a great deal of war talk, and a great deal of excitement. There was one young brave present whose father had been killed by a white man five years before. This man's blood was bad against white men, and he left the council calling for revenge.

Again I counseled peace, and I thought the danger was past. We had not complied with General Howard's order because we could not, but we intended to do so as soon as possible. I was leaving the council to kill beef for my family, when news came that the young man whose father had been killed had gone out with several other hot-blooded young braves and killed four white men. He rode up to the council and shouted: "Why do you sit here like women? The war has begun already." I was deeply grieved. All the lodges were moved except my brother's and my own. I saw clearly that the war was upon us when I learned that my young men had been secretly buying ammunition. I heard then that Too-hool-hool-suit, who had been imprisoned by General Howard, had succeeded in organizing a war party. I knew that their acts would involve all my people. I saw that the war could not be prevented. The time had passed. I counseled peace from the beginning. I knew that we were too weak to fight the United States. We had many grievances, but I knew that war would bring more. We had good white friends, who advised us against taking the war path. My friend and brother, Mr. Chapman, who has been with us since the surrender, told us just how the war would end. Mr. Chapman took sides against us, and helped General Howard. I do not blame him for doing so. He tried hard to prevent bloodshed. We hoped the white settlers would not join the soldiers. Before the war commenced we had discussed this matter all over, and many of my people were in favor of warning them that if they took no part against us they should not be molested in the event of war being begun by General Howard. This plan was voted down in the war council.

There were bad men among my people who had quarreled with white men, and they talked of their wrongs until they roused all the bad hearts in the council. Still I could not believe that they would begin the war. I know that my young men did a great wrong, but I ask, Who was first to blame? They had been insulted a thousand times; their fathers and brothers had been killed; their mothers and wives had been disgraced; they had been driven to madness by whisky sold to them by white men; they had been told by General Howard that all their horses and cattle which they had been unable to drive out of Wallowa were to fall into the hands of white men; and, added to all this, they were homeless and desperate.

I would have given my own life if I could have undone the killing of white men by my people. I blame my young men and I blame the white men. I blame General Howard for not giving my people time to get their stock away from Wallowa. I do not acknowledge that he had the right to order me to leave Wallowa at any time. I deny that either my father or myself ever sold that land. It is still our land. It may never again be our home, but my father sleeps there, and I love it as I love my mother. I left there, hoping to avoid bloodshed.

If General Howard had given me plenty of time to gather up my stock, and treated Too-hool-hool-suit as a man should be treated, there would have been no war.

My friends among white men have blamed me for the war. I am not to blame. When my young men began the killing, my heart was hurt. Although I did not justify them, I remembered all the insults I had endured, and my blood was on fire. Still I would have taken my people to the buffalo country without fighting, if possible.

I could see no other way to avoid a war. We moved over to White Bird Creek, sixteen miles away, and there encamped, intending to collect our stock before leaving; but the soldiers attacked us, and the first battle was fought. We numbered in that battle sixty men, and the soldiers a hundred. The fight lasted but a few minutes, when the soldiers retreated before us for twelve miles. They lost thirty-three killed, and had seven wounded. When an Indian fights, he only shoots to kill; but soldiers shoot at random. None of the soldiers were scalped. We do not believe in scalping, nor in killing wounded men. Soldiers do not kill many Indians unless they are wounded and left upon the battle field. Then they kill Indians.

Seven days after the first battle, General Howard arrived in the Nez Percés country, bringing seven hundred more soldiers. It was now war in earnest. We crossed the Salmon River, hoping General Howard would follow. We were not disappointed. He did follow us, and we got back between him and his supplies, and cut him off for three days. He sent out two companies to open the way. We attacked them, killing one officer, two guides, and ten men.

We withdrew, hoping the soldiers would follow, but they had got fighting enough for that day. They entrenched themselves, and next day we attacked them again. The battle lasted all day, and was renewed next morning. We killed four and wounded seven or eight.

About this time General Howard found out that we were in his rear. Five days later he attacked us with three hundred and fifty soldiers and settlers. We had two hundred and fifty warriors. The fight lasted twenty-seven hours. We lost four killed and several wounded. General Howard's loss was twenty-nine men killed and sixty wounded.

The following day the soldiers charged upon us, and we retreated with our families and stock a few miles, leaving eighty lodges to fall into General Howard's hands.

Finding that we were outnumbered, we retreated to Bitter Root Valley. Here another body of soldiers came upon us and demanded our surrender. We refused. They said, "You can not get by us." We answered, "We are going by you without fighting if you will let us, but we are going by you anyhow." We then made a treaty with these soldiers. We agreed not to molest any one, and they agreed that we might pass through the Bitter Root country in peace. We bought provisions and traded stock with white men there.

We understood that there was to be no more war. We intended to go peaceably to the buffalo country, and leave the question of returning to our country to be settled afterward.

With this understanding we traveled on for four days, and, thinking that the trouble was all over, we stopped and prepared tent poles to take with us. We started again, and at the end of two days we saw three white men passing our camp. Thinking that peace had been made, we did not molest them. We could have killed them or taken them prisoners, but we did not suspect them of being spies, which they were.

That night the soldiers surrounded our camp. About daybreak one of my men went out to look after his horse. The soldiers saw him and shot him down like a coyote. I have since learned that these soldiers were not those we had left behind. They had come upon us from another direction. The new white war chief's name was Gibbon. He charged upon us while some of my people were still asleep. We had a hard fight. Some of my men crept around and attacked the soldiers from the rear. In this battle we lost nearly all our lodges, but we finally drove General Gibbon back.

Finding that he was not able to capture us, he sent to his camp a few miles away for his big guns (cannons), but my men had captured them and all the ammunition. We damaged the big guns all we could, and carried away the powder and lead. In the fight with General Gibbon we lost fifty women and children and thirty fighting men. We remained long enough to bury our dead. The Nez Percés never make war on women and children; we could have killed a great many women and children while the war lasted, but we would feel ashamed to do so cowardly an act.

We never scalp our enemies, but when General Howard came up and joined General Gibbon, their Indian scouts dug up our dead and scalped them. I have been told that General Howard did not order this great shame to be done.

We retreated as rapidly as we could toward the buffalo country. After six days General Howard came close to us, and we went out and attacked him, and captured nearly all his horses and mules (about two hundred and fifty head). We then marched on to the Yellowstone Basin.

On the way we captured one white man and two white women. We released them at the end of three days. They were treated kindly. The women were not insulted. Can the white soldiers tell me of one time when Indian women were taken prisoners, and held three days and then released without being insulted? Were the Nez Percés women who fell into the hands of General Howard's soldiers treated with as much respect? I deny that a Nez Percé was ever guilty of such a crime.

A few days later we captured two more white men. One

of them stole a horse and escaped. We gave the other a poor horse and told him he was free.

Nine days' march brought us to the mouth of Clarke's Fork of the Yellowstone. We did not know what had become of General Howard, but we supposed that he had sent for more horses and mules. He did not come up, but another new war chief (General Sturgis) attacked us. We held him in check while we moved all our women and children and stock out of danger, leaving a few men to cover our retreat.

Several days passed, and we heard nothing of General Howard, or Gibbon, or Sturgis. We had repulsed each in turn, and began to feel secure, when another army, under General Miles, struck us. This was the fourth army, each of which outnumbered our fighting force, that we had encountered within sixty days.

We had no knowledge of General Miles' army until a short time before he made a charge upon us, cutting our camp in two, and capturing nearly all of our horses. About seventy men, myself among them, were cut off. My little daughter, twelve years old, was with me. I gave her a rope, and told her to catch a horse and join the others who were cut off from the camp. I have not seen her since, but I have learned that she is alive and well.

I thought of my wife and children, who were now surrounded by soldiers, and I resolved to go to them or die. With a prayer in my mouth to the Great Spirit Chief who rules above, I dashed unarmed through the line of soldiers. It seemed to me that there were guns on every side, before and behind me. My clothes were cut to pieces and my horse was wounded, but I was unhurt. As I reached the door of my lodge, my wife handed me my rifle, saying: "Here's your gun. Fight!"

The soldiers kept up a continuous fire. Six of my men were killed in one spot near me. Ten or twelve soldiers charged into our camp and got possession of two lodges, killing three Nez Percés and losing three of their men, who fell inside our lines. I called my men to drive them back. We fought at close range, not more than twenty steps apart, and drove the soldiers back upon their main line, leaving their dead in our hands. We secured their arms and ammunition. We lost, the first day and night, eighteen men and three women. General Miles lost twenty-six killed and forty wounded. The following day General Miles sent a messenger into my camp under protection of a white flag. I sent my friend Yellow Bull to meet him.

Yellow Bull understood the messenger to say that General Miles wished me to consider the situation; that he did not want to kill my people unnecessarily. Yellow Bull understood this to be a demand for me to surrender and save blood. Upon reporting this message to me, Yellow Bull said he wondered whether General Miles was in earnest. I sent him back with my answer, that I had not made up my mind, but would think about it and send word soon. A little later he sent some

Cheyenne scouts with another message. I went out to meet them. They said they believed that General Miles was sincere and really wanted peace. I walked on to General Miles' tent. He met me and we shook hands. He said, "Come, let us sit down by the fire and talk this matter over." I remained with him all night; next morning Yellow Bull came over to see if I was alive, and why I did not return.

General Miles would not let me leave the tent to see my friend alone.

Yellow Bull said to me: "They have got you in their power, and I am afraid they will never let you go again. I have an officer in our camp, and I will hold him until they let you go free."

I said: "I do not know what they mean to do with me, but if they kill me you must not kill the officer. It will do no good to avenge my death by killing him."

Yellow Bull returned to my camp. I did not make any agreement that day with General Miles. The battle was renewed while I was with him. I was very anxious about my people. I knew that we were near Sitting Bull's camp in King George's land, and I thought maybe the Nez Percés who had escaped would return with assistance. No great damage was done to either party during the night.

On the following morning I returned to my camp by agreement, meeting the officer who had been held a prisoner in my camp at the flag of truce. My people were divided about surrendering. We could have escaped from Bear Paw Mountain if we had left our wounded, old women, and children behind. We were unwilling to do this. We had never heard of a wounded Indian recovering while in the hands of white men.

On the evening of the fourth day General Howard came in with a small escort, together with my friend Chapman. We could now talk understandingly. General Miles said to me in plain words, "If you will come out and give up your arms, I will spare your lives and send you to your reservation." I do not know what passed between General Miles and General Howard.

I could not bear to see my wounded men and women suffer any longer; we had lost enough already. General Miles had promised that we might return to our own country with what stock we had left. I thought we could start again. I believed General Miles, or I never would have surrendered. I have heard that he has been censured for making the promise to return us to Lapwai. He could not have made any other terms with me at that time. I would have held him in check until my friends came to my assistance, and then neither of the generals nor their soldiers would have ever left Bear Paw Mountain alive.

On the fifth day I went to General Miles and gave up my gun, and said, "From where the sun now stands I will fight no more." My people needed rest—we wanted peace.

I was told we could go with General Miles to Tongue River and stay there until spring, when we would be sent back to our country.

Finally it was decided that we were to be taken to Tongue River. We had nothing to say about it. After our arrival at Tongue River, General Miles received orders to take us to Bismarck. The reason given was, that subsistence would be cheaper there.

General Miles was opposed to this order. He said: "You must not blame me. I have endeavored to keep my word, but the chief who is over me has given the order, and I must obey it or resign. That would do you no good. Some other officer would carry out the order."

I believe General Miles would have kept his word if he could have done so. I do not blame him for what we have suffered since the surrender. I do not know who is to blame. We gave up all our horses—over eleven hundred—and all our saddles—over one hundred —and we have not heard from them since. Somebody has got our horses.

General Miles turned my people over to another soldier, and we were taken to Bismarck. Captain Johnson, who now had charge of us, received an order to take us to Fort Leavenworth. At Leavenworth we were placed on a low river bottom, with no water except river water to drink and cook with. We had always lived in a healthy country, where the mountains were high and the water was cold and clear. Many of my people sickened and died, and we buried them in this strange land. I can not tell how much my heart suffered for my people while at Leavenworth. The Great Spirit Chief who rules above seemed to be looking some other way, and did not see what was being done to my people.

During the hot days (July, 1878) we received notice that we were to be moved farther away from our own country. We were not asked if we were willing to go. We were ordered to get into railroad cars. Three of my people died on the way to Baxter Springs. It was worse to die there than to die fighting in the mountains.

We were moved from Baxter Springs (Kansas) to the Indian Territory, and set down without our lodges. We had but little medicine, and we were nearly all sick. Seventy of my people have died since we moved there.

We had a great many visitors who have talked many ways. Some of the chiefs (General Fish and Colonel Stickney) from Washington came to see us, and selected land for us to live upon. We have not moved to that land, for it is not a good place to live.

The Commissioner Chief (E. A. Hayt) came to see us. I told him, as I told every one, that I expected General Miles' word would be carried out. He said it "could not be done; that white men now lived in my country and all the land was taken up; that, if I returned to Wallowa, I could not live in peace; that law-papers were out against my young men who began the war, and that the Government could not protect my people." This talk fell like a heavy stone upon my heart. I saw that I could not gain anything by talking to him. Other law chiefs (Congressional Committee) came to see me and said they would help me to get a healthy country. I did not know who to believe. The white people have too many chiefs. They do not understand each other. They do not all talk alike.

The Commissioner Chief (Mr. Hayt) invited me to go with him and hunt for a better home than we have now. I like the land we found (west of the Osage Reservation) better than any place I have seen in that country; but it is not a healthy land. There are no mountains and rivers. The water is warm. It is not a good country for stock. I do not believe my people can live there. I am afraid they will all die. The Indians who occupy that country are dying off. I promised Chief Hayt to go there, and do the best I could until the Government got ready to make good General Miles' word. I was not satisfied, but I could not help myself.

Then the Inspector Chief (General McNiel) came to my camp and we had a long talk. He said I ought to have a home in the mountain country north, and that he would write a letter to the Great Chief at Washington. Again the hope of seeing the mountains of Idaho and Oregon grew up in my heart.

At last I was granted permission to come to Washington and bring my friend Yellow Bull and our interpreter with me. I am glad we came. I have shaken hands with a great many friends, but there are some things I want to know which no one seems able to explain. I can not understand how the Government sends a man out to fight us, as it did General Miles, and then breaks his word. Such a government has something wrong about it. I can not understand why so many chiefs are allowed to talk so many different ways, and promise so many different things. I have seen the Great Father Chief (the President), the next Great Chief (Secretary of the Interior), the Commissioner Chief (Hayt), the Law Chief (General Butler), and many other law chiefs (Congressmen), and they all say they are my friends, and that I shall have justice, but while their mouths all talk right I do not understand why nothing is done for my people. I have heard talk and talk, but nothing is done. Good words do not last long unless they amount to something. Words do not pay for my dead people. They do not pay for my country, now overrun by white men. They do not protect my father's grave. They do not pay for all my horses and cattle. Good words will not give me back my children. Good words will not make good the promise of your War Chief General Miles. Good words will not give my people good health and stop them from dying. Good words will not get my people a home where they can live in peace and take care of themselves. I am tired of talk that comes to nothing. It makes my heart sick when I remember all the good words and all the broken promises. There has been too much talking by men who had no right to talk. Too many misrepresentations have been made, too many misunderstandings have come up between the white men about the Indians. If the white man wants to live in peace with the Indian he can live in peace. There need be no trouble. Treat all men alike. Give them the same law. Give them all an even chance to live and grow. All men were made by the same Great Spirit Chief. They are all brothers. The earth is the mother of all people, and all people should have equal rights upon it. You might as well expect the rivers to run backward as that any man who was born a free man should be contented when penned up and denied liberty to go where he pleases. If you tie a horse to a stake, do you expect he will grow fat? If you pen an Indian up on a small spot of earth, and compel him to stay there, he will not be contented, nor will he grow and prosper. I have asked some of the great white chiefs where they get their authority to say to the Indian that he shall stay in one place, while he sees white men going where they please. They can not tell me.

I only ask of the Government to be treated as all other men are treated. If I can not go to my own home, let me have a home in some country where my people will not die so fast. I would like to go to Bitter Root Valley. There my people would be healthy; where they are now they are dying. Three have died since I left my camp to come to Washington.

When I think of our condition my heart is heavy. I see men of my race treated as outlaws and driven from country to country, or shot down like animals.

I know that my race must change. We can not hold our own with the white men as we are. We only ask an even chance to live as other men live. We ask to be recognized as men. We ask that the same law shall work alike on all men. If the Indian breaks the law, punish him by the law. If the white man breaks the law, punish him also.

Let me be a free man—free to travel, free to stop, free to work, free to trade where I choose, free to choose my own teachers, free to follow the religion of my fathers, free to think and talk and act for myself—and I will obey every law, or submit to the penalty.

Whenever the white man treats an Indian as they treat each other, then we will have no more wars. We shall all be alike—brothers of one father and one mother, with one sky above us and one country around us, and one government for all. Then the Great Spirit Chief who rules above will smile upon this land, and send rain to wash out the bloody spots made by brothers' hands from the face of the earth. For this time the Indian race are waiting and praying. I hope no more groans of wounded men and women will ever go to the ear of the Great Spirit Chief above, and that all people may be one people.

In-mut-too-yah-lat-lat has spoken for his people.

Chief Joseph was the last of the great leaders to be subdued and sub-jected to the indignities the transplant American has reserved for the defeated within his borders, even as he has developed a capacity for restoring national pride and economic stability to the nations his superior technological skills allow him to bomb into submission on foreign shores. The surrender speech of Chief Joseph is indicative of the nobility of Native American leaders. And surely the quality of a people's leaders indicates the quality of a people, for leaders retain their positions only at the sufferance of those they lead; therefore they mirror the collective character. These are the words of Chief Joseph as he surrendered almost one hundred years ago. It had been a long, dismal century (1776-1877) for the Native American. The victim of the greatest act of aggression the world has ever known, the victim of a genocidal people hysterically determined to see themselves as superior creations of a god they had borrowed from the primitive and tribal Hebrews, the victim of a de-spoiler of the land and self, the Native American has been a paradigm of the classical tragic hero. Of noble birth, indeed, he has been reduced to low estate as a result of one overwhelming flaw. His flaw: honor and belief in the word. In a dishonest world where language is a weapon in the battle for possession, that is a tragic, tragic flaw.

The Surrender Speech of Chief Joseph

I am tired of fighting. Our chiefs are killed. Looking Glass is dead. Toohulhulsote is dead. The old men are all dead. It is the young men who say no and yes. He who led the young men is dead. It is cold and we have no blankets. The little children are freezing to death. My peo-ple, some of them, have run away to the hills and have no blankets, no food. No one knows where they are—perhaps they are freezing to death. I want to have time to look for my children and see how many of them I can find. Maybe I shall find them among the dead. Hear me, my chiefs, I am tired. My heart is sad and sick. From where the sun now stands I will fight no more forever.

Hear me, my chiefs! I am tired; my heart is sick and sad.

Chapter 6

To Golgotha and Back: Native American Religions After the Christian Invasion

Conquered peoples in all times, in all geographical areas experience a religious revival, a despairing resurgence of faith in the absence of hope. The Palestinian of the first centuries B.C. and A.D. is an excellent example of the anguish, the desperation, and the complexity of the cultural phenomenon of fragmentation that results from the superimposition of alien codes on a people in thrall. Finding his land appropriated by the technologically superior forces of Rome, he submitted in varying ways to edicts and decrees of his conquerors. He either allied himself with the Sadducees to reject oral laws, traditions, promises of hope in eternality, and a messiah because they were not specifically framed in the Old Testament which, they insisted, must be interpreted literally, or he sided with the Pharisees who interpreted the scriptures liberally, and adhered to oral laws and traditions which promised an afterlife and a messiah. Representatives on the theocratic right (the Sadducees) or the theocratic left (the Pharisees) appealed to the majority who were neither conservative nor liberal but who existed within the cultural dictates of the religious system as they lived out their lives of quiet desperation and hoped tomorrow would be better but expected it would be worse. The Sanhedrin, the supreme legislative council and highest ecclesiastical and secular tribunal of the Jews, was dominated by

313

the Sadducees but contained a representative, smaller number of Pharisees so that, torn by the ambitions of its membership, it debated and delayed important matters as it sought the economically expedient paths to coexistence with Caesar's legions. The people, weary of poverty, taxation, and oppression, gravitated to the fanatic but sincere fringe to the far left of the Pharisees, the prophets who sprang up like tares in the fertile gardens of discontent and depression.

And such a prophet was Zacharias, the father of John the Baptist, who prophesied over his newborn son:

Blessed be the Lord God of Israel; for he hath visited and redeemed his people, and hath raised up an horn of salvation for us in the house of his servant David; as he spake by the mouth of his holy prophets, which have been since the world began: That we should be saved from our enemies, and from the hand of all that hate us; to perform the mercy *promised* to our fathers, and to remember his holy covenant; the oath which he swore to our father Abraham, that he would grant unto us, that we being delivered out of the hand of our enemies might serve him without fear, in holiness and righteousness before him, all the days of our life. And thou, child, shalt be called the prophet of the Highest: for thou shalt go before the face of the Lord to prepare his ways; to give knowledge of salvation unto his people by the remission of their sins, through the tender mercy of our God; whereby the dayspring from on high hath visited us, to give light to them that sit in darkness, and *in* the shadow of death, to guide our feet into the way of peace.—Luke I:68-79

The advent of Christ was, in turn, prophesied by John and, on arrival at his years of ministry, Christ spoke in parables, ambiguities, and riddles that allowed one group to hear one thing, another group something else. The seeming failure of the ministry saw Christ on the cross at Golgotha and his followers, clothed in their invincible armor of faith, gathering to sing at the sign of the fish in Rome before they were massacred in the places of infamy that attest to the barbarous savagery of the world's most dominant and powerful culture—a culture that had waxed great as a result of its technological superiority, its insatiable appetite for lands it claimed by divine right, and a disregard for the cultures it deemed inferior. Itself decaying at the center, Rome touted its religion, its cultural superiority, its civilization as the most advanced, most noble, most artistically and technologically developed triumvirate the world had ever known or would ever know. And it closed its collective ears to the prophets of its own doom, its Cassandras. Incapable of living according to its ideals, inoperable in its far-reaching political interference with other nations, unable to provide stabilization and purpose for a frustrated and "fun loving" population that feasted on violence, nightmare, and horror, the empire finally crumbled before the refusal of a vanquished people to relinquish either its traditional religion or the ecumenical child it had spawned in that dark hour of greatest need for revitalized identity.

Small changes in nouns and religious affiliations could make the account fit other peoples in other times. The transplant American was a conquering army from Christian Europe. Settling into a vanquished land, he deemed the inhabitants inferior in every respect—from their tribal life patterns to their religions. Their arts were barbaric, their customs contemptible, their languages unrefined. Their land and its potential for exploitation were very desirable, and they could be utilized as slaves, as disinherited and powerless sources of new wealth for the civilized, refined, superior culture that dominated the world. Technological, religious, and artistic achievements of the vanquished peoples were beneath contempt, their dignity and sense of identity to be ignored.

And so they were. And so the prophets of the European American's own doom, after they had seen the pattern repeated, began their exhortations in the voices of Sidney Lanier in America and William Butler Yeats in England. Before their voices were raised, however, the Native American was conquered. He was given the choice of renouncing his religious concepts and embracing Christianity or dying by the transplant American's version of the sword. Many Native Americans died, for the land had that same covenantal quality that had existed in Palestine. Wah'kon-tah was an undeniable, unrenounceable reality without beginning, without end, without capacity to be destroyed by a self-deluding, self-aggrandizing, desperate group that had confused wealth, ease, and aspirations to luxury with dignity, honor, and identity; and time, as one of the more primitive and perceptive of the invaders was to say, is a stream man goes a-fishing in.

The Native American had always known the transcendental truth of Henry David Thoreau's statement in *Walden:*

The intellect is a cleaver; it discerns and rifts its way into the secret of things. I do not wish to be any more busy with my hands than is necessary. My head is hands and feet. I feel all my best faculties concentrated in it. My instinct tells me that my head is an organ for burrowing, as some creatures use their snout and fore paws, and with it I would mine and burrow my way through these hills. I think that the richest vein is somewhere hereabouts; so by the divining-rod and the thin rising vapors I judge; and here I will begin to mine.

The Indian's sacred lands were so integrally a part of his existence that, in the same indecision and confusion of values that marked the conduct of the Sanhedrin, the Native American delayed, compromised, sought security through accommodation and delusions of coexistence. And he saw himself torn between traditional values and ecumenical acculturation as Manito and Wah'kontah and the Kochinas merged with Jehovah and Christ to become neither one nor the other but some hybrid concept of the Great Spirit and some vague celestial geography called the happy hunting ground with the same promise of material reward the Christian had built into his eternal city with pearl-encrusted gates and streets paved with the yellow metal for which, on Earth, the transplant American would violate every religious rule and willingly forego any chance of ever seeing Heaven.

Religion, land, life—they went in that order as the Indian survived the unsuccessful battles for his land, for "life" was merely existence on some distant soil that remained Mother Earth beneath Father Sky but lacked the familiar haunts of the lesser divinities. And the revivalistic and messianic movements began.

The messianic movement among any people is the last, violent, desperate attempt to survive both physically and culturally, to retain life and identity; without identity, life becomes a despairing day-to-day search for some unknown reality that will make the daily search bearable—an endless cycle that lacks the satisfactions derived from commonality with the circular rhythms of the seasons or faith in the traditional patterns. Peter Farb explains the rise of such movements this way:

Every messianic movement known to history has arisen in a society that has been subjected to the severe stress of contact with an alien culture—involving military defeat, epidemic, and acculturation. The bewildered search for ways to counteract the threat may actually increase the stress, arousing anxiety over whether new solutions will be any better than the old. Once doubts arise about any aspect of the ancestral cultural system, there is yet increased stress due to fear that the entire cultural system may prove inadequate. At this point, the culture as a whole begins to break down, manifested by widespread alcoholism, apathy, disregard of kinship obligations and marriage rules, and intragroup violence.

Such behavior comes at the very time when the culture is least able to cope with it, and so the intensity of the stress increases still more. Ultimately, the inadequacy of the culture becomes apparent even to the most conservative of its members, and the culture may deteriorate to such an extent that it literally dies. The birth rate drops and the death rate rises; the society no longer possesses the will to resist, and it is fallen upon by predatory neighbors; the few survivors scatter and either gradually die out or are absorbed by other groups. The collapse may be forestalled or even averted if a revitalization or messianic movement arises that is acceptable to the culture. Such a movement depends upon the appearance of a particular personality at a certain precise time in the disintegration of the culture.

Almost every messianic movement known around the world came into being as the result of the hallucinatory visions of a prophet. One point must be emphasized about the prophet of the messianic movement: He is not a schizophrenic, as was so long assumed. A schizophrenic with religious paranoia will state that he is God, Jesus, the Great Spirit, or some other supernatural being. The prophet, on the other hand, never states that he is supernatural—only that he is or has been in contact with supernatural powers. (Of course, after his death, his disciples tend to deify him or at least to give him saintly status.)

Invariably the prophet emerges from his hallucinatory vision bearing a message from the supernatural that makes certain promises: the return of the bison herds, a happy hunting ground, or peace on earth and good will to men. Whatever the specific promises, the prophet offers a new power, a revitalization of the whole society. But to obtain these promises, the prophet says that certain rituals must be followed. These rituals may include dancing around a ghost pole or being baptized in water, but usually numerous other duties must be attended to day after day. At the same time that the prophet offers promises to the faithful, he also threatens punishment and catastrophe, such as world destruction or everlasting damnation. The prophet now declares the old ways dead and shifts attention to a new way or to a revised conception of an old part of the culture. To spread the word of what he has learned from his visions, he gathers about him disciples and missionaries.

The various prophets known to world history differed in their preaching methods, just as the American Indian prophets differed from each other. Some prophets spoke emotionally to large crowds, whereas others addressed themselves to small groups and left it to their disciples to carry the message. Some, like the Qumran sect that copied out the Dead Sea scrolls, appealed to a religious elite of particularly devout people, whereas others concerned themselves only with the downtrodden and exploited who shall inherit the earth.

What most impresses the people around the prophet is the personality change he has undergone during this time. In most cases, he lived in obscurity until he suddenly emerged as a prophet; the Indian prophets became cured of previous spiritual apathy, and those who had been alcoholics gave up the habit. The sudden transformation in personality may be due to changes produced in the body under physical and emotional stress, although more research on this point is needed. It is known, though, that individuals vary a great deal in the reaction of their metabolisms to stress. That alone would explain why, when stress reaches a certain intensity in the culture, only certain individuals feel called forth to become prophets while most do not. In any event, the prophet has emerged in a new cultural role, and his personality is liberated from the stress that called his response into being in the first place. Immune to the stress under which his brethren still suffer, he must to them appear supernatural.

The disciples who gather around the prophet also, like him, undergo a revitalizing personality change—as did Peter, to name one very familiar example. The prophet continues his spiritual leadership, but the disciples take upon themselves the practical tasks of organizing the campaign to establish the new movement. They convert large numbers of people, who in turn also undergo revitalizing personality transformations. If the messianic movement has been allowed to survive to this point by the oppressive, dominant culture that called it into being in the first place, a vital step must now be taken. The prophet must emphasize that he is only the intermediary between the converts and the supernatural being whose message he has been spreading. This step is essential, for it ensures the continuity of the new movement after its founding prophet dies. The prophet puts the converts and the supernatural being into close touch with each other by calling for certain symbolic duties the faithful must perform toward the supernatural being, such as eating peyote or partaking of bread and wine.

The new movement often has to resist both the oppressive alien culture and the opposition of factions within itself. The successful messianic movement meets this resistance by resorting to any one of a number of adaptations. It may change its teachings, as did the early Christians who gradually gave up Jewish rituals, such as circumcision. It may resort to political maneuvering and compromise. Most messianic movements, though, make the disastrous mistake that almost all Jewish and American Indian messianic movements did: They choose to fight. Islam alone succeeded by force of arms, whereas the success of the early Christians was their choice of universal peace as their weapon.

Once the messianic movement has won a large following, a new culture begins to emerge out of the death of the old—not only in religious affairs but in all aspects of economic, social, and political life as well. An organization with a secular and a sacerdotal hierarchy arises to perpetuate the new doctrine. The religion in that way becomes routinized in a stable culture. All routinized religions today (whether they be the Native American Church, Mohammedanism, Judaism, or Christianity) are successful descendants of what originated as messianic movements—that is, one personality's vision of a new way of life for a culture under extreme stress.

These steps apply equally to the messianic movement in Soviet Russia, even though it denies belief in the supernatural. Czarist Russia in 1917 was a society under extreme stress, disintegrating both on the war front and at home; in the previous decade it had suffered a humiliating defeat by the Japanese. There was unrest, and repressive measures were stern. A prophet, Lenin, arose; and he made a miraculous return from exile in Switzerland in a railroad car that traversed enemy territory. He preached his vision of Utopia, and he referred constantly to a revered, almost supernatural being named Karl Marx. The missionary fervor excited Lenin's close followers, and they in turn won adherents even among their former enemies in society. One element of the population in particular—the economically downtrodden—was appealed to, and it was promised a reward here on earth. But first these people had to perform certain rituals: convert to the new doctrine of Marx-Lenin; change the economic way of life; publicly confess errors, even if such confession resulted in martyrdom. After the prophet's death, a political organization of key disciples (Stalin, Trotsky, and others) continued his teachings and prepared a complex doctrine that admitted of no revisionism or deviation. The prophet himself was deified after death, as demonstrated today by the people paying homage at Lenin's tomb to the embalmed cadaver that, miraculously, is not heir to the flesh's corruption![1]

Farb's contention that the prophet's visions are hallucinatory, it should be noted, is merely an opinion. Undeniably, visions cannot be authenticated, but neither can atoms. Each is outside the realm of human observation, yet the effects of each are evident. The scientist accepts on faith in his own field that which the religionist might reject just as the religionist accepts on faith that which the scientist is apt to reject. To state categorically that visions are hallucinatory is to usurp the prerogatives of Orenda. Arguments in this area are profitless, for proof is denied all contenders. It is axiomatic, however, that every society honors its live conformists and its dead receivers of visions.

Attempts to reclaim the past, as if the present could be erased inevitably, led to failure for the messiahs, prophets, and people. One of the earliest prophets, Popé of the Tewa, succeeded at first but failed at last because he attempted to establish himself as virtual dictator, a political impossibility among the small tribes of the Pueblo who valued their individual existence and resisted the unification demanded by dictatorship. The initial uprising in 1680 destroyed the Catholic priests, their alien religion, and its cultural paraphernalia, and expelled the Spaniards who were not killed; but, in 1692, the Spanish returned with little difficulty, the cohesive power of Popé only a memory and the Pueblo incapable of resubmitting themselves to the indignity of mass power at the expense of individual group autonomy.

The longest, most successful messianic movement among the Native Americans began in Michigan when a nameless visionary, now called the Delaware Prophet, appeared in the Ohio Valley in 1762 and persuaded the Indians they needed neither the rum nor the gunpowder of the British to attain self-sufficiency. A return to the hunting and war weapons that had served them before the arrival of the white man would assure the removal of him and his devisiveness. The Ottawa Pontiac recognized the impracticability of the Delaware Prophet's exhortations but used the fervor they had generated to ally all of the tribes northwest of the Ohio River against

[1]Peter Farb, *Man's Rise to Civilization as Shown by the Indians of North America*...(New York, 1968), pp. 289–90.

the British and take eight of the ten forts (all but Detroit and Fort Pitt) on the Great Lakes. The Delaware Prophet had called for the expulsion of all whites; Pontiac twisted the words to mean only the British because he needed the support and powder of the French who promised aid but signed a treaty of peace with the British and attempted to remain friends with both for obvious tactical reasons. When the French finally refused to give their aid, Pontiac knew he could not take the remaining forts and, stunned by the defection of the French, he watched his Indian allies resume relations with the British until he was forced to negotiate with them in 1865. A Peoria assassin ended his life and lulled the messianic movement into forty years of fitful unrest until Elskwatawa (The Open Door) of the Shawnee declared himself a prophet and, with his widely respected brother Tecumtha, established Prophet's Town (Tippecanoe on the Wabash), a holy place where men worked hard, disdained alcohol, and subjected themselves to spartan discipline. From this base, Tecumtha traveled widely, exhorting the tribes to unite into one great state. The zeal of Elskwatawa, the organizational brilliance of Tecumtha worked to make the nation a seeming reality, but the ambitious governor of the Northwest Territory, William Henry Harrison, encouraged Tecumtha to believe the U.S. Government supported the effort as he simultaneously provoked the Prophet to attack the whites in Tecumtha's absence. At Tippecanoe on November 6, 1811, Harrison's and Elskwatawa's forces met. The governor's bullets would not be stopped by the magic spells of the Prophet, and the alliance of Tecumtha and the thousand warriors of Prophet's Town were scattered with the dream of an Indian nation centered in the Ohio Valley and the Great Lakes.

It seemed the transplant American would achieve by guile what bullets, rum, and smallpox had failed to accomplish. From the time of the Civil War, the official policy of the U.S. Government was, in essence: suppress the religious ceremonials of the Indian; force him to abandon all his old ways and become a farmer in spite of his religious objection to agricultural methods; destroy tribal holdings, and give the "surplus" to whites (see the Dawes Allotment Act of 1889); and, in the words of the Commissioner of Indian Affairs at the time, make the Indians "conform to the white man's ways, peaceably if they will, forceably if they must." Nor would the Indian henceforth be allowed to learn his own language. So pronounced the Commissioner of Indian Affairs in the following order:

It is believed that if any Indian vernacular is allowed to be taught by missionaries in schools on Indian reservations it will prejudice the pupil as well as his parents against the English language....This language which is good enough for a white man or a black man ought to be good enough for the red man. It is also believed that teaching an Indian youth in his own barbarous dialect is a positive detriment to him. The impracticability, if not impossibility, of civilizing the Indians of this country in any other tongue than our own would seem obvious.[2]

The last great resistance (for this burgeoning plan of cultural genocide was designed to replace the plan of extirpation which had failed) began with the birth of Smohalla about 1820. Of indeterminate tribal origin but probably a Sahaptin, Smohalla was born in the Rocky Mountains and educated by missionaries whose teachings were destined to provide the colorful aspects of his messianic career. When he was about forty years old, Smohalla and a rival shaman came to physical blows over their respective beliefs. Left for dead, Smohalla recovered and, after wandering the lands of the Southwest, eventually returned to his people and spread the news of his exchange with the "Great Spirit." The message he brought his people ("Return to your own religion!") was reinforced by their belief that Smohalla had died and been restored to life. And his frequent withdrawal into the visionary trance or dream state removed any lingering doubt. It also earned his followers the name "Dreamers," but so solidified them as a group that their active resistance to the U.S. Government's policy of forcing them to farm created problems that ultimately led to Chief Joseph's decision to flee into Canada with his Nez Percé to escape the cruel edict.

The story of that thousand-mile battle in 1877 is repugnant even to the most defensive transplant American. It began when the Nez Percé were told they would be moved from their Wallowa Valley in Oregon to a reservation in Idaho. Some acquiesced and signed a treaty, for, a proud and peaceful people, they had never raised arms against the white man; others resisted. Hinmaton-Yalaktit (Joseph) became chief and led the resistance after his father died and was buried in the beloved valley in 1873. However, the rich land was too great a temptation to whites who continued to pour into the valley, and in 1877, violence erupted.

Knowing his Nez Percé warriors were no match for the well-armed U.S. forces, Chief Joseph decided to take his people and

[2]Quoted in Edward E. Dale, *The Indians of the Southwest* (Norman, Oklahoma, 1949), pp. 185–86.

flee to sanctuary in Canada. On the long, grueling trip through Idaho, Wyoming, and Montana, the people were harassed and fired upon by the military forces of General O. O. Howard who had been ordered to return the Indians to the reservation or to make sure they did not cross the Canadian border. Outnumbered and under howitzer and Gatling gun siege, Chief Joseph's people fought valiantly but hopelessly before they surrendered almost in sight of the freedom of the border.

One of the white Cassandras wrote, in 1881,

Cheating, robbing, breaking promises—these three are clearly things which must cease to be done. One more thing, also, and that is the refusal of the protection of the law to the Indian's rights of property, "of life, liberty, and the pursuit of happiness." When these four things have ceased to be done, statesmanship, philanthropy, and Christianity can slowly and surely do the rest. Till these four things have ceased to be done, statesmanship and philanthropy alike must work in vain, and even Christianity can reap but small harvest.[3]

Sometime between 1868 and 1872 among the Paiute, a prophet named Tàvibo created a resurgence of hope with the report of a vision in which he had seen a giant earthquake swallow all men and disgorge only the Native American. Henceforth, peace and plenty would reign. Both a millenium and a "land of milk and honey" prophecy, its unfulfilled promise made Tàvibo's death in 1870 or 1871 particularly bitter in its attendant disappointments. While no recorded speeches or teachings of "The White Man" (as Tàvibo's name translates) exist, a summary letter from Captain J. M. Lee (who served under General Nelson A. Miles in the defeat of Chief Joseph and Geronimo) does exist. It was sent to James Mooney and included in the first chapter of his study, *The Ghost Dance Religion and the Sioux Outbreak of 1890.*

I was on Indian duty in Nevada in 1869, 1870, and 1871. When visiting Walker Lake reservation in 1869-70, I became acquainted with several superstitious beliefs then prevailing among the Paiute Indians. It was a rough, mountainous region roundabout, and mysterious happenings, according to tradition, always occurred when the prophet or medicine-men went up into the mountains and there received their revelations from the divine spirits. In the earlier part of the sixties the whites began to come in and appropriate much of the Indian country in Nevada, and in the usual course it turned out that the medicine-men or prophets were looked to for relief. The most influential went up alone into

[3]Helen Hunt Jackson, *A Century of Dishonor* (New York, 1881).

the mountain and there met the Great Spirit. He brought back with him no tablets of stone, but he was a messenger of good tidings to the effect that within a few moons there was to be a great upheaval or earthquake. All the improvements of the whites—all their houses, their goods, stores, etc.—would remain, but the whites would be swallowed up, while the Indians would be saved and permitted to enjoy the earth and all the fullness thereof, including anything left by the wicked whites. This revelation was duly proclaimed by the prophet, and attracted a few believers, but the doubting skeptics were too many, and they ridiculed the idea that the white man would fall into the holes and be swallowed up while the Indians would not. As the prophet could not enforce his belief, he went up into the mountain again and came back with a second revelation, which was that when the great disaster came, all, both Indians and whites, would be swallowed up or overwhelmed, but that at the end of three days (or a few days) the Indians would be resurrected in the flesh, and would live forever to enjoy the earth, with plenty of game, fish, and pine nuts, while their enemies, the whites, would be destroyed forever. There would thus be a final and eternal separation between Indians and whites.

This revelation, which seemed more reasonable, was rather popular for awhile, but as time wore along faith seemed to weaken and the prophet was without honor even in his own country. After much fasting and prayer, he made a third trip to the mountain, where he secured a final revelation or message to the people. The divine spirit had become so much incensed at the lack of faith in the prophecies, that it was revealed to his chosen one that those Indians who believed in the prophecy would be resurrected and be happy, but those who did not believe in it would stay in the ground and be damned forever with the whites.

It was not long after this that the prophet died, and the poor miserable Indians worried along for nearly two decades, eating grasshoppers, lizards, and fish, and trying to be civilized until the appearance of this new prophet Quoit-tsow, who is said to be the son, either actual or spiritual, of the first one.[4]

The claim of Tävibo is no more unbelievable than the claim of Moses that the Ten Commandments were delivered of Yaweh. And, certainly, the indicated skepticism of the people has its counterpart in the behavior of the followers of Moses who so irritated him that he broke the tablets in a fit of pique and had to make a second trip himself. If the earthquake vision seems a bit surrealistic, hallucinatory, and superstitious, compare it with this account:

And I saw an angel come down from heaven, having the key of the bottomless pit and a great chain in his hand. And he laid hold on the dragon, that old serpent, which is the Devil, and Satan, and bound him a thousand years, and cast him into the bottomless pit, and shut him up, and set a seal upon him, that

---

[4]*Fourteenth Annual Report of the Bureau of Ethnology to the Secretary of the Smithsonian Institution, 1892–93* (Washington, 1896).

he should deceive the nations no more, till the thousand years should be fulfilled: and after that he must be loosed a little season. And I saw thrones, and they sat upon them, and judgment was given unto them: and I saw the souls of them that were beheaded for the witness of Jesus, and for the word of God, and which had not worshipped the beast, neither his image, neither had received his mark upon their foreheads, or in their hands; and they lived and reigned with Christ a thousand years. But the rest of the dead lived not again until the thousand years were finished. This is the first resurrection. Blessed and holy is he that hath part in the first resurrection: on such the second death hath no power, but they shall be priests of God and of Christ, and shall reign with him a thousand years. And when the thousand years are expired, Satan shall be loosed out of his prison, and shall go out to deceive the nations which are in the four quarters of the earth, Gog and Magog, to gather them together to battle: the number of whom is as the sand of the sea. And they went up on the breadth of the earth, and compassed the camp of the saints about, and the beloved city: and fire came down from God out of heaven, and devoured them. And the devil that deceived them was cast into the lake of fire and brimstone, where the beast and the false prophet are, and shall be tormented day and night for ever and ever.

Fanatical, hysterical, frenzied? No less so than the vision of Tàvibo. Generations of acceptance of this passage as "divine revelation" create, at worst, a response of noblesse oblige in the inheritor of the Christian tradition, and he dismisses the passage as "symbolic, of course" because to do less would be an exhibition of bad taste. Yet he, the chronic defender of religious tolerance, will brand the visions of a man he denigrates as "Pagan" as the ravings of a madman or the lies of a charlatan. Not even his noblesse oblige will conceal his distress at a "pagan's" dismissing the words of St. John the Divine as they are recorded in Revelations 20:1-10.

At about the time of Tàvibo's death, a second prophet assumed the mantle. Mooney also reports an account of Tàvibo's inheritor, Waugh-zee-waugh-ber. The account is "from a letter addressed to the Commissioner of Indian Affairs under date of November 19, 1890, by Mr. Frank Campbell."

Eighteen years ago I was resident farmer on Walker Lake Indian reserve, Nevada. I had previously been connected with the Indian service at the reserve for ten years, was familiar with the Paiute customs, and personally acquainted with all the Indians in that region. In 1872 an Indian commenced preaching a new religion at that reserve that caused a profound sensation among the Paiute. For several months I was kept in ignorance of the cause of the excitement— which was remarkable, considering the confidence they had always reposed in me. They no doubt expected me to ridicule the sayings of the new messiah, as I had always labored among them to break down their superstitious beliefs. When finally I was made acquainted with the true facts of the case, I told them the preachings of Waugh-zee-waugh-ber were good and no harm could come from it. Indian emissaries visited the reserve from Idaho, Oregon, and other places, to investigate the new religion. I visited the Indian camp while the prophet was in a trance and remained until he came to. In accordance with instructions, the Indians gathered around him and joined in a song that was to guide the spirit back to the body. Upon reanimation he gave a long account of his visit to the Supreme Ruler, who was then on the way with all the spirits of the departed dead to again reside upon this earth and change it into a paradise. Life was to be eternal, and no distinction was to exist between races.

This morning's press dispatches contain an account of Porcupine's visit to Walker Lake...that proves to me that the religion started at Walker Lake eighteen years ago is the same that is now agitating the Indian world. There is nothing in it to cause trouble between whites and Indians unless the new messiah is misquoted and his doctrine misconstrued. I left Walker Lake reserve in June, 1873, and at the time supposed this craze would die out, but have several times since been reminded by Nevada papers and letters that it was gradually spreading.

The vision of Waugh-zee-waugh-ber was, specifically, that an enormous train would bring the dead and notify all Indians of its arrival with a great explosion. Song and dance (the magic incantation of the word) would speed the day. The people sang and danced, but time passed; the great train did not arrive. The Union Pacific Railroad had made its first transcontinental run shortly before, and none would deny the obvious connection. It is obvious that prophets and messiahs are confined to their experience or to the technological realities of their time—as obvious as Christ's limited observations about the destruction of the temple or his vague answers about the date of the end of the world.

The Mormons of an earlier decade had been granted some very specific prophecies by their founder, Joseph Smith. According to his 1843 prophecy, in his eighty-fifth year (1890) he would see the messiah in the flesh. He had earlier prophesied a New Jerusalem in the desert where all the faithful would gather, including the lost tribes of Israel—in his opinion, the Native Americans. The Latter-day Saints of Jesus Christ were, in short, ready for Wovoka.

The son of an assistant of either Tävibo or Waugh-zee-waugh-ber (this point will probably never be satisfactorily settled), Wovoka was a quiet, sincere prophet of nonviolence. James Mooney sought out the man who said "he believed it was better for the Indians to follow the white man's road and to adopt the habits of civilization," who disavowed any connection with the ghost dance shirt, and who "makes no claim to be Christ, the Son of God, as has been so often asserted in print. He does claim to be a prophet who has received a divine revelation."

The confusion about Wovoka's parentage did not seem to exist in his mind, and the accounts earlier noted here suggest Wovoka knew more about his parentage than anyone else, especially if one notes Lee's phrase, "son, either actual or spiritual." To an Indian, no confusion exists, and Wovoka's own autobiographical sketch as he delivered it to Mooney seems best evidence:

He said he was about 35 years of age, fixing the date from a noted battle between the Paiute and the whites near Pyramid Lake, in 1860, at which time he said he was about the size of his little boy, who appeared to be of about 4 years. His father, Tàvibo, "White Man," was not a preacher, but was a *capita* (from the Spanish *capitan*) or petty chief, and was a dreamer and invulnerable. His own proper name from boyhood was Wovoka or Wüvoka, "The Cutter," but a few years ago he had assumed the name of his paternal grandfather, Kwohitsauq, or "Big Rumbling Belly." After the death of his father he had been taken into the family of a white farmer, David Wilson, who had given him the name of Jack Wilson, by which he is commonly known among the whites. He thus has three distinct names, Wovoka, Kwohitsauq, and Jack Wilson. He stated positively that he was a full-blood, a statement borne out by his appearance. The impression that he is a half-blood may have arisen from the fact that his father's name was "White Man" and that he has a white man's name. His followers, both in his own and in all the other tribes, commonly refer to him as "our father." He has never been away from Mason Valley and speaks only his own Paiute language, with some little knowledge of English.... He had given the dance to his people about four years before, but had received his great revelation about two years previously. On this occasion "the sun died" (was eclipsed) and he fell asleep in the daytime and was taken up to the other world. Here he saw God, with all the people who had died long ago engaged in their oldtime sports and occupations, all happy and forever young. It was a pleasant land and full of game. After showing him all, God told him he must go back and tell his people they must be good and love one another, have no quarreling and live in peace with the whites; that they must work, and not lie or steal; that they must put away all the old practices that savored of war; that if they faithfully obeyed his instructions they would at last be reunited with their friends in this other world, where there would be no more death or sickness or old age. He was then given the dance which he was commanded to bring back to his people. By performing this dance at intervals, for five consecutive days each time, they would secure this happiness to themselves and hasten the event. Finally God gave him control over the elements so that he could make it rain or snow or be dry at will, and appointed him his deputy to take charge of affairs in the west, while "Governor Harrison" would attend to matters in the east, and he, God, would look after the world above. He then returned to earth and began to preach as he was directed, convincing the people by exercising the wonderful powers that had been given him.

Frank Campbell's observation that "There is nothing in it to cause trouble between whites and Indians unless the new messiah is misquoted and his doctrine misconstrued" was obviously accurate. But Wovoka was misquoted, his doctrine was misconstrued. Oppression breeds hope, and hope misquotes and misconstrues. Changing as it swept from tribe to tribe, the doctrine assumed proportions outside Wovoka's teaching: the buffalo would return in their earlier massive numbers; magic shirts inspired by vision and decorated with symbols from the dream would have the power to stop bullets; the dead would return to swell the warrior forces. The Indians of the West had been driven to desperation. As Chief Luther Standing Bear of the Oglala Sioux charges in his autobiography:

We did not think of the great open plains, the beautiful rolling hills, the winding streams with tangled growth as "wild." Only to the white man was nature a "wilderness" and only to him was the land "infested" with "wild" animals and "savage" people. To us it was tame. Earth was bountiful and we were surrounded with the blessings of the Great Mystery. Not until the hairy man from the east came and with brutal frenzy heaped injustices upon us and the families we loved was it "wild" for us. When the very animals of the forest began fleeing from his approach, then it was that for us the "Wild West" began.[5]

That desperation translated itself into determination as military and religious leaders saw in the fervor of the Ghost Dance a unifying force that would allow the Sioux, the Cheyenne, the Kiowa, the Arapaho, the Paiute, the Washo, the Apache, and the Caddo to band in one mighty effort to rid the western lands of the white man. Even that coalition of warrior people would have been difficult to provoke to action had not the blundering policies of the newly elected president of the United States, Benjamin Harrison, brought about the death of Sitting Bull. At any rate, the Ghost Dance Movement ended at Wounded Knee.

  The visionary Wovoka had seen his messianic doctrines misquoted and misconstrued to bring destruction rather than salvation to his people. Himself defeated, he could only add this postscript to the blasted hopes of his Mason Valley followers:

Hoo-oo! My children, my children. In days behind many times I called you to travel the hunting trail or to follow the war trail. Now those trails are choked with sand; they are covered with grass, the young men cannot find them. My children, today I call upon you to travel a new trail, the only trail now open—the White Man's Road.

  In spite of the failure of the messiahs and prophets, some Native American religions survived and are practiced today much as they were centuries ago, notably the Hopi and the Navajo.

[5]*Land of the Spotted Eagle* (Boston and New York, 1933), p. xix.

Many Native Americans, unable to resist the threats or the degenerative time changes of the proselyting white man, became "Christians," their belief an admixture of the best elements of Christianity and their original religions—an admixture that makes them vulnerable in their ambivalences, for time creates a rationalization about belief that blinds the practitioner to any but his need for personal accommodation.

Still other people managed to survive by accepting a "new religion" such as that set down in the Gaiwiio or teachings of the Seneca prophet Handsome Lake, born in 1735, half brother of Cornplanter. We know little of his biography except that which is suggested in his code. He had, obviously, been an alcoholic, an invalid for four years, and a recipient of visions—visions which healed him and made him a temperance reformer in the dark days that befell the Iroquois Confederation in the early nineteenth century. In spite of the opposition of such luminaries as Red Jacket and his own brother, Cornplanter, whether or not he was influenced by his Philadelphia-educated nephew, Henry O'Bail, despite the attacks of skeptics, his "new religion" created a new cohesion among his people. With his grandson, Sosheowa, he prevailed so that when he died the Six Nations saw fit to mark his tomb with a granite marker.

And, finally, there is the religion of Peyotism which gave rise to the Native American Church. The inoffensive looking button of the peyote cactus contains both stimulants and sedatives related to strychnine and morphine. Laws respecting the use of peyote trace back to 1899 when the Sessions Laws of what is now Oklahoma forbade its use. The year Oklahoma became a state (1907) three Indians were fined for use of peyote. Partially as a result of the testimony of Comanche Quanah Parker, the law was repealed in 1908. Outlawed in 1917 by Colorado, Utah, and Nevada, "peyote is not regarded as a narcotic drug, and its use is not prohibited by the Federal Government" according to *Bulletin on Narcotics*, IX, No. 2, April-June, 1959, page 18. Other states passed anti-peyote laws in 1920 (Kansas), 1923 (Arizona, Montana, South Dakota, North Dakota), 1924 (Iowa), 1929 (Wyoming and New Mexico with New Mexico amending the law in 1959 to permit ritual use), 1935 (Idaho), and 1937 (Texas).

The religious significance of peyote is bitterly contested, the most liberal and lucid opinion to date being written by the Honorable Yale McFate, Superior Court of Coconino County, Flagstaff, Arizona, July 26, 1960:

Peyote is not a narcotic. It is not habit-forming....There are about 225,000 members of the organized church, known as the Native American Church, which adheres to this practice....The use of peyote is essential to the existence of the peyote religion. Without it, the practice of the religion would be effectively prevented....It is significant that many states which formerly outlawed the use of peyote have abolished or amended their laws to permit its use for religious purposes. It is also significant that the Federal Government has in nowise prevented the use of peyote by Indians or others.

That the Native American Church is the major religious affiliation among more than fifty groups of Native Americans, that they invariably dissuade white participation though they usually welcome blacks, that Peyotism is a Pan-Indian movement—all suggest the genesis of problems and misunderstandings. The anthropologist, psychologist, and ethnologist will decide, and probably accurately, that the movement is an outgrowth of the Ghost Dance Movement which failed. They will, and again accurately, find the psychological state of the Native American and the youth cult of the 1960s-70s analogous, even interdependent, as the alienated young transplant American sought at least spiritual alliance with the tribal cohesiveness of the Native American, adopting his clothing and hair styles and pursuing his literary-historical fragments. We wonder if those future seekers after truth will blame the Indian, rationalize their findings, or create fanciful explanations. We are satisfied they will not hear the Cassandra-voiced Ernest Thompson Seton and Julia M. Seton who, in 1937, noted in *The Gospel of the Redman: An Indian Bible:*

The Civilization of the Whiteman is a failure; it is visibly crumbling around us. It has failed at every crucial test. No one who measures things by results can question this fundamental statement.

Apparently, the money-madness is the main cause of it all. We know that such a thing was unknown among the Indians. Their big menace was failure of food supply, and against this they prepared by a storage plan that was effectual.

What is Civilization? Literally, it is a system by which men can live in a large group (a city, or *civitas*) and enjoy all the benefits without suffering the evils that result from such association....

How are we going to appraise the value of a Civilization? By certain yard measures that are founded on human nature, and which remorselessly investigate the fundamentals of the man-mind and the man-needs.

First of these is: Does your Civilization guarantee to you absolute freedom of action so long as you do not encroach on the equal right of your neighbour to do the same thing?

Does your system work for the greatest happiness of the greatest number?

Is your Civilization characterized by justice in the courts and gentleness in the streets?

Are its largest efforts to relieve suffering and misery?

Does your Civilization grant to every individual the force and rights of manhood?

Does your system guarantee absolute freedom of religion?

Is everyone in your community guaranteed food, shelter, protection, dignity, so long as your group has these things in its gift?

Does your system guarantee the tribal control of tribal interests?

Does your system guarantee to each man one vote; but so much influence as his character can command?

Does your system guarantee to each man the product of his industry?

Does your system accept the fact that material things are of doubtful or transient value, that the things of the spirit are all that are enduring and worth while?

Does your system set larger value on kindness than on rigorous justice?

Does your system discourage large material possessions in one man?

Does your system provide for the sick, the helpless, the weak, the old and the stranger?

Does your system guarantee the integrity of the natural group called the family?

Does your system recognize and further the fundamental thought that the chief duty of man is the attainment of manhood, which means the perfect and harmonious development of every part and power that goes to make a man; and the consecration of that manhood to the service of one's people?

By every one of these tests, the White Civilization is a failure.

How is it that we of the Whiteman's way have just as much food in the land as we ever had, just as much wealth as ever we had, just as much need for labour, just as much material of every kind, just as much readiness to work; and yet we are facing a breakdown because we cannot co-ordinate these things into effective action?

Our system has broken down—our Civilization is a failure. Wherever pushed to a logical conclusion, it makes one millionaire and a million paupers. There is no complete happiness under its blight.

Men of the White Race! We speak now as representative of the most heroic race the world has ever seen, the most physically perfect race the world has ever seen, the most spiritual Civilization the world had ever seen.

We offer you the Message of the Redman, the Creed of Manhood. We advocate his culture as an improvement on our own, if perchance by belated repentance, remorse, restitution, and justification, we may save ourselves from Divine vengeance and total destruction, as did the Ninevites in their final stance; so that we may have a chance to begin again with a better, higher thought.[6]

[6]London, pp. 105–08. Available in a 1958 edition from Seton Village Press, Seton Village, Santa Fe, N.M.

Two Accounts
of Pontiac's Recounting
of the Delaware Prophet's
Appearance before
"The Great Spirit"

I

A Delaware Indian conceived an eager desire to learn wisdom from the Master of Life; but, being ignorant where to find him, he had recourse to fasting, dreaming, and magical incantations. By these means it was revealed to him, that, by moving forward in a straight, undeviating course, he would reach the abode of the Great Spirit. He told his purpose to no one, and having provided the equipments of a hunter— gun, powder-horn, ammunition, and a kettle for preparing his food— he set out on his errand. For some time he journeyed on in high hope and confidence. On the evening of the eighth day, he stopped by the side of a brook at the edge of a meadow, where he began to make ready his evening meal, when, looking up, he saw three large openings in the woods before him, and three well-beaten paths which entered them. He was much surprised; but his wonder increased, when, after it had grown dark, the three paths were more clearly visible than ever. Remembering the important object of his journey, he could neither rest nor sleep; and, leaving his fire, he crossed the meadow, and entered the largest of the three openings. He had advanced but a short distance into the forest, when a bright flame sprang out of the ground before him, and arrested his steps. In great amazement, he turned back, and entered the second path, where the same wonderful phenomenon again encountered him; and now, in terror and bewilderment, yet still resolved to persevere, he took the last of the three paths. On this he journeyed a whole day without interruption, when at length, emerging from the forest, he saw before him a vast mountain, of dazzling whiteness. So precipitous was the ascent that the Indian thought it hopeless to go farther, and looked around him in despair; at that moment, he saw, seated at some distance above, the figure of a beautiful woman arrayed in white, who arose as he looked upon her, and thus accosted him:

"How can you hope, encumbered as you are, to succeed in your design? Go down to the foot of the mountain, throw away your gun, your ammunition, your provisions, and your clothing; wash yourself in the stream which flows there, and you will then be prepared to stand before the Master of Life."

The Indian obeyed, and again began to ascend among the rocks, while the woman, seeing him still discouraged, laughed at his faintness of heart, and told him that, if he wished for success, he must climb by the aid of one hand and one foot only. After great toil and suffering, he at length found himself at the summit. The woman had disappeared, and he was left alone. A rich and beautiful plain lay before him, and at a little distance he saw three great villages, far superior to the squalid wigwams of the Delawares. As he approached the largest, and stood hesitating whether he should enter, a man gorgeously attired stepped forth, and, taking him by the hand, welcomed him to the celestial abode. He then conducted him into the presence of the Great Spirit, where the Indian stood confounded at the unspeakable splendor which surrounded him. The Great Spirit bade him be seated, and thus addressed him:

"I am the Maker of heaven and earth, the trees, lakes, rivers, and all things else. I am the Maker of mankind; and because I love you, you must do my will. The land on which you live I have made for you, and not for others. Why do you suffer the white men to dwell among you? My children, you have forgotten the customs and traditions of your forefathers. Why do you not clothe yourselves in skins, as they did, and use the bows and arrows, and the stone-pointed lances, which they used? You have bought guns, knives, kettles, and blankets, from the white men, until you can no longer do without them; and, what is worse, you have drunk the poison fire-water, which turns you into fools. Fling all these things away; live as your wise forefathers lived before you. And as for these English—these dogs dressed in red, who have come to rob you of your hunting-grounds, and drive away the game—you must lift the hatchet against them. Wipe them from the face of the earth, and then you will win my favor back again, and once more be happy and prosperous. The children of your great father, the King of France, are not like the English. Never forget that they are your brethren. They are very dear to me, for they love the red men, and understand the true mode of worshipping me."

—From Francis Parkman's *The Conspiracy of Pontiac,* Volume 1 (Champlain edition), 1898.

*In the first version, there is a general confusion between "the Great
Spirit" and "the Master of Life." A translation problem earlier noted,
a further word is in order here as the concept is central to the works
in this chapter. In Bulletin 43 of the Bureau of American Ethnology,
John R. Swanton cites the work of the Frenchman DuPratz among the
Natchez of the lower Mississippi valley. We have stated the Native American had no concept that can be translated as "the Great Spirit." Perhaps
the reason will become apparent in DuPratz's words:*

I wished to know first of the guardian of the temple what he and his fellow
countrymen thought of God. In the common [i.e., Mobilian] language *coustiné*
signifies "spirit," *tchito*, "great," and as all the natives, whatever language they
speak, employ the words Great Spirit to express the word God. I asked him in
the Natchez language what he thought of the Great Spirit, *Coyocop-cliguip*, because in their language, which I knew passably, *coyocop* signifies "spirit," and
cliguip signifies "great." I was mistaken, however, for just as in French the word
grand does not always signify the height or the length, but the qualities revealed, as when one says *un grand roi, un grand général*, in the same way the
word *cliguip* has the two significations, and in spite of that I had not yet at-
tained by this word to the idea they have of God. The guardian of the temple
then told me that they did not call him so but *Coyocop-chill*. To give an accurate idea of what this word *chill* signifies I will make use of an example.
The Natchez call common fire *oüa*, they call the sun *oüa-chill*, the very great
fire, the supreme fire. Thus in giving to God the name *Coyocop-chill* they mean
the spirit infinitely great, the spirit *par excellence*, and the spirit according to
their way of thinking, as far above other spirits as the sun by means of his heat
exceeds the fiery element. I think myself obliged to give this explanation and
to adduce this example in order to develop the idea which they have of God
through the name which they give him.

II

I am the Master of Life, whom thou desirest to know and to whom thou
wouldst speak. Listen well to what I am going to say to thee and all thy
red brethren. I am He who made heaven and earth, the trees, lakes,
rivers, all men, and all that thou seest, and all that thou hast seen on
earth. Because [I have done this and because] I love you, you must do
what I say and [leave undone] what I hate. I do not like that you drink
until you lose your reason, as you do; or that you fight with each other;
or that you take two wives, or run after the wives of others; you do not
well; I hate that. You must have but one wife, and keep her until death.
When you are going to war, you juggle, join the medicine dance, and
believe that I am speaking. You are mistaken, it is to Manitou to whom
you speak; it is a bad spirit who whispers to you nothing but evil, and
to whom you listen because you do not know me well. This land, where
you live, I have made for you and not for others. How comes it that
you suffer the whites on your lands? Can't you do without them? I

know that those whom you call the children of your Great Father supply your wants, but if you were not bad, as you are, you would well do without them. You might live wholly as you did before you knew them. Before those whom you call your brothers came on your lands, did you not live by bow and arrow? You had no need of gun nor powder, nor the rest of their things, and nevertheless you caught animals to live and clothe yourselves with their skins, but when I saw that you went to the bad, I called back the animals into the depths of the woods, so that you had need of your brothers to have your wants supplied and cover you. You have only to become good and do what I want, and I shall send back to you the animals to live on. I do not forbid you, for all that, to suffer amongst you the children of your father [the French]. I love them, they know me and pray to me, and I give them their necessities and all that they bring to you, but as regards those who have come to trouble your country [the British], drive them out, make war to them! I love them not, they know me not, they are my enemies and the enemies of your brothers! Send them back to the country which I made for them! There let them remain.

> —From journal or history of "A Conspiracy by the Indians against the English and of the Siege of the Fort Detroit, by Four Different Nations Beginning on the 7th of May, 1763." Written by an unknown French author, possibly Robert Navarre.

Admiration for the impassioned plea of the prophet of "the Dreamers," Smohalla, is widespread. It is summarized by Hartley Burr Alexander in Volume X of The Mythology of All Races *(New York, 1964), page 91: "...from a chieftain of the far West, the prophet Smohalla, comes perhaps the most eloquent expression of the sense of Earth's motherhood in Occidental literature." We wonder only why Dr. Alexander included the disclaimer "perhaps."*

Smohalla Speaks

My young men shall never work. Men who work cannot dream, and wisdom comes in dreams.

You ask me to plow the ground. Shall I take a knife and tear my mother's breast? Then when I die she will not take me to her bosom to rest.

You ask me to dig for stone. Shall I dig under her skin for bones? Then when I die I cannot enter her body to be born again.

You ask me to cut grass and make hay and sell it, and be rich like the white men. But how dare I cut off my mother's hair?

It is a bad law, and my people cannot obey it. I want my people to stay with me here. All the dead men will come to life again. We must wait here in the house of our fathers and be ready to meet them in the body of our mother.

The Ghost Dance Religion

The transplant American is, by nature, revivalistic. His fundamentalism creates a fervor and fire in him that smolders all week before flaming brightly in his weekly religious observation—an observation that frequently approaches frenzy in his response to the evangelistic or apocalyptic sermon and the stirring rhythms of "The Battle Hymn of the Republic," "How Great Thou Art," and "Marching to Zion." Nostalgia pervades "The Old Rugged Cross," "Nearer, My God, to Thee," and "The Little Brown Church in the Wildwood." Promise of a brighter day lifts hopes in "Whispering Hope," "In the Sweet By and By," and "The Doxology." Then, periodically, he erupts into a week of revival as Oral Roberts or Billy Graham crusades into town and flagellates the flagging, rejuvenates the rejected, and rearms the apostate. Even the formal, ritualistic, and restrained religions offer mysticism that floats heavenward on incense and music that entrances.

If anyone should understand the appeal of the Ghost Dance, it is that messianically oriented Christian who lives in anticipation of rejoining his relatives in heaven, of basking in the beneficence of a fatherly god, and of sharing in the brotherhood of Christ. And perhaps he understood the appeals too well, seeing his own primitive needs and aspirations in the movement that he viewed as a threat. Perhaps he realized his messianic aspirations ended inevitably in a violent insistence that others share his enthusiasm and knowledge of righteousness and right. Perhaps he transferred his own zeal, projecting it as a horrible possibility: The

Native American might use his rebirth of hope against the white who had achieved dominance through such a religious route. He need not have worried. The Native American never proselyted, never sought converts, never engaged in missionary activities. Nor did he ever use religion as an excuse for aggression. He was too civilized for such barbarism.

It is easy to understand, to appreciate, to respond to the literature of the Ghost Dance if the religious responses engendered by Christianity are allowed to manifest themselves in relation to the Ghost Dance. And they will unless they are deliberately inhibited, for hope and promise have an appeal for all people.

The literature of the Ghost Dance Religion in this section is from *The Ghost-Dance Religion and the Sioux Outbreak of 1890* by James Mooney (Part 2 of the *Fourteenth Annual Report of the Bureau of Ethnology to the Secretary of the Smithsonian Institution*, 1892-92, pages 641-1110.) Excerpted and rearranged to create a greater sense of cohesion, the material should reveal the depth and beauty of this religion of pacifism—this religion that was another tragic fatality in the transplant American's much vaunted history of religious tolerance.

James Mooney was a nineteenth-century ethnologist who visited the prophet Wovoka, recorded and translated the Ghost Dance songs of the various tribes, and persuaded the Native American leaders that he was not antagonistic to their beliefs—persuaded them so completely that they trusted him enough to share the following letters from Wovoka. He did not violate their trust, for they empowered him to take the letters to Washington and there attempt to explain the peaceful nature of their religion and attest to their dedication to its principles. He did those things. If he failed to understand the beauty of the religion or the significance of some of the songs, his cultural heritage rather than his personal integrity created the failure. And that failure is both understandable and forgivable.

Sent to leaders of the Arapaho and Cheyenne delegations after they had visited with Wovoka and returned to their people, the following is a free rendering.

The Messiah Letter

When you get home you must make a dance to continue five days. Dance four successive nights, and the last night keep up the dance until the morning of the fifth day, when all must bathe in the river and then disperse to their homes. You must all do in the same way.

I, Jack Wilson, love you all, and my heart is full of gladness for the gifts you have brought me. When you get home I shall give you a good cloud [rain?] which will make you feel good. I give you a good spirit and give you all good paint. I want you to come again in three months, some from each tribe there [the Indian Territory].

There will be a good deal of snow this year and some rain. In the fall there will be such a rain as I have never given you before.

Grandfather [a universal title of reverence among Indians and here meaning the messiah] says, when your friends die you must not cry. You must not hurt anybody or do harm to anyone. You must not fight. Do right always. It will give you satisfaction in life. This young man has a good father and mother. [Possibly this refers to Casper Edson, the young Arapaho who wrote down this message of Wovoka for the delegation.]

Do not tell the white people about this. Jesus is now upon the earth. He appears like a cloud. The dead are all alive again. I do not know when they will be here; maybe this fall or in the spring. When the time comes there will be no more sickness and everyone will be young again.

Do not refuse to work for the whites and do not make any trouble with them until you leave them. When the earth shakes [at the coming of the new world] do not be afraid. It will not hurt you.

I want you to dance every six weeks. Make a feast at the dance and have food that everybody may eat. Then bathe in the water. That is all. You will receive good words again from me some time. Do not tell lies.

Among the northern Cheyenne, Porcupine was a major figure in the Ghost Dance. He volunteered the following account of his first view of Wovoka to one Major Carroll, the commander of Camp Crook at Tongue River agency, Montana. The account is dated June 15, 1890. It has that same simplicity and sincerity that characterizes the four gospels of the New Testament. It also has as much integrity. (The "Fish-eaters" are Paiute.)

The Truth according to Porcupine of the Cheyenne

What I am going to say is the truth. The two men sitting near me were with me, and will bear witness that I speak the truth. I and my people have been living in ignorance until I went and found out the truth. All the whites and Indians are brothers, I was told there. I never knew this before.

The Fish-eaters near Pyramid Lake told me that Christ had appeared on earth again. They said Christ knew he was coming; that eleven of his children were also coming from a far land. It appeared that Christ had sent for me to go there, and that was why unconsciously I took my journey. It had been foreordained. Christ had summoned myself and others from all heathen tribes, from two or three or four from each of fifteen or sixteen different tribes. There were more different languages than I ever heard before and I did not understand any of them. They told me when I got there that my great father was there also, but did not know who he was. The people assembled called a council, and the chief's son went to see the Great Father [messiah], who sent word to us to remain fourteen days in that camp and that he would come to see us. He sent me a small package of something white to eat that I did not know the name of. There were a great many people in the council, and this white food was divided among them. The food was a big white nut. Then I went to the agency at Walker lake and they told us Christ would be there in two days. At the end of two days, on the third morning, hundreds of people gathered at this place. They cleared off a place near the agency in the form of a circus ring and we all gathered there. This space was perfectly cleared of grass, etc. We waited there till late in the evening anxious to see Christ. Just before sundown I saw a great many people, mostly Indians, coming dressed in white men's clothes. The Christ was with them. They all formed in this ring around it. They put up sheets all around the circle, as they had no tents. Just after dark some of the Indians told me that the Christ [Father] was arrived. I looked around to find him, and finally saw him sitting on one side of the ring. They all started toward him to see him. They made a big fire to throw light on him. I never looked around, but went forward, and when I saw him I bent my head. I had always thought the Great Father was a white man, but this man looked like an Indian. He sat there a long time and nobody went up to speak to him. He sat with his head bowed all the time. After awhile he rose and said he was very glad to see his children. "I have sent for you and am glad to see you. I am going to talk to you after awhile about your relatives who are dead and gone. My children, I want you to listen to all I have to say to you. I will teach you, too, how to dance a dance, and I want you to dance it. Get ready for your dance and then, when the dance is over, I will talk to you." He was dressed in a white coat with stripes. The rest of his dress was a white man's except that he had on a pair of moccasins. Then he commenced our dance, everybody joining in, the Christ singing while we danced. We danced till late in the night, when he told us we had danced enough.

The next morning, after breakfast was over, we went into the circle and spread canvas over it on the ground, the Christ standing in the midst of us. He told us he was going away that day, but would be back that next morning and talk to us.

In the night when I first saw him I thought he was an Indian, but the next day when I could see better he looked different. He was not so dark as an Indian, nor so light as a white man. He had no beard or whiskers, but very heavy eyebrows. He was a good-looking man. We were crowded up very close. We had been told that nobody was to talk, and even if we whispered the Christ would know it. I had heard that Christ had been crucified, and I looked to see, and I saw a scar on his wrist and one on his face, and he seemed to be the man. I could not see his feet. He would talk to us all day.

That evening we all assembled again to see him depart. When we were assembled, he began to sing, and he commenced to tremble all over, violently for a while, and then sat down. We danced all that night, the Christ lying down beside us apparently dead.

The next morning when we went to eat breakfast, the Christ was with us. After breakfast four heralds went around and called out that the Christ was back with us and wanted to talk with us. The circle was prepared again. The people assembled, and Christ came among us and sat down. He said he wanted to talk to us again and for us to listen. He said: "I am the man who made everything you see around you. I am not lying to you, my children. I made this earth and everything on it. I have been to heaven and seen your dead friends and have seen my own father and mother. In the beginning, after God made the earth, they sent me back to teach the people, and when I came back on earth the people were afraid of me and treated me badly. This is what they did to me [showing his scars]. I did not try to defend myself. I found my children were bad, so went back to heaven and left them. I told them that in so many hundred years I would come back to see my children. At the end of this time I was sent back to try to teach them. My father told me the earth was getting old and worn out, and the people getting bad, and that I was to renew everything as it used to be, and make it better."

He told us also that all our dead were to be resurrected; that they were all to come back to earth, and that as the earth was too small for them and us, he would do away with heaven, and make the earth itself large enough to contain us all; that we must tell all the people we meet about these things. He spoke to us about fighting, and said that was bad, and we must keep from it; that the earth was to be all good hereafter, and we must all be friends with one another. He said that in the fall of the year the youth of all the good people would be renewed, so that nobody would be more than 40 years old, and that if they behaved themselves well after this the youth of everyone would be renewed in the spring. He said if we were all good he would send people among us who could heal all our wounds and sickness by mere touch, and that we would live forever. He told us not to quarrel, or fight, nor strike each other, nor shoot one another; that the whites and Indians were to be all one people. He said if any man disobeyed what he ordered, his tribe would be wiped from the face of the earth; that we must believe everything he said, and that we must not doubt him, or say he lied; that if we did, he would know it; that he would know our thoughts and actions, in no matter what part of the world we might be.

When I heard this from the Christ, and came back home to tell it to my people, I thought they would listen. Where I went to there were lots of white people, but I never had one of them say an unkind word to me. I thought all of your people knew all of this I have told you of, but it seems you do not.

Ever since the Christ I speak of talked to me I have thought what he said was good. I see nothing bad in it. When I got back, I knew my people were bad, and had heard nothing of all this, so I got them together and told them of it and warned them to listen to it for their own good. I talked to them for four nights and five days. I told them just what I have told you here today. I told them what I said were the words of God Almighty, who was looking down on them. I wish some of you had been up in our camp here to have heard my words to the

Cheyennes. The only bad thing that there has been in it at all was this: I had just told my people that the Christ would visit the sins of any Indian upon the whole tribe, when the recent trouble [killing of Ferguson] occurred. If any one of you think I am not telling the truth, you can go and see this man I speak of for yourselves. I will go with you, and I would like one or two of my people who doubt me to go with me.

The Christ talked to us all in our respective tongues. You can see this man in your sleep any time you want after you have seen him and shaken hands with him once. Through him you can go to heaven and meet your friends. Since my return I have seen him often in my sleep. About the time the soldiers went up the Rosebud I was lying in my lodge asleep, when this man appeared and told me that the Indians had gotten into trouble, and I was frightened. The next night he appeared to me and told me that everything would come out all right.

The following account was written by an Ogalala Sioux named George Sword in the Teton Dakota dialect and translated by another Native American whose identity is not recorded.

The Truth according to George Sword

In the story of ghost dancing, the Ogalala heard that the Son of God was truly on earth in the west from their country. This was in the year 1889. The first people knew about the messiah to be on earth were the Shoshoni and Arapaho. So in 1889 Good Thunder with four or five others visited the place where Son of God said to be. These people went there without permission. They said the messiah was there at the place, but he was there to help the Indians and not the whites; so this made the Indians happy to find out this. Good Thunder, Cloud Horse, Yellow Knife, and Short Bull visited the place again in 1890 and saw the messiah. Their story of visit to the messiah is as follows:

"From the country where the Arapaho and Shoshoni we start in the direction of northwest in train for five nights and arrived at the foot of the Rocky mountains. Here we saw him and also several tribes of Indians. The people said that the messiah will come at a place in the woods where the place was prepare for him. When we went to the place a smoke descended from heaven to the place where he was to come. When the smoke disappeared, there was a man of about forty, which was the Son of God. The man said:

"My grandchildren! I am glad you have come far away to see your relatives. This are your people who have come back from your country." When he said he wanted us to go with him, we looked and we saw a land created across the ocean on which all the nations of Indians were coming home, but, as the messiah looked at the land which was created and reached across the ocean, again disappeared, saying that it was not time for that to take place. The messiah then gave to Good Thunder some paints—Indian paint and a white paint—a green grass [sagebrush twigs?]; and said, "My grandchildren, when you get home, go to farming and send all your children to school. And on way home if you kill any buffalo cut the head, the tail, and the four feet and leave them, and that buffalo will come to live again. When the soldiers of the white people chief want to arrest me, I shall stretch out my arms, which will knock them to nothingness, or, if not that, the earth will open and swallow them in. My father commanded me to visit the Indians on a purpose. I have came to the white people first, but they not good. They killed me, and you can see the marks of my wounds on my feet, my hands, and on my back. My father has given you life—your old life—and you have come to see your friends, but you will not take me home with you at this time. I want you to tell when you get home your people to follow my examples. Any one Indian does not obey me and tries to be on white's side will be covered over by a new land that is to come over this old one. You will, all the people, use the paints and grass I give you. In the spring when the green grass comes, your people who have gone before you will come back, and you shall see your friends then, for you have come to my call."

The people from every tipi send for us to visit them. They are people who died many years ago. Chasing Hawk, who died not long ago, was there, and we went to his tipi. He was living with his wife, who was killed in war long ago. They live in a buffalo skin tipi—a very large one—and he wanted all his friends to go there to live. A son of Good Thunder who died in war long ago was one who also took us to his tipi so his father saw him. When coming we come to a herd of buffaloes. We killed one and took everything except the four feet, head, and tail, and when we came a little ways from it there was the buffaloes come to life again and went off. This was one of the messiah's word came to truth. The messiah said, "I will short your journey when you feel tired of the long ways, if you call upon me." This we did when we were tired. The night came upon us, we stopped at a place, and we called upon the messiah to help us, because we were tired of long journey. We went to sleep and in the morning we found ourselves at a great distance from where we stopped.

One of the Sioux leaders who had visited Wovoka and later became one of the prime leaders in the dance was Short Bull. On October 31, 1890, he delivered this sermon at Red Leaf camp on Pine Ridge Reservation.

The Sermon
of Short Bull

My friends and relations: I will soon start this thing in running order. I have told you that this would come to pass in two seasons, but since the whites are interfering so much, I will advance the time from what my father above told me to do, so the time will be shorter. Therefore you must not be afraid of anything. Some of my relations have no ears, so I will have them blown away.

Now, there will be a tree sprout up, and there all the members of our religion and the tribe must gather together. That will be the place where we will see our dead relations. But before this time we must dance the balance of this moon, at the end of which time the earth will shiver very hard. Whenever this thing occurs, I will start the wind to blow. We are the ones who will then see our fathers, mothers, and everybody. We, the tribe of Indians, are the ones who are living a sacred life. God, our father himself, has told and commanded and shown me to do these things.

Our father in heaven has placed a mark at each point of the four winds. First, a clay pipe, which lies at the setting of the sun and represents the Sioux tribe. Second, there is a holy arrow lying at the north, which represents the Cheyenne tribe. Third, at the rising of the sun there lies hail, representing the Arapaho tribe. Fourth, there lies a pipe and nice feather at the south, which represents the Crow tribe. My father has shown me these things, therefore we must continue this dance. If the soldiers surround you four deep, three of you, on whom I have put holy shirts, will sing a song, which I have taught you, around them, when some of them will drop dead. Then the rest will start to run, but their horses will sink into the earth. The riders will jump from their horses, but they will sink into the earth also. Then you can do as you desire with them. Now, you must know this, that all the soldiers and that race will be dead. There will be only five thousand of them left living on the earth. My friends and relations, this is straight and true.

Now, we must gather at Pass creek where the tree is sprouting. There we will go among our dead relations. You must not take any earthly things with you. Then the men must take off all their clothing and the women must do the same. No one shall be ashamed of exposing their persons. My father above has told us to do this, and we must do as he says. You must not be afraid of anything. The guns are the only things we are afraid of, but they belong to our father in heaven. He will see that they do no harm. Whatever white men may tell you, do not listen to them, my relations. This is all. I will now raise my hand up to my father and close what he has said to you through me.

Songs of the Ghost Dance

Birth of the New Earth

(A Paiute Sequence)

INCANTATION TO NATURE TO REJOIN MAN

Fog! Fog!
Lightning! Lightning!
Whirlwind! Whirlwind!

WIND RISES FIRST IN THE HIGH PLACES

There is dust from the whirlwind,
There is dust from the whirlwind,
There is dust from the whirlwind.
The whirlwind on the mountain,
The whirlwind on the mountain,
The whirlwind on the mountain.

THEN IT VIBRATES IN ROCKS

The rocks are ringing,
The rocks are ringing,
The rocks are ringing.
They are ringing in the mountains,
They are ringing in the mountains,
They are ringing in the mountains.

AND IT BREAKS THEIR RESISTANCE

The black rock, the black rock,
The black rock, the black rock,
The rock is broken, the rock is broken,
The rock is broken, the rock is broken.

WITH THE SPEED OF WIND, AS CONCEALING
AS SNOW, NEW EARTH COVERS THE OLD

       The whirlwind! The whirlwind!
       The whirlwind! The whirlwind!
The snowy earth comes gliding, the snowy earth
  comes gliding;
The snowy earth comes gliding, the snowy earth
  comes gliding.

NEW GROWTH COVERS NEW EARTH

The cottonwoods are growing tall,
The cottonwoods are growing tall,
The cottonwoods are growing tall.
They are growing tall and verdant,
They are growing tall and verdant,
They are growing tall and verdant.

ALL CREATURES AGAIN SHARE THE EARTH
IN THEIR JOY

A slender antelope, a slender antelope,
A slender antelope, a slender antelope,
He is wallowing upon the ground,
He is wallowing upon the ground,
He is wallowing upon the ground,
He is wallowing upon the ground.

In Faith and in Wind

(A Kiowa Sequence)

THE WAY IT WILL HAPPEN; PRAY TO SPEED THE DAY

The father will descend,
The father will descend.
The earth will tremble,
The earth will tremble.
Everybody will arise,
Everybody will arise.
Stretch out your hands,
Stretch out your hands.

THE QUICK AND THE DEAD WILL BE ONE

Ä'häyä' Ehä'eho'! Ä'häyä' Ehä'eho'!
E'häyä' Ehä'eho'! E'häyä' Ehä'eho'!
The father shows me the road,
The father shows me the road.
I went to see my friends,
I went to see my friends.
I went to see the dances,
I went to see the dances.

IT WILL BE THE WORK OF THE FATHER, NOT MAN

The spirit army is approaching,
The spirit army is approaching.
The whole world is moving onward,
The whole world is moving onward.
See! Everybody is standing watching,
See! Everybody is standing watching.
Let us all pray,
Let us all pray.

THE FATHER WILL PITY THE LEAST ONE

My father has much pity for us,
My father has much pity for us.
I hold out my hands toward him and cry,
I hold out my hands toward him and cry.
In my poverty I hold out my hands toward him and cry,
In my poverty I hold out my hands toward him and cry.

THE LEAST SHARE HIS COMPASSION

Heyĕ′ heyĕ′ heyĕ′ heyĕ′ Äho′ho′!
Heyĕ′ heyĕ′ heyĕ′ heyĕ′ Äho′ho′!
Because I am poor,
Because I am poor,
I pray for every living creature,
I pray for every living creature.
Äo′ñyo! Äo′ñyo!

THE OLD WAYS WILL RETURN

He makes me dance with arrows,
He makes me dance with arrows.
He calls the bow my father,
He calls the bow my father.
Grandmother, persevere,
Grandmother, persevere.

I TRUST IT IS HAPPENING

The spirit host is advancing, they say,
The spirit host is advancing, they say.
They are coming with the buffalo, they say,
They are coming with the buffalo, they say.
They are coming with the (new) earth, they say,
They are coming with the (new) earth, they say.

AND I WAIT WITH THE WIND AND MY FAITH

The wind, that wind
Shakes my tipi, shakes my tipi,
And sings a song for me,
And sings a song for me.

Promise, Fulfillment, and Thanks

(A Sioux Sequence)

THE FATHER COMES SINGING

There is the father coming,
There is the father coming.
The father says this as he comes,
The father says this as he comes,
"You shall live," he says as he comes,
"You shall live," he says as he comes.

HE PROMISES REUNION

The father says so—*E'yayo!*
The father says so—*E'yayo!*
The father says so,
The father says so.
You shall see your grandfather—*E'yayo'!*
You shall see your grandfather—*E'yayo'!*
The father says so,
The father says so.
You shall see your kindred—*E'yayo'!*
You shall see your kindred—*E'yayo'!*
The father says so,
The father says so.

PEACE AND TRUTH WILL RETURN

My son, let me grasp your hand,
My son, let me grasp your hand,
Says the father,
Says the father.
You shall live,
You shall live,
Says the father,
Says the father.

I bring you a pipe,
I bring you a pipe,
Says the father,
Says the father.
By means of it you shall live,
By means of it you shall live,
Says the father,
Says the father.

MEN WILL LIVE AS THEY SHOULD

I love my children—*Ye'ye'!*
I love my children—*Ye'ye'!*
You shall grow to be a nation—*Ye'ye'!*
You shall grow to be a nation—*Ye'ye'!*
Says the father, says the father.
Haye'ye' E'yayo'yo'! Haye'ye' E'yayo'yo'!

THE LAND WILL BE FRUITFUL AGAIN

This is to be my work—*Yo'yoyo'!*
This is to be my work—*Yo'yoyo'!*
All that grows upon the earth is mine—*Yo'yoyo'!*
All that grows upon the earth is mine—*Yo'yoyo'!*
Says the father—*Yo'yoyo'!*
Says the father—*Yo'yoyo'!*
E'ya Yo'yoyo'!
E'ya Yo'yoyo'!

MY GREAT GIFTS ARE LIFE AND PEACE

It is I who make these sacred things,
Says the father, says the father.
It is I who make the sacred shirt,
Says the father, says the father.
It is I who made the pipe,
Says the father, says the father.

THE POWER OF THE FATHER IS AWESOME

You see what I can do—*Ye'yeye'!*
You see what I can do—*Ye'yeye'!*
You see them, you see them,
Ha'eye'ya he'yeye'! Ha'eye'ya he'yeye'!

THANKS TO THE FATHER FOR GIFTS OF LIFE

It was the father who gave us these things—*Ye'ye'ye'*!
It was the father who gave us these things—*Ye'ye'ye'*!
It was the father who gave us fire—*Ye'ye'ye'*!
It was the father who gave us fire—*Ye'ye'ye'*!
The father gave it to us—*Ye'ye'ye'*!
The father gave it to us—*Ye'ye'ye'*!

A Vision of the New World

(A Cheyenne Sequence)

THE WHITE MAN'S GOD HAS FORSAKEN HIM, BLESSED US

The devil—*Hi'hi'hai'-yai'*!
The devil—*Hi'hi'hai'-yai'*!
We have put him aside—*Hi'hi'hai'-yai'*!
We have put him aside—*Hi'hi'hai'-yai'*!
The White Man Above—*Hi'hi'hai'-yai'*!
The White Man Above—*Hi'hi'hai'-yai'*!
He is our father—*Hi'hi'hai'-yai'*!
He is our father—*Hi'hi'hai'-yai'*!
He has blest us—*Hi'hi'hai'-yai'*!
He has blest us—*Hi'hi'hai'-yai'*!

THE SPIRITS ARE HASTENING THE FATHER

My children, I am now humming—*He'eye'*!
My children, I am now humming—*He'eye'*!
Your children, your children,
They are crying—*He'eye'*!
They are crying—*He'eye'*!
They are hurrying me along,
They are hurrying me along.

GAMES WITH FRIENDS, REUNION WITH FAMILIES

(Composed by Mo ki, "Little Woman," a leader in the Cheyenne Ghost Dance and wife of Grant Left-hand.)

My comrade—*I'yahe'yahe'e'!*
My comrade—*I'yahe'yahe'e'!*
Let us go and play shinny—*Ahe'e'ye'!*
Let us go and play shinny—*Ahe'e'ye'!*
Let us go look for our mother—*Ahe'e'ye'!*
Let us go look for our mother—*Ahe'e'ye'!*
Our father tells us to do it—*Ahe'e'ye'!*
Our father tells us to do it—*Ahe'e'ye'!*

SONG OF THE QUICK AND THE DEAD

Yani'tsini'hawa'na!
Yani'tsini'hawa'na!
We shall live again,
We shall live again.

THE FATHER COMES RIDING THE WHIRLWIND

I am coming in sight—*Ehe'ee'ye'!*
I am coming in sight—*Ehe'ee'ye'!*
I bring the whirlwind with me—*E'yahe'eye'!*
I bring the whirlwind with me—*E'yahe'eye'!*
That you may see each other—
That you may see each other.

THE NEW EARTH HUMS AS IT COVERS THE OLD

(Composed by Porcupine, great leader of the Ghost Dance among the northern Cheyenne)

Our father has come,
Our father has come,
The earth has come,
The earth has come,
It is rising—*Eye'ye'!*
It is rising—*Eye'ye'!*
It is humming—*Ahe'e'ye'!*
It is humming—*Ahe'e'ye'!*

BATHING IN THE SPIRIT WORLD RIVERS
BRINGS FORGETTING

My father—*E'yehe'! E'he'eye'!*
My father—*E'yehe'! E'he'eye'!*
When I first met him—*Ehe'eye'!*
When I first met him—*Ehe'eye'!*
"In the blue-green water—*He'eye'!*
"In the blue-green water—*He'eye'!*
You must take a bath"—*He'eye'!*
You must take a bath"—*He'eye'!*
Thus he told me, thus he told me—*He'!*

The Resounding Song

(An Arapaho Sequence)

SONG OF THE FATHER DISAPPOINTED BY WHITES

(Composed by Nawat, "Left Hand," chief of the southern Arapaho)

My children, when at first I liked the whites,
My children, when at first I liked the whites,
I gave them fruits,
I gave them fruits.

THE FATHER'S SONG OF REJECTION

He'yoho'ho'! He'yoho'ho'!
The yellow-hide, the white-skin (man).
I have now put him aside—
I have now put him aside—
I have no more sympathy with him,
I have no more sympathy with him.
He'yoho'ho'! He'yoho'ho'!

SONG OF THE THUNDERBIRD DELIVERING REJECTION TO THE WHITES

I circle around—
I circle around
The boundaries of the earth,
The boundaries of the earth—
Wearing the long wing feathers as I fly,
Wearing the long wing feathers as I fly.

THE MESSAGE DELIVERED IN THUNDER

My children, my children,
It is I who make the thunder as I circle about—
    The thunder as I circle about.
My children, my children.
It is I who make the loud thunder as I circle about—
    The loud thunder as I circle about.

THE CROW SPREADS GOOD NEWS TO THE PEOPLE

I

My children, my children,
I am flying about the earth,
I am flying about the earth.
I am a bird, my children,
I am a bird, my children,
Says the father,
Says the father.

II

Stand ready,
Stand ready.
(So that when) the crow calls you,
(So that when) the crow calls you.
You will see him,
You will see him.

SONG OF UNSHAKABLE FAITH

The rock, the rock,
I am standing upon it,
I am standing upon it.
By its means I saw our father,
By its means I saw our father.

SONG TO SPEED THE DAY OF DELIVERANCE

Father, have pity on me,
Father, have pity on me;
I am crying for thirst,
I am crying for thirst;
All is gone—I have nothing to eat,
All is gone—I have nothing to eat.

ENCOURAGEMENT FROM THE MESSIAH
TO PERSEVERE

My children, my children,
I take pity on those who have been taught,
I take pity on those who have been taught,
Because they push on hard,
Because they push on hard.
Says our father,
Says our father.

SONG OF RENEWAL: THE GHOST CLEANSES
THE LIVING WITH CEREMONIAL PAINT

The *Hanahawunĕn* gave to me,
The *Hanahawunĕn* gave to me,
His paint—He made me clean,
His paint—He made me clean.

SITTING BULL'S APOSTOLIC SONG OF
THE CROW

(A messenger from the dead)

My father did not recognize me (at first),
My father did not recognize me (at first).
When again he saw me,
When again he saw me,
He said, "You are the offspring of a crow,"
He said, "You are the offspring of a crow."

SONG TO RECALL THE DEAD

The sacred pipe tells me—*E'yahe'eye!*
The sacred pipe tells me—*E'yahe'eye!*
Our father—*Yahe'eye'!*
Our father—*Yahe'eye'!*
We shall surely be put again (with our friends)—*E'yahe'eye!*
We shall surely be put again (with our friends)—*E'yahe'eye!*
Our father—*E'yahe'eye!*
Our father—*E'yahe'eye!*

THE ARRIVAL OF THE GHOSTS

The father showed me,
The father showed me,
Where they were coming down,
Where they were coming down.

SONG OF THE GHOST ARMY LED BY THE MESSIAH

(Brought to the southern Arapaho from the North by
Sitting Bull)

He! When I met him approaching—
He! When I met him approaching—
My children, my children—
I then saw the multitude plainly,
I then saw the multitude plainly.

SONG OF THE NEW WORLD QUAKING AND COVERING THE OLD LIKE A SHELL

My children, my children,
Look! the earth is about to move,
Look! the earth is about to move.
My father tells me so,
My father tells me so.

SONG OF THE WHITES ABANDONED ON THE OLD WORLD IN DARKNESS AS THE INDIANS MOVE UP TO THE NEW

I'yehe'! my children—*Uhi'yeye'heye'!*
I'yehe'! my children—*Uhi'yehe'heye'!*
I'yehe'! we have rendered them desolate—*Eye'äe'yuhe'yu!*
I'yehe'! we have rendered them desolate—*Eye'äe'yuhe'yu!*
The whites are crazy—*Ahe'yuhe'yu!*

THE OLD LIFE IS RESTORED

The seven venerable *Chǐ'nachichǐ'bät* priests—
The seven venerable *Chǐ'nachichǐ'bät* priests—
We see them,
We see them.
They all wear it on their heads—
They all wear it on their heads—
The Thunderbird,
The Thunderbird.
Then I wept,
Then I wept.

RETURNING TO CAMP AFTER THE WHITE MAN IS GONE AND BUFFALO AGAIN COVER THE PLAINS

How bright is the moonlight!
How bright is the moonlight!
Tonight as I ride with my load of buffalo beef,
Tonight as I ride with my load of buffalo beef.

SONG OF THE PERFECT NEW WORLD

(There) is a good river,
(There) is a good river,
Where there is no timber—
Where there is no timber—
But thunder-berries are there,
But thunder-berries are there.

SONG OF THE NEW COVENANT (THE PIPE) AFTER THE NEW WORLD COVERS THE OLD

O, my children! O, my children!
Here is another of your pipes—*He'eye'!*
Here is another of your pipes—*He'eye'!*
Look! thus I shouted—*He'eye'!*
Look! thus I shouted—*He'eye'!*
When I moved the earth—*He'eye'!*
When I moved the earth—*He'eye'!*

IN PRAISE OF THE FATHER

Father, now I am singing it—*Hǐ'nǐ'ni!*
Father, now I am singing it—*Hǐ'nǐ'ni!*
That loudest song of all,
That loudest song of all—
That resounding song—*Hǐ'nǐ'ni!*
That resounding song—*Hǐ'nǐ'ni!*

The slaughter at Wounded Knee provoked a spate of hysterical editorials in transplant American newspapers. Sympathy was not with the victims of the massacre. One such editorial appeared in the Chicago Tribune *and elicited this response from a Sioux. The paper printed it.*

A Letter to the Editor
of the
Chicago Tribune, 1890

(Masse Hadjo)

You say, "If the United States army would kill a thousand or so of the dancing Indians there would be no trouble." I judge by the above language you are a "Christian," and are disposed to do all in your power to advance the cause of Christ. You are doubtless a worshiper of the white man's Saviour, but are unwilling that the Indians should have a "Messiah" of their own.

The Indians have never taken kindly to the Christian religion as preached and practiced by the whites. Do you know why this is the case? Because the Good Father of all has given us a better religion—a religion that is all good and no bad, a religion that is adapted to our wants. You say if we are good, obey the Ten Commandments and never sin any more, we may be permitted eventually to sit upon a white rock and sing praises to God forevermore, and look down upon our heathen fathers, mothers, brothers and sisters who are howling in hell.

It won't do. The code of morals as practiced by the white race will not compare with the morals of the Indians. We pay no lawyers or preachers, but we have not one-tenth part of the crime that you do. If our Messiah does come we shall not try to force you into our belief. We will never burn innocent women at the stake or pull men to pieces with horses because they refuse to join in our ghost dances. You white people had a Messiah, and if history is to be believed nearly every nation has had one. You had twelve Apostles; we have only eleven, and some of those are already in the military guard-house. We also had a

Virgin Mary and she is in the guard-house. You are anxious to get hold of our Messiah, so you can put him in irons. This you may do—in fact, you may crucify him as you did that other one, but you cannot convert the Indians to the Christian religion until you contaminate them with the blood of the white man. The white man's heaven is repulsive to the Indian nature, and if the white man's hell suits you, why, you keep it. I think there will be white rogues enough to fill it.

Some Native Americans have resisted the inroads of Christianity, retaining their identity through their religions. Among the Navaho, ritual practices and chants as old as time indicate the strong bond between the people and their concept of the beautiful. One such chant, "All Is Well," embodies beauty with that same secure joy the Judeo-Christian finds in the Psalms. The chant is designed for the correcting of mistakes; the incantory power of the words eradicates error and the results of error.

One of the Night Chants, the Chant of All Is Well

This covers it all,
The Earth and the Most High Power Whose Ways Are
  Beautiful.
All is beautiful before me,
All is beautiful behind me,
All is beautiful below me,
All is beautiful above me,
All is beautiful all around me.

This covers it all,
The Skies and the Most High Power Whose Ways Are
  Beautiful.
All is beautiful....

This covers it all,
The Mountains and the Most High Power Whose Ways
    Are Beautiful.
All is beautiful....

This covers it all,
The Water and the Most High Power Whose Ways Are
    Beautiful.
All is beautiful....

This covers it all,
The Darkness and the Most High Power Whose Ways
    Are Beautiful.
All is beautiful....

This covers it all,
The Dawn and the Most High Power Whose Ways Are
    Beautiful.
All is beautiful....

This covers it all,
Hasjelti and the Most High Power Whose Ways Are
    Beautiful.
All is beautiful.

This covers it all,
Hasjohon and the Most High Power Whose Ways Are
    Beautiful.
All is beautiful....

This covers it all,
The White Corn and the Most High Power Whose Ways
    Are Beautiful.
All is beautiful....

This covers it all,
The Yellow Corn and the Most High Power Whose Ways
    Are Beautiful.
All is beautiful....

This covers it all,
The Pollen and the Most High Power Whose Ways Are
    Beautiful.
All is beautiful....

Recorded at the end of the nineteenth century, these planting songs of the Navaho are unchanged today—but, then, the Navaho resisted the ecumenical movement others would have forced on them. They felt ecumenism means the ultimate death of faith, and, without faith, there will not be rain, will not be corn, will not be life. The body is served by such rituals as these; the man is served; continuation is served. The songs are not presented here in proper sequence, nor are all of the songs presented. One of the songs is not even a part of the actual sequence— being in the religious works outside the sequence—but is included here to make a more cohesive sense of completion for the reader unfamiliar with the religion of the Navaho.

In the Garden of the Home God

I

The sacred blue corn-seed I am planting,
In one night it will grow and flourish,
In one night the corn increases,
In the garden of the Home God.

The sacred white corn-seed I am planting,
In one day it will grow and ripen,
In one day the corn increases,
In its beauty it increases.

II

With this it grows, with this it grows,
The dark cloud, with this it grows.
The dew thereof, with this it grows,
The blue corn, with this it grows.

III

This it eats, this it eats,
The dark cloud,
Its dew
The blue corn eats,
This it eats.

This it eats, this it eats,
The dark mist,
Its dew
The white corn eats,
This it eats.

IV

The great corn plant is with the bean,
Its rootlets now are with the bean,
Its leaf tips now are with the bean,
Its dewdrops now are with the bean,
Its tassel now is with the bean,
Its pollen now is with the bean,
And now its silk is with the bean,
And now its grain is with the bean.

The great true plant is with the bean,
Its rootlets now are with the bean,
Its leaf tips now are with the bean,
Its dewdrops now are with the bean,
Its tassel now is with the bean,
Its pollen now is with the bean,
And now its silk is with the bean,
And now its grain is with the bean.

V

Truly in the East
The white bean
And the great corn plant
Are tied with the white lightning.
Listen! It approaches! [It = rain]
The voice of the bluebird is heard.

Truly in the East
The white bean
And the great squash
Are tied with the rainbow.
Listen! It approaches!
The voice of the bluebird is heard.

VI

On your farm the cloud is level with the corn,
On your farm the cloud is level with the corn,
On your farm the mist is level with the plant,
On your farm the mist is level with the pollen.

VII

From the East,
Through the middle of your field,
Your corn moves. It walks.

From the West,
Through the middle of your field,
Your corn moves. It walks.

VIII

The corn grows up.
    The waters of the dark clouds drop, drop.
The rain descends.
    The waters from the corn leaves drop, drop.
The rain descends.
    The waters from the plants drop, drop.
The corn grows up.
    The waters of the dark mists drop, drop.

IX

From the top of the great corn plant the water gurgles,
   I hear it;
Around the roots the water foams, I hear it;
Around the roots of the plants it foams, I hear it;
From their tops the water foams, I hear it.

X

Shall I cull this fruit
Of the great corn plant?
Shall you break it? Shall I break it?
Shall I break it? Shall you break it?
    Shall I? Shall you?

Shall I cull this fruit
Of the great squash vine?
Shall you pick it up? Shall I pick it up?
Shall I pick it up? Shall you pick it up?
    Shall I? Shall You?

XI

I pulled it with my hand.
The great corn plant I scatter around.
I pulled it with my hand.
The standing plants are scattered around.

XII

Since the ancient days, I have planted,
Since the time of the emergence, I have planted,
The great corn plant, I have planted,
Its roots, I have planted,
The tips of its leaves, I have planted,
Its dew, I have planted,
Its tassel, I have planted,
Its pollen, I have planted,
Its silk, I have planted,
Its seed, I have planted.

Since the ancient days, I have planted,
Since the time of the emergence, I have planted,
The great squash vine, I have planted,
Its seed, I have planted,
Its silk, I have planted,
Its pollen, I have planted,
Its tassel, I have planted,
Its dew, I have planted,
The tips of its leaves, I have planted,
Its roots, I have planted.

In all literature it would be difficult if not impossible to find a more beautiful statement, chant, hymn—call it what you will—than "Beauty-way." Its usage among the Navaho is specific, but it can serve as a prayer, a statement to the dead, a song of self-searching. In short, it is so universal in the responses it elicits that it can stand alone for anyone of any faith who is aesthetically or sensitively ready to listen. The last line ("In beauty it is finished") is comparable to the idea embodied in the word Amen—please let it be so.

Beautyway

from *The Night Chant*

Tségihi.
House made of dawn,
House made of evening light,
House made of dark cloud,
House made of male rain,
House made of dark mist,
House made of female rain,
House made of pollen,
House made of grasshoppers,
Dark cloud is at the door.
The trail out of it is dark cloud.
The zigzag lightning stands high upon it.
Male deity!
Your offering I make.
I have prepared a smoke for you.
Restore my feet for me,
Restore my legs for me,
Restore my body for me,
Restore my mind for me,
Restore my voice for me.
This very day take out your spell for me.
Your spell remove for me.
You have taken it away for me;
Far off it has gone.
Happily I recover.
Happily my interior becomes cool.

Happily I go forth.
My interior feeling cool, may I walk.
No longer sore, may I walk.
Impervious to pain, may I walk.
With lively feelings, may I walk.
As it used to be long ago, may I walk.
Happily may I walk.
Happily, with abundant dark clouds, may I walk.
Happily, with abundant showers, may I walk.
Happily, with abundant plants, may I walk.
Happily, on a trail of pollen, may I walk.
Happily may I walk.
Being as it used to be long ago, may I walk.
May it be beautiful before me,
May it be beautiful behind me,
May it be beautiful below me,
May it be beautiful above me.
May it be beautiful all around me.
In beauty it is finished.

The Code of Handsome Lake

The Longhouse religion that is seated in the Code of Handsome Lake (Skaniadariio), the Seneca Prophet, has been, almost from its inception, a part of the slow movement toward Pan-Indianism, both religious and secular. Religious because it restrengthened the weakening ties among the nations of the Iroquois Confederation, the movement was also secular because, as a result of the efforts of Arthur C. Parker who was instrumental in the translation and publication of the Code, another cohesive force was brought to bear against the combined destructive efforts of the non-Native American groups bent on destroying the identity of the American Indian so he would melt into the mass of men and disappear as a constant reminder of the religious failure of the nation that saw itself the result of living the Christian life.

Although Parker himself saw Pan-Indianism as a secular movement and attempted to develop the Society of American Indians (of which he became president) along those lines, he knew (as did everyone else) that the "civilizing" process was at heart the Christianizing process: The Indians should abandon tribal dress (it was "barbaric"), cut their hair in the white mode, forswear dancing (the fundamentalist of an earlier day, like many of his present-day counterparts, viewed the dance as some sexually arousing form of sin-inducing anarchy that released primitive passion), work hard (for the Puritan Ethic joy of keeping busy to avoid introspection or self-analysis), make cleanliness a fetish (superficial appearances counted far more than spiritual decay), deify money (even if the white messiah expressly forbade such deification), aspire to ownership of private property (thereby removing the pagan concept of Mother Earth and sundering the identification with the soil as flesh of the collective ancestor), live in houses (to wall out community reliance), make the father preempt (thereby emulating the anthropomorphic Elohim and drifting away from other "pagan" gods), and embrace temperance (thereby facing the nightmare of the sterile existence without even temporary escape, for confronting terror strengthens the soul). To be civilized was to be Christian, for the "American virtues" were the corruptions of that Oriental Hebraism that had brought the transplant American to his spiritual confusion, and his "Christian Charity" insisted all be allowed to share his spiritual unhappiness and loss of allegiance to a land of long origin. And, if any resisted the nightmare of fragmentation that such precepts delivered, he would have to be forced into the "good life" because, in a democracy, everyone should have equal rights—at least the rights that insured a loss of personal and cultural identity—in short, one's heritage. By encouraging the preservation of Gaiwiio, Parker encouraged the secular strengthening of Pan-Indianism, for the secular and the religious cannot really be separated in one's concept of self.

Parker's friend, Alanson Skinner, seemed to realize such truths more readily than Parker. Reviewing Parker's *The Code of Handsome Lake, the Seneca Prophet,* Skinner wrote in the *American Anthropologist,* XVII, 1915:

One point that Mr. Parker does not mention is this: Almost since our first contact with the Indians of North America there has been a constant succession of Messianic or revealed religions…The two to make the most lasting, if not the most profound, impressions were the Peyote (miscalled "mescal") and the Code of Handsome Lake. Both aim at the suppression of drunkenness particularly, both seem to uphold some ancient practices and condemn others.

If the old religions could not withstand Christianity, perhaps some compromise between the two might be effective. And a people's religion must originate from themselves, be theirs rather than the creation of some distant, alien culture, for religion serves a culture in its geographical setting, serves the needs engendered by that geography and the peculiar personality of the unique group. The intrusion of the whites had changed the spiritual geography of the Native American even as it had changed his actual geography. Handsome Lake evolved a compromise code that would allow his people to "be" Indian with loss—a state preferable to becoming Christianized out of existence.

The following excerpts from the code called Gaiwiio reveal the method.

Now This Is Gaiwiio

SECTION 7

"Now another message.

"The Creator has ordered that man and wife should rear their children well, love them and keep them in health. This is the Creator's rule. We, the messengers, have seen both men and women desert each other when children come. The woman discovers that the man, her husband, loves his child and she is very jealous and spreads evil reports of him. She does this for an excuse before the world to leave him. Thus the messengers say that the Creator desires men and women to cease such mischief."

So they said and he said. Eniaiehuk.

SECTION 14

"Now another message.

"This is what your people do.

"An old woman punished her children unjustly. The Creator is sad because of such things and bids us tell you that such practices must cease." So they said.

"Now this is the way ordained by the Creator: Talk slowly and kindly to children and never punish them unjustly. When a child will not obey let the mother say, 'Come to the water and I will immerse you'. If after this warning the child is still obstinate she must take it to the water's edge and say, 'Do you now obey?' and she must say so again and if at the third time there is no obedience then the child must be thrust in the water. But if the child cries for mercy it must have it and the woman must not throw it into the water. If she does she does evil."

So they said and he said. Eniaiehuk.

SECTION 15

"Now another message of things not right.

"Parents disregard the warnings of their children. When a child says, 'Mother, I want you to stop wrongdoing', the child speaks straight words and the Creator says that the child speaks right and the mother must obey. Furthermore the Creator proclaims that such words from a child are wonderful and that the mother who disregards them takes the wicked part. The mother may reply, 'Daughter, stop your noise. I know better than you. I am the older and you are but a child. Think not that you can influence me by your speaking'. Now when you tell this message to your people say that it is wrong to speak to children in such words."

So they said and he said. Eniaiehuk.

SECTION 16

"Now another message.

"Tell your people that the Creator is sad because of what they are doing.

"Some people live together well as man and wife and family, but the man of the family uses strong drink. Then when he comes home he lifts up his child to fondle it and he is drunk. Now we, the messengers of the Creator, say that this is not right for if a man filled with strong drink touches his child he burns its blood. Tell your people to heed this warning."

So they said and he said. Eniaiehuk.

SECTION 17

"Now another message.

"Some people live together righteously as man and wife according as the Creator ordained, but they have no child. When this is so let this be the way: If the wife's sister has children, of these let the wife without issue take from one to three and rear them and thereby fulfil her duty to the Creator. Moreover when a woman takes children she must rear them well as if born of herself. We, the messengers, say that you must tell this to your people."

So they said and he said. Eniaiehuk.

SECTION 19

"Now another message.

"Now the Creator of mankind ordained that people should live to an old age. He appointed that when a woman becomes old she should be without strength and unable to work. Now the Creator says that it is a great wrong to be unkind to our grandmothers. The Creator forbids unkindness to the old. We, the messengers, say it. The Creator appointed this way: he designed that an old woman should be as a child again and when she becomes so the Creator wishes the grandchildren to help her, for only because she is, they are. Whosoever does right to the aged does right in the sight of the Creator."

So they said and he said. Eniaiehuk.

SECTION 21

"Now another message.

"Now this is right.

"When a woman hears children playing near her lodge she must call them in and ask them to eat. The Creator says that this is right for some children are of poor parents and have little to eat. The Creator loves poor children and whosoever feeds the poor and unfortunate does right before him."

So they said and he said. Eniaiehuk.

SECTION 25

"Now another message.

"Three things that our younger brethren (the white people) do are right to follow.

"Now, the first. The white man works on a tract of cultivated ground and harvests food for his family. So if he should die they still have the ground for help. If any of your people have cultivated ground let them not be proud on that account. If one is proud there is sin within him but if there be no pride there is no sin.

"Now, the second thing. It is the way a white man builds a house. He builds one warm and fine appearing so if he dies the family has the house for help. Whoso among you does this does right, always providing there is no pride. If there is pride it is evil but if there is none, it is well.

"Now the third. The white man keeps horses and cattle. Now there is no evil in this for they are a help to his family. So if he dies his family has the stock for help. Now all this is right if there is no pride. No evil will follow this practice if the animals are well fed, treated kindly and not overworked. Tell this to your people."

So they said and he said. Eniaiehuk.

SECTION 26

"Now another message to tell your relatives.

"This concerns education. It is concerning studying in English schools.

"Now let the Council appoint twelve people to study, two from each nation of the six. So many white people are about you that you must study to know their ways."

So they said and he said. Eniaiehuk.

SECTION 29

"Now another message for you to tell your people.

"It is not right for you to have so many dances and dance songs.

"A man calls a dance in honor of some totem animal from which he desires favor or power. This is very wrong, for you do not know what injury it may work upon other people.

"Tell your people that these things must cease. Tell them to repent and cease."

So they said and he said. Eniaiehuk.

"Now this shall be the way: They who belong to these totem animal societies must throw tobacco and disband." So they said. "Now in those days when the head men heard this message they said at once, in anger, 'We disband', and they said this without holding a ceremony as the messenger had directed."

Eniaiehuk.

SECTION 34

"Now another message to tell your people.

"Now the messengers said that this thing was beyond the control of Indians.

"At some future day the wild animals will become extinct. Now when that day comes the people will raise cattle and swine for feast food at the thanksgivings."

So they said and he said. Eniaiehuk.

SECTION 38

"Now another message for your people.

"If all the world would repent the earth would become as new again. Because of sin the under-world is crumbling with decay. The world is full of sin. Truly, this is so."

So they said and he said. Eniaiehuk.

SECTION 43

"Now another message to tell your people.

"Good food is turned into evil drink. Now some have said that there is no harm in partaking of fermented liquids.

"Then let this plan be followed: let men gather in two parties, one having a feast of food, apples and corn, and the other have cider and whiskey. Let the parties be equally divided and matched and let them commence their feasting at the same time. When the feast is finished you will see those who drank the fermented juices murder one of their own party but not so with those who ate food only."

So they said and he said. Eniaiehuk.

SECTION 44

"Now another message for your people.

"You have had the constant fear that the white race would exterminate you. The Creator will care for his Oñgwe̱'oⁿwe (real people)."

So they said and he said. Eniaiehuk.

SECTION 50

"Now another message to tell your people.

1 "Now we are of the mind that the cold of winter will take life away. Many will be taken away because of the changing cold. Moreover some will freeze because they are filled with strong drink. Then again when the earth grows warm and the warm changes come, many will perish because of strong drink. Now the Creator never intended that variations of weather and season, warm and cold, should cause death."

2 "The Creator made the waters of the earth, the rivers and lakes. These too will cause death and some filled with strong drink will be swallowed up by the waters."

3 "And now more. The Creator made fire and this will also cause death and some filled with strong drink will be destroyed by the flames."

"Verily he has said and ordained that they who disobey Gai'wiio' should fall into hardships."

So they said and he said. Eniaiehuk.

SECTION 60

"Now another message.

"It is a custom for thanksgiving to be made over the hills of planted corn. Let the head one of the family make an invocation over the planted hills that the corn may continue to support life. Now this will be a right thing and whosoever asks the help of the Creator will receive it."

So they said and he said. Eniaiehuk.

SECTION 62

"Now another message.

"Now there are some who have boasted that they could drink all the strong drink in the world. Now we, the messengers, say that they who thus idly boast will never live to accomplish what they boast. White men will ever distil the evil liquor."

So they said and he said. Eniaiehuk.

SECTION 65

"Now another message.

"It has been a custom when a person knows of a healing herb to ask payment for giving it to a patient. Now we say that this is not right. It is not right to demand compensation for treating the sick. If such is done it adds greater afflictions to the sick one. The Creator has given different people knowledge of different things and it is the Creator's desire that men should employ their knowledge to help one another, especially those who are afflicted. Now moreover the person helped out ought only to give tobacco for an offering."

So they said and he said. Eniaiehuk.

SECTION 70

"Now another message.

"Now we say that you must tell your friends and relatives that there will be a time when all the earth will withhold its sustaining foods. Then will come the end of the world and those who refuse to believe in Gai'wiio' will suffer great hardships."

So they said and he said. Eniaiehuk.

SECTION 71

"Now another message.

"Now we think that a time will come when a great plague will kill many people and no one will know its cause. Then will you know that the end is near and those who do not believe will suffer great hardships."

So they said and he said. Eniaiehuk.

SECTION 77

"Now another message.

"Now we think that when the end comes the earth will be destroyed by fire and not one upon it will escape for all the earth will be enveloped in flames and all those who refuse to believe in Gai'wiio' will be in it."

So they said and he said. Eniaiehuk.

SECTION 80

"Now another message.

"Every person has a song to sing when the time comes to leave the earth. When a person is departing he must sing that song and continue to sing on his journey to the other world. They will do this who have repented and who believe in Gai'wiio'."

So they said and he said. Eniaiehuk.

SECTION 95

"So they proceeded on their journey and had not gone far when they came to a halt.

"Then the messengers pointed out a certain spot and said, 'Watch attentively,' and beheld a man carrying loads of dirt and depositing them in a certain spot. He carried the earth in a wheelbarrow and his task was a hard one. Then he knew that the name of the man was Sagoyewat'ha, a chief.

"Then asked the messengers, 'What did you see?'

"He answered, 'I beheld a man carrying dirt in a wheelbarrow and that man had a laborious task. His name was Sagoyewat'ha, a chief.'

"Then answered the messengers, 'You have spoken truly. Sagoyewat'ha is the name of the man who carries the dirt. It is true that his work is laborious and this is for a punishment for he was the one who first gave his consent to the sale of Indian reservations. It is said that there is hardship for those who part with their lands for money or trade. So now you have seen the doom of those who repent not. Their eternity will be one of punishment.'"

So they said and he said. Eniaiehuk.

SECTION 104

"Now he saw a certain nude woman coming out from a crowd and in all the hair of her body were writhing serpents. Her cheeks were parched to the bone where she had been wont to color them and likewise where her hair was parted there was no flesh. Now she was greatly ashamed but she would not cover her nakedness. So in this condition he saw her.

"Then said the four messengers, 'Saw thou that woman? In life she was wont to give on'oityi'yĕnde, [secret powders] to men to attract them to her. So you have seen the punishment meted out to those who do this and do not repent.'"

So they said. Eniaiehuk.

SECTION 124

"Thus it happened in the past and it is the truth.

"'I must now take up my final journey to the new world,' he thought, and he was greatly troubled and longed for the home of his childhood and pined to return.

"Then came the four messengers to him and said, 'The children will comfort you in your distress for they are without sin.

They will elect a certain one from among them to plead that you continue to abide among them.'"

So they said. Eniaiehuk.

"Now it happened that it came to pass that all the children assembled and their spokesman did his utmost to exact a promise from Ganio'dai'io'. So great was his grief that after he had spoken a short time he could no longer plead. Then another boy was appointed by the children, a boy not bashful but rough and bold. So he, too, endeavored to persuade Ganio'dai'io', but it was a difficult task for him and he could scarcely speak, but he did. Then Ganio'dai'io' made an answer to the children. He rose and exhorted them to ever be faithful and a great multitude heard him and wept." Eniaiehuk.

Attempts to unify tribes, recall the lost sense of identity, reestablish some of the lost pride, and create a sense of "Indianness" are obvious parts of the Pan-Indian movement in the latter part of the nineteenth century and all of the twentieth. One magazine that tried to do these things was The Narragansett Dawn *published in Oakland, Rhode Island, under the editorship of Princess Red Wing of the Seven Crescents, Royal House of Pokanoket, Narragansett Tribe of the Wampanoag Nation. Two articles from Volume 1, No. 8, December, 1935, indicate the gradations of Christianization among the people. These articles are relatively representative and might have come from almost any tribe.*

Religion or Salvation

Eagle Eye

What church shall I join? Who is right? This is the question we hear so often, and it only goes to prove that the questioners are not satisfied in their own hearts as to their religion. It proves that they have not known Christ as their personal Savior. In the old dispensation you were justified in having a question, but in this new dispensation, the Holy Ghost will teach and guide every child of God, in the path of Truth and Righteousness. So, if you have not had a change of heart or accepted Christ as your Savior, do not join any church, for religion without Christianity is a farce. There are the St. Simonians, Samaritans, Shakers, Baptists, Second Adventists, Methodists, Presbyterians, Puritans, Quakers, Catholics, Spiritualists, Mormans, Congregationalists, Nazarenes, Dutch Reformed, Episcopalians, and any number of others which I have not mentioned, that you may join, but they cannot save you. Religion will not save you. What you need is salvation through Jesus Christ, for this means a restful, happy, contented life, free from world control and deliverance from the folly of fashion and slavery of the world's opinion.

The reason why some never get on the straight and narrow path is because they have their eyes on worldly objects or persons and cannot see Christ. I remember myself, seven years ago, I never gave God a thought. The things that concerned me were, did I have money enough to stay in a game of cards, hope I don't run out of tobacco, hope I make a good impression, and I'll go to church because I call myself a Christian. I was born in a Christian country so I am all right.

But when God showed me myself, I saw nothing but hell ahead for me. I went to the alter 14 or 15 times publicly before the truth dawned upon me. Since I have been to Him a countless number of times to thank Him, praise Him and to ask for wisdom and forgiveness. I know now the Words of the Bible are true. There is an element of gloom in all false religions. Paganism is a barrel of horrors. The God of Confucious frowned upon its victims with blind fate; Mohammidism promises nothing to those exhausted with sin in this world but an eternity of the same passional indulgences. The papacy prostrates its devotees with fastings, kneelings, merciless taxations of the poor man's wages, and tugs until they sweat from January until December trying to pull its dead priests and archbishops out of purgatory.

But God intended our religion should have grand characteristics of cheerfulness and happiness; St. Paul struck the key note when he said, "Rejoice evermore and again I say, rejoice." And Paul could rejoice because he gave up his religion for Salvation, when God met him on his way to Damascus.

History of the Indian's Religion

Princess Red Wing

The subject of "The History of the Indian's Religion," makes a beautiful story, because it goes into every phase of his daily life. He did not pack it into one hour on Sunday. We who are collecting and preserving the history of the Indian from his own unwritten book, find that his religion was a true and deep understanding of the Creator of all things, *A Good Spirit*, with an evil spirit to combat.

They sought, they found and solved the mysteries of life through nature. They heard the unsung music and fashioned their hearts to its tune. They sensed the unspoken verse and all life to them was a poem. They felt the oneness with an unseen God. The Indian could put forth his hand and touch the lovely flowers, not made by man; he could cut down the mighty trees which swayed in the breeze unaided by man. He learned centuries ago that herbs and roots, barks and berries, soothed and sustained life. All these were wonderful to him. His seeds placed in the ground turned into fruit for his maintenance. It was the work of an unseen being, a Creator, who should be pleased and praised. They believed one so mighty to create could destroy if they displeased Him. They knew the animals, understood their life and some hidden instinct taught them the appreciation of it. But man could master the most fierce of animals, because they understood their traits, haunts and could reckon their mating time. The fur on the foxes' backs told them of the forthcoming season.

They listened to the winds which brought relief in summer, the snow, hail and storms in winter. They understood it and man could protect himself from it. They could protect themselves from the sun, which was also their great gift from the Creator. No! They figured, all these things are not God. Man cannot hide himself from Manitou. These are the works of Manitou for the good of man. They looked up to the sky, and said the habitation of the Good Spirit must be above the bright blue, for He is high above the earth and all things about the earth. The sun, the moon, the winds are all the Good Spirit's ways of speaking to man. The vegetation, the animals and minerals are his ways of feeding and caring for man without showing Himself directly. And so, to the old Indian of these parts, He was Manitou, dwelling in the skies, high above all things, all powerful, the Good Spirit, who assisted them in the hereafter.

Down somewhere under the earth dwelt the evil spirit and his agents. The Indians were very sincere in their belief that if they did not please, worship, praise, fear, and trust the Good Spirit, they would leave a loop hole for the agents of the evil spirit. They believed the wages of sin were death through the evil spirit. America's great nature poet [William Cullen Bryant] touched a true cord in the Indian's faith when he wrote:

> So live that when thy summons come
> To join that innumerable caravan
> Which moves to that mysterious realm
> Where each shall take up his place
> In the quiet chambers of death
> Go thou not, like a quarry slave
> At night, scourged to his dungeon
> But like one soothed and sustained
> By an unfaltering trust, approach thy grave
> Like he who wraps his couch covers about him
> And lies down to pleasant dreams.

It was from the keen understanding of nature that this poet wrote; and it was deep understanding of the great issues of life that the Indian of long ago, found his unfaltering trust in the Great Spirit. Their faith not only soothed, sustained, but it called forth the best that a man could give to life, in order to obtain the best that life could give to him.

They prided themselves on being strong of character and muscle, brave in danger and wise in the knowledge of the elements. The younger generation worked to this end. As very young children, they were taught, to be strong of character, one does not lie or rob his brother, or break a promise; to be strong of muscle, he must take care of his body and mind his diet.

Very young they learned what a grand thing it was to be brave and thus through common sense protect themselves against dangers. They were given beads and trinkets for deeds of bravery and words of wisdom. Parents gloried in the smartness of a youngster, who learned a good name was earned by working for it.

When a boy was about 15 summers, his father took him aside and explained, that he must go forth into the forest and hills and seek for himself the great mysteries of life. What he was to see or to find, he was not told. But that which he did see, hear or feel, he must hide in his heart forever, because it was to be his symbol of life, his communication and understanding with the Great Spirit. He took his bow and arrows, but he could not shoot for food. He must not eat until he had talked with his God. Sometimes these young lads were gone 3 or 4 days. They wandered, searching about the forests, praying for a sign from heaven, begging for understanding. They killed dangerous animals, they sat down by the brooks to ponder about the future and life in general. Tired, weak and hungry, they slept under the stars and God gave them vision. For as truly as Christ speaks to the sinsick souls of to-day who really seek Him, a living Spirit, guided, protected and spoke to those young lads of yore, who never went back to the village until they understood. As the light of knowledge dawned upon their young brains, they arose to conquer or kill anything in their path. That which inspired him to action became his symbol. If it were a black bear, he killed it and took it home. The bear became his crest which would be seen on his jacket and home, while his name would become Black Bear. Thus they left their childhood names and gained a new name.

Einstein, the great German scientist says, "There lays a deep meaning in the fact that the children of every civilized nation of the world are fond of playing Indians." But when your son plays Indian, he is not the little sore eyed, ragged Navajo or Pawnee or Sioux of to-day but the son of a great chief of yester-year, who at the break of each grey dawn, parted the doorway of his abode and went forth to meet his God alone. He lifted his eyes unto the hills and his heart to the living God of the universe and there found strength and wisdom for the day. His religion was a mixture of philosophy, psychology, and Christian Science. They believed all life's miseries came from butting their little wills against the great Divine Will. To them two wrongs could never make a right. Educated intelligent people of to-day thought so when they voted to bring back liquor. They shout on the air repeal will save the country, wipe out crime, end depression and stop accidents. Did it?

Better we to-day think like the old, old Indian—let each individual search himself for what evil he can right and repent to help his chief in difficult times. You know, the Indian thought it his sacred duty to uphold his chief and to support him in all measures. If he were upset, sick or unreasonable each man searched his own soul to see what sacrifice he could make to drive away the evil spirits that were troubling their chief. And when he was well and the village prosperous and the harvests good they all prayed, gave thanks and had many ceremonies to please the Great Spirit. They played ball and tried to excell in athletics to please Manitou.

One of the fundamental items in the Indians faith is his belief in unity, fraternities or brotherhoods. Mr. J. Howard McGrath, a leader among the Foresters of America once said, the Indian is the father of brotherhoods here. The Foresters, the Red Men, The Woodmen and other lodges and associations have formed their by-laws on those found existing among the Indians before the white man came. In those long ago days the Indians united in tribes and the tribes in Pow Wows or greater meetings, to ward off dangers or to generate power that one tribe alone could not master. The Iroquois called together the first great league of nations here in America and the colonies, settled for different purposes along the Atlantic coast followed their example and united to conquer the Indians and later the British and thus was born our own United States.

The individual Indian was subjective to his chief and the chief to the Grand Sachem, who had his council, to whom he listened; and together these men, wise in the nature of the spirits, the forests, the chase and the very elements, ruled the tribes. They decreed justice to please the Great Spirit. One having committed an evil deed was possessed by the evil spirit and must be dealt with accordingly, else destruction or ill luck come upon all. That one must go out alone to fast and pray on a high hill, with only the trees and rocks to hear his lamentations. He would then be still and perhaps even fall asleep while he awaited the will of Manitou. Perhaps he would be made to suffer long. Manitou was all merciful, and if one really repented and suffered long and deep in his heart for the evil deed, his heart would be purged from sin and he could go back rejoicing to his people and be successful. But if he were so bad that the Good Spirit hid His face, they believed that it would thunder and lightning to show the wrath of Manitou. The evil one must then make great sacrifices, and his tribe must give offerings and have prayers for him. All were concerned until the evil spirits were driven out.

Good acts they believed would bring blessings from the Great Spirit to them and to all. When in doubt, they meditated alone for days as to-day one prays for guidance from God.

Long ago you never found half a village hungry, jobless and homeless, while the other half lived in luxury. The chief saw to it that everybody worked, co-operated and made the village liveable and prosperous. If crops were poor, all suffered alike and long were their prayers and appeals to the Great Spirit.

Do we blame the ills of our country on ourselves? Do we think because our front pages are splashed with the red blood of murder, robbery, crime, accidents, pledges and depression that we as individuals are to blame, that our country is not a purer place?

The Indian did. That was the basis of his brotherhood. They saw themselves first, and tried to make that self with the help of Manitou, something bigger, better and more helpful to the glory of his tribe and his chief a more glorious leader. If it were proven a chief was not brave enough to lay down his life for any one of his people he would quickly be removed from his position and exiled. It was a part of their religion to help each young man thinking of marriage to first build his abode. The women helped the young marriageable daughters to fill their hope chests with useful house utensils. Her parents gave a festival for her often until she were chosen by some young brave. This was called the festival of the pure maiden and here she made her vows to remain pure until marriage. If these vows were broken she welcomed the arrow to her heart rather than deceive a brave in marriage. These young people never went to school but their training began at an early age in the homes. The first thing the young child learned was to thank God for food and rejoice in life. He knew almost before he could talk that he must not displease the Good Spirit. He must stick close to mother and her teachings, else some harm come to him. Indian Mothers were responsible for the spiritual well being of the tribe.

Zitkala-Sä (Gertrude Bonnin), a Dakota Sioux, was a contemporary of Charles A. Eastman. She did not convert to Christianity for reasons she set forth in the following article published in the December, 1902, issue of the Atlantic Monthly. *Her books* Old Indian Legends *and* American Indian Stories *are, unfortunately, out of print. A teacher, she possessed a rare genius for creating understanding between transplant and Native American children.*

Why I Am a Pagan

Gertrude Bonnin
(Zitkala-Sä)

When the spirit swells my breast I love to roam leisurely among the green hills; or sometimes, sitting on the brink of the murmuring Missouri, I marvel at the great blue overhead. With half closed eyes I watch the huge cloud shadows in their noiseless play upon the high bluffs opposite me, while into my ear ripple the sweet, soft cadences of the river's song. Folded hands lie in my lap, for the time forgot. My heart and I lie small upon the earth like a grain of throbbing sand. Drifting clouds and tinkling waters, together with the warmth of a genial summer day, bespeak with eloquence the loving Mystery round about us. During the idle while I sat upon the sunny river brink, I grew somewhat, though my response be not so clearly manifest as in the green grass fringing the edge of the high bluff back of me.

At length retracing the uncertain footpath scaling the precipitous embankment, I seek the level lands where grow the wild prairie flowers. And they, the lovely little folk, soothe my soul with their perfumed breath.

Their quaint round faces of varied hue convince the heart which leaps with glad surprise that they, too, are living symbols of omnipotent thought. With a child's eager eye I drink in the myriad star shapes wrought in luxuriant color upon the green. Beautiful is the spiritual essence they embody.

I leave them nodding in the breeze, but take along with me their impress upon my heart. I pause to rest me upon a rock embedded on the side of a foothill facing the low river bottom. Here the Stone-Boy, of whom the American aborigine tells, frolics about, shooting his baby arrows and shouting aloud with glee at the tiny shafts of lightning that flash from the flying arrow-beaks. What an ideal warrior he became, baffling the siege of the pests of all the land till he triumphed over their united attack. And here he lay,—Inyan our great-great-grandfather, older than the hill he rested on, older than the race of men who love to tell of his wonderful career.

Interwoven with the thread of this Indian legend of the rock, I fain would trace a subtle knowledge of the native folk which enabled them to recognize a kinship to any and all parts of this vast universe. By the leading of an ancient trail I move toward the Indian village.

With the strong, happy sense that both great and small are so surely enfolded in His magnitude that, without a miss, each has his allotted individual ground of opportunities, I am buoyant with good nature.

Yellow Breast, swaying upon the slender stem of a wild sunflower, warbles a sweet assurance of this as I pass near by. Breaking off the clear crystal song, he turns his wee head from side to side eyeing me wisely as slowly I plod with moccasined feet. Then again he yields himself to his song of joy. Flit, flit hither and yon, he fills the summer sky with his swift, sweet melody. And truly does it seem his vigorous freedom lies more in his little spirit than in his wing.

With these thoughts I reach the log cabin whither I am strongly drawn by the tie of a child to an aged mother. Out bounds my four-footed friend to meet me, frisking about my path with unmistakable delight. Chän is a black shaggy dog, "a thorough bred little mongrel" of whom I am very fond. Chän seems to understand many words in Sioux, and will go to her mat even when I whisper the word, though generally I think she is guided by the tone of the voice. Often she tries to imitate the sliding inflection and long drawn out voice to the amusement of our guests, but her articulation is quite beyond any ear. In both my hands I hold her shaggy head and gaze into her large brown eyes. At once the dilated pupils contract into tiny black dots, as if the roguish spirit within would evade my questioning.

Finally resuming the chair at my desk I feel in keen sympathy with my fellow creatures, for I seem to see clearly again that all are akin.

The racial lines, which once were bitterly real, now serve nothing more than marking out a living mosaic of human beings. And even here men of the same color are like the ivory keys of one instrument where each resembles all the rest, yet varies from them in pitch and quality of voice. And those creatures who are for a time mere echoes of another's note are not unlike the fable of the thin sick man whose distorted shadow, dressed like a real creature, came to the old master to make him follow as a shadow. Thus with a compassion for all echoes in human guise, I greet the solemn-faced "native preacher" whom I find awaiting me. I listen with respect for God's creature, though he mouth most strangely the jangling phrases of a bigoted creed.

As our tribe is one large family, where every person is related to all the others, he addressed me: —

"Cousin, I came from the morning church service to talk with you."

"Yes?" I said interrogatively, as he paused for some word from me.

Shifting uneasily about in the straight-backed chair he sat upon, he began: "Every holy day (Sunday) I look about our little God's house, and not seeing you there, I am disappointed. This is why I come to-day. Cousin, as I watch you from afar, I see no unbecoming behavior and hear only good reports of you, which all the more burns me with the wish that you were a church member. Cousin, I was taught long years ago by kind missionaries to read the holy book. These godly men taught me also the folly of our old beliefs.

"There is one God who gives reward or punishment to the race of dead men. In the upper region the Christian dead are gathered in unceasing song and prayer. In the deep pit below, the sinful ones dance in torturing flames.

"Think upon these things, my cousin, and choose now to avoid the after-doom of hell fire!" Then followed a long silence in which he clasped tighter and unclasped again his interlocked fingers.

Like instantaneous lightning flashes came pictures of my own mother's making, for she, too, is now a follower of the new superstition.

"Knocking out the chinking of our log cabin, some evil hand thrust in a burning taper of braided dry grass, but failed of his intent, for the fire died out and the half burned brand fell inward to the floor. Directly above it, on a shelf, lay the holy book. This is what we found after our return from a several days' visit. Surely some great power is hid in the sacred book!"

Brushing away from my eyes many like pictures, I offered midday meal to the converted Indian sitting wordless and with downcast face. No sooner had he risen from the table with "Cousin, I have relished it," than the church bell rang.

Thither he hurried forth with his afternoon sermon. I watched him as he hastened along, his eyes bent fast upon the dusty road till he disappeared at the end of a quarter of a mile.

The little incident recalled to mind the copy of a missionary paper brought to my notice a few days ago, in which a "Christian" pugilist commented upon a recent article of mine, grossly perverting the spirit of my pen. Still I would not forget that the pale-faced missionary and the hoodooed aborigine are both God's creatures, though small indeed their own conceptions of Infinite Love. A wee child toddling in a wonder world, I prefer to their dogma my excursions into the natural gardens where the voice of the Great Spirit is heard in the twittering of birds, the rippling of mighty waters, and the sweet breathing of flowers. If this is Paganism, then at present, at least, I am a Pagan.

The Peyote Religion

In the review of *The Code of Handsome Lake, the Seneca Prophet,* noted earlier in this chapter, Alanson Skinner continued:

The Peyote religion differs from the Code of Handsome Lake in many ways, particularly in that it offers, in the Peyote "button," a substitute for liquor, which it is said, successfully kills the desire for alcohol. The Peyote teachings have been far more prosperous and popular than the Code of Handsome Lake, having spread like wildfire over many tribes of the West, and are now working eastward and northward, while that of Handsome Lake has always been confined to the Iroquois. Peyote is, however, still a comparatively young religion.

The Peyote religion is sixty years older than it was when those words were written. It began before the Ghost Dance; it survived the Ghost Dance.

Not at variance with Christianity, Peyotism was flexible enough to incorporate or ignore Christianity, depending upon the group of Peyotists. Peyotists and Christians alike agreed that alcoholism is a major evil. And temperance is, if there is *one*, the major tenet of Peyotism. The Christian sects deem the peyote button as great an evil as alcohol—if not a greater one—and they continue to attempt its suppression.

"The last great chief of the Comanches," Quanah Parker, and John Wilson (Moonhead), a leader of the Caddo in the Ghost Dance, embraced Peyotism and did much to spread it in Oklahoma and New Mexico. In the first decade of the twentieth century, it spread rapidly into Arizona, Iowa, Nebraska, Wisconsin, and Wyoming. John Rave, a Winnebago, brought it to his people who established the Union Church and shared their beliefs with such

Omahas as Hiram Chase, a lawyer, who urged the foundation of a church on Mormon administrative principles.

Inevitably, a bill (HR 2614, 1918) was introduced into Congress to outlaw peyote. Carl M. Hayden of Arizona was its author and the hearings brought such notables as Gertrude Bonnin and Charles A. Eastman into determined alliance with Hayden because they foresaw peyote as an addictive that would prove harmful to all Americans. Such anthropologists as James Mooney, Francis LaFlesche (himself an Omaha), and Truman Michelson argued against the bill on various grounds. Pro-peyote forces argued the cult was a respectable religion of some antiquity; anti-peyote forces argued the cult sought to legalize drug addiction.

It was James Mooney who, in 1918, persuaded the Peyotists to apply for a charter so they could call on their right of religious freedom under the national Constitution. And so the Native American Church was incorporated in Oklahoma on October 10, 1918.

By 1934, the Native American Church of Oklahoma was ready to move for national federation in a Central Council of the Native American Church. The statement of purposes in the amended charter filed on April 24, 1934, reads as follows:

This corporation is formed for the purpose of jointly combining, because of our relationship to our forefathers, to push forward our religious worship. Founded upon the four great Primal Laws of God—Love, Faith, Hope and Charity.

The American Indian recognizing the sacramental use of the Earthly plant known as Peyote; with its teachings of love of God and right-living, which embodies morality, sobriety, kindness and brotherly love for all mankind. Including therein the various members of the Faith in the State of Oklahoma, with the right to own and hold property for the purposes herein stated that he may conduct its business or hold services according to the rituals of the Unwritten Code, as given to him by his Maker, the creator of the Universe, God Almighty.

—Amended Articles of Incorporation, Native American Church. Oklahoma.

The Christian opposition to the cult became secular as transplant American youth created the drug cult of the second half of the twentieth century, and alarmed elders sought any source but self on which to place the blame for the defection of youth from the "traditional" values. The Native American, beginning to become legally sophisticated, learning how to speak "with forked tongue" in self-defense had, for a change, out-maneuvered his white neighbor. The fight is, by no means, over; the Native American is, by no means, unified by the Native American Church. But the messianic movements have caused Pan-Indianism to work as it never has before. It blurs tribal identities by making the Native American melt into a cohesive whole for political strength, but it gives a people who number only one-half of one percent of the total population a small power base.

Whether or not peyote is addictive seems irrelevant in one sense. A dominant oppression creates a kind of righteous power in the transplant American, and there can be no argument that ambition, self-righteousness, and power have always been destructively addictive. That which lessens his ignoble attacks on human dignity (which, of course, includes his own) can only be, ultimately, to his advantage. He will not like the feeling of being helped in spite of his wishes, of being improved when he feels he is already perfected. But he may learn something about religious tolerance in process. The two accounts which follow should prove helpful, for they are in the tradition of *The Confessions* of Saint Augustine and the book of The Acts of the Apostles in the New Testament. Before reading John Rave's account, it might be well to reread Acts 9: 1-20 for comparative purposes:

And Saul, yet breathing out threatenings and slaughter against the disciples of the Lord, went unto the high priest, and desired of him letters to Damascus to the synagogues, that if he found any of this way, whether they were men or women, he might bring them bound unto Jerusalem. And as he journeyed, he came near Damascus: and suddenly there shined round about him a light from heaven: and he fell to the earth, and heard a voice saying unto him, Saul, Saul, why persecutest thou me. And he said, Who art thou, Lord? And the Lord said, I am Jesus whom thou persecutest: *it is* hard for thee to kick against the pricks. And he trembling and astonished said, Lord, what wilt thou have me to do? And the Lord *said* unto him, Arise, and go into the city, and it shall be told thee what thou must do. And the men which journeyed with him stood speechless, hearing a voice, but seeing no man. And Saul arose from the earth; and when his eyes were opened, he saw no man: but they led him by the hand, and brought *him* into Damascus. And he was three days without sight, and neither did eat nor drink. And there was a certain disciple at Damascus named Ananias; and to him said the Lord in a vision, Ananias. And he said, Behold, I *am here*, Lord. And the Lord *said* unto him, Arise, and go into the street which is called Straight, and enquire in the house of Judas for *one* called Saul, of Tarsus: for, behold, he prayeth, and hath seen in a vision a man named Ananias coming in, and putting *his* hand on him, that he might receive his sight. Then Ananias answered, Lord I have heard by many of this man, how much evil he hath done to thy saints at Jerusalem: and here he hath authority from the chief priests to bind all that call on thy name. But the Lord said unto him, Go thy way: for he is a chosen vessel unto me, to bear my name before the Gentiles, and kings, and the children of Israel. For I will show him how great things he must suffer for my name's sake. And Ananias went his way, and entered into the house; and putting his hands on him said, Brother Saul, the Lord, *even* Jesus, that appeared unto thee in the way as thou camest, hath sent me, that thou mightest receive thy sight, and be filled with the Holy Ghost. And immediately there fell from his eyes as it had been scales: and he received sight forthwith, and arose, and was baptized. And when he had received meat, he was strengthened. Then was Saul certain days with the disciples which were at Damascus. And straightway he preached Christ in the synagogues, that he is the Son of God.

The Peyote Cult
and My Conversion

John Rave
(Winnebago)

During 1893-94 I was in Oklahoma with peyote eaters.

In the middle of the night we were to eat peyote. We ate it and I also did. It was the middle of the night when I got frightened, for a live thing seemed to have entered me. "Why did I do it?" I thought to myself. I should not have done it, for right at the beginning I have harmed myself. Indeed, I should not have done it. I am sure it will injure me. The best thing will be for me to vomit it up. Well, now, I will try it. After a few attempts I gave up. I thought to myself, "Well, now you have done it. You have been going around trying everything and now you have done something that has harmed you. What is it? It seems to be alive and moving around in my stomach. If only some of my own people were here! That would have been better. Now no one will know what has happened to me. I have killed myself."

Just then the object was about to come out. It seemed almost out and I put out my hand to feel it, but then it went back again. "O, my, I should never have done it from the beginning. Never again will I do it. I am surely going to die."

As we continued it became day and we laughed. Before that I had been unable to laugh.

The following night we were to eat peyote again. I thought to myself, "Last night it almost harmed me." "Well, let us do it again," they said. "All right, I'll do it." So there we ate seven peyote apiece.

Suddenly I saw a big snake. I was very much frightened. Then another one came crawling over me. "My God! where are these coming from?" There at my back there seemed to be something. So I looked around and I saw a snake about to swallow me entirely. It had legs and arms and a long tail. The end of this tail was like a spear. "O, my God! I am surely going to die now," I thought. Then I looked again in another direction and I saw a man with horns and long claws and with a spear in his hand. He jumped for me and I threw myself on the ground. He missed me. Then I looked back and this time he started back, but it seemed to me that he was directing his spear at me. Again I threw myself on the ground and he missed me. There seemed to be no possible escape for me. Then suddenly it occurred to me, "Perhaps it is this peyote that is doing this thing to me?" "Help me, O medicine, help me! It is you who are doing this and you are holy! It is not these frightful visions that are causing this. I should have known that you were doing it. Help me!" Then my suffering stopped. "As long as the earth shall last, that long will I make use of you, O medicine!"

This had lasted a night and a day. For a whole night I had not slept at all.

Then we breakfasted. Then I said, when we were through, "Let us eat peyote again to-night." That evening I ate eight peyote.

In the middle of the night I saw God. To God living up above, our Father, I prayed. "Have mercy upon me! Give me knowledge that I may not say and do evil things. To you, O God, I am trying to pray. Do thou, O Son of God, help me, too. This religion, let me know. Help me, O medicine, grandfather, help me! Let me know this religion!" Thus I spoke and sat very quiet. And then I beheld the morning star and it was good to look upon. The light was good to look upon. I had been frightened during the night but now I was happy. Now as the light appeared, it seemed to me that nothing would be invisible to me. I seemed to see everything clearly. Then I thought of my home and as I looked around, there I saw the house in which I lived far away among the Winnebago, quite close to me. There at the window I saw my children playing. Then I saw a man going to my house carrying a jug of whisky. Then he gave them something to drink and the one that had brought the whisky got drunk and bothered my people. Finally he ran away. "So, that is what they are doing," I thought to myself. Then I beheld my wife come and stand outside of the door, wearing a red blanket. She was thinking of going to the flagpole and was wondering which road she should take. "If I take this road I am likely to meet some people, but if I take the other road, I am not likely to meet anyone."

Indeed, it is good. They are all well — my brother, my sister, my father, my mother. I felt very good indeed. O medicine, grandfather, most assuredly you are holy! All that is connected with you, that I would like to know and that I would like to understand. Help me! I give myself up to you entirely!

For three days and three nights I had been eating medicine, and for three days and three nights I had not slept. Throughout all the years that I had lived on earth, I now realized that I had never known anything holy. Now, for the first time, I knew it. Would that some of the Winnebagoes might also know it!

Many years ago I had been sick and it looked as if this illness were going to kill me. I tried all the Indian doctors and then I tried all of the white man's medicines, but they were of no avail. "I am doomed. I wonder whether I will be alive next year." Such were the thoughts that came to me. As soon as I ate the peyote, however, I got over my sickness. After that I was not sick again. My wife had suffered from the same disease, and I told her that if she ate this medicine it would surely cure her. But she was afraid, although she had never seen it before. She knew that I used it, but nevertheless she was afraid of it. Her sickness was getting worse and worse and one day I said to her, "You are sick. It is going to be very difficult, but try this medicine anyhow. It will ease you." Finally she ate it. I had told her to eat it and then to wash herself and comb her hair and she would get well, and now she is well. Then I painted her face and took my gourd and began singing very much. Then I stopped. "Indeed, you are right," she said, "for now I am well." From that day on to the present time she has been well. Now she is very happy.

Black Water-spirit at about that time was having a hemorrhage and I wanted him to eat the peyote. "Well, I am not going to live anyhow," he said. "Well, eat this medicine soon then and you will get cured." Consumptives never were cured before this and now for the first time one was cured. Black Water-spirit is living to-day and is very well.

There was a man named Walking-Priest and he was very fond of whisky; he chewed and he smoked and he gambled. He was very fond of women. He did everything that was bad. Then I gave him some of the peyote and he ate it and he gave up all the bad things he was doing. He had had a very dangerous disease and had even had murder in his heart. But to-day he is living a good life. That is his desire.

Whoever has any bad thoughts, if he will eat this peyote he will abandon all his bad habits. It is a cure for everything bad.

To-day the Indians say that only God is holy. One of the Winnebagoes has told me, "Really, the life that I led was a very bad one. Never again will I do it. This medicine is good and I will always use it." John Harrison and Squeaking-Wings were prominent members of the medicine dance; they thought much of themselves as did all the members of the medicine dance. They knew everything connected with this medicine dance. Both of them were gamblers and were rich because they had won very much in gambling. Their parents had acquired great possessions by giving medicines to the people. They were rich and they believed that they had a right to be selfish with their possessions. Then they ate peyote and ever since that time they have been followers of this medicine. They were really very ill and now they have been cured of it. Now if there are any men that might be taken as examples of the peyote, it is these three. Even if a man were blind and only heard about them he would realize that if any medicine were good, it is this medicine. It is a cure for all evil. Before, I had thought that I knew something but I really knew nothing. It is only now that I have real knowledge. In my former life I was like one blind and deaf. My heart ached when I thought of what I had been doing. Never again will I do it. This medicine alone is holy and has made me good and has rid me of all evil. The one whom they call God has given me this. That I know positively. Let them all come here; men and women; let them bring with them all that they desire; let them bring with them their diseases. If they come here they will get well. This is all true; it is all true. Bring whatever desires you possess along with you and then come and eat or drink this medicine. This is life, the only life. Then you will learn something about yourself, so come. Even if you are not told anything about your-self, nevertheless you will learn something of yourself. Come with your disease, for this medicine will cure it. Whatever you have, come and eat this medicine and you will have true knowledge once and for all. Learn of this medicine yourself through actual experience.

    If you just hear about it you are not likely to try it. If you desire real knowledge about it try it yourself, for then you will learn of things that you had never known before. In no other way will you ever be happy. I know that all sorts of excuses will run through your mind for not partaking of it, but if you wish to learn of something good, try this. Perhaps you will think to yourself that it will be too difficult and this will seem an excuse to you for not trying it. But why should you act thus? If you partake of it, even if you feel some uncertainty about its accomplishing all the good that has been said of it, I know that you will say to yourself, "Well, this life is good enough." After you have taken it for the first time, it will seem as if they are digging a grave for you, that you are about to die; and you will not want to take it again. "It is bad," you will think to yourself. You will believe that you are go-ing to die and you will want to know what is going to happen to you. The coffin will be set before you and then you will see your body. If you wish to inquire further about where you are going then you will learn something you have not known. Two roads there are, one leading to a hole in the earth and the other extending up above. You will learn something that you had not known before. Of the two roads, one is dark and the other is light. You must choose one of these while you are alive and so must you decide whether you wish to continue in your evil ways or whether you will abandon them. These are the two roads.

The Peyote people see them. They claim that only if you weep and repent will you be able to obtain knowledge. Do not, as I said before, listen to others talking about it, but try the medicine yourself. That is the only way to find out. No other medicine can accomplish what this has done. If, therefore, you make use of it, you will live. After they have eaten peyote people throw aside all the (evil) ceremonies that they were accustomed to perform before. Only by eating the peyote will you learn what is truly holy. That is what I am trying to learn myself.

It is now 23 years since I first ate peyote, and I am still doing it (1912). Before that my heart was filled with murderous thoughts. I wanted to kill my brother and my sister. It seemed to me that my heart would not feel good until I killed one of them. All my thoughts were fixed on the warpath. This is all I thought of. Now I know that it was because the evil spirit possessed me that I felt that way. I was suffering from a disease. I even desired to kill myself; I did not care to live. That feeling, too, was caused by this evil spirit living within me. Then I ate this medicine and everything changed. The brother and sister I wanted to kill before I became attached to and I wanted them to live. The medicine had accomplished this.

The Old People Were Right

Don C. Talayesva (Sun Chief, Hopi)

My earliest memories of my real grandfather, Homikniwa, are full of kind feelings. I slept with him much of the time. In the mornings before sunrise he sang to me and told me stories. He took me to his fields, where I helped him to work or slept under a peach tree. Whenever he saw me make a circle on the ground he stepped cautiously around it, saying that he had to watch me lest I block his path with my antelope power. He kept reminding me of this power. He also took me through the fields to collect healing herbs. I watched him sprinkle corn meal and pray to the Sun god before picking off leaves or berries or digging medicine roots. Whenever mothers brought their sick children to our house, I watched him take their pinches of meal, step outside, pray, and sprinkle them to the Sun god, moon, or stars, and to his special medicine god. Then he would return to the patient, blow upon his hands, and begin his treatment. He was respected by all. Even Mr. Voth, the missionary, came to him to learn about plants and herbs. He taught the white man many things. He also taught me almost all I ever learned about plants.

Mr. Voth and the Christians came to Oraibi and preached Jesus in the plaza where the Katcinas danced. The old people paid no attention, but we children were told to accept any gifts and clothing. Mr. Voth never preached Christ to me alone but talked to us in groups. He said that Jesus Christ was our Saviour and suffered for our sins. He told us that Jesus was a good shepherd and that we were sheep or goats. We were to ask Jesus for whatever we wanted. Oranges and candy looked pretty good to me so I prayed for them. I said, "Jesus, give me some oranges and candy." Then I looked up into the sky but I never saw him throw anything down to me. Mr. Voth claimed that our gods were no good but the old people pointed out to us that when the Katcinas danced in the plaza it often rained. Even as a child I was taught that the missionaries had no business condemning our gods and that it might cause droughts and famine.

When I began to run around, I first wore shirts, without pants, which the missionaries gave us. We were told that Whites (*Bahanas*) did not like to see us naked. But we boys went without clothes most of the time unless someone warned us that Whites were climbing the mesa. We were always on the lookout for them. One day my father made shirts for my brother and me out of a couple of flour sacks. There was a beautiful deer's head printed on the backs. The other children stared at us with eyes shining, while we felt happy and up-to-date. But I was careless, and my mother sometimes scolded or spanked me for getting my clothes dirty. I did not seem to mind dirt.

In the summer Katcinas with great heads and fine clothes came into the plaza and danced. They almost never spoke but sang a great deal. An old man, called the Father of the Katcinas, sprinkled corn meal upon them, and our mothers carried loads of food to their resting place just outside the village. My father and others dressed as clowns and played funny jokes in the plaza. The Katcinas usually gave us gifts. At about sundown the old man, their "Father," asked them to go home and send us rain. They marched away toward the San Francisco mountains in the west. Everybody knew they were spirit gods.

In late summer when I was perhaps four, the men in the Snake and Antelope societies placed signs outside their kivas and our parents warned us to stay away. For several days the men came out in fancy costumes, lined up, and marched off the mesa in search of snakes.

I wished to follow them and was told that some day I might be chosen as a Snake man. In the evenings the people told how many snakes had been caught and that some were large rattlers. We knew snakes were spirit gods who bring rains and never harm anyone with a good heart. We were told never to act silly and scream or yell like Whites when a snake goes toward them. My grandfather said that such foolish behavior spoiled the ceremony. When snakes were pleased with their treatment they were quiet and would bring rain as a reward.

On the last day of the ceremony great crowds of Whites and strange Indians came to Oraibi. They climbed over housetops, stood in doorways, and crowded into the plaza near the Snake kiva to see everything. Late in the afternoon the Antelope men entered the plaza in fine costumes and marched around the Snake house (*kisi*) four times, stamping their feet before it. Then the Snake members, painted and finely dressed, came with lively steps and circled the kisi in the same manner. Soon they were dancing with big live snakes in their hands and between their teeth. Some snakes wriggled and stuck out their tongues but others were quiet. My grandfather said later that dancers with the best hearts had the quietest snakes. When the serpents were placed in a circle on the ground they ran in every direction before the snake catcher could get them. Some Whites yelled and jumped back shamefully. A bull snake came toward me at the edge of the plaza. I did not cry but I was ready to run when the snake catcher picked it up. He was brave and had a good heart. I wanted to be a Snake man. . . .

One winter morning in February I saw a tall, strange Katcina (Hahai-i) coming into the village from the north side, blowing a bone whistle and uttering a long drawn "Hu-hu-huhuhu." When he entered the plaza women and children threw pinches of corn meal upon him and took springs of green corn and of spruce boughs from his tray. Two other Katcinas joined him near the kiva. Some men came out of the Powamu kiva where they were holding a ceremony, blew tobacco smoke on the backs of the Katcinas, and sprinkled them with corn meal. A number of different Katcinas, some running cross-legged (*hüüve*), came through the streets handing out gifts. Some of us received bows, arrows, rattles, and Katcina dolls (*tiku*). Other Katcinas came into the village bringing bean sprouts in baskets. We were in the plaza watching them. Suddenly my mother threw a blanket over my head. When she uncovered me the Katcinas were all gone and the people were looking up into the sky and watching them fly about—they said. I looked up but could see nothing. My mother laughed and said that I must be blind.

I later saw some giantlike Katcinas (Nataskas) stalking into the village with long, black bills and big sawlike teeth. One carried a rope to lasso disobedient children. He stopped at a certain house and called for a boy. "You have been naughty," he scolded. "You fight with other children. You kill chickens. You pay no attention to the old people. We have come to get you and eat you." The boy cried and promised to behave better. The giants became angrier and threatened to tie him up and take him away. But the boy's parents begged for his life and offered fresh meat in his place. The giant reached out his hand as if to grab the boy but took the meat instead. Placing it in his basket, he warned the boy that he would get just one more chance to change his conduct. I was frightened and got out of sight. I heard that sometimes these giants captured boys and really ate them....

As far back as I can remember, I noticed that my father, mother, and grandfather would take a little food before eating and put it aside. They said that it was to feed the Sun and other gods who protected us. Sometimes I heard them speak to these gods, inviting them to eat. They were especially careful to do this on dance days. Whenever my father asked the gods for anything, he fed them first. Sometimes he would take a bit of food, step outside and throw it to the Sun, then ask for something. We were told that there was no need to speak out loud in thanking our gods at the three daily meals. We could pray in our hearts: "Now this meal is prepared for me. I will put it into my body to make myself strong for work. May my Spirit Guide protect me...."

By the time I was six, I had learned to find my way about the mesa and to avoid graves, shrines, and harmful plants, to size up people, and to watch out for witches. I was above average height and in good health. My hair was clipped just above my eyes, but left long in back and tied in a knot at the nape of my neck. I had almost lost one eye. I wore silver earrings, a missionary shirt or one made of a flour sack, and was always bare-legged, except for a blanket in cold weather. When no Whites were present, I went naked. I slept out on the house-top in summer and sometimes in the kiva with other boys in winter. I could help plant and weed, went out herding with my father, and was a kiva trader. I owned a dog and a cat, a small bow made by my father, and a few good arrows. Sometimes I carried stolen matches tucked in the hem of my shirt collar. I could ride a tame burro, kill a kangaroo rat, and catch small birds, but I could not make fire with a drill and I was not a good runner like the other fellows. At the races people teased me and said that my feet turned out so far that I pinched my anus as I ran. But I had made a name for myself by healing people; and I had almost stopped running after my mother for her milk....

A few years before my birth the United States Government had built a boarding school at the Keams Canyon Agency. At first our chief, Lololomai, had not wanted to send Oraibi children, but chiefs from other villages came and persuaded him to accept clothes, tools, and other supplies, and to let them go. Most of the people disliked this and refused to cooperate. Troops came to Oraibi several times to take the children by force and carry them off in wagons. The people said that it was a terrible sight to see Negro soldiers come and tear children from their parents. Some boys later escaped from Keams Canyon and returned home on foot, a distance of forty miles.

Some years later a day school was opened at the foot of the mesa in New Oraibi, where there were a trading post, a post office, and a few government buildings. Some parents were permitted to send their children to this school. When my sister started, the teacher cut her hair, burned all her clothes, and gave her a new outfit and a new name, Nellie. She did not like school, stopped going after a few weeks, and tried to keep out of sight of the Whites who might force her to return. About a year later she was sent to the New Oraibi spring to fetch water in a ceremonial gourd for the Ooqol society and was captured by the school principal who permitted her to take the water up to the village, but compelled her to return to school after the ceremony was over. The teachers had then forgotten her old name, Nellie, and called her Gladys. Although my brother was two years older than I, he had managed to keep out of school until about a year after I started, but he had to be careful not to be seen by Whites. When finally he did enter the day school at New Oraibi, they cut his hair, burned his clothes, and named him Ira.

In 1899 it was decided that I should go to school. I was willing to try it but I did not want a policeman to come for me and I did not want my shirt taken from my back and burned. So one morning in September I left it off, wrapped myself in my Navaho blanket, the one my grandfather had given me, and went down the mesa barefoot and bareheaded. . . .

In May we had a Decoration Day celebration. We stuck little flags in our caps, took bunches of flowers, and marched out to the graves of two soldiers who had come out here to fight the Hopi and had died.

On June the fourteenth my father came for me and we returned home, riding burros and bringing presents of calico, lamps, shovels, axes, and other tools. It was a joy to get home again, to see all my folks, and to tell about my experiences at school. I had learned many English words and could recite part of the Ten Commandments. I knew how to sleep on a bed, pray to Jesus, comb my hair, eat with a knife and fork, and use a toilet. I had learned that the world is round instead of flat, that it is indecent to go naked in the presence of girls, and to eat the testes of sheep or goats. I had also learned that a person thinks with his head instead of his heart. . . .

By the end of summer I had had enough of hoeing weeds and tending sheep. Helping my father was hard work and I thought it was better to be educated. My grandfather agreed that it was useful to know something of the white man's ways, but said that he feared I might neglect the Hopi rules which were more important. He cautioned me that if I had bad dreams while at school, I should spit four times in order to drive them from my mind and counteract their evil influences.

Before sunrise on the tenth of September the police came to Oraibi and surrounded the village, with the intention of capturing the children of the Hostile families and taking them to school by force. They herded us all together at the east edge of the mesa. Although I had planned to go later, they put me with the others. The people were excited, the children and the mothers were crying, and the men wanted to fight. I was not much afraid because I had learned a little about education and knew that the police had not come without orders. One of the captured boys was Dick, the son of "Uncle Joe" who had stirred up most of the trouble among the Hostiles. I was glad. Clara, the granddaughter of Chief Lolulomai, was also taken. The Chief went up to Mr. Burton, who was writing our names down on a piece of paper, and said, "This girl must be left here until she is older." She was allowed to return to her mother. They also captured my clan brother Archie, the son of my mother's sister, Nuvahunka.

When Mr. Burton saw me in the group, he said, "Well, well, what are you doing here? I thought you were back in school at the agency." I told him that I was glad to go with him. This seemed to please him, and he let me go to my house to get my things. When I returned with a bag of fresh peaches, I discovered that they had marched the children to New Oraibi to be placed in the wagons. I followed and found my grandfather in a group near the wagons. When I noticed how crowded the wagons were, I asked Mr. Burton if I might ride a horse. He sent me with Archie, Dick, and my grandfather to ask the police. Two of them were my clan uncles, Adam from First Mesa and Secavaima from Shipaulovi. I walked up to Adam, smiling, shook hands with him, and introduced my clan brother Archie. "You don't need to fear us," said my uncle, "we are policemen." I asked him whether Archie and I might ride double on horseback to the Agency. They laughed and said that I had a brave heart. They warned me that the Hostiles might follow us on the road and give battle, but they were only teasing. . . .

Within a few days the teachers gave us a test on the multiplication tables and sent me back from the sixth into the fourth grade. Ira, my brother, was put in the second grade and we were given part-time jobs in the bakery. Besides going regularly to classes, we joined athletic clubs and debating societies, and attended many socials, including square dances. I was also taken into the Y. M. C. A. by two Hopi boys, Adolph Hoye and Harry McClain, who led me into a room and had me sign my name before I knew what I was getting into. I had no idea that I was committing myself to Christianity. They had me attend the meetings every Thursday evening and gave me a prize for learning the names of all the books of the Bible. They also urged me to memorize Scripture verses, which I did during the week ends, and won a Bible.

At the Y. M. C. A. meetings we were expected to stand on our feet and testify for Jesus Christ. I prepared a little sermon which

I could get up and repeat: "Well, my partners, I am asked to speak a few words for Jesus. I am glad that I came to Sherman and learned to read and cipher. Now I discover that Jesus was a good writer. So I am thankful that Uncle Sam taught me to read in order that I may understand the Scriptures and take my steps along God's road. When I get a clear understanding of the Gospel I shall return home and preach it to my people in darkness. I will teach them all I know about Jesus Christ, the Heavenly Father, and the Holy Ghost. So I advise you boys to do your best and pray to God to give us a good understanding. Then we will be ready for Jesus to come and take us up to heaven. I don't want any of my friends to be thrown into the lake of hell fire where there is suffering and sorrow forever. Amen." At that time I was half-Christian and half-heathen and often wished that there were some magic that could change my skin into that of a white man.

I learned to preach pretty well, and to cuss too. The Hopi language has no curse words in it. But at Sherman even the Y. M. C. A. and the Catholic boys cussed like hell. At first so much of it made me tired; but when I got into the habit myself it was all right. When I wanted anything I would say, "give me that God-damn thing." But I soon learned when and where it was appropriate to curse....

I could not put off initiation into the Wowochim. My father, grandfather, and two great-uncles urged me to forget about school and become a man. They said it would please the gods, prepare me for ceremonial work, put me in line to become Chief of the Sun Clan, and fit me for a higher place in life after death. Talasvuyauoma, the big War Chief, advised me to join the men's society without delay. My ceremonial father, clan fathers, mother, godmother, clan mothers, and other relatives encouraged me; and they implied that any boy who did not seek membership in the Wowochim proved himself to be either incompetent or kahopi. They said that only hopeless cripples like Naquima or young men who had been spoiled by Christianity failed to take this important step into manhood....

The seventh day was spent in paho making. After prayers to the Sun god and breakfast, the men let down their long hair. We all undressed except for the loincloth or, in some cases kilt, arranged ourselves in rows in the lower section of the kiva, and began making pahos with feathers, native string, herbs, and willow sticks. I had never done this work before, and had to be instructed by my ceremonial father, who spoke in a whisper because of the presence of ancestral spirits. I made first the prayer arrow, then soft prayer feathers for my Guardian Spirit, the Spider Woman, Masau'u, the Twin War gods, the sun, moon, stars, and all the springs, oceans, and rivers about which I had heard. Then I made prayer offerings for the Six-Point-Cloud-People, for our dear ones who had recently departed, and for all the other spirits that

I could remember. I also made them for all the members of my family, my special friends, the livestock, dogs, cats, houses, trees, and other objects of value. I thought about each god, spirit, person, or object while I made a paho for him. I learned that this is the most important work in the world, that the gods and the spirits are holding out their hands for pahos, and that if the Soyal should fail, life for the Hopi might end. We were instructed to keep our minds pure and filled with these thoughts while we worked and wished strongly for rain, good crops, and long life. If a sexual thought had come into my mind, I would have tried to free myself of it and would not have mentioned the subject to a fellow member even to relieve him of hiccoughs—an excellent remedy on other occasions.

When the pahos and the prayer feathers were finished, they were placed on the floor, where a little honey was spat on them and the makers smoked over them before tying them into little bundles and hanging them on the kiva wall. When our work was over at sunset— for it is a rule that paho making must cease at that hour—we swept the floor, gathered up the trash carefully, sprinkled it with corn meal, and threw it into a gully, where the rains could take it into the valley over our farms. We had worked all day without eating, and the Special Officers had eaten nothing since the night before. When we had finished our lifeless meal, food was brought for the priests, and we sang, as on other nights, while they ate. Then we practiced our Katcina songs and dances, keeping an eye on the Great Dipper stars.

Some Soyal members set to work making *hihikwispi* (something to breathe upon), consisting of four cornhusks tied at tip and stub on a string, about twelve inches apart. At the point of every husk was fastened an eagle prayer feather, together with a feather of six other birds. The four husks were placed one within another, the long string folded into the upper one, and the packages put away for use the next day.

When the Great Dipper stars reached the appointed position, we sang our prayer songs again for two hours as on the preceding night, with the women participating. I was so tired and drowsy that they called me sleepyhead and poured water on me to keep me awake until the ceremony was completed....

Before dawn we took our prayer offerings to our relatives who had washed their heads and were ready with happy hearts for the Paho Planting ceremony. At sunrise the entire village, including babies on their mothers' backs, assembled at the east edge of the mesa, thrust many hundreds of pahos into the ground, and sprinkled them with meal. The people who belonged to my father's clan placed their pahos at a spot called Bow Height (*Awatobi*), because the Sand Clan came from Awatobi, a village now in ruins. Many men and boys, including myself, placed pahos on the Antelope shrine in order to have success in hunting.

As we returned to the village, one could see hundreds of willow switches standing three or four feet high with seven or eight turkey, hawk, eagle, or other soft feathers attached to them three or four inches apart. No chicken or crow feathers were ever used. Fathers who had sons less than a year old planted little crooked pahos for them in order that they might thrive, be happy, and live long. Most of the prayer feathers were fastened to the long sticks for our departed dear ones. The short double pahos were made for all the dead and for the Six-Point-Cloud-People who send rain. It is our belief that the spirit gods and our ancestors come with outstretched hands, seeking pahos in exchange for the blessings of health and long life, and that if they find none they turn away sorrowful. We know that they take with them only the souls of the pahos....

I had learned a great lesson and now knew that the ceremonies handed down by our fathers mean life and security, both now and hereafter. I regretted that I had ever joined the Y. M. C. A. and decided to set myself against Christianity once and for all. I could see that the old people were right when they insisted that Jesus Christ might do for modern Whites in a good climate, but that the Hopi gods had brought success to us in the desert ever since the world began.

Vine Deloria, Jr. is a Standing Rock Sioux, the author of Custer Died for Your Sins *and* We Talk, You Listen, *books written to present a new, truthful version of history and to raise the social consciousness of the transplant American. When the Forum for Contemporary History began its series of monthly letters from world leaders (political, religious, and scholarly), it chose Vine Deloria, Jr. to inaugurate the venture. His letter, appropriately, closes this section.*

An Open Letter to the

Heads of the Christian

Churches in America

VINE DELORIA, Jr.
Bellingham, Washington

January 28, 1972

Dear Fellow Citizen,

I want to share with you an open letter to the Heads of the Christian Churches in America.

It may seem strange to be receiving a letter concerning political matters from an American Indian. But when you understand the nature of my request you will see that it is to you gentlemen alone that we must turn for an answer to our question.

Nearly five centuries ago the European nations, thrilled with the discovery of a large and unknown world to the west, embarked upon the systematic exploration and conquest of the newly discovered continents which have since come to be known as North and South America. These nations were initially spurred on by the thought of inexhaustible riches to be gained through commerce with the nations of the west. It was not long, however, before questions of a theological nature arose. Who were these newly discovered peoples? What rights did they possess? How were they to be treated?

A gradual consensus of the learned scholars of Christendom decided that the peoples inhabiting the western continents were to be treated with respect BUT, that the peoples of the Americas were to have lands and rights only with respect to those nations which claimed the exclusive rights to deal with them. A bargain was struck, therefore, among the Christian nations of western Europe, that whoever discovered lands inhabited by non-Christian peoples would have the exclusive right to "extinguish" such title as against any other Christian nation.

The pattern was thus set that while other nations of the world were to have their lands confirmed to them, the aboriginal peoples of the western hemisphere were to have title and right to their lands only at the pleasure of the Christian nations which chose to recognize those titles. Thinking themselves justified by the god they worshipped, the nations of Europe proceeded to subdue both the lands and peoples of the western continents. They came to regard their actions as the inevitable result of the foreordained plan of God for the future history of the world.

The initial struggle for the right to rule the eastern seacoast of North America involved England, France, Sweden, Holland. After several centuries of struggle England stood supreme upon the shores of the Atlantic. But this success was temporary. Almost immediately following the triumph of England over France the English colonists conducted a successful revolution against their mother country. The colonists established a government in which the major documents of state proclaimed the right of every man to choose his own religion, to pick his own vocation, to have rights to his own property, his home, his job, and his time to be determined by himself.

In those days we inhabited and owned the continent upon which you now live. We followed our own laws and the dictates of our consciences and traditions of our tribes. We were powerful in those days and

could easily have snuffed out the tiny settlements
along the coast. But we were told that red men and
white men could live in peace in such a large country
provided each respected the laws and customs of the
other. We were content with this agreement.

In the years that followed, another doctrine
arose from the minds of Christian men. This doctrine
announced that America, the new country, had a
"Manifest Destiny". It was God's will, we were told,
indeed, the people of America were told, that Christian civilization should extend from coast to coast;
from "sea to shining sea" as it were. Everything non-
Christian and lacking the customs and attributes of
Christian civilization was to be pushed from the
inevitable path of progress.

In 1787, the Congress of the United States declared that the "utmost good faith" would be shown
the Indian tribes of the continent. Congress disclaimed any treachery or deceit in its dealings with
us and promised that only in just wars would our lands
be taken from us. You gentlemen know, as well as we
do, what the result has been. I need not labor the
point of perfidy and injustice with you. Since it is
a matter of historical fact it is sufficient that we
recognize the past for what it has been and not dwell
on it but rather find those answers which will ensure
that mistakes of the past are not continuously
repeated in the future.

It is for that reason that I have chosen to
address you gentlemen as representatives of Christendom. I seek only your honest response and heartfelt
consideration of my questions. It is not the docu-
mented and footnoted answers that you can use to
justify your position that I seek to invoke, but the
beginning of honest inquiry by yourselves into the
nature of your situation. And that situation is that
I believe that you have taught mankind to find its
identity in a re-writing of history and not an affir-
mation of it. It is this tendency, more than any
other, that now confronts American Indian people in
their relations with the United States government.
We are content to live under the laws of this country.
But the United States government has learned to continually change those laws with respect to us by
viewing its own history as it chooses to view it and
not as it was. And I would be so bold as to suggest
that the government learned to do this by following
the lead of its religious community.

Early missionaries, for example, told us the
story of Adam and Eve. They went on at great length
with the stories of Jonah and the Whale. They regaled
us with accounts of the Resurrection, the Exodus, and
the Tower of Babel. We recognized these stories as
myths by which a people explain how they came to
consciousness as a national community. When we tried
to explain our myths the missionaries grew angry and
accused us of believing superstitions.

You gentlemen and your predecessors told us
that God has given man a command in the Garden of Eden
that he should subdue the earth. Out of this command
came the vast industrial machine of modern America.
We replied that the Great Spirit gave certain lands
to each tribe to use, that no one tribe could own the
lands exclusively against any other, that the plants
and animals, even the rivers, mountains and valleys,
each had a right to its own existence because it was
made for that existence by the Great Spirit.

At each point and in every aspect you refused
to confront our ideas but chose instead to force your
opinions, myths, and superstitions on us. You have
never chosen to know us. You have only come to us to
confront and conquer us. And it is this tendency to
continually pervert the experiences of life that you
have passed on to the federal government that has
created our present difficulty. As years have passed
and memories have dimmed we have been told that our
treaties and agreements did not ever mean what they
appear to mean. We are told that promises made upon
the most solemn occasions were mere subterfuges to
gain time or to pacify the tribes. We are told that
obligations of the United States were necessary con-
veniences to the settling of the west -- a mission
ultimately deriving from the Divine command of Eden.

Wishing that something happened long ago does not
change what did happen at that time. Believing in
myths does not give them historical reality. Indeed,
it shields one from ever knowing that reality or from
learning from it. So it is with government, so it is
with religion.

For nearly a century your own scholars have been
pointing out that the best estimates of history are
that no Garden of Eden existed, that the Tower of
Babel was at best an effort to explain the multiplicity
of languages and nations to be found on earth. More
recently Biblical criticism has pointed out that
Jesus in all probability did not rise from the dead

in bodily form. He did not ascend to heaven by leaving the earth in a cloud. (Indeed, with escape
velocity of the planet set at some 25,000 miles per
hour, conceiving the cloud alone takes some
imagination.)

All indications appear to be that while Christianity has certain religious forms that provide a
satisfactory religious experience for a segment of
mankind, it is hardly the final answer either to man's
experience on earth or to his status in any life hereafter. Believing in the Divinity of Jesus does not
alter the historical facts of his existence. A theory
of history, no matter how broad, is not a historical
explanation of the things that have happened if it
cannot account for what has in fact happened.

At one time in man's history the explanations
given by Christianity were sufficient to cover man's
knowledge of his world. This is no longer true.
The ruins of the past civilizations of the Orient and
the western hemispheres alone suffice to reject the
traditional Christian interpretation of history as the
specific plan of a particular God to do a particular
thing with a particular people. You gentlemen know
this far better than I. But you continue to perpetuate
the traditional interpretation of the world as it has
been taught to you. You surely realize the inadequacy
of the Christian interpretation of man's historical
experience.

You do not lack faith in your religion. In
many instances you have gone the extra mile to attempt
to make amends for errors of the past. The only white
men willing to help the Cherokee Nation in its conflict
with Georgia were missionaries. The final and significant force brought to bear for Civil Rights of the
Black man was the effort made by Christians, most of
them white Christians of western European background.

You lack credibility.

Not so much in what you do. You lack credibility
in what you say. And so long as you feel no need to
present a credible and comprehensible understanding of
man's history the governments of the societies in which
you live will see no need to have credibility in what
they do.

This is our problem. It is the crisis of western
man. Whether we like it or not we are inevitably tied
to the fate of western man who has invaded our lands
and among whom we now dwell. When he falls we believe
we shall still survive. But we know it will be at a
terrible cost.

The present position of the United States government is that it holds our lands and communities as its wards. When this doctrine is traced to its origin it lands comfortably within the Doctrine of Discovery and the United States claims its rights over us not by right of conquest but by right of having succeeded to the rights of Great Britain to extinguish our titles to lands. We are completely helpless to ever maintain our lands, our communities and cultures so long as the major reason that they are protected is to enable the United States to one day extinguish them as its legal right against the other Christian nations.

We have been placed beyond the remedies of the Constitution of the United States because the Doctrine of Discovery has never been disclaimed either by the governments of the Christian nations of the world or by the leaders of the Christian churches of the world. And more especially by the leaders of the Christian churches of this country. No effort has been made by Christians to undo the wrongs that were done, albeit mistakenly, and which are perpetuated because Christians refuse to measure their own understanding of the world by the facts of the world in which we all live.

A disclaimer of the traditional Christian understanding of history would carry with it the demand by the peoples of the west that all institutions honestly attempt to appraise the present situation in its true historical light. The American experience would not then appear inevitable. The novelty of the establishment of a democracy would be understood in its own light. The mythology of American history would be seen as merely mythology. The Custers, Chivingtons and Calleys would be seen for what they were. We could all come to the necessity of facing ourselves for what we are. We would no longer have a God busily endorsing and applauding the things that we are doing. We would have to be on God's side in our dealings with other peoples instead of being so sure that God is automatically on our side.

If nothing is certain, then Congress would have no excuse for not dealing justly with us, for industrial and technological progress would not have divine sanction over us. At present the Black Mesa on the Navajo-Hopi reservation in Arizona is being destroyed because it has been said that it is inevitable that more people will need more electrical power and burning the coal deposits of those reservations for power is the cheapest way to get the power needed. The project is justified as the inevitable result of

American progress. But is this kind of progress
ultimately inevitable or have we been trained to
believe it is?

We watch as species after species of wild life
is destroyed by man. We always considered the birds
and animals as brothers, joint creatures of one
creation. But you have told us that this is not so.
You have maintained that God gave man dominion over
the animals in the Garden of Eden. You have justified
the destruction of God's creation and his creatures as
the inevitable consequences of Christian history.
You do not yet raise your voices in protest at this
destruction because it is intimately tied in with your
command to subdue the earth.

The poverty we presently endure, the confiscation
of our lands, the destruction of animals we once
enjoyed, the obliteration of our valleys and rivers,
the exploitation of our holy places as tourist traps,
all of these things might have occurred anyway. We
might even have done these things eventually, although
according to our beliefs this would have been the
gravest of sins. But we would never have deliberately
done these things as a religious command and when our
myths no longer served our purposes we would have
found new myths, new songs and ceremonies, new revelations, to incorporate into our understanding of
ourselves so that we would not be blindly led to
destruction because we could not afford to face the
truth of our own situation.

It may be that we cannot change the past but we
can certainly begin to try to understand it. We have
only to stand today for the things that are right and
which we know are right. If promises have been made,
those promises must be kept. If mistakes are made
they must be corrected. If the lands of aboriginal
peoples were wrongly taken by a Christian mandate then
what remains of those lands must not be continually
taken once the mistake is known.

It remains to you as honest men to ponder what
your predecessors have created and what, by your
silence, you now endorse. If your understanding of
history cannot account for the experiences of mankind
then your duty to mankind is clear. You must announce
the errors that have led men astray from themselves
and lead the search for that understanding or that
religious interpretation that can bring them to understand themselves, their fellow men, and the creation
in which they live.

Political institutions are viable under most circumstances. But they operate according to their understanding of the world in which they exist. In every era of man's existence religions have acted to give to political institutions the justification, incentive, and heart to exist. If we have political institutions that do not serve us today it is because our religious institutions have not called those governments and the peoples who run them to a greater vision of humanity. Justice has become merely justification of man's condition and not a call for the integrity resulting from credibility or the expansion of man's vision of himself.

Christianity once had a message of the dignity of man. And this is my final question to you. At what point can we as peoples of the creation look to Christianity to demand from the political structures of the world our dignity as human beings? At what point can we become men and not mere appendages of the Christian Doctrine of Discovery?

Sincerely Yours,

Vine Deloria, Jr.

Vine Deloria, Jr.
A Sioux Indian

Chapter 7

Memories Miserable and Magnificent: Biography and Autobiography

Biography and autobiography are, almost invariably, the late arrivals in a people's literature, following the creative poetic and fictional forms and the history of events rather than the history of persons. The reasons are obvious enough, the main one being that biography as a component of early literature (religion, culture tales, epics) is so fictionalized, so romanticized, so collective in its attribution of characteristics and deeds to one man that it in no way fulfills the functions of biography; and autobiography doesn't even exist until much later because the fit subjects of autobiography are too busy making history to spend time writing their own even if they have the literary talent required by the form.

The earliest biographies in any people's history are concerned with religious personages or historically vital people who have so shaped the course of events that their lives are indicative of the times they helped create. Naturally enough, early biographies are usually laudatory and commemorative, the facts being shaped to conceal undesirable aspects of the biographee's life and conduct, or they are condemnatory and commemorative, the facts being shaped to emphasize or exaggerate aspects that make the biographee more villainous than he was in actuality.

That commemorative aspect creates a second characteristic of biography: didacticism of a moralistic nature. The reader "learns" something of value about the man, his relation to his time, and his desirable or undesirable influence on history. One of the more common criticisms of biographies is that they reveal more about the biases of the biographer than they reveal about the character of the biographee. The objectivity that, ideally, should characterize biography or history is almost impossible to achieve. The main reason for this is that a writer must have a personal, compelling reason to want to create a record in the first place. Such involvement does not, ordinarily, encourage objectivity.

Utilizing some of the allied forms of biography—anecdotes, memoirs, journals, diaries, recollections of acquaintances of the subject—the biographer attempts to see the life of the biographee in relationship to historical events, intellectual currents of the time, and the political machinations that too often remain eternally unrecorded. Out of the welter of "facts" which are already distortions because they have been strained through the viewpoints of the original observers, he must extract dominant, motivating characteristics and historical trends that, combined and artfully presented, create a sense of the cohesion and flow of events and ideas in time. The complexities of the human animal, the accidents of history will not be honestly shaped to prove a thesis, to create truth that can be stated in the prospectus for a study. But that is the nature of the form, and it is the best form we have for the purpose; so we work with the imperfections it creates.

Nor can a third aspect of biography be ignored. It may even be the most vital aspect. A nagging curiosity, a rampant rage to be privy to the recesses of another person's life and mind goads civilized man. The dullness of his life creates a compulsion to live vicariously in the shadows of lives that seem exciting, dangerous, untrammelled, or dominant in time. Questions that personal restraint makes unaskable are posed silently, and to satisfy their curiosity biographer and reader scuttle through the historical middens like rats seeking tidbits.

The reader of biography expects certain conventional demands to be met by the biographer. As the account is historical, the history must be either accurate or inaccurate in desirable ways. The history of the period must serve as a backdrop against which the biographee moves, while the social and political institutions of the time must be analyzed only as they shape and change the man or are shaped and changed by him. In short, biography is a man's history; it is not a history of a country, a people, a culture. The man's personality must serve as the core around which events and trends and movements flow together and merge to form a sense of cohesion in the juices and pulp that create the fruity body of the work, always taking their flavor and sweetness or bitterness from the character at the center. A pervasive thesis usually binds the ingredients together: "History conspired to shape this man" or "This man so dominated his time that he shaped history" or "When history and this man collided, each was so strong that the lives of all succeeding men were changed by the impact."

In the English-speaking world, Boswell's study of Dr. Samuel Johnson set the acceptable pattern for the biography, but it was Dr. Johnson's *Lives of the Poets* which elevated biography above mere historical account and entrenched it in the realm of literature. Johnson's refinement of the presentation, Boswell's formula for presenting the trivial as an illumination of the important, and an intellectually stimulating climate—all combined to perfect biography in the eighteenth century. The moral righteousness, the defensive prudery, the narrowing perspective of Victorian England returned the form to the level of hagiography perfected by Plutarch and the church-produced lives of the saints. Biographies were "authorized" with the understanding that facts would be manipulated to create a desirable conclusion whether it was accurate or inaccurate. Then, when the full impact of Freud and the expanding sciences of anthropology and ethnology were manifest in the twentieth century, an apparent truth without regard for moral restraint or discretion assumed domination. At least it assumed domination in works devoted to those culturally desirable heroes and antiheroes who fostered the myth of the melting pot, the rationalization for "progress," and the defense of the cultural superiority of the ascendant group.

The "objective" biography concerned with the white figure and written by the white biographer was, indeed, an historical-psychological study. That same "objective" biography of the figure from the black or red ranks inevitably assumed the proportions of a clinical study of a culturally inferior creature, no matter how "dedicated" or "sensitive" the biographer might be. Some of the great studies of the Native American which pass for biography are characterized by an approach that suggests he is "interesting" as a case history, but case histories detail the man removed from the human sphere, the man residing in a twilight zone it is titillating to visit as long as one does not have to live there beyond the time of field work.

Native American biographies by Native American biographers are relatively rare even now. Happily, some do exist, for the numbers of Indians who have mastered the Eurasian forms of literature are quite large in relation to the total number of Indians in America.

Autobiography is quite another matter.

At any time, among any people, the autobiography is a bit on the suspect side. Who would get an honest picture of the genocidal, economically irresponsible, licentious (by Judeo-Christian standards) Benjamin Franklin, for instance, from his widely admired autobiography? The choices a biographer makes for inclusion or omission are infinitely more objective than those made by the author of any autobiography. Self-defense takes curious forms, of course, and one assumes Franklin's autobiography is as accurate and objective as is St. Augustine's or Casanova's—but for entirely different reasons.

Among the Native American autobiographies, the reader finds many "as told to" notices. How much of those autobiographies is representative of the thinking of the Indian and how much is representative of the white amanuensis is far more apparent to the Indian reader than to the white reader. Shades of cultural thought, programmed phraseology, an inability to hear with an ear shaped by one religious background no matter how highly trained by another are apparent in the best of the "as told to" works. The collaborative efforts of Crashing Thunder and Paul Radin, Black Elk and John Neihardt, and "a Papago Woman" and Ruth Underhill are, by all odds, the most faithful in this group.

Such autobiographers as Ohiyesa (Charles A. Eastman), Zitkala-Ša (Gertrude Bonnin), Chief Standing Bear, and Kaibah (Kay Bennett) reveal the historically recalled past of a people and weave it into the present realities of their lives with as much insight and literary ability as one might want. Explanations of religious beliefs, philosophy, and the Indian version of certain historical events make these works engrossing accounts as well as literary treasures. The English-speaking world would be a poorer place had not such autobiographers as Isadora Duncan, Anthony Trollope, and Henry Adams recorded their unique visions of self, including in process their view of the world in which they lived. It would be correspondingly poorer had not the Indian autobiographers shared their lives and worlds. Perhaps it would be even poorer because what they have recorded could not have been recorded by the white author. What would we not give for an autobiography from the time of Christ? Or Homer? Or Cleopatra? Even biased autobiography is more revealing than the most objective history written two centuries after the facts.

The following excerpts reveal a great deal about the biographer and the biographee. The Sioux Eastman visits Rain-in-the-Face, a great warrior of Eastman's own tribe. The Cherokee Yellow Bird creates a near-fantasy in his assessment of the Mexican outlaw Murieta, possibly because Yellow Bird had seen his own people dispossessed, had himself killed a man, had seen his father stabbed to death, and therefore could understandably romanticize another minority representative. And Osage John Joseph Mathews strikes a nice balance in his presentation of the Indian Agent, Major Laban J. Miles, and the Osage Gray Bird.

The autobiographical excerpts seem to us important statements that are both beautifully presented and charmingly honest. Unquestionably the work of the Indian subjects of the autobiographies (which not all ethnological autobiographies are), they are characteristic expressions of attitudes about the past, the present, and the future. Lost innocence and the heroic figure pervade the nostalgic account of the Sioux Ohiyesa. Quiet refusal to abandon the old rites resides in Tlakodlas' account of the potlatch that so angers the missionary and the Indian Agent. Love of the land and fear for the plundered planet sound a warning none should miss in Ojibwa Grey Owl's record of the beaver leaving their foster parents, Grey Owl and his wife Anaharee, themselves wanderers of a dying wilderness.

Rain-in-the-Face

Charles A. Eastman
(Ohiyesa, Sioux)

The noted Sioux warrior, Rain-in-the-Face, whose name once carried terror to every part of the frontier, died at his home on the Standing Rock reserve in North Dakota on September 14, 1905. About two months before his death I went to see him for the last time, where he lay upon the bed of sickness from which he never rose again, and drew from him his life-history.

It had been my experience that you cannot induce an Indian to tell a story, or even his own name, by asking him directly.

"Friend," I said, "even if a man is on a hot trail, he stops for a smoke! In the good old days, before the charge there was a smoke. At home, by the fireside, when the old men were asked to tell their brave deeds, again the pipe was passed. So come, let us smoke now to the memory of the old days!"

He took of my tobacco and filled his long pipe, and we smoked. Then I told an old mirthful story to get him in the humor of relating his own history.

The old man lay upon an iron bedstead, covered by a red blanket, in a corner of the little log cabin. He was all alone that day; only an old dog lay silent and watchful at his master's feet.

Finally he looked up and said with a pleasant smile:

"True, friend; it is the old custom to retrace one's trail before leaving it forever! I know that I am at the door of the spirit home.

"I was born near the forks of the Cheyenne River, about seventy years ago. My father was not a chief; my grandfather was not a chief, but a good hunter and a feastmaker. On my mother's side I had some noted ancestors, but they left me no chieftainship. I had to work for my reputation.

"When I was a boy, I loved to fight," he continued. "In all our boyish games I had the name of being hard to handle, and I took much pride in the fact.

"I was about ten years old when we encountered a band of Cheyennes. They were on friendly terms with us, but we boys always indulged in sham fights on such occasions, and this time I got in an honest fight with a Cheyenne boy older than I. I got the best of the boy,

414

but he hit me hard in the face several times, and my face was all spattered with blood and streaked where the paint had been washed away. The Sioux boys whooped and yelled:

"'His enemy is down, and his face is spattered as if with rain! Rain-in-the-Face! His name shall be Rain-in-the-Face!'

"Afterwards, when I was a young man, we went on a war-path against the Gros Ventres. We stole some of their horses, but were overtaken and had to abandon the horses and fight for our lives. I had wished my face to represent the sun when partly covered with dark-ness, so I painted it half black, half red. We fought all day in the rain, and my face was partly washed and streaked with red and black: so again I was christened Rain-in-the-Face. We considered it an honor-able name.

"I had been on many warpaths, but was not especially successful until about the time the Sioux began to fight with the white man. One of the most daring attacks that we ever made was at Fort Totten, North Dakota, in the summer of 1866.

"Hóhay, the Assiniboine captive of Sitting Bull, was the leader in this raid. Wapáypay, the Fearless Bear, who was afterward hanged at Yankton, was the bravest man among us. He dared Hóhay to make the charge. Hóhay accepted the challenge, and in turn dared the other to ride with him through the agency and right under the walls of the fort, which was well garrisoned and strong.

"Wapáypay and I in those days called each other 'brother-friend.' It was a life-and-death vow. What one does the other must do; and that meant that I must be in the forefront of the charge, and if he is killed, I must fight until I die also!

"I prepared for death. I painted as usual like an eclipse of the sun, half black and half red."

His eyes gleamed and his face lighted up remarkably as he talked, pushing his black hair back from his forehead with a ner-vous gesture.

"Now the signal for the charge was given! I started even with Wapáypay, but his horse was faster than mine, so he left me a little behind as we neared the fort. This was bad for me, for by that time the soldiers had somewhat recovered from the surprise and were aiming better.

"Their big gun talked very loud, but my Wapáypay was leading on, leaning forward on his fleet pony like a flying squirrel on a smooth log! He held his rawhide shield on the right side, a little to the front, and so did I. Our warwhoop was like the coyotes singing in the evening, when they smell blood!

"The soldiers' guns talked fast, but few were hurt. Their big gun was like a toothless old dog, who only makes himself hotter the more noise he makes," he remarked with some humor.

"How much harm we did I do not know, but we made things lively for a time; and the white men acted as people do when a swarm of angry bees get into camp. We made a successful retreat, but some of the reservation Indians followed us yelling, until Hóhay told them that he did not wish to fight with the captives of the white man, for there would be no honor in that. There was blood running down my leg, and I found that both my horse and I were slightly wounded.

"Some two years later we attacked a fort west of the Black Hills [Fort Phil Kearny, Wyoming]. It was there we killed one hundred soldiers. [The military reports say eighty men, under the command of Captain Fetterman—not one left alive to tell the tale!] Nearly every band of the Sioux nation was represented in that fight—Red Cloud, Spotted Tail, Crazy Horse, Sitting Bull, Big Foot, and all our great chiefs were there. Of course such men as I were then comparatively unknown. However, there were many noted young warriors, among them Sword, the younger Young-Man-Afraid, American Horse [afterward chief], Crow King, and others.

"This was the plan decided upon after many councils. The main war party lay in ambush, and a few of the bravest young men were appointed to attack the woodchoppers who were cutting logs to complete the building of the fort. We were told not to kill these men, but to chase them into the fort and retreat slowly, defying the white men; and if the soldiers should follow, we were to lead them into the ambush. They took our bait exactly as we had hoped! It was a matter of a very few minutes, for every soldier lay dead in a shorter time than it takes to annihilate a small herd of buffalo.

"This attack was hastened because most of the Sioux on the Missouri River and eastward had begun to talk of suing for peace. But even this did not stop the peace movement. The very next year a treaty was signed at Fort Rice, Dakota Territory, by nearly all the Sioux chiefs, in which it was agreed on the part of the Great Father in Washington that all the country north of the Republican River in Nebraska, including the Black Hills and the Big Horn Mountains, was to be always Sioux country, and no white man should intrude upon it without our permission. Even with this agreement Sitting Bull and Crazy Horse were not satisfied, and they would not sign.

"Up to this time I had fought in some important battles, but had achieved no great deed. I was ambitious to make a name for myself. I joined war parties against the Crows, Mandans, Gros Ventres, and Pawnees, and gained some little distinction.

"It was when the white men found the yellow metal in our country, and came in great numbers, driving away our game, that we took up arms against them for the last time. I must say here that the chiefs who were loudest for war were among the first to submit and accept reservation life. Spotted Tail was a great warrior, yet he was one of the first to yield, because he was promised by the Chief Soldiers that they would make him chief of all the Sioux. Ugh! he would have stayed with Sitting Bull to the last had it not been for his ambition.

"About this time we young warriors began to watch the trails of the white men into the Black Hills, and when we saw a wagon coming we would hide at the crossing and kill them all without much trouble. We did this to discourage the whites from coming into our country without our permission. It was the duty of our Great Father at Washington, by the agreement of 1868, to keep his white children away.

"During the troublesome time after this treaty, which no one seemed to respect, either white or Indian [but the whites broke it first], I was like many other young men—much on the warpath, but with little honor. I had not yet become noted for any great deed. Finally, Wapáypay and I way-laid and killed a white soldier on his way from the fort to his home in the east.

"There were a few Indians who were liars, and never on the warpath, playing 'good Indian' with the Indian agents and the war chiefs at the forts. Some of this faithless set betrayed me, and told more than I ever did. I was seized and taken to the fort near Bismarck, North Dakota [Fort Abraham Lincoln], by a brother [Tom Custer] of the Long-Haired War Chief, and imprisoned there. These same lying Indians, who were selling their services as scouts to the white man, told me that I was to be shot to death, or else hanged upon a tree. I answered that I was not afraid to die.

"However, there was an old soldier who used to bring my food and stand guard over me—he was a white man, it is true, but he had an Indian heart! He came to me one day and unfastened the iron chain and ball with which they had locked my leg, saying by signs and what little Sioux he could muster:

"'Go, friend! take the chain and ball with you. I shall shoot, but the voice of the gun will lie.'

"When he had made me understand, you may guess that I ran my best! I was almost over the bank when he fired his piece at me several times, but I had already gained cover and was safe. I have never told this before, and would not, lest it should do him an injury, but he was an old man then, and I am sure he must be dead long since. That old soldier taught me that some of the white people have hearts," he added, quite seriously.

"I went back to Standing Rock in the night, and I had to hide for several days in the woods, where food was brought to me by my relatives. The Indian police were ordered to retake me, and they pretended to hunt for me, but really they did not, for if they had found me I would have died with one or two of them, and they knew it! In a few days I departed with several others, and we rejoined the hostile camp on the Powder River and made some trouble for the men who were building the great iron track north of us [Northern Pacific].

"In the spring the hostile Sioux got together again upon the Tongue River. It was one of the greatest camps of the Sioux that I ever saw. There were some Northern Cheyennes with us, under Two Moon, and a few Santee Sioux, renegades from Canada, under Inkpaduta, who had killed white people in Iowa long before. We had decided to fight the white soldiers until no warrior should be left."

At this point Rain-in-the-Face took up his tobacco pouch and began again to fill his pipe.

"Of course the younger warriors were delighted with the prospect of a great fight! Our scouts had discovered piles of oats for horses and other supplies near the Missouri River. They had been brought by the white man's fire-boats. Presently they reported a great army about a day's travel to the south, with Shoshone and Crow scouts.

"There was excitement among the people, and a great council was held. Many spoke. I was asked the condition of those Indians who had gone upon the reservation, and I told them truly that they were nothing more than prisoners. It was decided to go out and meet Three Stars [General Crook] at a safe distance from our camp.

"We met him on the Little Rosebud. I believe that if we had waited and allowed him to make the attack, he would have fared no better than Custer. He was too strongly fortified where he was, and I think, too, that he was saved partly by his Indian allies, for the scouts discovered us first and fought us first, thus giving him time to make his preparations. I think he was more wise than brave! After we had left that neighborhood he might have pushed on and connected with the Long-Haired Chief. That would have saved Custer and perhaps won the day.

"When we crossed from Tongue River to the Little Big Horn, on account of the scarcity of game, we did not anticipate any more trouble. Our runners had discovered that Crook had retraced his trail to Goose Creek, and we did not suppose that the white men would care to follow us farther into the rough country.

"Suddenly the Long-Haired Chief appeared with his men! It was a surprise."

"What part of the camp were you in when the soldiers attacked the lower end?" I asked.

"I had been invited to a feast at one of the young men's lodges [a sort of club]. There was a certain warrior who was making preparations to go against the Crows, and I had decided to go also," he said.

"While I was eating my meat we heard the war cry! We

all rushed out, and saw a warrior riding at top speed from the lower camp, giving the warning as he came. Then we heard the reports of the soldiers' guns, which sounded differently from the guns fired by our people in battle.

"I ran to my teepee and seized my gun, a bow, and a quiver full of arrows. I already had my stone war club, for you know we usually carry those by way of ornament. Just as I was about to set out to meet Reno, a body of soldiers appeared nearly opposite us, at the edge of a long line of cliffs across the river.

"All of us who were mounted and ready immediately started down the stream toward the ford. There were Ogallalas, Minneconjous, Cheyennes, and some Unkpapas, and those around me seemed to be nearly all very young men.

"'Behold, there is among us a young woman!' I shouted. 'Let no young man hide behind her garment!' I knew that would make those young men brave.

"The woman was Tashenamani, or Moving Robe, whose brother had just been killed in the fight with Three Stars. Holding her brother's war staff over her head, and leaning forward upon her charger, she looked as pretty as a bird. Always when there is a woman in the charge, it causes the warriors to vie with one another in displaying their valor," he added.

"The foremost warriors had almost surrounded the white men, and more were continually crossing the stream. The soldiers had dismounted, and were firing into the camp from the top of the cliff."

"My friend, was Sitting Bull in this fight?" I inquired.

"I did not see him there, but I learned afterward that he was among those who met Reno, and that was three or four of the white man's miles from Custer's position. Later he joined the attack upon Custer, but was not among the foremost.

"When the troops were surrounded on two sides, with the river on the third, the order came to charge! There were many very young men, some of whom had only a war staff or a stone war club in hand, who plunged into the column, knocking the men over and stampeding their horses.

"The soldiers had mounted and started back, but when the onset came they dismounted again and separated into several divisions, facing different ways. They fired as fast as they could load their guns, while we used chiefly arrows and war clubs. There seemed to be two distinct movements among the Indians. One body moved continually in a circle, while the other rode directly into and through the troops.

"Presently some of the soldiers remounted and fled along the ridge toward Reno's position; but they were followed by our warriors, like hundreds of blackbirds after a hawk. A larger body remained together at the upper end of a little ravine, and fought bravely until they were cut to pieces. I had always thought that white men were cowards, but I had a great respect for them after this day.

"It is generally said that a young man with nothing but a war staff in his hand broke through the column and knocked down the leader very early in the fight. We supposed him to be the leader, because he stood up in full view, swinging his big knife [sword] over his head, and talking loud. Some one unknown afterwards shot the chief, and he was probably killed also; for if not, he would have told of the deed, and called others to witness it. So it is that no one knows who killed the Long-Haired Chief [General Custer].

"After the first rush was over, *coups* were counted as usual on the bodies of the slain. You know four *coups* [or blows] can be counted on the body of an enemy, and whoever counts the first one [touches it for the first time] is entitled to the 'first feather.'

"There was an Indian here called Appearing Elk, who died a short time ago. He was slightly wounded in the charge. He had some of the weapons of the Long-Haired Chief, and the Indians used to say jokingly after we came upon the reservation that Appearing Elk must have killed the Chief, because he had his sword! However, the scramble for plunder did not begin until all were dead. I do not think he killed Custer, and if he had, the time to claim the honor was immediately after the fight.

"Many lies have been told of me. Some say that I killed the Chief, and others that I cut out the heart of his brother [Tom Custer], because he had caused me to be imprisoned. Why, in that fight the excitement was so great that we scarcely recognized our nearest friends! Everything was done like lightning. After the battle we young men were chasing horses all over the prairie, while the old men and women plundered the bodies; and if any mutilating was done, it was by the old men.

"I have lived peaceably ever since we came upon the reservation. No one can say that Rain-in-the-Face has broken the rules of the Great Father. I fought for my people and my country. When we were conquered I remained silent, as a warrior should. Rain-in-the-Face was killed when he put down his weapons before the Great Father. His spirit was gone then; only his poor body lived on, but now it is almost ready to lie down for the last time. Ho, hechetu! [It is well.]"

Concerning the Life and Character of Joaquín Murieta

Yellow Bird, Cherokee
(John Rollin Ridge)

I sit down to write somewhat concerning the life and character of *Joaquín Murieta*, a man as remarkable in the annals of crime as any of the renowned robbers of the Old or New World, who have preceded him; and I do this, not for the purpose of ministering to any depraved taste for the dark and horrible in human action, but rather to contribute my mite to those materials out of which the early history of California shall one day be composed. The character of this truly wonderful man was nothing more than a natural production of the social and moral condition of the country in which he lived, acting upon certain peculiar circumstances favorable to such a result, and, consequently, his individual history is a part of the most valuable history of the State.

There were two Joaquíns, bearing the various surnames of Murieta, O'Comorenia, Valenzuela, Botellier, and Carillo—so that it was supposed there were no less than five sanguinary devils ranging the country at one and the same time. It is now fully ascertained that there were only two, whose proper names were Joaquín Murieta and Joaquín Valenzuela, the latter being nothing more than a distinguished subordinate to the first, who is the Rinaldo Rinaldini of California.

Joaquín Murieta was a Mexican, born in the province of Sonora of respectable parents and educated in the schools of Mexico. While growing up, he was remarkable for a very mild and peaceable disposition, and gave no sign of that indomitable and daring spirit which afterwards characterized him. Those who knew him in his school-boy days speak affectionately of his generous and noble nature at that period of his life and can scarcely credit the fact that the renowned and bloody bandit of California was one and the same being. At an early age of his manhood—indeed, while he was yet scarcely more than a boy—he became tired of the uncertain state of affairs in his own country, the usurpations and revolutions which were of such common occurrence, and resolved to try his fortunes among the American people, of whom he had formed the most favorable opinion from an acquaintance with the few whom he had met in his own native land. The war with Mexico had been fought, and California belonged to the United States. Disgusted with the conduct of his degenerate countrymen and fired with enthusiastic admiration of the American character, the youthful Joaquín left his home with a buoyant heart and full of the exhilarating spirit of adventure. The first that we hear of him in the Golden State is that, in the spring of 1850, he is engaged in the honest occupation of a miner in the Stanislaus placers, then reckoned among the richest portions of the mines. He was then eighteen years of age, a little over the medium height, slenderly but gracefully built, and active as a young tiger. His complexion was neither very dark or very light, but clear and brilliant, and his countenance is pronounced to have been, at that time, exceedingly handsome and attractive. His large black eyes, kindling with the enthusiasm of his earnest nature, his firm and well-formed mouth, his well-shaped head from which the long, glossy, black hair hung down over his shoulders, his silvery voice full of generous utterance, and the frank and cordial bearing which distinguished him made him beloved by all with whom he came in contact. He had the confidence and respect of the whole community around him, and was fast amassing a fortune from his rich mining claim. He had built him a comfortable mining residence in which he had domiciled his heart's treasure—a beautiful Sonorian girl, who had followed the young adventurer in all his wanderings with that devotedness of passion which belongs to the dark-eyed damsels of Mexico. It was at this moment of peace and felicity that a blight came over the young man's prospects. The country was then full of lawless and desperate men, who bore the name of Americans but failed to support the honor and dignity of that title. A feeling was prevalent among this class of contempt for any and all Mexicans, whom they looked upon as no better than conquered subjects of the United States, having no rights which could stand before a haughtier and superior race. They made no exceptions. If the proud blood of the Castilians mounted to the cheek of a partial descendant of the Mexiques, showing that he had inherited the old chivalrous spirit of his Spanish ancestry, they looked upon it as a saucy presumption in one so inferior to them. The prejudice of color, the antipathy of races, which are always stronger and bitterer with the ignorant and unlettered, they could not overcome, or if they could, would not, because it afforded them a convenient excuse for their unmanly cruelty and oppression. A band of these lawless men, having the brute power to do as they pleased, visited Joaquín's house and peremptorily bade him leave his claim, as they would allow no Mexicans to work in that region. Upon his remonstrating against such outrageous conduct, they struck him violently over the face, and, being physically superior, compelled him to swallow his wrath. Not content with this, they tied him hand and foot and ravished his mistress before his eyes. They left him, but the soul of the young man was from that moment darkened. It was the first injury he had ever received at the hands of the Americans, whom he had always hitherto respected, and it wrung him to the soul as a deeper and deadlier wrong from that very circumstance. He departed with his weeping and almost heartbroken mistress for a more northern portion of the mines; and the next we hear of him, he is cultivating a little farm on the banks of a beautiful stream that watered a fertile valley, far out in the seclusion of the mountains. Here he might hope for peace—here he might forget the past, and again be happy. But his dream was not destined to last. A company of unprincipled Americans—shame that there should be such bearing the name!—saw his retreat, coveted his little home surrounded by its fertile tract of land, and drove him from it, with no other excuse than that he was "an infernal Mexican intruder!" Joaquín's blood boiled in his veins, but his spirit was still unbroken, nor had the iron so far entered his soul as to sear up the innate sensitiveness to honor and right which reigned in his bosom. Twice broken up in his honest pursuit of fortune, he resolved still to labor on with unflinching brow and with that true *moral* bravery, which throws its redeeming light forward upon his subsequently dark and criminal career. How deep must have been the anguish of that young heart and how strongly rooted the native honesty of his soul, none can know or imagine but they who have been tried in a like manner. He bundled up his little movable property, still accompanied by his faithful bosom-friend, and again started forth to strike once more, like a brave and honest man, for fortune and for happiness.

The Indian Agent Visits Gray Bird

John Joseph Mathews
(Osage)

The Major came finally to a clear stream bordered by elms, then turned down it toward the river. Dry cottonwood leaves floated and turned on the surface of the clear water, and the elms had begun to drop their leaves. Along the sides of the hill the sumac bushes were becoming crimson, though not flaming; they had just begun to attract attention. A band of white-tailed deer started off through the trees as the buggy creaked its way over the rocks, but they stopped suddenly and facing the Major watched his movements with wide-eyed wonder, but not too concerned to stamp occasionally the vicious autumn flies from their slender legs.

Soon he came to thick timber; the kind that grows in the rich alluvium of river valleys. Then very soon in a group of big oaks he saw the large lodge of Gray Bird looming among the dark, gray boles of the trees. There was tranquillity in this timbered valley; Gray Bird choosing to live away from the village with his two wives. His horse was hobbled and was busily grazing near the spring, the hair still stiff and whitish from sweat.

At the noise of the Major's approach Gray Bird came out of the lodge, and behind him came his wives. Though they did not smile, their faces showed expressions of welcome as the Major drove his mules under a large tree and unhitched them, taking a sack of oats out from the rear of the buggy with which to feed them. On these trips he always carried feed for his mules as the Indians provided no food for their horses.

Gray Bird came up to him and said: "My friend it is good that you have come." They went into the lodge where the usual fire was burning in the center. The lodge of Gray Bird was a large one, about thirty feet long by fourteen feet wide, the Major thought, but this space did not seem too large for the many things which it contained. There were piles of corn and vegetables, and quite a large pile of jerked beef, which had been taken down from the rack back of the lodge, where it had been drying. There were lounging pallets covered with skin, and many black pots and other utensils. There was an atmosphere of activity, as the women were preparing for the ceremony which was to take place about four or five miles distant, the next day.

The sun was almost set and the air had the sharpness of autumn. The fire in the center of the lodge seemed cozy as it crackled under the large pot in which vegetables were cooking. One of the women spread a blanket near the fire and Gray Bird without ceremony sat down drawing his feet under his legs, with his characteristically quick movements. The Major sat down on the other half of the blanket and they began to talk of things which had happened since their last visit together. The women busied themselves preparing the supper, placing it on another blanket on the other side of the fire. It consisted of the usual broiled beef, vegetables, fried bread and black coffee. Suddenly with what seemed like one movement Gray Bird was on his feet, and with a wave of his hand to the Major said, "How." They moved over to the other blanket where their supper was set and ate in silence.

After he had finished Gray Bird wiped his mouth with a great red handkerchief. He looked over at the Major, and with little wrinkles gathered at the corners of his eyes, said in English: "My women don't cook good, ain't it." The Major smiled in appreciation of the joke and the two wives giggled.

The men arose and went down to look at Gray Bird's vegetables and corn. The Major thought there was about half an acre, and that there was enough corn when dried to supply them for the winter, as they had no children. The sun had set and the air was uncomfortably cool, and the silence was almost complete except for the quavering complaint of a screech owl. The flaming western horizon could be seen through the large trees. As they came back toward the lodge, Gray Bird picked up some soft wood for the fire, which during the time between supper and bedtime must be kept fed with light wood so there would always be a bright blaze by which to see.

When they reached the lodge the women had prepared the beds, one for the Major between the fire and the entrance, and one for Gray Bird on the other side of the fire. Their own beds they prepared in the rear of the lodge back of their husband. They sat for a few minutes in silence, then Gray Bird said: "My friend, tonight it is good that we go to sleep. Tomorrow will be making of medicine man. When we come back tomorrow night we will have much to talk about."

The Major enjoyed talking to Gray Bird, but tonight he felt tired and the warm fire had made him drowsy. But after rolling in his blanket he lay awake for some time watching the fire die; watching the miniature explosions when the sparks flew out in all directions.

Just before it died into glowing coals it suddenly brightened and revealed the dark form of Gray Bird rolled in his blanket. He heard Gray Bird's horse as he jumped in his hobbles from grass tuft to grass tuft, and the fretful movements of one of his mules. He thought he heard the distant, long-drawn-out howl of a wolf, but he was not sure. Then suddenly a barred owl startled the silence with his booming voice. After this the silence seemed to become more intense, and during this intenseness he fell into sound sleep.

The Major awoke when the east was just turning red. He looked over at Gray Bird's bed but saw that it was empty, and it suddenly dawned on him that Gray Bird had got up to greet the sun with chant. In his drowsy semi-consciousness he thought that he had heard the chant; perhaps from some high place near the lodge. This prayer to the rising sun had always fascinated him; like most Indian customs it seemed to have such a simple beauty, that fascination which the paganism of Greece and Rome held for people, he thought.

He arose and walked out in front of the lodge. He saw one of the women coming with wood. He walked toward the spring to wash. The morning was sharp and the air carried the delightful scents of the bottoms; of frost touched walnuts and the very pleasing aroma of dying vegetation; an odor almost pungent. The little pool into which the spring flowed had a thin coating of ice around the edges, ribbed and veined like the web of a spider, and as the cold water touched his face youth seemed to flood his body and he felt inexhaustible.

Breakfast over, the four of them set out for the meeting place. For some time before they saw the lodges, they could hear the slow, muffled beating of the great kettle drum. A slow continuous TUM-tum-TUM-tum-TUM-tum-TUM-tum. Like the cosmic pulse; the pulse of the prairie and the blackjack hills.

When the party arrived they found that perhaps a hundred Indians had gathered, and were moving around in a shady grove. In the center of the grove an open lodge had been erected, in which the drummers had already taken their places, the chanters standing near them.

TUM-tum-TUM-tum-TUM-tum—then the singers broke out into a low chant, in harmony with these heart throbs of the earth; chanting their prayers to Wah'Kon-Tah, so that he might know that his children were gathered here for grave purpose. The chanting was spasmodic but the drum beats continued on as an undertone to the activity.

Aside from the rest was a group of medicine men, their faces painted with lines and daubs, which were symbolical of many things. Their faces were not masked, as they were not playing rôles in which they represented mysteries; they were simply praying for the attention of the Great Spirit. Several of them carried sacred bundles and rattles; dried bladders in which small pebbles had been placed. Among them stood the man who was to be initiated, and occasionally the group would break into a chant.

A short distance away from this group was a post about four feet high, and perched upon it was an elongated dove. No ordinary dove ever grew to such proportions, and the Major guessed it was the result of sewing two stuffed doves together, so that they gave the impression of one very long one. The dove faced the east. He seemed to have none of the timidity of a live dove, sitting with frightened glances and close-drawn feathers. Yet he did not resemble the usual, crudely mounted dove, with pop eyes and legs coming out from under the tail, seeming to droop from some incurable illness. This symbol faced the sun unblinking with an air of aloofness and gravity which fitted him perfectly for the rôle he was playing.

Soon the people began to take their places, assembling back of the dove, and as they assembled the medicine men began to chant again and the drum beats swelled slightly in volume, as though to remind the applicant of the responsibility that was about to be placed upon him. As the drums beat this warning to him, the medicine men began to chant fragments of the songs he must learn. As the chanting stopped the drum beats became more subdued, rising at intervals to keep this applicant's mind on the seriousness of his position.

Presently the medicine men came and sat down back of the drummers, followed by six witnesses who came in sedately and sat down in a row behind the medicine men. For some minutes everyone waited, during which time there were certain formalities among the medicine men. Gravely they sat there, and leisurely they performed certain things which the ceremony demanded; grave formalities to the slow throbbing of the drum.

The sun climbed higher and cast deep shadows on the tall grasses, that had begun to turn brown at the top. Soon all movement had stopped and everyone had found his place, and there was a period filled with expectancy. The Major saw several of the men he didn't know, turn questioning eyes toward him; slyly and cautiously they threw these glances thinking that he did not see them. To one less observant it would have appeared that he, the only white man present, was totally ignored.

Then the drums throbbed louder and the singers began to chant. One of the witnesses got up slowly and walked toward the dove. He carried in one hand a bundle of little sticks, about the size of a pencil. Solemnly he came before the dove and stood motionless for a few seconds. Then with great gravity he addressed the dove thus: "Fly away to Wah'Kon-Tah and tell him. Tell him worthiness of this one who wishes to become medicine man. Tell him I know this thing. Tell him this. One time we were in country of Kaw across river. We were hunting. Wounded bull was charging warrior whose horse had stepped into hole. This man rushed up and stabbed this bull. Tell him I know this thing." Saying this, he threw down one of the sticks at the foot of the pole. He stood like a statue while the singers chanted with increased volume, and the drums became louder and more insistent.

During this interval when the drums beat louder and the chanters raised their voices, Wah'Kon-Tah was being given time to consider these deeds.

Suddenly the drums fell back to their throbbing, and the singers lowered their voices and chanted softly, and the witness began to talk to the dove, "Fly away to Wah'Kon-Tah and tell him. Tell him this. One time we were on great plains far to west. There were many buffalo that season. There were many tribes there hunting buffalo. There were Pawnee and Cheyenne and many others. This man wounded bull and this bull ran toward where woman was skinning buffalo. He killed this bull. He looked for his wife to come but he was far behind. He thought he would get on his horse and go for more buffalo. He saw woman standing there. This woman was not skinning buffalo. He said to this woman, 'You cannot find arrows of your man?' and this woman said, 'I have no man.' This man answered. 'Take that bull I have killed. Look well at my arrows. When you find arrows marked as they are marked, you will know that I have killed buffalo. You will know that buffalo is yours when you find my arrows.'" The witness threw down another stick and the low chanting swelled; the drum beats became louder.

After some time he had thrown down all of his sticks, and he came gravely back to his seat. As soon as he was seated several men in charge of the ceremony came up to him, and gave him a blanket and some leggings. These things had been agreed upon as payment for his service in testifying for the applicant.

When the drum beats had become low again and the chanting became a murmur, another witness got up and went up to the dove, also telling of the deeds of the applicant.

When the sun stood in mid-sky, there was a recess, and there was much to eat; great pieces of beef that had been broiled over a fire, soup, fried bread and black coffee.

All afternoon the ceremony went on, and the people sat gravely and watched. The singers chanted, and as an undertone was the slow pulse beats of the drum.

The sun swung toward the west, and the shadows lengthened on the grass. Then the sun set in a blaze of red and the air became chilled. The drum beats stopped, and the people seemed to melt into the darkening woods; silently, and with dignity they disappeared, leaving the open ceremonial lodge, standing silently in the chilled twilight.

Back at Gray Bird's lodge the Major again fed his mules, and the women prepared something to eat, and prepared the beds as they had done the night before. The Major and Gray Bird sat silent for a long time, the fire lighting their faces. Then Gray Bird said: "My friend this ceremony which you have seen. I believe you think it is not good. You are my friend. I will talk about this thing that is in my mind. Long time ago I went through this ceremony. It cost me many ponies. It cost me forty ponies, I believe. I found my witnesses and I said to them you will say this thing for me. And they said yes we will do this thing for you, but you must give us this or that, and I say good. Every time I had to give something to medicine men. Every time I had to pay for these services. I learned songs and all these things that have been known by our people for long time. But I know all this and my mind has not changed. It is still like fog in morning, and many things I do not understand. Many things which trouble my mind. But these medicine men, they do things which are magic, and people say that is good. Medicine man tells people to do these things and people say that is good we will do it. For many years it is like this, but I do not know about these things."

For a long time they sat, then Gray Bird rose quickly to his feet. He stepped to the entrance of the lodge and went out, and the Major could see him through the door, as he stood looking into the sky. Then he came back and unceremoniously rolled into his blankets. The Major rolled into his blankets on the other side of the fire. Gray Bird's wives had gone to bed sometime earlier.

Soon Gray Bird began to stir, and rolled over on his back. He seemed to be thinking about something. He began to talk: "My friend I have thought much about this thing. I have thought much about spirit of man. I don't know what white man thinks about this. I've heard white man say much about brain but I don't know. I do not believe that home of spirit of man is in head. I will show you what I mean.

"Sometime when I go hunting I kill deer. I come back and I am very happy. I say there will be plenty of venison. But soon I pass lodge of woman. This woman has lost his man. This woman has some small children and there is no man to hunt for him. I stop at lodge of woman who has lost his man and I cut off big piece of this venison. I say I have brought you something to eat. As I walk away my heart swells. I put my hand on my heart and I can feel it swell. I feel happy and I am glad to see anybody. I feel of my head. But I cannot feel any change in my head. It feels same. My heart is only thing that changes. Then I go out hunting again and I kill deer. I am happy. Soon I pass this lodge of woman who has no man. I say my heart is heavy for this woman. I look at venison and I say we need all this venison. I walk on and I do not cut off piece of this venison for woman. My heart seems to become very small. I put my hand on my heart and it seems to have gone away. I can feel nothing there. I do not want to see anyone. I am not happy. When I put my hand to my head I do not feel anything. It has not changed. That is what I think about this thing. Home of spirit is in heart. This I believe. I would like to know what white man thinks about this thing."

The Major thought for some time. He remembered the study of this matter under a very dear professor, who referred many times to the great English philosopher, Doctor Locke, and his ideas of the relationship of mind to matter. He felt that he had never been able to come to any conclusion about the problem. In fact he had forgotten about it in the busy life since his university days. He suddenly realized that here was an Indian in the Osage reservation, with no books in the long winter evenings troubling his mind about matters which scientists over the world had discussed. He remembered that he had also thought such things important during his university days, but one out in the world seemed to worry very little about it, and when he answered Gray Bird's question he said: "This thing you have asked me is very difficult. I believe that I do not know about this. But I believe, that which you believe about this thing is good."

There was another silence, then Gray Bird continued: "A thing has been bothering my mind since you were here." This time the Major knew by the inflection that the matter was not grave, and he waited for a joke. "My wives, I do not know about them. In other times when wood is needed for fire, they go out and get this wood. They hitch up team and go out and get this wood for fire. If I wanted horse they would go and get horse and have it ready for me. Many times when I would come home tired they take horse, and take off saddle and put it away. Now I do not understand. When wood is small they say to me, 'There is very little wood—you must get some wood'. And they say when I come to lodge and ask them to put horse away, 'We are busy—put it away yourself.' My mind is troubled about this thing—I do not know about this."

The Major had noticed that the women had been listening to their conservation all evening, and after Gray Bird had stopped talking he could hear suppressed giggling in the back of the lodge. He raised his voice a little and addressed the women, "Wetunka, what is trouble?" One of the women spoke. "He thinks he is great man now, our husband. Many times he has gone with you to these places to get money for payments. He has become very proud and has changed much since he goes with you to all these places. He comes to us and says he must have shirts. He says to us he wants shirts in many colors. He says he will not wear shirts which we make from skin of deer. He must have shirts which trader sells. We must spend much time dressing him when he goes to these places with you. When he goes to dances it is good.

We dress him in all of his things and paint his face. But this thing when he goes many times to Agency, and when he goes many time to these places with you he must have many new shirts. He must have shirts to take along with him so he will have shirt to put on when he gets to these places. All day we are busy making these shirts for him. We cannot do other things when we are doing this."

There was humor in the situation as the four of them lay there in the darkness. Gray Bird could laugh at himself and his playing the rôle of dandy, and no one enjoyed the situation more than he. He was thinking of his wives' baffled attempts to play their part of the tradition, in keeping their warrior well equipped. The wives on the other hand, saw the humor of this great man who was only a boy, with the vanity of a boy. The delightful situation pleased the Major immensely. He had always remarked Gray Bird's magnificence on the trips out of the Reservation. He always rode good horses and his body was straight, and everything he did was with those quick movements of the wolf.

Gray Bird broke the silence in English. He spoke English only when he wished to make some satirical observation to some other Indian or to a close friend, "My wife he not good, ain't it?" The answer which he seemed to be expecting came promptly from one of the women who spoke also in English: "Hunh, shuh, he's crazy. I bet you don't blame us that-a-way; it's his fault. He ain't got no right to say things like that." There was no sound of laughter, though the atmosphere was charged.

Gray Bird turned over in his blanket and silence came into the dark lodge. The fire had died down, the wood used for the purpose of lighting the lodge had burned quickly. Outside a heavy, autumnal silence crept over the great oaks. A chill silence under the blinking stars.

The Potlatch,
a Kwakiutl Institution

Tlakodlas
(Charles James Nowell, Kwakiutl)

Maybe I was twelve years old when my father took sick. He wanted to
have a talk with me, so my brother came and took me out of school.
My brother sent three of the boys to come and get me. He got one of the
Hunt family to write a letter to Mr. Hall so I could go. Mr. Hall didn't
seem to mind my going. He never even told me to come right back. I
went to Fort Rupert, and, as soon as I get there, my father calls me to
go to his bedside, and told me he is going to leave us, and told me to
remember what he has taught me regarding potlatches. He told me to do
the same as my brother does—that he is always loaning out blankets to
other people, and that is the only way to get more blankets. "If you
will spend your earnings foolishly, you will be no good. They will not
look upon you as they are looking upon your brother. Most of all I want
to say is, I know you have been to school, and I think the only way for
you to remember the main positions and all the ancestors is for you to
write them down, because it seems to me that everybody is forgetting
all their ancestors and names. I have often heard people make mistakes.
The first thing, you will write down our ancestors till now." So I did—all
our ancestors right down to him. He then told me to write down the
names we should use and told me about the positions in our clan, and
told me who had that position and why we should use it. Then he begin
to talk about the dances and the dance names, and, when he finish that,
he lay down and slept. He lose his breath talking to me, and, when he
lay down to sleep, he died. He was going to talk about our relatives,
but before he finished his breath gave out, and he died.

What became of those papers I wrote I don't know. It was
my brother that looked after it. It must have been burnt when they
burnt all my brother's clothing, according to the custom of the Indians,
that they have to take everything that a man used for clothing and burn
it after the funeral. I was so busy when my brother died, I didn't have a
chance to go and watch.

After my father died, they put him in a long coffin, and it was cedar boards nailed together, and they buried him in the ground in back of the porch. My brother had to pay Mr. Hunt one pair of blankets for a place to bury him in the graveyard. Four days after, my brother gave the potlatch, and that is the time he put me in my father's position in our clan—number three position.

When my father died I was old enough to have my position in my clan. My brother give a potlatch and announce my new name, Tlakodlas, which means "where you get your coppers from." After this two men are sent to go and invite me to a feast, and my brother gives them a blanket each. Then I go with these two men. I don't like to go—I would rather play than go to a feast. When the two men get to the front of the building where the feast is, one of them speaks to the people, saying that I have come to join the feast and that my seat should be open where I am going to sit. When I sit down, the chief of my clan gets up again, and tells the Kwekas to sit up and sing my brother's potlatch song. They begin to sing, and then after the singing, our chief announces that I am going to give a feast or a potlatch soon. After that, I am a man—not any more a child. They now have to remember me on every feast.

When I was in the third position in the first clan of the Kwekas, before I was married, a nephew of mine, Nulis, who was older than me belonged to our clan, but his position was way lower, gave a potlatch after he sold a copper. When he was giving it to all the other tribes who came to Fort Rupert, he told the people of how we stand, and we are from one family in the olden days, that he has a right to be in one of our grandfather's positions, and that he wants to be put on the third position of our clan, and I was to be the fourth, which was a man called Likiosa who was a little older than me and was related to me, and we all just go down one so he can have my position. My brother wasn't at Fort Rupert. He was at Alert Bay working for the new Indian agent, Mr. Pidcock, and while he was talking to the people about this position, somebody told me to stand up and tell him I don't want him to come in front of me until my brother comes back, and agree to what he says.

When my brother comes back to Fort Rupert, there was another potlatch from other peoples to the Fort Ruperts, and this Nulis stood up and says, when the potlatch comes to my place, "Now give me my share on this position where I am now going to be." My brother stood up and told him he has heard about what he said, and that he doesn't agree with him. "If you had spoken to me beforehand," he says, "I might have agreed, but you have tried to steal the position away when I wasn't here, and so I am telling you by the face of all these people, that you are not going to get that position." Nulis says, "If you don't agree to that, then I'll be on the fourth position." Likiosa got up and says,

"No, I'm not going to have you come in front of me." He then turned around to the Fort Ruperts and tells them to stand up and sing his potlatch song that he is going to give a potlatch. When we finish with this song, Nulis also told us to sing his song, that he is going to give another potlatch. They went on for so many years giving potlatches, Likiosa and Nulis. When they went to other potlatches, they were given gifts—both together, so they wouldn't quarrel in the potlatch. Finally Nulis won out and took the position away from Likiosa.

When my brother wanted me to get my share, in anybody's potlatch, he gave a potlatch of blankets and told the people that this potlatch has been given away by his son. From now on I receive my gifts from the other people and use them for myself. That means that I am old enough to look after them myself. That was when I was quite grown up but before I was married. Maybe I was eighteen or twenty. At this potlatch he announced my name, Tlakodlas, the same as the second, and put me in my position in the clan. My brother was the first, and I was the third. I took my father's position, and the rest of our family was way down about thirty or more after me. My next oldest brother was on that place that I took, and he died about a year before this. If he hadn't died, I would have been in the lower position that I was in when I was called to the feast.

When I was receiving gifts from potlatches, I had to look after that and not spend it foolishly. I had to loan some of it out to other people. My brother showed me how to do this. When I loan out money, they promise to pay double the amount when they pay it back, because that is the custom of the Indians, and any time I want to give a potlatch, I have to collect what I loaned out. In collecting it, I have to call my people into my house and have a meal there. That is the time I tell them I want to give a potlatch and want to collect what I loaned out. I loaned out to anybody, but I only call my own clan to collect it. They will send two men out to other houses to collect my money. They come back with the payment, and when they get it all in, then they begin to make speeches, and they begin to sing my own potlatch song. After singing, they say that I am going to give blankets away. I would do this as often as I could collect enough to give a potlatch.

What Boy Would Not Be an Indian?

Charles A. Eastman
(Ohiyesa, Sioux)

What boy would not be an Indian for a while when he thinks of the freest life in the world? This life was mine. Every day there was a real hunt. There was real game. Occasionally there was a medicine dance away off in the woods where no one could disturb us, in which the boys impersonated their elders, Brave Bull, Standing Elk, High Hawk, Medicine Bear, and the rest. They painted and imitated their fathers and grandfathers to the minutest detail, and accurately too, because they had seen the real thing all their lives.

We were not only good mimics but we were close students of nature. We studied the habits of animals just as you study your books. We watched the men of our people and represented them in our play; then learned to emulate them in our lives.

No people have a better use of their five senses than the children of the wilderness. We could smell as well as hear and see. We could feel and taste as well as we could see and hear. Nowhere has the memory been more fully developed than in the wild life, and I can still see wherein I owe much to my early training.

Of course I myself do not remember when I first saw the day, but my brothers have often recalled the event with much mirth; for it was a custom of the Sioux that when a boy was born his brother must plunge into the water, or roll in the snow naked if it was winter time; and if he was not big enough to do either of these himself, water was thrown on him. If the new-born had a sister, she must be immersed. The idea was that a warrior had come to camp, and the other children must display some act of hardihood.

I was so unfortunate as to be the youngest of five children who, soon after I was born, were left motherless. I had to bear the humiliating name "Hakadah," meaning "the pitiful last," until I should earn a more dignified and appropriate name. I was regarded as little more than a plaything by the rest of the children.

My mother, who was known as the handsomest woman of all the Spirit Lake and Leaf Dweller Sioux, was dangerously ill, and one

435

of the medicine men who attended her said: "Another medicine man has come into existence, but the mother must die. Therefore let him bear the name 'Mysterious Medicine.'" But one of the bystanders hastily interfered, saying that an uncle of the child already bore that name, so, for the time, I was only "Hakadah."

My beautiful mother, sometimes called the "Demi-Goddess" of the Sioux, who tradition says had every feature of a Caucasian descent with the exception of her luxuriant black hair and deep black eyes, held me tightly to her bosom upon her death-bed, while she whispered a few words to her mother-in-law. She said: "I give you this boy for your own. I cannot trust my own mother with him; she will neglect him and he will surely die."

The woman to whom these words were spoken was below the average in stature, remarkably active for her age (she was then fully sixty), and possessed of as much goodness as intelligence. My mother's judgment concerning her own mother was well founded, for soon after her death that old lady appeared, and declared that Hakadah was too young to live without a mother. She offered to keep me until I died, and then she would put me in my mother's grave. Of course my other grandmother denounced the suggestion as a very wicked one, and refused to give me up.

The babe was done up as usual in a movable cradle made from an oak board two and a half feet long and one and a half feet wide. On one side of it was nailed with brass-headed tacks the richly-embroidered sack, which was open in front and laced up and down with buckskin strings. Over the arms of the infant was a wooden bow, the ends of which were firmly attached to the board, so that if the cradle should fall the child's head and face would be protected. On this bow were hung curious playthings—strings of artistically carved bones and hoofs of deer, which rattled when the little hands moved them.

In this upright cradle I lived, played and slept the greater part of the time during the first few months of my life. Whether I was made to lean against a lodge pole or was suspended from a bough of a tree, while my grandmother cut wood, or whether I was carried on her back, or conveniently balanced by another child in a similar cradle hung on the opposite side of a pony, I was still in my oaken bed.

This grandmother, who had already lived through sixty years of hardships, was a wonder to the young maidens of the tribe. She showed no less enthusiasm over Hakadah than she had done when she held her first-born, the boy's father, in her arms. Every little attention that is due to a loved child she performed with much skill and devotion. She made all my scanty garments and my tiny moccasins with a great deal of taste. It was said by all that I could not have had more attention had my mother been living.

Uncheedah (grandmother) was a great singer. Sometimes, when Hakadah wakened too early in the morning, she would sing to him something like the following lullaby:

> Sleep, sleep, my boy, the Chippewas
>   Are far away—are far away.
> Sleep, sleep, my boy; prepare to meet
>   The foe by day—the foe by day!
> The cowards will not dare to fight
>   Till morning break—till morning break.
> Sleep, sleep, my child, while still 'tis night;
>   Then bravely wake—then bravely wake!

The Dakota women were wont to cut and bring their fuel from the woods and, in fact, to perform most of the drudgery of the camp. This of necessity fell to their lot, because the men must follow the game during the day. Very often my grandmother carried me with her on these excursions; and while she worked it was her habit to suspend me from a wild grape vine or a springy bough, so that the least breeze would swing the cradle to and fro.

She has told me that when I had grown old enough to take notice, I was apparently capable of holding extended conversations in an unknown dialect with birds and red squirrels. Once I fell asleep in my cradle, suspended five or six feet from the ground, while Uncheedah was some distance away, gathering birch bark for a canoe. A squirrel had found it convenient to come upon the bow of my cradle and nibble his hickory nut, until he awoke me by dropping the crumbs of his meal. My disapproval of his intrusion was so decided that he had to take a sudden and quick flight to another bough, and from there he began to pour out his wrath upon me, while I continued my objections to his presence so audibly that Uncheedah soon came to my rescue, and compelled the bold intruder to go away. It was a common thing for birds to alight on my cradle in the woods.

My food was, at first, a troublesome question for my kind foster-mother. She cooked some wild rice and strained it, and mixed it with broth made from choice venison. She also pounded dried venison almost to a flour, and kept it in water till the nourishing juices were extracted, then mixed with it some pounded maize, which was browned before pounding. This soup of wild rice, pounded venison and maize was my main-stay. But soon my teeth came—much earlier than the white children usually cut theirs; and then my good nurse gave me a little more varied food, and I did all my own grinding.

After I left my cradle, I almost walked away from it, she told me. She then began calling my attention to natural objects. Whenever I heard the song of a bird, she would tell me what bird it came from, something after this fashion:

"Hakadah, listen to Shechoka (the robin) calling his mate. He says he has just found something good to eat." Or "Listen to Oopehanska (the thrush); he is singing for his little wife. He will sing his best." When in the evening the whippoorwill started his song with vim, no further than a stone's throw from our tent in the woods, she would say to me:

"Hush! It may be an Ojibway scout!"

Again, when I waked at midnight, she would say:

"Do not cry! Hinakaga (the owl) is watching you from the tree-top."

I usually covered up my head, for I had perfect faith in my grandmother's admonitions, and she had given me a dreadful idea of this bird. It was one of her legends that a little boy was once standing just outside of the teepee (tent), crying vigorously for his mother, when Hinakaga swooped down in the darkness and carried the poor little fellow up into the trees. It was well known that the hoot of the owl was commonly imitated by Indian scouts when on the war-path. There had been dreadful massacres immediately following this call. Therefore it was deemed wise to impress the sound early upon the mind of the child.

Indian children were trained so that they hardly ever cried much in the night. This was very expedient and necessary in their exposed life. In my infancy it was my grandmother's custom to put me to sleep, as she said, with the birds, and to waken me with them, until it became a habit. She did this with an object in view. An Indian must always rise early. In the first place, as a hunter, he finds his game best at daybreak. Secondly, other tribes, when on the war-path, usually make their attack very early in the morning. Even when our people are moving about leisurely, we like to rise before daybreak, in order to travel when the air is cool, and unobserved, perchance, by our enemies.

As a little child, it was instilled into me to be silent and reticent. This was one of the most important traits to form in the character of the Indian. As a hunter and warrior it was considered absolutely necessary to him, and was thought to lay the foundations of patience and self-control. There are times when boisterous mirth is indulged in by our people, but the rule is gravity and decorum.

After all, my babyhood was full of interest and the beginnings of life's realities. The spirit of daring was already whispered into my ears. The value of the eagle feather as worn by the warrior had caught my eye. One day, when I was left alone, at scarcely two years of age, I took my uncle's war bonnet and plucked out all its eagle feathers to decorate my dog and myself. So soon the life that was about me had made its impress, and already I desired intensely to comply with all of its demands.

The Beaver and
That Long Wailing Cry

Grey Owl
(Wa-sha-quon-asin, Ojibwa)

An official of the Company, not willing to see us camping out in tents, allotted to our use a small snug cabin on the shores of Lake Touladi. This camp, known as the "Half-way," became our home until we should choose to move.

Here we turned the beaver loose, and they spent their nights exploring the new waters, sleeping in the camp by day. We had many visitors, being now only five miles from Cabano, and were very contented, save for the cloud that hung heavy over the hearts of two of us. But this setback had somehow made me more determined than ever to carry on. The sacrifice at Birch Lake was not to be in vain, and never again would I desert my post and let those dependent on me foot the bill. That it should happen again was unthinkable. With set purpose and design I commenced again to write, and got away another article, though I doubted its acceptance for my new pen seemed somehow filled with a melancholy that flowed out of it into nearly every line.

Meanwhile we kept close watch on the beaver, as the region was full of travellers, river drivers and habitants. They were good company on their frequent visits and seemed very friendly towards us, but Dave, who spoke French fluently, overheard more than one scrap of conversation concerning the beaver that put us doubly on our guard. And the three of us took turns to patrol the neighbourhood, so that they were never beyond earshot at any hour. Our charges were not hard to keep track of, as they were always creating a commotion at some point or another. They built themselves a funny little beaver house a short distance away where the water was open and the soil clear of snow. They cut and slashed small poplars and willows in all directions, and their cries and slashings and other uproar could be heard at almost any time. Just about daybreak they would scratch and call out at the door, and being let in would come into our beds and go to sleep. They awoke about noon, and, without waiting to eat, scampered off to the big doings outside. They had made another partition for themselves of firewood, but they did not go behind it much, preferring our beds to rest in, and as beaver live twenty or thirty years it looked as though we would have to spend the rest of our lives sleeping on the floor.

At this time there came to live with us an old man who had for many years trapped muskrats on these lakes. This hunt was his by right and he depended on it. On account of the danger to the beaver his coming meant only one thing—we must move. So David went out to Cabano intending, with his knowledge of French, to seek a job, while Anahareo and I collected the beaver, loaded them into the barrel, and catching a passing team moved everything to a little lake that lay beside the road, still nearer to the town. Here, under some big elms, we made camp, while McGinnis and McGinty disported themselves around an old beaver house and dam that stood at the foot of the little pond. There was plenty of feed and water and these old works besides, and they would be well fixed here until I could locate another colony in which to introduce them. When our work was finished, we went down to the lake and called them. They came racing over and tumbled their black dumpy bodies all about our feet, labouring under some great excitement, doubtless on account of the old beaver works. They calmed down a little to eat some sticks of candy, still jabbering away in concert, telling us, no doubt, about their discoveries, and the new estate that had fallen to them with all its ready-made castle and appurtenances. They were hardly able to contain themselves, and after a few moments of gambolling with us, during which they pulled strongly at our legs and charged back and forth as if to have us join in the fun, they hurried off to their small properties like a pair of kids to a circus, two absurd but happy little creatures enjoying their new freedom to the utmost, and who from now on would live as they were intended to.

It was almost a year since we had found them, two tiny helpless orphans at the point of death, and this celebration seemed a fitting anniversary. And my heart warmed the more towards them as I reflected that in their new-found self-sufficiency and independence, they still retained that child-like attachment to ourselves that we had feared to lose.

Once during the evening they came bustling up to camp, and coming inside combed themselves and talked loudly and long, and roamed around the tent as of yore, evidently recognising it, which was not remarkable as it had been their only home for half their lives. They smelled at the stove in which they had so many adventures, and McGinnis burnt his nose on it, while McGinty upset the grub-box, disclosing the bannock of which they ate a goodly portion and altogether seemed very much at home in these familiar surroundings. They had their usual petting party and even slept a while, and it was all so like those eventful days on the Birch Lake trail that seemed now so far away, that we were glad to be back in the old tent again with the little stove going and our two small friends beside us in its glow. Soon they headed for their lake, two gnome-like capering little figures that alternately bounced and waddled side by side down the water trail, and we followed them to the landing as we always did, and somehow wished that they were small again.

We watched the two V's forging ahead towards the ancient beaver lodge until they disappeared into the dusk. And in the starlight, the wake of their passing made pale rippling bands of silver that spread wide behind them, and touched the shore at last, and so were lost. Once, in answer to a call, a long clear note came back to us, followed by another in a different key. And the two voices blended and intermingled like a part-song in the stillness of the little lonesome pond, and echoed back and forth in the surrounding hills and faded to a whisper, and died.

And that long wailing cry from out the darkness was the last sound we ever heard them make.

We never saw them any more.

This knowledge did not come to us at once, but was slowly borne upon us with the slow immutable passage of the days. One evening passed with no ripple to break the glassy surface of the water, no eager response in answer to our calling. A second night passed, a third and yet a fourth, and there came no racket on the water, no cheerful chattering, no familiar small brown bodies trotted up the water trail on happy visits. The rain washed away their tracks; their sticks of candy wasted quite away. At the Half-way their small works had been removed, and the unfinished lodge had been submerged and soon was swept away. There was nothing left of them, nothing at all. It was as if they had never been.

That they should follow the Spring flood to the mouth of any stream was inevitable; but their return, in a country of this nature, was just as sure.

We followed the stream up to its source and down to the mouth, caving in through snow banks undermined by its flood, wallowing in slush on broken snowshoes, calling, calling—We scoured the whole neighbouring district. We covered the shores of Touladi foot by foot, and followed every creek. We did this until the possiblities were exhausted, while all around us shots resounded and tracks of men crisscrossed in all directions. Anything could have happened; once we found a deer half skinned, the hunters disturbed by our coming; here and there traps were laying set, regardless of season. I doubt if they ever reached the mouth. Tame as they were they would be easy victims, and one man with a club could have killed them anywhere, they who so much craved affection and needed so little to be happy. And we could only hope that they had passed together to the Great Beyond, side by side as they had lived, and that in their last moments they had known it was not we who took their lives away.

A good-natured and deeply religious people these, nonetheless more than one of them had intimated that little would be added to us in the hereafter for our consideration to creatures having neither speech nor a soul. Their principles would include no mercy to an animal. Some were sure the beaver had been killed, others were as certain they had not. We could not know and we carried on our ceaseless, hopeless quest.

The canoe was forty miles away and we needed to prosecute our search. We walked in and paddled back eighty miles in three days. On the river bank stood the tent poles of our camps. At one we saw a little pen of sticks, made before the days of the famous coach; a happy camp it had been. We passed the spot where they had so nearly drowned and had been saved, passed it swiftly, never speaking. That night we slept out on the beach of Temiscouata, too tired to walk the five miles to our camp. The next day we resumed our search. For many more days we ranged the countryside. We scarcely ate; our sleep was troubled and our waking hours full of sorrow. Often we made long trips to inspect some hide we heard of; McGinnis had a burnt nose and some grey hairs, McGinty was jet black. We found, mercifully, no such skins. We questioned travellers, followed some, one or two we searched. We went armed; we made enemies. A grim and silent search it had become. Constantly we got false leads, and momentarily buoyed up, followed them to inevitable disappointment. Sometimes, towards the last, we acted on the impulse of some foolish dream, a vision conjured up by fatigue and hunger and restless haunted slumber. There was little that escaped us, and we found beaver that no one knew even existed.

And all the time we travelled we kept some dainties in the tent and on the landing; but no one ever ate them, ever came for them.

And Anahareo grew gaunt and pale and hollow cheeked; her eyes began to have a strained and hungry look. Once she said, "I wonder what we have done. Anything else in all the world could have happened to us—anything but this." And again "We thought we would always have them" and in her sleep she said, "They loved us."

And we hoped on long after we knew that there was nothing left to hope for. We sat at nights in the darkness by our unhappy camp beneath the elm trees, waiting, watching, listening for a well remembered cry of greeting, or the thump of clumsy plodding feet that never came, never would come. And we saw nothing save the still lake and the silent ring of trees, heard nothing but the tiny murmur of the brook. The leaves came, and grass grew undisturbed on the ancient beaver house; the pond dried to a marsh and only the stream remained, running slowly through it.

And at last we knew that they were gone forever, into the darkness from whence they came, two random spirits from the Land of Shadows that had wandered in and stayed a little time, and wandered back again, that had passed like the forgotten winds of yesterday, had vanished like the figment of a dream.

And they left behind them no sign, no trace, save an empty barrel with a hole in it that sat beside the lake, and dried and warped and fell apart, and became a heap of staves and rusty hoops.

And the aged trees whose great drooping crowns loomed high above our heads, standing omniscient in the wisdom of the ages, seemed to brood and to whisper, and look down upon our useless vigil, in a mighty and compassionate comprehension. And they stood about us in a serried dark array, as though to shield us and this spot from further spoilation by the civilization that could be at once so benignant and so ruthless. For they were of the Wild as we were, the Wild to which in our desolation we turned for a solace and a refuge, that ageless Wilderness that had ever been and would, somewhere, always be, long after we had followed our little lost companions and were gone.

And in the grove of stately elms the little tin stove was placed high in a hidden spot with its door open, faced towards the lake. So that the small wandering spirits that might sometimes be lonely would see, and remember, and sometimes enter in, as they had done in life when they were small. And so the stove that knew so many tales might learn another and a last one, a tale of which the end is lost forever, a story we could never, never know.

For we are Indian, and have perhaps some queer ideas; yet who among you having a faith of any kind, will deny us our own strange fancies and tell us we are wrong, or say us no.

The camp beneath the elms is far away. Yet memories linger on, and that last long haunting cry rings often in our ears.

We sometimes hear it in the storm, and in the still of evening; at dawn in the song of the birds, and in the melancholy calling of a loon, half-heard and distant in the night. It wails in the minor cadences of an Indian chant, and swells in the deep notes of an organ played softly by a master hand; it mutters in the sound of sleepy streams, and murmurs in the rumour of the river, in the endless tolling of the waves upon a lake-shore—each and everyone a note from the composite of Nature's harmony, chords struck at random from the mighty Symphony of the Infinite that echoes forever on, down the resounding Halls of Time.

Chapter 8

Anguished, Angry, Articulate: Current Voices in Poetry, Prose, and Protest

After Wounded Knee, Indian resistance to assimilation, to extirpation, to human indignity was to take new form. The white American's most powerful weapon had always been words, not because he viewed them as magic but because he used them ambivalently, ambiguously, ambitiously. They would assure, on the one hand, that he believed "all men are created equal" even as they threatened, "The only good Indians I ever saw were dead." The first statement comes from the U.S. Constitution, the second from General Philip Sheridan whose job it was to enforce the Constitution. Words could promise, "The utmost good faith shall always be observed towards the Indians; their land and property shall never be taken from them without their consent; and in their property, rights and liberty, they shall never be invaded or disturbed, unless in just and lawful wars." That promise was made by the Congress of the United States in 1789. The Supreme Court decision on Worcester *vs.* Georgia in 1832 held, "The Cherokee Nation, then, is a distinct community...in which the laws of Georgia can have no force, and which the citizens of Georgia have no right to enter, but with the assent of the Cherokees...or in conformity with treaties, and with the Acts of Congress."

The Trail of Tears indicated something about the transplant American's regard for the sanctity of his word and his laws. In short, his government was his agent; it did his bidding. If its word was worthless, its laws inconsequential, the people it represented were neither truthful nor trustworthy. They were, despite their pious use of words to assert their allegiance to their god and their ideals, men of no faith, of no religious conviction, of no value or worth if they were to be judged by their acts. And how else does one judge except by a man's acts in relation to his stated ideals?

But there was no way to restrain the barbarian who had come to these shores. Murder, rape, pillage, deceit, and cleverness had been handmaidens to his aggressive appropriation of land through military force, his destruction of the peoples' religion and the imposition of his own upon them on pain of death, his unsuccessful but stated attempts to achieve genocide on a continental scale. In later years, when he had appropriated a continent, achieved genocide in 1700 cases, and become the self-proclaimed democratic protector of the world, he would decry the attempted genocide of the German Jew, the land appropriations of any number of countries which at least had historical precedence as an argument for agression, religious suppression and attempts to deprive various peoples of their "right" to choice of ideologies.

America's word was propagandized sacred, "commitments" being the ritual abracadabra which neither the United States citizen nor the political friend or foe trusted, the word having no magical powers at home, the word having constantly been profaned, the word having lost simple respectability. Nor could incantory repetition make the word magic, for magic requires faith, and faith requires trust. The magic visions of the transplant American had been revealed as the distractions of legerdemain; the visionaries had been unmasked as charlatans seeking ambitious ends. The Native American began to realize that "civilized" is not synonymous with "virtuous" or "honorable" or "trustworthy"; rather, it is merely indicative of "having an advanced culture" and "advanced" is synonymous with "technological." The technologically oriented man could not justify the "polite, refined, well-bred" associations with the word, for they are moral rather than technological in concept. His religion had become a social institution rather than a moral code by which he lived. And he dismissed such writers as Charles Sheldon with technologically conceived words out of literary criticism when, in such works as *In His Steps,* such writers had sought to make him aware of his sundered values.

The twentieth-century Native American suffered his last and greatest defeat at the hands of the transplant American. He began to see the word as neither magic nor sacred; it was merely a tool used in the art of rationalization, a tool used in the craft of craft. He even began to see why the mystic visionaries among English language writers were so chronically misunderstood. D. H. Lawrence, James Joyce, Ernest Hemingway, Hart Crane, T. S. Eliot—the literary gods of the transplant American, disillusioned with the dehumanizing results of a technological debasing, had turned, in one way or another, to the primitive rituals and literatures and beliefs in a vain attempt to reestablish some part of the broken link between themselves and the Great Mystery.

But the word was English. Had there ever been the concept that it was magic? When Saint John averred, "In the beginning was the Word, and the Word was with God, and the Word was God," he was not speaking of the English word. Perhaps it had always lacked magic, had always been merely a technological achievement designed for attaining power rather than receiving it. Perhaps that was what Sun Chief meant when, in his autobiography,[1] he recalled the training he received at the Sherman Institute in Riverside, California: "I had learned many English words and could recite part of the Ten Commandments. I knew how to sleep on a bed, pray to Jesus, comb my hair, eat with a knife and fork, and use a toilet....I had also learned that a person thinks with his head instead of his heart."

The new Native American writers are caught in the web of language. Some of them speak only English, for they, like the editors of this book, were denied their native tongues by a society that considered them "rude and barbaric" and by their own realization that communication must be with the transplant American in his language, for he does, at heart, consider any language but English "foreign" and touts it as the "greatest language in the world" because it has a larger vocabulary. Not recognizing the obvious possibility that his own limited vocabulary cuts him away from the communication possibilities in that elaborate language, he still resents hearing any language but English spoken in America because, as Archie Bunker would say, "Why can't *they* use *our* language if they're going to live in our country? If they want to speak some foreign language, let them go back to where they came from." The new Native Ameri-

---

[1]Don C. Talayesva, *Sun Chief: The Autobiography of a Hopi Indian*, ed. Lee W. Simmons (New Haven, 1942).

can writer *is* where he came from so he must use an alien language and he must use it well, for his message is automatically resented no matter how articulate and eloquent it is. An accusation resides in the most natural presentation, for his subject matter must spring from his heritage and his heritage accuses.

That heritage also makes him sensitive to language in ways the transplant is not sensitive. Poetry springs naturally into English prose when the heritage of thought process is basically poetic, when it relies on the rhythms of seasons even in urban areas. Generations of response cannot be exorcised by machine rhythms overnight. Even the pedigreed poodle still burrows a protective hole in the leaves before he lies down on the brocaded couch in an air-conditioned apartment. And that sensitivity to language, that poetic presentation alienates many transplant American readers because it suggests that same awareness that makes Hemingway's "simple" line so easy to read, the total composition so baffling. N. Scott Momaday's Pulitzer Prize winning novel *House Made of Dawn* was criticized for its lack of clarity and economy[2] by one reviewer, by another for "plenty of haze in the telling of this tale."[3] Lucidity and economy are seldom so apparent in American novels as they are in *House Made of Dawn,* but the "haze" which seems to create murkiness for the white reviewers is the autumnal mist that lingers after one great cultural fire has died down, the spring fog that results when a cooling earth's fires are fed to warmth in some new morning. Old traditions, awarenesses, ties with nature's realities — the Indian past — must be combined with new germinations of tradition, new growing awareness, accommodation with the white perversions of nature and natural man — the American present. In the successful wedding of the two, a language (English) that is strident, harsh, and cacaphonous to the sensitive ears of people who have known transplant American and British repression (the East Indian, the Oriental, the African, for example) must be gentled with intuitive wisdoms sprung from the land and sensitivity to the demands of the language. If the resultant prose seems "hazy," it is probably due to the same causes that make passages from D. H. Lawrence's *The Fox* or Eudora Welty's short stories so frustrating to some reviewers, so rewarding for others. Momaday is still too close to his heritage of belief in the power of the word to mechanize his writing into the "lucid" line of

[2]William James Smith in *Commonweal,* September 20, 1968, p. 636.
[3]Marshall Sprague, *New York Times Book Review,* June 9, 1968, p. 5.

expository arbitrariness that characterizes much transplant American literature.

When deliverance is a protested *fait accompli*, as it is in such a novel as James Dickey's well-received work, the mists that gentle the heart's acceptance are absent, for intellectual acceptance demands oversimplified and apparent metaphor. When metaphor is established as a consequence of the sensitivity of the writer to two cultures and completed by the sensitivity of the reader rejecting the absolutes of one dominant culture, the smoke from their fires may be obscuring to the reviewer who lacks a knowledge of spiritual kindlings. Nor can he be told how to be sensitive to language or to the soul of man, for he considers himself to be. His innocence is, unfortunately, the gaucherie of naïveté rather than the simplicity of unformed insight.

The poetry of some contemporary Native Americans reveals very clearly the problems inherent in conveying cultural awareness in a language antithetical to the culture's survival. Truth stated in a spiritually alien medium becomes denunciatory or apologetic to the ear which, attuned only to the one language, cannot hear the cadences of thought that underlie the spontaneous overflow of emotion and response borne on the unarticulated language pattern of the Native American writer. Even if he knows only English, his inherited and unconsciously sublimated urge to employ the polysynthetic structure of Native American languages comes forth in the overlaid phrasings of Buffy-Sainte Marie's "My country 'tis of thy people you're dying" or James Welch's old man who "painted the cry of a goose so long, it floated off the canvas into thin air." The phrasal bursts of sound that approximate whole sentences in English may have sounded like ughs and grunts to the Euro-American ear attuned only to the logical and unsubtle clusterings of the English sentence, but they were, and are, magic islands of thought sent into the sea of air like puffs of smoke released in intermittent bursts to create a sustained communication; the smoke signal is language visible in pattern. That the transplant American considered anything that lovely barbaric is no judgment of the Indian languages. It is a self-analysis indicating an incapacity for receipt of the beautiful.

And it is observable in contemporary Native American writings when they are not self-consciously English, when the language is English but the underlying communication is remembered Indianness. To listen for the voice out of Wah'kon-tah that drifts through the English phrasings is to hear language enriched beyond its spiritual bounds. Unfortunately, the ear that cannot hear it in the Indian's line cannot hear it in Hemingway's or Lawrence's either. Nor is the failure caused exclusively by otic insensitivity; its greater genesis lies in an insensitivity to a richer viewpoint, one aware of the limited biases but capable of transcending them and sending back messages from an emotional-spiritual-intellectual distance beyond them.

It is a Native American poet, James Welch, who seems to summarize the problem best. In "Snow Country Weavers," he asks:

> Say this: say in my mind
>
> I saw your spiders weaving threads
> to bandage up the day. And more,
> those webs were filled with words
> that tumbled meaning into wind.[4]

Spiders can weave threads to bandage up the day when the day reveals a world that flows from the past into the inevitable future, the present being the rich gift of the landscape. Unfortunately, the transplant American does not often see that world. One of his own very sensitive spokesmen, D. H. Lawrence, once theorized on this dreadful truth:

The American landscape has never been at one with the white man. Never. And white men have probably never felt so bitter anywhere, as here in America, where the very landscape in its very beauty seems a bit devilish and grinning, opposed to us.

The desire to extirpate the Indian. And the contradictory desire to glorify him. Both are rampant still, today....

But you have there the myth of the essential white America. All the other stuff, the love, the democracy...is a sort of by-play. The essential American soul is hard, isolated, stoic, and a killer. It has never yet melted.[5]

A Native American spokesman, Benny Bearskin (Winnebago) would not agree that the transplant American possesses the "essential American soul." The *essential* one is that Native American soul that, in the words of the urbanized Chicago Bearskin, has "a deep attachment for the land." And that deep attachment creates a basic pride which, he says, is essential because, "If you don't have that pride, well, then you have no identity."

---

[4] *South Dakota Review*, Summer, 1969, p. 28.

[5] Cited in Paul Jacobs and Saul Landau, *To Serve the Devil. Volume I: Natives and Slaves* (New York, 1971), pp. xxxiv–xxxv.

That identity is apparent in the works of the Native American voices of the twentieth century. In the main, they have escaped the damages Bearskin says happen "in between" two cultures:

There are some areas where the transition from Indian culture to white culture is going on, and some of the children are born into a situation where the old values are already lost. There being no basic economies in these areas, there's much poverty. And nothing of the white culture is available to them. So they're lost in between.

And it is this type of young Indian who is ashamed he is an Indian. Because he doesn't realize, there's nobody ever told him: his ancestors were a noble race of men, who developed over many centuries a way of life, primitive though it was; it existed without prisons, hospitals, jails, courts or anything, or insane asylums or currency or anything. Yet an Indian back in those days was able to live from babyhood till all the hair on his head became white, and he lived a life of complete fulfillment. With no regrets at the end. You rarely see that in this day and age....

I think those Indians who retain the greatest amount of their cultural heritage are really very fortunate, because they feel that it's more important to retain one's dignity and integrity and go through life in this manner, than spending all their energy on an accumulation of material wealth. They find this a frustrating situation. I think the Indian is the only nationality under the system who has resisted this melting-pot concept. Everybody else want to jump in, they view this idea, jumping in and becoming American or losing identity.[6]

The voices in this chapter have not lost their identity. In fact, they have recovered that part of themselves that the years between 1492 and 1900 almost extirpated. It simply would not die as long as blood tells the heart what to know about identity.

[6]Studs Terkel, "Benny Bearskin, 45," *Division Street: America* (New York, 1967).

New Poets in the Land

TED BERRIGAN *is of Irish and Choctaw parentage. Born in Providence, Rhode Island, he is the editor of* "C," A Journal of Poetry *and of* "C" Press Publications. *His work appears regularly in magazines and reviews, and he has three volumes of poetry to his credit.* BYRON BLACK *was a student at the University of Texas when* "I, the Fake Mad Bomber" *was published in* Prairie Schooner. BRUCE IGNACIO *is a Ute.* PATTY HARJO *is Seneca-Cayuga-Quapaw.* CHIRON KHANSHENDEL *(Schiacalega), is a pen name of Bronwen Elizabeth Edwards, a Hopi-Comanche.* PETER LaFARGE *was born in Colorado and was a popular folk song composer and singer.* ALONZO LOPEZ *is a Papago who was a student at Yale when he wrote these poems.* EMERSON BLACK-HORSE MITCHELL *is a Navaho author. His* Miracle Hill, the Story of a Navaho Boy *was published by the University of Oklahoma Press.* N. SCOTT MOMADAY *is the son of a Kiowa father and a Cherokee mother. His widely acclaimed novel,* House Made of Dawn *was a 1969 Pulitzer Prize winner.* SOGE TRACK *is a Sioux-Pueblo.* SIMON J. ORTIZ'S *people live atop a sandstone monolith 300 feet high at Acu, New Mexico.* "And the Land Is Just as Dry" *is a memorial poem to Ira Hayes, Indian hero of the Mount Suribachi flag-raising group who died an alcoholic, unremembered by the nation that had earlier honored him.* NORMAN H. RUSSELL *is of Cherokee ancestry and a college professor.* JAMES WELCH *has received wide recognition as an American poet. Born on a Blackfoot reservation, he is, it seems to us, one of the most lyrical poets in the nation.*

Peace

Ted Berrigan

What to do
    when the days' heavy heart
                having risen, late
in the already darkening East
      & prepared at any moment to sink into the West
surprises suddenly,
       & settles, for a time,
                  at a lovely place
where mellow light spreads
          evenly
             from face to face?
The day's usual aggressive
        contrary beat
             now softly dropped
into a regular pace
        the head riding gently its personal place
where pistons feel like legs
         on feelings met like lace.
                  Why,
take a walk, then,
        across this town. It's a pleasure
to meet the one certain person you've been counting on
          to take your measure
who will smile, & love you, sweetly, at your leisure.
                And if
she turns your head around
        like any other man,
           go home
and make yourself a sandwich
        of toasted bread, & ham
           with butter
lots of it
     & have a diet cola,
        & sit down
& write this,
     because you can.

Presence

Ted Berrigan

and I am lost in the ringing elevator
he waggles   the fat whiteness of milk
sweeping me to the top
one is reminded of constellations
there there were pine needles
dreams of symbolism
the part that goes over the fence last
star light   the cord "reaches"
it was turkey
sheepish lights   you turned me on
reflecting dilemmas   majorities
Bildungsroman of the bathrobe ride
and the briny sound of the alarm
a funny feeling prompted me out of bed
Love
the top had been "sliced"
ribbons your presence on the white and green sheet
I asked for a Hook-and-Ladder
takes   The End.
in the ideal society pants

Now   we can make some explosions
shine like money
Francis is not diminutive   thanks
others are less legs
thighs wings breast
Caress the window grease, John
as you are not yet 12
19?   40?   who pulls me down?
that night we slept reverently   (you lust
I must lust in-
vigorating   the sixteen genre
dragon   bottle-opener
spiral cuff-link aerial
facade of the wonderful orient word
"doilies"
Overhead the moon is out
blacking my shoes, face

we were all livid, numinous

Things whip toward the center
licking the palate of his headache
this indicates your future
meditates on his wish which is
hooked onto the top and draped archly

Childhood fuses   a mystery play
Take off your beautiful blouse, you foolish girl!
which ribbons the marvelous laurel   the loop-
Are you list-   with this ring I
eye thee
(that was later, out west, after more baseball
some turkey
a wristwatch, dictionary, sniper suit, rifle
to "meditate"
(is there room in the tune to atune in?)

They were incensed at his arrival
Now we are glad   it was stinky
some paint them black in the face to be quaint or
    something
one symbol fact seems valid
I don't know
all hate it to be right
on the cards
which are sometimes funky (aesthetic) having
snow of feet and that a domination.
Then we had presence.

I, the Fake Mad Bomber and Walking It Home Again

Byron Black

First comes the cold,
and puffing as classes change
fast as the frames of a film
and dried old sarcophagi of professors reel on
trot placidly Latin with its dust and their rot.

Then dives the red sun
crashes like the stock market, in black
"the day was fine" as Wm. says
and the Tower stands impudent, one wants to slap it down
before the blast-off into stone-gray space.

Brisk bright day
Wm. and I walking fast,
we smile at lurid tales which shock like adders

Dark people with the faces of bulldogs
gruffly waddle past, Chryslers with the scream of a rocket
charge us jousting, we hurry fast
to the flap and claw of the Night Hawk

where dark hamburgers from the heart of a living vulture
are served by an Aztec princess
"the hamburger don't come with onions"
(pimples as jewels, and the pop of gum)
And the white bourgeois, slimy smiles
slide in with assuredness of talkative slugs, to music
   of the bank

outside the brightwork of their gaudy Cadillacs
wails like a chrome banshee toward the cool evening,
   and sad glass eyes,
And I thanking Wm. we part
he for home
and I full of cheer and good meat

head for my place, legs flashing
the power of wet muscles
sends an electric orgasm,
and as approaching Red River, now dry
beside the stadium where Christians are devourers
the night breaks
I know myself as the Fake Mad Bomber
and light a black cigar in the dark to prove it.

Lost

Bruce Ignacio

I know not of my forefathers
nor of their beliefs
For I was brought up in the city.
Our home seemed smothered and surrounded
as were other homes on city sites.
When the rain came
I would slush my way to school
as though the street were a wading pool.
Those streets were always crowded.
I brushed by people with every step,
Covered my nose once in awhile,
Gasping against the smell of perspiration on humid days.
Lights flashed everywhere
until my head became a signal, flashing on and off.
Noise so unbearable
I wished the whole place would come to a standstill,
leaving only peace and quiet

And still, would I like this kind of life? . . .
The life of my forefathers
who wandered, not knowing where they were going,
but just moving, further and further
from where they had been,
To be in quiet,
to kind of be lost in their dreams and wishing,
as I have been to this day,
I awake.

Musings

Patty Harjo

Walk proud, walk straight, let your thoughts race
with the blue wind, but do not bare your soul to
your enemies.

The black mountain lion called night devours the
white rabbit of day. And the icy cold wind blows
over the still-warm, brown earth.

In restless dreams I called out his name,
Waking, I do not remember.

In my score of years
I have known not love
except wind, earth and darkness.

Grebes at Sunset

Chiron Khanshendel

The grebes' mad wings
        sucking air
thru the long
        flight-feathers all evening
long bidding the sun
        farewell...

the sheltered
        Eucalyptus trees hide
where the tides cannot
        reach, above on a
crumbling cliff
        away from the
water that will soon
        be their purgatory...

The ocean showered with
  twilight pigments
is the new moon's
  special child.

Vision of a Past Warrior

Peter LaFarge

I have within me such a dream of pain
That all my silver horseman hopes rust still—
Beyond quick silver mountains, on the plain,
The buffalo are gone, none left to kill.

I see the plains grow blackened with that dawn,
No robes for winter warmth, no meat to eat—
The ghost white buffalos' medicine gone.
No hope for Indians then: I see defeat.

Then there will be changes to another way,
We will fight battles that are legends long.
But of all our glory none will stay—
Who will remember that I sang this song?

I Am Crying from Thirst

Alonzo Lopez

I am crying from thirst.
I am singing for rain.
I am dancing for rain.
The sky begins to weep,
  for it sees me
  singing and dancing
  on the dry, cracked
  earth.

Direction

Alonzo Lopez

I was directed by my grandfather
To the East,
    so I might have the power of the bear;
To the South,
    so I might have the courage of the eagle;
To the West,
    so I might have the wisdom of the owl;
To the North,
    so I might have the craftiness of the fox;
To the Earth,
    so I might receive her fruit;
To the Sky,
    so I might lead a life of innocence.

The New Direction

Emerson Blackhorse Mitchell

This vanishing old road,
    Through hail-like dust storm,
It stings and scratches,
    Stuffy, I cannot breathe.

Here once walked my ancestors,
    I was told by the old ones,
One can dig at the very spot,
    And find forgotten implements.

Wasting no time I urged on,
    Where I'd stop I knew not,
Startled I listened to the wind,
    It whistled, screamed, cried,
"You! Go back, not this path!"

Then I recalled this trail
     Swept away by the north wind,
It wasn't for me to follow,
     The trail of the Long Walk.

Deciding between two cultures,
     I gave a second thought,
Reluctantly I took the new one,
     The paved rainbow highway.
I had found a new direction

Angle of Geese

N. Scott Momaday

     How shall we adorn
Recognition with our speech?
     And the dead firstborn
Keeps at the fore of the tongue.

     Custom intervenes;
We are civil, something more:
     More than language means,
The mute presence mulls and marks.

     Almost of a mind,
We take measure of the loss;
     I am slow to find
The mere margin of repose.

     And one November
It was longer in the watch,
     As if forever,
Of the huge ancestral goose.

     So much symmetry!
Like the pale angle of time
     And eternity.
The great shape labored and fell.

     Quit of hope and hurt,
It held the motionless gaze,
     Wide of time, alert,
On the dark distant flurry.

Before an Old Painting of the Crucifixion

N. Scott Momaday

The Mission Carmel,
June, 1960

I ponder how He died, despairing once.
I've heard the cry subside in vacant skies,
In clearings where no other was. Despair,
Which, in the vibrant wake of utterance,
Resides in desolate calm, preoccupies,
Though it is still. There is no solace there.

That calm inhabits wilderness, the sea,
And where no peace inheres but solitude;
Near death it most impends. It was for Him,
Absurd and public in His agony,
Inscrutably itself, nor misconstrued,
Nor metaphrased in art or pseudonym:

A vague contagion. Old, the mural fades...
Reminded of the fainter sea I scanned,
I recollect: How mute in constancy!
I could not leave the wall of palisades
Till cormorants returned my eyes on land.
The mural but implies eternity:

Not death, but silence after death is change.
Judean hills, the endless afternoon,
The farther groves and arbors seasonless
But fix the mind within the moment's range.
Where evening would obscure our sorrow soon,
There shines too much a sterile loveliness.

No imprecisions of commingled shade,
No shimmering deceptions of the sun,
Herein no semblances remark the cold
Unhindered swell of time, for time is stayed.
The Passion wanes into oblivion,
And time and timelessness confuse, I'm told.

Indian Love Letter

Soge Track

Lady of the crescent moon
tonight I look at the sky
You are not there
You are not mad at me, are you?
"You are angry at the people,
Yes, I know."

>   they are changing
>   be not too hard

If you were taken to
the mission school,
not because you wanted,
but someone thought it best for you
you too would change.

They came out of nowhere
telling us how to eat our food
how to build our homes
how to plant our crops.
Need I say more of what they did?
All is new—the old ways are nothing.

>   they are changing
>   be not too hard

I talk to them
they turn their heads.
Do not be hurt—you have me
I live by the old ways
I will not change.

Tonight—my prayer plumes in hand
with the white shell things—
to the silent place I will go
(It is for you I go, please be there.)
Oh! Lady of the crescent moon
with the corn-silk hair—I love you

>   they are changing
>   be not too hard

And the Land Is Just as Dry

line from song by Peter LaFarge

Simon J. Ortiz

the horizons are still mine
the ragged peaks
the cactus the brush the hard brittle plants
these are mine yours
we must be humble with them

the green fields
a few a very few
Interstate highway 10 to tucson
sacaton, bapchule,
my home is right there
off the road to tucson
before the junction
on the map it is yellow
and dry, very dry
breathe tough swallow
look for rain and rain

used to know ira he said
his tongue slow spit on his lips
in mesa used to chop cotton
coming into phoenix from north
you pass by john jacobs farm
many of the people there
they live in one room shacks
they're provided for by john jacobs
pays them about $5 per day in sun
enough for quart of wine on friday
ira got his water alright
used to know him in mesa in the sun
my home is brown adobe
and tin roof and lots of children
broken down cars the pink ford
up on those railroad ties

still paying for it
and it's been two years since
it ran motor burned out
had to pull it back from phoenix

gila river the sign states
at the bridge full of brush
and sand and where's the water
the water which you think about
sometimes in empty desperation
it's in those green very green fields
which are not mine

you call me a drunk indian go ahead

Ten O'Clock News

Simon J. Ortiz

berstein disc jockey
telling about indians
on ten o'clock news
o they have been screwed
i know everybody's talking
about indians yesterday
murdering conquest the buffalo
in those hills in kansas
railroad hustling progress
today maybe tomorrow in
ghost dance dreams we'll
find out berstein doesn't know
what indians say these days
in wino translations
he doesn't know that and even
indians sometimes don't know
because they believe in trains
and what berstein tells them
on ten o'clock news

Smoking My Prayers

Simon J. Ortiz

now that i have lighted my smoke
i am motioning to the east
i am walking in thought that direction
i am listening for your voices
i am occurring in my mind
    this instance that i am here
now that i have breathed inwards
i am seeing the mountains east
i am travelling to that place of birth
i am aware of your voices
i am thinking of your relationship with me
    this time in the morning that we are together
now that i have breathed outwards
i am letting you take my breath
i am moving for your sake
i am hearing the voices of your children
i am not myself but yourself now
    at this time your spirit has captured mine
now that i am taking breath in again
i have arrived back from that place of birth
i have travelled fast and surely
i have heard what you wanted me to hear
i have become whole and strong with yourself

    this morning i am living with your breath.

This Preparation

Simon J. Ortiz

these sticks i am holding
i cut down at the creek.
i have just come from there.
i listened to the creek
speaking to the world,
i did my praying,
and then i took my knife
and cut the sticks.
there is some sorrow in leaving
fresh wounds in growing things,
but my praying has relieved
some of my sorrow. prayers
make things possible, my uncle said.
before i left i listened again
for words the creek was telling,
and i smelled its smell which
are words also. and then
i tied my sticks into a bundle
and came home, each step a prayer
for this morning and a safe return.
my son is sleeping still
in this quietness, my wife
is stirring at her cooking,
and i am making this preparation.
i wish to make my praying
into these sticks like gods have taught.

i have many friends

Norman H. Russell

when i am in the forest in the day
the birds come and speak messages to me
the birds tell me of an enemy

when i lie asleep in the night
the insects talk my safety about me
when an enemy comes they are still

i have few enemies
i have many friends

the birds have their enemies
the insects have their enemies
i wish to tell them of their enemies
i wish to tell them i am their friend
i wish to thank them for my life
which they have given me over and over again.

this is a sign

Norman H. Russell

there is dew on the grass
this is a sign
the edge of the sky is white
this is a sign
the sun is dustred coming up
this is a sign

then the morning comes
and the sun burns brighter
lines of little clouds rise
out of the earths edge
this too is a sign

now we wait in the dry grass
now we wait in the hot sand
my sheep my dogs and i
watching the sky

the signs tell rain
but the signs have told rain before
and there has been no rain

the bellies of the sheep are thin
my eyes go blind
the dogs are dying.

In My Lifetime

James Welch

This day the children of Speakthunder
run the wrong man, a saint unable
to love a weasel way, able only to smile
and drink the wind that makes the others go.
Trees are ancient in his breath.
His bleeding feet tell a story of run
the sacred way, chase the antelope naked
till it drops, the odor of run
quiet in his blood. He watches cactus
jump against the moon. Moon is speaking
woman to the ancient fire. Always woman.

His sins were numerous, this wrong man.
Buttes were good to listen from. With thunder-
hands his father shaped the dust, circled
fire, tumbled up the wind to make a fool.
Now the fool is dead. His bones go back
so scarred in time, the buttes are young to look
for signs that say a man could love his fate,
that winter in the blood is one sad thing.

His sins—I don't explain. Desperate in my song,
I run these woman hills, translate wind
to mean a kind of life, the children of Speakthunder
are never wrong and I am rhythm to strong medicine.

The Versatile Historian

James Welch

I came through autumn forests needing
wind that needed fire. Sun on larch,
fir, the ponderosa told me to forget
the friends I needed years ago.
Sky is all the rage in country steeped
in lore, the troubled Indians wise within
their graves. The chanting clouds
crowded against the lowest peak. I sang
of trouble to the north. Sleeping weasels robbed
my songs of real words. Everywhere, rhythm raged.
Sun beneath my feet, I became
the statue needing friends in wind
that needed fire, mountains to bang against.

Snow Country Weavers

James Welch

A time to tell you things are well.
Birds flew south a year ago.
One returned, a blue-winged teal
wild with news of his mother's love.

Mention me to friends. Say
wolves are dying at my door,
the winter drives them from their meat.
Say this: say in my mind

I saw your spiders weaving threads
to bandage up the day. And more,
those webs were filled with words
that tumbled meaning into wind.

An Alien Form Mastered: Fiction

The Lakota chief and writer Standing Bear introduced Juanita Platero, a Navaho, and Siyowin Miller, a white. In collaboration, they write fiction detailing the search for identity in two worlds. Theirs is a sympathetic and sensitive relationship as "Chee's Daughter" reveals.

Chee's Daughter

Juanita Platero and Siyowin Miller

The hat told the story, the big, black, drooping Stetson. It was not at the proper angle, the proper rakish angle for so young a Navaho. There was no song, and that was not in keeping either. There should have been at least a humming, a faint, all-to-himself "he he he heya," for it was a good horse he was riding, a slender-legged, high-stepping buckskin that would race the wind with light knee-urging. This was a day for singing, a warm winter day, when the touch of the sun upon the back belied the snow high on distant mountains.

Wind warmed by the sun touched his high-boned cheeks like flicker feathers, and still he rode on silently, deeper into Little Canyon, until the red rock walls rose straight upward from the stream bed and only a narrow piece of blue sky hung above. Abruptly the sky widened where the canyon walls were pushed back to make a wide place, as though in ancient times an angry stream had tried to go all ways at once.

This was home—this wide place in the canyon—levels of jagged rock and levels of rich red earth. This was home to Chee, the rider of the buckskin, as it had been to many generations before him.

He stopped his horse at the stream and sat looking across the narrow ribbon of water to the bare-branched peach trees. He was seeing them each springtime with their age-gnarled limbs transfigured beneath veils of blossom pink; he was seeing them in autumn laden with their yellow fruit, small and sweet. Then his eyes searched out the indistinct furrows of the fields beside the stream, where each year the corn and beans and squash drank thirstily of the overflow from summer rains. Chee was trying to outweigh today's bitter betrayal of hope by gathering to himself these reminders of the integrity of the land.

Land did not cheat! His mind lingered deliberately on all the days spent here in the sun caring for the young plants, his songs to the earth and to the life springing from it— "...In the middle of the wide field... Yellow Corn Boy...He has started both ways...," then the harvest and repayment in full measure. Here was the old feeling of wholeness and of oneness with the sun and earth and growing things.

Chee urged the buckskin toward the family compound where, secure in a recess of overhanging rock, was his mother's dome-shaped hogan, red rock and red adobe like the ground on which it nestled. Not far from the hogan was the half-circle of brush like a dark shadow against the canyon wall—corral for sheep and goats. Farther from the hogan, in full circle, stood the horse corral made of heavy cedar branches sternly interlocked. Chee's long thin lips curved into a smile as he passed his daughter's tiny hogan squatted like a round Pueblo oven beside the corral. He remembered the summer day when together they sat back on their heels and plastered wet adobe all about the circling wall of rock and the woven dome of piñon twigs. How his family laughed when the Little One herded the bewildered chickens into her tiny hogan as the first snow fell.

Then the smile faded from Chee's lips and his eyes darkened as he tied his horse to a corral post and turned to the strangely empty compound. "Someone has told them," he thought, "and they are inside weeping." He passed his mother's deserted loom on the south side of the hogan and pulled the rude wooden door toward him, bowing his head, hunching his shoulders to get inside.

His mother sat sideways by the center fire, her feet drawn up under her full skirts. Her hands were busy kneading dough in the chipped white basin. With her head down, her voice was muffled when she said, "The meal will soon be ready, son."

Chee passed his father sitting against the wall, hat over his eyes as though asleep. He passed his older sister who sat turning mutton ribs on a crude wire grill over the coals, noticed tears dropping on her hands. "She cared more for my wife than I realized," he thought.

Then because something must be said sometime, he tossed the black Stetson upon a bulging sack of wool and said, "You have heard, then." He could not shut from his mind how confidently he had set the handsome new hat on his head that very morning, slanting the wide brim over one eye: he was going to see his wife and today he would ask the doctors about bringing her home; last week she had looked so much better.

His sister nodded but did not speak. His mother sniffled and passed her velveteen sleeve beneath her nose. Chee sat down, leaning against the wall. "I suppose I was a fool for hoping all the time. I should have expected this. Few of our people get well from the coughing sickness. But *she* seemed to be getting better."

His mother was crying aloud now and blowing her nose noisily on her skirt. His father sat up, speaking gently to her.

Chee shifted his position and started a cigarette. His mind turned back to the Little One. At least she was too small to understand what had happened, the Little One who had been born three years before in the sanitarium where his wife was being treated for the coughing sickness, the Little One he had brought home to his mother's hogan to be nursed by his sister whose baby was a few months older. As she grew fat-cheeked and sturdy-legged, she followed him about like a shadow; somehow her baby mind had grasped that of all those at the hogan who cared for her and played with her, he—Chee—belonged most to her. She sat cross-legged at his elbow when he worked silver at the forge; she rode before him in the saddle when he drove the horses to water; often she lay wakeful on her sheep-pelts until he stretched out for the night in the darkened hogan and she could snuggle warm against him.

Chee blew smoke slowly and some of the sadness left his dark eyes as he said, "It is not as bad as it might be. It is not as though we are left with nothing."

Chee's sister arose, sobs catching in her throat, and rushed past him out the doorway. Chee sat upright, a terrible fear possessing him. For a moment his mouth could make no sound. Then: "The Little One! Mother, where is she?"

His mother turned her stricken face to him. "Your wife's people came after her this morning. They heard yesterday of their daughter's death through the trader at Red Sands."

Chee started to protest but his mother shook her head slowly. "I didn't expect they would want the Little One either. But there is nothing you can do. She is a girl child and belongs to her mother's people; it is custom."

Frowning, Chee got to his feet, grinding his cigarette into the dirt floor. "Custom! When did my wife's parents begin thinking about custom? Why, the hogan where they live doesn't even face the East!" He started toward the door. "Perhaps I can overtake them. Perhaps they don't realize how much we want her with us. I'll ask them to give my daughter back to me. Surely they won't refuse."

His mother stopped him gently with her outstretched hand. "You couldn't overtake them now. They were in the trader's car. Eat and rest, and think more about this."

"Have you forgotten how things have always been between you and your wife's people?" his father said.

That night, Chee's thoughts were troubled—half-forgotten incidents became disturbingly vivid—but early the next morning he saddled the buckskin and set out for the settlement of Red Sands. Even though his father-in-law, Old Man Fat, might laugh, Chee knew that he must talk to him. There were some things to which Old Man Fat might listen.

Chee rode the first part of the fifteen miles to Red Sands expectantly. The sight of sandstone buttes near Cottonwood Spring reddening in the morning sun brought a song almost to his lips. He twirled his reins in salute to the small boy herding sheep toward many-colored Butterfly Mountain, watched with pleasure the feathers of smoke rising against tree-darkened western mesas from the hogans sheltered there. But as he approached the familiar settlement sprawled in mushroom growth along the highway, he began to feel as though a scene from a bad dream was becoming real.

Several cars were parked around the trading store which was built like two log hogans side by side, with red gas pumps in front and a sign across the tarpaper roofs: *Red Sands Trading Post—Groceries Gasoline Cold Drinks Sandwiches Indian Curios.* Back of the trading post an unpainted frame house and outbuildings squatted on the drab, treeless land. Chee and the Little One's mother had lived there when they stayed with his wife's people. That was according to custom—living with one's wife's people—but Chee had never been convinced that it was custom alone which prompted Old Man Fat and his wife to insist that their daughter bring her husband to live at the trading post.

Beside the Post was a large hogan of logs, with brightly painted pseudo-Navaho designs on the roof—a hogan with smoke-smudged windows and a garish blue door which faced north to the highway. Old Man Fat had offered Chee a hogan like this one. The trader would build it if he and his wife would live there and Chee would work at his forge making silver jewelry where tourists could watch him. But Chee had asked instead for a piece of land for a cornfield and help in building a hogan far back from the highway and a corral for the sheep he had brought to this marriage.

A cold wind blowing down from the mountains began to whistle about Chee's ears. It flapped the gaudy Navaho rugs which were hung in one long bright line to attract tourists. It swayed the sign *Navaho Weaver at Work* beside the loom where Old Man Fat's wife sat hunched in her striped blanket, patting the colored thread of a design into place with a wooden comb. Tourists stood watching the weaver. More tourists stood in a knot before the hogan where the sign said: *See Inside a Real Navaho Home 25¢.*

Then the knot seemed to unravel as a few people returned to their cars; some had cameras; and there against the blue door Chee saw the Little One standing uncertainly. The wind was plucking at her new purple blouse and wide green skirt; it freed truant strands of soft dark hair from the meager queue into which it had been tied with white yarn.

"Isn't she cunning!" one of the women tourists was saying as she turned away.

Chee's lips tightened as he began to look around for Old Man Fat. Finally he saw him passing among the tourists collecting coins.

Then the Little One saw Chee. The uncertainty left her face and she darted through the crowd as her father swung down from his horse. Chee lifted her in his arms, hugging her tight. While he listened to her breathless chatter, he watched Old Man Fat bearing down on them, scowling.

As his father-in-law walked heavily across the gravelled lot, Chee was reminded of a statement his mother sometimes made: "When you see a fat Navaho, you see one who hasn't worked for what he has."

Old Man Fat was fattest in the middle. There was indolence in his walk even though he seemed to hurry, indolence in his cheeks so plump they made his eyes squint, eyes now smoldering with anger.

Some of the tourists were getting into their cars and driving away. The old man said belligerently to Chee, "Why do you come here? To spoil our business? To drive people away?"

"I came to talk with you," Chee answered, trying to keep his voice steady as he faced the old man.

"We have nothing to talk about," Old Man Fat blustered and did not offer to touch Chee's extended hand.

"It's about the Little One." Chee settled his daughter more comfortably against his hip as he weighed carefully all the words he had planned to say. "We are going to miss her very much. It wouldn't be so bad if we knew that *part* of each year she could be with us. That might help you too. You and your wife are no longer young people and you have no young ones here to depend upon." Chee chose his next words remembering the thriftlessness of his wife's parents, and their greed. "Perhaps we could share the care of this little one. Things are good with us. So much snow this year will make lots of grass for the sheep. We have good land for corn and melons."

Chee's words did not have the expected effect. Old Man Fat was enraged. "Farmers, all of you! Long-haired farmers! Do you think everyone must bend his back over the short-handled hoe in order to have food to eat?" His tone changed as he began to brag a little. "We not only have all the things from cans at the trader's, but when the Pueblos come past here on their way to town we buy their salty jerked mutton, young corn for roasting, dried sweet peaches."

Chee's dark eyes surveyed the land along the highway as the old man continued to brag about being "progressive." *He* no longer was tied to the land. He and his wife made money easily and could *buy* all the things they wanted. Chee realized too late that he had stumbled into the old argument between himself and his wife's parents. They had never understood his feeling about the land—that a man took care of his land and it in turn took care of him. Old Man Fat and his wife scoffed at him, called him a Pueblo farmer, all during that summer when he planted and weeded and harvested. Yet they ate the green corn in their mutton stews, and the chili paste from the fresh ripe chilis, and the tortillas from the cornmeal his wife ground. None of this working and sweating in the sun for Old Man Fat, who talked proudly of his easy way of living—collecting money from the trader who rented this strip of land beside the highway, collecting money from the tourists.

Yet Chee had once won that argument. His wife had shared his belief in the integrity of the earth, that jobs and people might fail one but the earth never would. After that first year she had turned from her own people and gone with Chee to Little Canyon.

Old Man Fat was reaching for the Little One. "Don't be coming here with plans for my daughter's daughter," he warned. "If you try to make trouble, I'll take the case to the government man in town."

The impulse was strong in Chee to turn and ride off while he still had the Little One in his arms. But he knew his time of victory would be short. His own family would uphold the old custom of children, especially girl children, belonging to the mother's people. He would have to give his daughter up if the case were brought before the Headman of Little Canyon, and certainly he would have no better chance before a strange white man in town.

He handed the bewildered Little One to her grandfather who stood watching every movement suspiciously. Chee asked, "If I brought you a few things for the Little One, would that be making trouble? Some velvet for a blouse, or some of the jerky she likes so well...this summer's melon?"

Old Man Fat backed away from him. "Well," he hesitated, as some of the anger disappeared from his face and beads of greed shone in his eyes. "Well," he repeated. Then as the Little One began to squirm in his arms and cry, he said, "No! No! Stay away from here, you and all your family."

The sense of his failure deepened as Chee rode back to Little Canyon. But it was not until he sat with his family that evening in the hogan, while the familiar bustle of meal preparing went on about him, that he began to doubt the wisdom of the things he'd always believed. He smelled the coffee boiling and the oily fragrance of chili powder dusted into the bubbling pot of stew; he watched his mother turning round crusty fried bread in the small black skillet. All around him was plenty—a half of mutton hanging near the door, bright strings of chili drying, corn hanging by the braided husks, cloth bags of dried peaches. Yet in his heart was nothing.

He heard the familiar sounds of the sheep outside the hogan, the splash of water as his father filled the long drinking trough from the water barrel. When his father came in, Chee could not bring himself to tell a second time of the day's happenings. He watched his wiry, soft-spoken father while his mother told the story, saw his father's queue of graying hair quiver as he nodded his head with sympathetic exclamations.

Chee's doubting, acrid thoughts kept forming: Was it wisdom his father had passed on to him or was his inheritance only the stubbornness of a long-haired Navaho resisting change? Take care of the land and it will take care of you. True, the land had always given him food, but now food was not enough. Perhaps if he had gone to school he would have learned a different kind of wisdom, something to help him now. A schoolboy might even be able to speak convincingly to this government man whom Old Man Fat threatened to call, instead of sitting here like a clod of earth itself—Pueblo farmer indeed. What had the land to give that would restore his daughter?

In the days that followed, Chee herded sheep. He got up in the half-light, drank the hot coffee his mother had ready, then started the flock moving. It was necessary to drive the sheep a long way from the hogan to find good winter forage. Sometimes Chee met friends or relatives who were on their way to town or to the road camp where they hoped to get work; then there was friendly banter and an exchange of news. But most of the days seemed endless; he could not walk far enough or fast enough from his memories of the Little One or from his bitter thoughts. Sometimes it seemed his daughter trudged beside him, so real he could almost hear her footsteps—the muffled pad-pad of little feet clad in deerhide. In the glare of a snow bank he would see her vivid face, brown eyes sparkling. Mingling with the tinkle of sheep bells he heard her laughter.

When, weary of following the small sharp hoof marks that crossed and recrossed in the snow, he sat down in the shelter of a rock, it was only to be reminded that in his thoughts he had forsaken his brotherhood with the earth and sun and growing things. If he remembered times when he had flung himself against the earth to rest, to lie there in the sun until he could no longer feel where he left off and the earth began, it was to remember also that now he sat like an alien against the same earth; the belonging-together was gone. The earth was one thing and he was another.

It was during the days when he herded sheep that Chee decided he must leave Little Canyon. Perhaps he would take a job silversmithing for one of the traders in town. Perhaps, even though he spoke little English, he could get a job at the road camp with his cousins; he would ask them about it.

Springtime transformed the mesas. The peach trees in the canyon were shedding fragrance and pink blossoms on the gentled wind. The sheep no longer foraged for the yellow seeds of chamiso but ranged near the hogan with the long-legged new lambs, eating tender young grass.

Chee was near the hogan on the day his cousins rode up with the message for which he waited. He had been watching with mixed emotions while his father and his sister's husband cleared the fields beside the stream.

"The boss at the camp says he needs an extra hand, but he wants to know if you'll be willing to go with the camp when they move it to the other side of the town?" The tall cousin shifted his weight in the saddle.

The other cousin took up the explanation. "The work near here will last only until the new cut-off beyond Red Sands is finished. After that, the work will be too far away for you to get back here often."

That was what Chee had wanted—to get away from Little Canyon—yet he found himself not so interested in the job beyond town as in this new cut-off which was almost finished. He pulled a blade of grass, split it thoughtfully down the center as he asked questions of his cousins. Finally he said: "I need to think more about this. If I decide on this job I'll ride over."

Before his cousins were out of sight down the canyon Chee was walking toward the fields, a bold plan shaping in his mind. As the plan began to flourish, wild and hardy as young tumbleweed, Chee added his own voice softly to the song his father was singing: "...In the middle of the wide field...Yellow Corn Boy...I wish to put in."

Chee walked slowly around the field, the rich red earth yielding to his footsteps. His plan depended upon this land and upon the things he remembered most about his wife's people.

Through planting time Chee worked zealously and tirelessly. He spoke little of the large new field he was planting because he felt so strongly that just now this was something between himself and the land. The first days he was ever stooping, piercing the ground with the pointed stick, placing the corn kernels there, walking around the field and through it, singing, "...His track leads into the ground... Yellow Corn Boy...his track leads into the ground." After that, each day Chee walked through his field watching for the tips of green to break through; first a few spikes in the center and then more and more until the corn in all parts of the field was above ground. Surely, Chee thought, if he sang the proper songs, if he cared for this land faithfully, it would not forsake him now, even though through the lonely days of winter he had betrayed the goodness of the earth in his thoughts.

Through the summer Chee worked long days, the sun hot upon his back, pulling weeds from around young corn plants; he planted squash and pumpkin; he terraced a small piece of land near his mother's hogan and planted carrots and onions and the moisture-loving chili. He was increasingly restless. Finally he told his family what he hoped the harvest from this land would bring him. Then the whole family waited with him, watching the corn: the slender graceful plants that waved green arms and bent to embrace each other as young winds wandered through the field, the maturing plants flaunting their pollen-laden tassels in the sun, the tall and sturdy parent corn with new-formed ears and a froth of purple, red and yellow corn-beards against the dusty emerald of broad leaves.

Summer was almost over when Chee slung the bulging packs across two pack ponies. His mother helped him tie the heavy rolled pack behind the saddle of the buckskin. Chee knotted the new yellow kerchief about his neck a little tighter, gave the broad black hat brim an extra tug, but these were only gestures of assurance and he knew it. The land had not failed him. That part was done. But this he was riding into? Who could tell?

When Chee arrived at Red Sands, it was as he had expected to find it—no cars on the highway. His cousins had told him that even the Pueblo farmers were using the new cut-off to town. The barren gravel around the Red Sands Trading Post was deserted. A sign banged against the dismantled gas pumps *Closed until further notice*.

Old Man Fat came from the crude summer shelter built beside the log hogan from a few branches of scrub cedar and the sides of wooden crates. He seemed almost friendly when he saw Chee.

"Get down, my son," he said, eyeing the bulging packs. There was no bluster in his voice today and his face sagged, looking somewhat saddened; perhaps because his cheeks were no longer quite full enough to push his eyes upward at the corners. "You are going on a journey?"

Chee shook his head. "Our fields gave us so much this year, I thought to sell or trade this to the trader. I didn't know he was no longer here."

Old Man Fat sighed, his voice dropping to an injured tone. "He says he and his wife are going to rest this winter; then after that he'll build a place up on the new highway."

Chee moved as though to be traveling on, then jerked his head toward the pack ponies. "Anything you need?"

"I'll ask my wife," Old Man Fat said as he led the way to the shelter. "Maybe she has a little money. Things have not been too good with us since the trader closed. Only a few tourists come this way." He shrugged his shoulders. "And with the trader gone—no credit."

Chee was not deceived by his father-in-law's unexpected confidences. He recognized them as a hopeful bid for sympathy and, if possible, something for nothing. Chee made no answer. He was think-

ing that so far he had been right about his wife's parents: their thriftlessness had left them with no resources to last until Old Man Fat found
another easy way of making a living.

Old Man Fat's Wife was in the shelter working at her loom.
She turned rather wearily when her husband asked with noticeable
deference if she would give him money to buy supplies. Chee surmised
that the only income here was from his mother-in-law's weaving.

She peered around the corner of the shelter at the laden
ponies, and then she looked at Chee. "What do you have there, my son?"

Chee smiled to himself as he turned to pull the pack from
one of the ponies, dragged it to the shelter where he untied the ropes.
Pumpkins and hardshelled squash tumbled out, and the ears of corn—
pale yellow husks fitting firmly over plump ripe kernels, blue corn,
red corn, yellow corn, many-colored corn, ears and ears of it—tumbled
into every corner of the shelter.

"Yooooh," Old Man Fat's Wife exclaimed as she took some
of the ears in her hands. Then she glanced up at her son-in-law. "But
we have no money for all this. We have sold almost everything we own—
even the brass bed that stood in the hogan."

Old Man Fat's brass bed. Chee concealed his amusement
as he started back for another pack. That must have been a hard parting. Then he stopped, for, coming from the cool darkness of the hogan
was the Little One, rubbing her eyes as though she had been asleep.
She stood for a moment in the doorway and Chee saw that she was
dirty, barefoot, her hair uncombed, her little blouse shorn of all its
silver buttons. Then she ran toward Chee, her arms outstretched. Heed-
less of Old Man Fat and his wife, her father caught her in his arms,
her hair falling in a dark cloud across his face, the sweetness of her
laughter warm against his shoulder.

It was the haste within him to get this slow waiting game
played through to the finish that made Chee speak unwisely. It was
the desire to swing her before him in the saddle and ride fast to Little
Canyon that prompted his words. "The money doesn't matter. You still
have something...."

Chee knew immediately that he had overspoken. The old
woman looked from him to the corn spread before her. Unfriendliness
began to harden in his father-in-law's face. All the old arguments between himself and his wife's people came pushing and crowding in
between them now.

Old Man Fat began kicking the ears of corn back onto
the canvas as he eyed Chee angrily. "And you rode all the way over
here thinking that for a little food we would give up our daughter's
daughter?"

Chee did not wait for the old man to reach for the Little
One. He walked dazedly to the shelter, rubbing his cheek against her
soft dark hair and put her gently into her grandmother's lap. Then he

turned back to the horses. He had failed. By his own haste he had failed. He swung into the saddle, his hand touching the roll behind it. Should he ride on into town?

Then he dismounted, scarcely glancing at Old Man Fat, who stood uncertainly at the corner of the shelter, listening to his wife. "Give me a hand with this other pack of corn, Grandfather," Chee said, carefully keeping the small bit of hope from his voice.

Puzzled, but willing, Old Man Fat helped carry the other pack to the shelter, opening it to find more corn as well as carrots and round pale yellow onions. Chee went back for the roll behind the buckskin's saddle and carried it to the entrance of the shelter where he cut the ropes and gave the canvas a nudge with his toe. Tins of coffee rolled out, small plump cloth bags; jerked meat from several butcherings spilled from a flour sack, and bright red chilis splashed like flames against the dust.

"I will leave all this anyhow," Chee told them. "I would not want my daughter nor even you old people to go hungry."

Old Man Fat picked up a shiny tin of coffee, then put it down. With trembling hands he began to untie one of the cloth bags—dried sweet peaches.

The Little One had wriggled from her grandmother's lap, unheeded, and was on her knees, digging her hands into the jerked meat.

"There is almost enough food here to last all winter," Old Man Fat's Wife sought the eyes of her husband.

Chee said, "I meant it to be enough. But that was when I thought you might send the Little One back with me." He looked down at his daughter noisily sucking jerky. Her mouth, both fists were full of it. "I am sorry that you feel you cannot bear to part with her."

Old Man Fat's Wife brushed a straggly wisp of gray hair from her forehead as she turned to look at the Little One. Old Man Fat was looking too. And it was not a thing to see. For in that moment the Little One ceased to be their daughter's daughter and became just another mouth to feed.

"And why not?" the old woman asked wearily.

Chee was settled in the saddle, the barefooted Little One before him. He urged the buckskin faster, and his daughter clutched his shirtfront. The purpling mesas fling back the echo: "...My corn embrace each other. In the middle of the wide field...Yellow Corn Boy embrace each other."

As a student, Navaho Emerson Blackhorse Mitchell was fortunate to have T. D. Allen, a white teacher at the Institute of American Indian Arts in Santa Fe, as mentor and friend. Guiding the developing boy, Don Allen allowed him that freedom that would prompt Mitchell to dedicate his book, Miracle Hill, the Story of a Navajo Boy, *"To the memory of Don Allen, who said, 'Make them smell, taste, feel, and hear the story.'" The following excerpt is the last chapter of this lyrical work.*

Miracle Hill

Emerson Blackhorse Mitchell

Broneco, still lying in bed early in the morning, begin to smile. Then he sat up in bed. Feeling weightless, he felt his chest, astonished, sensing that something has happen during the night. He looked at himself in the mirror and saw that his hair was more darker than he thought he had seemed the day before.

"I can't believe it. I just can't believe it," he thought, feeling his hair. Ghastly the room looked.

Looking out the window made a lot of difference. Broneco's eyes twinkled, blinking his eyes to clear the blurs, he listen to all kinds of sounds out there beyond the many rolling hills. The air smelled in the odor of freshness and of the cold rain that night. Hearing the ripples of the dripping rain water falling every seconds, dripping down from the roof. Broneco's mind was clear. He felt his head. It was cold.

The wind was blowing softly and gentle. The water forming between the window screen stopped. Broneco listened to the tiny drops of rain water falling outside. It made an unusual musical sound. Could hear the rooster flapping its wing, hens pecking insects, and pulling worms out of the moist area in the yard. Broneco looked at the dresser top and saw the papers scattered about in the room. The picture of Grandmother on the dresser look as though she was going to smile.

Broneco, still blinking his eyes, wondered about his Grandmother. All the things she used to talk about once—a better improvements on the old house, a separate rooms for each, and a new dining room with a large living room window.

These things ringed through Broneco's ears. Secondly, remembering Grandmother used to ride her gray donkey. The days were wonderful then. Those days were long in past for Broneco, herding sheep for a whole day, having all kinds of joyful games. He recalled his forgotten history of the past.

He looked out the window, staring far in the great distance. The mountains were hidden underneath the misty fogs. The sounding of the thunder. The flashing of the lightning, striking about the mountains. It looked as if somewhere in a swampy country. The fog covered the mountain tops.

Feeling much secure of rest, Broneco got out of bed and stretch his arms high into the empty atmosphere of the room, almost touching the ceiling above him. Then decided to pick up the scattered materials of papers which were all blown on the floor. He walked around in the room. After finishing and replacing items neatly back in its order properly, Broneco pick the picture off the dresser and held it close to his chest.

The cool blowing air made the curtains twisting and drifting gently. The sun was now peering over the East Mesa. Broneco placed the picture back upon the dresser and opened the door.

Without making any sort of a sound, he creep out. Standing out in the front of the main kitchen door, Broneco faced east. Walking farther away from the house he stood there. Reaching into his pocket he drew out a small bag. Untying it, he held it steady in his hand.

Waiting in that tedious hour for the wind to calm and stillness, he drew his small finger into the bag. There, a grains of yellowish, golden corn pollen he held to the East. Broneco stood facing the bright rays of the morning sun, sensed that the air was still now.

Looking among the heavy thick clouds gradually opening into the blue heaven of the universe, Broneco stared at the opening of the dark clouds as though expecting an object to appear before him in the opening. His eyes begin to glow in chills of tears. Broneco choked in whispers of speech:

Wondering of the yonder distance,
Thinking, When will I reach there?

The wind whispers in my ear,
I hear the songs of old ones.

My loneliness I wrap around me,
It is my striped blanket.

Sending out touching wishes,
To the world beyond hands' reach.

The bluebird that flies above,
Leads me to my friend, the white man.

At last, I know the all of me —
Out there, beyond, and here upon my hill.

"I'll come again, Miracle Hill," said Broneco as the pollen at the tip of his small finger descends.

Broneco turned clock-wisely, walked back to the entrance, then into the kitchen, passing on to the bedroom of his own.

Annie and Auntie were still giving off their soft buzzing snores.

Broneco opened the door to the south. Standing under the porch, he faced the hill in fear and expecting a miracle.

The glorifying hill was now covered with green grass. The gray-sided hill no longer showed. Broneco, winking his eyes, stared at the hill. He couldn't believe it. Looking toward the corral now, he could hear the different bells jingling and tinkling on the neck of the sheep.

Shaking themselves, the sprinkle of rain water dropped. The dogs sat before the gateway to the corral as though they were smiling.

Broneco walked through the puddles of water, then right on, passing the water. The permeating fruit odor on the yucca plant where were now ripen, as Broneco can see since they were falling off and the smell of it. Walking through the small garden bed, the morning glory on the side of the wall. They also, were showing their respective colors of variations in blue, pink, and white.

Broneco could smell the sweetness of the circulating odor in the air. The wild flowers Annie used to water were blooming at last. Glancing here and there, it was amazing. Broneco, strolling about the house, kept seeing different things.

The sagebrush, neatly trimmed, has overgrown again, but this time it was showing its frisky seed pods in rough formation in groups. Interesting it looked as Broneco walked through the growing flowers and others blooming in decorative shades.

The sun was now high in the sky. Broneco looked to the south again. "I'll never forget my first white friend," he thought. "If Dale was still here in this community, I would shake his hands and thank him for what he once tried to teach me, sitting under the tree with him. But, those days are over. Now I must use white man's method to explore their dignity."

Just then, Broneco saw his cat, Moon, upon the heated side of the roof, all curl up. Moon was wet, as Broneco can see, since his soft furs was still shining in the sunlight, bristling.

"Moon, will you come down? Who do you think you are, sitting upon the roof?"

"A cat on the hot tin roof," said Annie, teasing her brother from the kitchen window as she was lighting up the stove.

Broneco furiously turned his head toward the roof, facing Moon who was now licking his paw, pointing south toward the hill. Broneco, for a moment, thought Moon was speaking.

"What did you say?" asked Broneco in fear.

"No, it was me, Broneco," said Annie from the kitchen window.

Broneco didn't smile, instead ignore Annie. Now she was fixing herself a breakfast, including Broneco's and her mother. The near tree in heavy coated leaves kept waving. Resting under the shade of the tree, Broneco stared at the hill.

The voice of the wind upon the hill seems to whisper. "Come, Little One, for you may find your happiness here upon me, the miracle hill. For I am the mother earth who rules nature. Come."

Then Broneco remembered, "I must tell my Aunt and Annie about the dream I had last night before I forget." He went rushing into the kitchen.

Annie's mother was pouring herself a cup of fresh coffee. Broneco seated himself besides his aunt. Annie placed the prepared breakfast on the table and also seated herself besides Broneco.

Broneco pulled the shades aside and, glancing out, kept looking at the hill.

"I see the hill is covered with verdant green," Annie's mother said. "Water still rushing in the rivulet stream down the hill, yet they are slowing their speed. Out there beyond, I also see the land with fertile soil," she said. Then, turning around again, poured another cup of coffee.

"I got something to tell you this morning," said Broneco.

"What is it?" asked Auntie, anxiously to know.

"It's about the dream I had last night."

"What about the dream—bad, good, or bad?"

"It was a good dream."

"Then tell us about your wonderful dream," she said.

"I dreamed that I was walking toward the hill. Then I was upon the hill. I met a stranger. Facing away from me, he stood."

"Said anything at all?" Auntie asked.

"He didn't say anything. Just when he was turning around to face me, the dropping of the rain water from the window splashed on my face and wake me up. I didn't see who, or what he looked like," said Broneco, finishing his dream story.

Annie didn't say anything about the hill. She only went on eating her morning breakfast.

"Yes, it's a miracle, since everythings this morning seems to be different," said Auntie.

"You ought to look around out in the yard this morning. It look just beautiful and every flower that Annie watered for the last six week in this drying desert country are sprouting and blooming. Especially the morning glory on the side of the house," said Broneco.

Attached to their deep conversation, Broneco didn't know it was getting late for the sheep to graze out in the open country as usual. When he remembered, he went out to the corral and opened the gate.

Walking through the corral, the sheep moved out into the open freedom. They scattered on the side of the sandy hills. As hungry as they are, they eat to their mouthful of greens to satisfy their appetite. They nibbled on the small gray greasewoods.

Broneco walked back to the house. Entering the gate, he looked at the hill again.

While out in the yard, Annie and her mother were picking off the fruit from the yucca plant. Carefully they picked the fruit off, making sure that the pointed needle will not puncture their hands.

Broneco crossed the small wooden bridge. The clear water in the dammed area glimmered during each blow of the air. The tree kept waving its heavy leafs. Moon was now climbing up the tree, using his sharp claws.

Broneco went back into the house. Entering his room, he picked up his summer shoes and a white shirt together with dark-colored slack. He changed his clothes in the room and combed his hair neatly.

"I'm going to the hill and sniff the great-spirit air," he thought. Taking up more of his time, he fixed his dark blue tie and walked into the bedroom. Glancing on the chest drawer, he decided to close the drawer. He saw his grandfather's picture in the unfolded photo album. Broneco held it in his hand and smiled.

"I'm going to the hill where once you told me that I will find cheerfulness there on the hill. I remember the cheerfulness you talked of. I remember," he said, placing the picture back in the chest drawer, then closing it afterward.

Standing under the porch, giving a little stretch and a deep breath of fresh air, he walked across the small wooden bridge. Reaching the post, Broneco lean on it.

Standing there, Broneco begin to think of his youthful days again. The land was wide then, now the days for Broneco were short. For many ways, Broneco wanted to spend his time at home with his family. Now, was it the time to stay with the family?

Thinking back in the month of December, during the winter of nineteen hundred and sixty-three, Broneco recalled the day he stood before his grandmother, for the last time, speaking to her. It brought deep sorrows which formed tears in Broneco's eyes. Blinking his eyes, the drop of tears dried within his eyes.

Watching the corral over the south side of the hill, Broneco could smell the drying scent of odor in the corral and its surrounding.

Sniffing and wrinkling his nose, he glance about the area, searching with his eyes.

Broneco kept recalling the past and its history. "The world out there and beyond the hands' reach..." Broneco thought about it again.

These objects in the distance used to make Broneco wondered. The yonder hill made Broneco think more and more about the civilization where there was cheerfulness, where there was lot of interesting things—the city, the school, the piano, the writing on his manuelscripts. Broneco held onto the post quietly.

The post was cold from the night's rain. Still covered with twinkling bubbles of water. Feeling the post, Broneco could feel the texture of morning dews. Along the side of the twenty-gallon barrel, there were moss of green color, the water dripping down into the pan below. Then Broneco look over to the horse corral where Grandmother's donkey used to scratch himself against the rusty post.

Broneco could still picture the sacrificed gray donkey during the death of his Grandmother. The stable still full of dry hay made Broneco lonely.

Ever since the gate was close, only the big glossy dark blue rooster flies upon the gate when the light begin to show. There he would flutter his wing and cock early in the morning, but this morning he didn't cock because of the heavy rain that night.

Broneco smiled a little when he saw the rooster walking across the open area in the yard. He looked weary, stretching his wing high, trying to flutter the dews of his wet wing.

The bells on the few sheep kept jingling within the gray greasewoods. The dogs wrestling among the moisted sandy hill, crawling and barking. Broneco glanced back to the hill.

The wind was quiet, except once in awhile, the cool blowing air blew wildly. The sun was now high up in the blue heaven. Far to the west, the clouds started moving toward the north. They looked as though a giant sheep grazing in the meadow, nibbling on prairie grass, moving slowly to another grazing country. Broneco's eyes dimmed, looking about.

Along the side of the fence, the tumbleweeds stack—the most enemy of many human beings who lives on the prairie—pointing their needles outward, turning their gray long-stretching arms into the greenish shades. Then, hearing the birds tweeting in the trees, seems to brighten up the day. Broneco grinned and faced the trees, wondering what kind of birds were up in the tree, singing their harmonized music that he never heard before. He like the sound of the birds singing in the treetops.

Just then, Annie and Auntie came around the corner of the house on the east side. In their hands, carrying shovel. Digging fresh dirt onto a new position to hold the rain water for a longer lasting to keep the trees soaked with plenty of water for at least a few more days. Making a new dam, they worked together.

Broneco still holding the cold post, feeling the texture of the post again, gently rubbing it with his fingers. His cat, Moon, came across the wooden bridge, welcoming him. Rolling himself at the edge of Broneco's feet, he played.

"Go play with Annie, Moon." said Broneco, speaking to his cat.

But Moon didn't listen to Broneco. He went rolling himself, scratching Broneco's feet.

Broneco looked to where once the family sat together, eating early in the morning, talking together. What he sees there is only the wash away fireplace. Farther he looked into the distance. He saw the two rolling hills, and the wide wash area. Now he remembered once racing along the side of that particular wash. Riding his horse, Pinto, which he owned once. Broneco picture himself receiving the necklace on his Grandmother's birthday.

Then, recalling the day he first killed a gray fox, when he used to carry his bow which he no longer carry in the year of nineteen hundred and sixty-four. He rested his head against the post. Thinking of the past wasn't a happy feeling. Those days were wonderful, but those days happened in the past. The time was now nine-thirty. The sun was high off from the East Mesa.

Broneco shutted his eyes, listen to the sounds around the house. The sounds became present from the past, but it made no difference. It was present. Barking of the dogs far over the hills kept reminding him of the day he was getting ready to go to school. He had almost forgotten his mother, Emma, since he never seen her for a long time now. He kept thinking about all the things that happened in the past. He felt tears and sorrow inside his heart.

But then he thought, "Why should I think of the past which exist no more?" He straighten up. "This should be the day I feel stronger and happy about all the things that had renewed by the heavy rain last night. I should be happy and thankful for the rain. It brought the nature's cheerfulness to all the plain that was starving from the hunger for thirst. Even the surrounding things are cheering up, full of pride. Then, why shouldn't I be happy?"

Broneco lifted his head and looked toward the hill—the hill in the distance as if someone was going to appear at the top. He stared away from the hill, still holding onto the cold post. He whispered, "It's been a long time since I've seen Johnnie. I wish I could see him again, just to greet him with the word of welcome. I wondered whereabouts is he."

Broneco squeeze his hands together against the roughness of the post. Now his mind seems to clear.

"The dream last night. I wonder if it's true?" he asked himself several times. "I wonder if it is someone living or is he just another dream spirit," thought again Broneco, standing straight and looking at the hill.

Annie and Auntie were now worried about Broneco been standing out there for the whole hour. Annie and Auntie went back inside the house and sat by the window, waiting for Broneco to come inside the house.

Auntie decided to go outside to see if anything was wrong with Broneco, so she did. "Come, my child, come inside the house and have a cup of coffee. Might feel better then," she said.

Broneco reached for his aunt's hand and said, "One minute."

"Is there something wrong?" she asked curiously.

"No, Auntie, I was just thinking."

"Thinking?"

"Yes," said Broneco.

Then she smiles and crossed the small wooden bridge. Quietly close the door behind her and entered the kitchen.

Broneco waited. Sometimes he had a strange attitude and difficult to understand. Again, he was strange, but he seems to smile. He would never show a single otherwise.

Waiting another few minutes, Broneco wondered why he was known as a "mystery boy," and the other, "the unknown boy," then there was another one by the name of "Little One."

Recalling his given name from distance relatives, Broneco almost giggled. Even in the heart of civilize American people, he played joke with other people. He did play his part of being a mystery boy to his people, yet his white friend were too smart to play with.

He started to walk, passing the garden, leaving his tracks in the moist wet earth. Walking a little ways, he stopped and reached down to the ground and dipped the fertile soil into the palm of his hand. Cupping a handful of soil, he kept rubbing it together, feeling the moisture of the dirt.

He looked toward the hill and walked on in a shuffle, shifting the dirt in his hand. Engaged to the hill, his memories kept recollecting in dreams of flowing fog mist. Picturing the forgotten history, again the distance remind him of the day he sat with his grandfather, many years ago. When Broneco was five, he used to think that the world was small. He remembered since he was four.

Slowly he walked, approaching the first rising hill. He stopped to caught his breath. Stepping on, he stroll, crossing the second low flat stretching hill, he begin to fear and, startled, glancing at the hill.

Come to the third rolling hill. Broneco's frightening fear deformed in his nerve. Although the chills of fever left his body, he kept refusing to reach his fourth hill. Squeezing the displaced tangled fingers against the other, his nerves were now alert and aware. Forgetting about the existing world and the gifts it contained, Broneco was now whispering the word, "Miracle Hill."

He stood at the foot of the high slanting hill. The fear was now gone. Again, the wind began to whisper through the stunted and rusty arid brush. Whishing of the cool summer air blew upon Broneco, waked him out of his numbness into a pleasant alertness. He glanced beyond.

There, the stranger stood, faced away from Broneco!

Broneco, thinking it must be the blurrness, doubted the object. He rubbed, blinked, and winked his eyes. The object was still there.

Broneco, curiously, glanced to the left of him, remembering the magic tea growing there once. It was an unbelievable sight, the tea was there. Showing its glorifying tiny yellow berries in the form of bells, struck immediate attention in Broneco's eyes on the side of the hill. Waving in the stiff formation, it vibrated in silent still.

Broneco tried to speak, but the word couldn't come out. The stranger seems to smile as Broneco bowed his head down, looking at his feet, thinking, "What in the world is happening to me? Am I fainting to die?" He whisper the words clearly, at last.

"No, brother, it's me," he heard.

"For heaven sake! God of All Mighty, help me," said Broneco, thinking he was dying as the earth bounds to whirl in a spin. He thought this was the end of his life.

He glanced toward the house and saw that, in the north, the clouds of fog like cotton still remain. The rainbow showing its four different colors in red, blue, yellow, and dark purple. Though it was far in the great distance, the rainbow seems to be nearer. Then sees the sheep, grazing along the sandy hill, nibbling on the green prairie grass. The grass waving and glimmering, as Broneco never before has seen the old place looked so in tiding of green.

Broneco bited his lip and faced the stranger again. He looked straight at the stranger's face and spoke. "Is this the end of my days?"

The stranger only smiled as of before, and then answered, "No, it is only the beginning."

And then the stranger was the great rock, standing in the far distance among the dark southwestern mountain about fourteen miles away. Showing its terrifying sight, it stood high and great.

Although it stood far away in the great distance, it looked as though it was nearby, just behind the horizontal hill. In the foggy white mist, it showed its unforgettable memories, since Broneco's time of birth. It looked like a ship caught in a waving sea of rolling tide, during a heavy hurricane storm for an endless hours.

Broneco, blinking his eyes, watched the great standing rock, remembering again of his youthful days. "I used to think of that distance standing rock when I was young and away from the civilization. I guess I was still untame, living among the nature's gift and half wild yet."

When he was five and a months old, he used to think and wonder of the far standing rock in the shade of heavy ash color, intercepting the clear horizontal prairie. Isolated and alone it stood, yet known to all its surrounding. "Yes, I was young then," he thought.

He transposed his eye vision into a distance where he couldn't see no farther. Going beyond this point, Broneco, curious of his yonder mountain, then thought, "If I ever reach that far mountain, there will be another mountain."

Now, on this hill, Broneco knew that he must be going on to explored something more valuable than the first. Coming to the top of this small ordinary gray and sun-baking arid desert hill of his traditional life, Broneco was now amazed. It was there—another mountain.

"At last, I know a little, I have accomplished, and achieve the knowledge and wisdom of my distance friends. Ever I shall use their tongue to understand and to communicate, exchange gifts, for their tongue is the barrier of destruction to my people. Now, I have learn their signs and ways of living, I can see another mountain."

Now, Broneco turned, leaving his footprints on the Miracle Hill. The wind blew for once again, blowing, singing the ancient songs.

The birds in the near treetop of the yard sang their best melody of music. Broneco left the hill thinking, "It's been a lonely years. Miracle Hill, in the glory of hope, I thank thee. I will always return and share the nature's airy freedom upon you."

Leaving the hill behind in a far distance, showing its merry sight. No longer after, Broneco ever would be lonely. Till this present day, the wind still whispers, singing the songs of the old ones. This is the Miracle Hill, and Broneco walks on, learning about the world beyond hands' reach.

With the exception of Vine Deloria, Jr., N. Scott Momaday is the most widely published and read Native American author in the United States. His Kiowa-Cherokee parentage, his Ph.D. from Stanford University, his professorial position at the Santa Barbara campus of the University of California—all combine to make him sensitive to the Indian mind, the white mind, and the language that he uses to reach both. In The Way to Rainy Mountain, *published in 1969, Momaday recalls the legends of his people and his own boyhood, weaving them together like some ritual chant of a bygone day.* House Made of Dawn, *from which this excerpt comes, received the Pulitzer Prize in 1969. Deloria assaults the intellect frontally; Momaday persuades the conscience to assault its owner. Each is remarkably effective.*

Flight on the Wind

N. Scott Momaday

He had seen a strange thing, an eagle overhead with its talons closed upon a snake. It was an awful, holy sight, full of magic and meaning.

The Eagle Watchers Society was the sixth to go into the kiva at the summer and autumn rain retreats. It was an important society, and it stood apart from the others in a certain way. This difference—this superiority—had come about a long time ago. Before the middle of the last century there was received into the population of the town a small group of immigrants from the Tanoan city of Bahkyula, a distance of seventy or eighty miles to the east. These immigrants were a wretched people, for they had experienced great suffering. Their land bordered upon the Southern Plains, and for many years they had been an easy mark for marauding bands of buffalo hunters and thieves. They had endured every kind of persecution until one day they could stand no more and their spirit broke. They gave themselves up to despair and were then at the mercy of the first alien wind. But it was not a human enemy that overcame them at last; it was a plague. They were struck down by so deadly a disease that, when the epidemic abated, there were fewer than twenty survivors in all. And this remainder, too, should surely have perished among the ruins of Bahkyula had it not been for these *patrones*, these distant relatives who took them in at the certain risk of their own lives and the lives of their children and grandchildren. It is said that the cacique himself went out to welcome and escort the visitors in. The people of the town must have looked narrowly at those stricken souls who walked slowly towards them, wild in their eyes with grief and desperation. The Bahkyush immigrants brought with them little more than the clothes on their backs, but even in this moment of deep hurt and humiliation, they thought of themselves as a people. They carried three things that should serve thereafter to signal who they were: a sacred flute; the bull mask of Pecos; and the little wooden statue of their patroness *Maria de los Angeles*, whom they called Porcingula. Now, after the intervening years and generations, the ancient blood of this forgotten tribe still ran in the veins of men.

The Eagle Watchers Society was the principal ceremonial organization of the Bahkyush. Its chief, Patiestewa, and all its members were direct descendants of those old men and women who had made that journey along the edge of oblivion. There was a look about these men, even now. It was as if, conscious of having come so close to extinction, they had got a keener sense of humility than their benefactors, and paradoxically a greater sense of pride. Both attributes could be seen in such a man as old Patiestewa. He was hard, and he appeared to have seen more of life than had other men. In their uttermost peril long ago, the Bahkyush had been fashioned into seers and soothsayers. They had acquired a tragic sense, which gave to them as a race so much dignity and bearing. They were medicine men; they were rainmakers and eagle hunters.

He was not thinking of the eagles. He had been walking since daybreak down from the mountain where that year he had broken a horse for the rancher John Raymond. By the middle of the morning he was on the rim of the Valle Grande, a great volcanic crater that lay high up on the western slope of the range. It was the right eye of the earth, held open to the sun. Of all the places that he knew, this valley alone could reflect the great spatial majesty of the sky. It was scooped out of the dark peaks like the well of a great, gathering storm, deep umber and blue and smoke-colored. The view across the diameter was magnificent; it was an unbelievably great expanse. As many times as he had been there in the past, each first new sight of it always brought him up short, and he had to catch his breath. Just there, it seemed, a strange and brilliant light lay upon the world, and all the objects in the landscape were washed clean and set away in the distance. In the morning sunlight the Valle Grande was dappled with the shadows of clouds and vibrant with rolling winter grass. The clouds were always there, huge, sharply described, and shining in the pure air. But the great feature of the valley was its size. It was too great for the eye to hold, strangely beautiful and full of distance. Such vastness makes for illusion, a kind of illusion that comprehends reality, and where it exists there is always wonder and exhilaration. He looked at the facets of a boulder that lay balanced on the edge of the land, and the first thing beyond, the vague, misty field out of which it stood, was the floor of the valley itself, pale and blue-green, miles away. He shifted the focus of his gaze, and he could just make out the clusters of dots that were cattle grazing along the river in the faraway plain.

Then he saw the eagles across the distance, two of them, riding low in the depths and rising diagonally towards him. He did not know what they were at first, and he stood watching them, their far, silent flight erratic and wild in the bright morning. They rose and swung across the skyline, veering close at last, and he knelt down behind the rock, dumb with pleasure and excitement, holding on to them with his eyes.

They were golden eagles, a male and a female, in their mating flight. They were cavorting, spinning and spiralling on the cold, clear columns of air, and they were beautiful. They swooped and hovered, leaning on the air, and swung close together, feinting and screaming with delight. The female was full-grown, and the span of her broad wings was greater than any man's height. There was a fine flourish to her motion: she was deceptively, incredibly fast, and her pivots and wheels were wide and full-blown. But her great weight was streamlined, perfectly controlled. She carried a rattlesnake; it hung shining from her feet, limp and curving out in the trail of her flight. Suddenly her wings and tail fanned, catching full on the wind, and for an instant she was still, widespread and spectral in the blue, while her mate flared past and away, turning round in the distance to look for her. Then she began to beat upward at an angle from the rim until she was small in the sky, and she let go of the snake. It fell, slowly, writhing and rolling, floating out like a bit of silver thread against the wide backdrop of the land. She held still above, buoyed up on the cold current, her crop and hackles gleaming like copper in the sun. The male swerved and sailed. He was younger than she and a little more than half as large. He was quicker, tighter in his moves. He let the carrion drift by; then suddenly he gathered himself and stooped, sliding down in a blur of motion to the strike. He hit the snake in the head, with not the slightest deflection of his course or speed, cracking its long body like a whip. Then he rolled and swung upward in a great pendulum arc, riding out his momentum. At the top of his glide he let go of the snake in turn, but the female did not go for it. Instead she soared out over the plain, nearly out of sight, like a mote receding into the haze of the far mountain. The male followed, and he watched them go, straining to see, saw them veer once, dip and disappear.

Now there was the business of the society. It was getting on towards the end of November, and the eagle hunters were getting ready to set forth to the mountains. He brooded for a time, full of a strange longing; then one day he went to old Patiestewa and told him of what he had seen. "I think you had better let me go," he said. The old chief closed his eyes and thought about it for a long time. Then he answered: "Yes, I had better let you go."

The next day the Bahkyush eagle watchers started out on foot, he among them, northward through the canyon and into the high timber beyond. They were gone for days, holding up here and there at the holy places where they must pray and make their offerings. Early in the morning they came out of the trees on the edge of the Valle Grande. The land fell and reached away in the early light as far as the eye could see, the hills folding together and the gray grass rolling in the plain, and they began the descent. At midmorning they came to the lower meadows in the basin. It was clear and cold, and the air was thin and sharp like a shard of glass. They needed bait, and they circled out and apart, forming a ring. When the circle was formed, they converged slowly towards the center, clapping and calling out in a high, flat voice that carried only a little way. And as they closed, rabbits began to jump up from the grass and bound. They got away at first, many of them, while the men were still a distance apart, but gradually the ring grew small and the rabbits crept to the center and hid away in the brush. Now and then one of them tried to break away, and the nearest man threw his stick after it. These weapons were small curved clubs, and they were thrown with deadly accuracy by the eagle hunters, so that when the ring was of a certain size and the men only a few feet apart, very few of the animals got away.

He bent close to the ground, his arm cocked and shaking with tension. A great jackrabbit buck bounded from the grass, straight past him. It struck the ground beyond and sprang again, nearly thirty feet through the air. He spun round and hurled the stick. It struck the jackrabbit a glancing blow just as it bounded again, and it slumped in the air and fell heavily to the ground.

The clapping and calling had stopped. He could feel his heart beating and the sweat growing cold on his skin. There was something like remorse or disappointment now that the rabbits were still and strewn about on the ground. He picked one of the dead animals from the brush—it was warm and soft, its eyes shining like porcelain, full of the dull lustre of death—then the great buck, which was not dead but only stunned and frozen with fear. He felt the warm living weight of it in his hands; it was brittle with life, taut with hard, sinewy strength.

When he had bound the bait together and placed it in the sack, he gathered bunches of tall grass and cut a number of evergreen boughs from a thicket in the plain; these he tied in a bundle and carried in a sling on his back. He went to the river and washed his head in order to purify himself. When all was ready, he waved to the others and started off alone to the cliffs. When he came to the first plateau he rested and looked across the valley. The sun was high, and all around there was a pale, dry uniformity of light, a winter glare on the clouds and peaks. He could see a crow circling low in the distance. Higher on the land, where a great slab of white rock protruded from the mountain, he saw the eagle-hunt house; he headed for it. The house was a small tower of stone, built round a pit, hollow and open at the top. Near it was a shrine, a stone shelf in which there was a slight depression. There he placed a prayer offering. He got into the house, and with boughs he made a latticework of beams across the top and covered it with grass. When it was finished there was a small opening at the center. Through it he raised the rabbits and laid them down on the boughs. He could see here and there through the screen, but his line of vision was vertical, or nearly so, and his quarry would come from the sun. He began to sing, now and then calling out, low in his throat.

      The eagles soared southward, high above the Valle Grande. They were almost too high to be seen. From their vantage point the land below reached away on either side to the long, crooked tributaries of the range; down the great open corridor to the south were the wooded slopes and the canyon, the desert and the far end of the earth bending on the sky. They caught sight of the rabbits and were deflected. They veered and banked, lowering themselves into the crater, gathering speed. By the time he knew of their presence, they were low and coming fast on either side of the pit, swooping with blinding speed. The male caught hold of the air and fell off, touching upon the face of the cliff in order to flush the rabbits, while the female hurtled in to take her prey on the run. Nothing happened; the rabbits did not move. She overshot the trap and screamed. She was enraged and she hurled herself around in the air. She swung back with a great clamor of her wings and fell with fury on the bait. He saw her in the instant she struck. Her foot flashed out and one of her talons laid the jackrabbit open the length of its body. It stiffened and jerked, and her other foot took hold of its skull and crushed it. In that split second when the center of her weight touched down upon the trap he reached for her. His hands closed upon her legs and he drew her down with all of his strength. For one instant only did she recoil, splashing her great wings down upon the beams and boughs—and she very nearly broke from his grasp; but then she was down in the darkness of the well, hooded, and she was still.

      At dusk he met with the other hunters in the plain. San Juanito, too, had got an eagle, but it was an aged male and poor by comparison. They gathered round the old eagle and spoke to it, bidding it return with their good will and sorrow to the eagles of the crags. They fixed a prayer plume to its leg and let it go. He watched it back away and crouch on the ground, glaring, full of fear and suspicion. Then it took leave of the ground and beat upward, clattering through the still shadows of the valley. It gathered speed, driving higher and higher until it reached the shafts of reddish-gold final light that lay like bars across the crater. The light caught it up and set a dark blaze upon it. It levelled off and sailed. Then it was gone from sight, but he looked after it for a time. He could see it still in the mind's eye and hear in his memory the awful whisper of its flight on the wind. He felt the great weight of the bird which he held in the sack. The dusk was fading quickly into night, and the others could not see that his eyes were filled with tears.

That night, while the others ate by the fire, he stole away to look at the great bird. He drew the sack open; the bird shivered, he thought, and drew itself up. Bound and helpless, his eagle seemed drab and shapeless in the moonlight, too large and ungainly for flight. The sight of it filled him with shame and disgust. He took hold of its throat in the darkness and cut off its breath

Half Creek, half Mexican, Durango Mendoza is a native of Oklahoma. As a student at the University of Missouri, he won the Mahan Fiction Contest with "Summer Water and Shirley." Death is seldom treated this sensitively in any literature.

Summer Water and Shirley

Durango Mendoza

It was in the summer that had burned every stalk of corn and every blade of grass and dried up the creek until it only flowed in trickles across the ford below the house where in the pools the boy could scoop up fish in a dishpan.

The boy lived with his mother and his sister, Shirley, and the three smaller children eleven miles from Weleetka, and near Lthwathlee Indian church where it was Eighth Sunday meeting and everyone was there. The boy and his family stayed at the camp house of his dead father's people.

Shirley and her brother, who was two years older and twelve, had just escaped the deacon and were lying on the brown, sun-scorched grass behind the last camp house. They were out of breath and giggled as they peeped above the slope and saw the figure of the deacon, Hardy Eagle, walking toward the church house.

"Boy, we sure out-fooled him, huh?" Shirley laughed lightly and jabbed her elbow in her brother's shaking side. "Whew!" She ran her slim hand over her eyes and squinted at the sky. They both lay back and watched the cloudless sky until the heat in their blood went down and their breath slowed to normal. They lay there on the hot grass until the sun became too much for them.

"Hey, let's go down to the branch and find a pool to wade in, okay?" She had rolled over suddenly and spoke directly into the boy's ear.

"I don't think we better. Mama said to stay around the church grounds."

"Aw, you're just afraid."

"No, it's just that—"

"'Mama said to stay around the church grounds!' Fraidy-cat, I'll go by myself then." She sat up and looked at him. He didn't move and she sighed. Then she nudged him. "Hey." She nudged him again and assumed a stage whisper. "Looky there! See that old man coming out of the woods?"

The boy looked and saw the old man shuffling slowly through the high johnson grass between the woods and the clearing for the church grounds. He was very old and still wore his hair in the old way.

"Who is he?" Shirley whispered. "Who is he?"

"I can't tell yet. The heat makes everything blurry." The boy was looking intently at the old man who was moving slowly in the weltering heat through the swaying grass that moved with the sound of light tinsel in the dry wind.

"Let's go sneak through the grass and scare him," Shirley suggested. "I bet that'd make him even run." She moved her arms as if she were galloping and broke down into giggles. "Come on," she said, getting to one knee.

"Wait!" He pulled her back.

"What do you mean, 'wait'? He'll be out of the grass pretty soon and we won't—" She broke off. "What's the matter? What're you doing?"

The boy had started to crawl away on his hands and knees and was motioning for her to follow. "Come on, Shirley," he whispered. "That's old Ansul Middlecreek!"

"Who's *he?*"

"Don't you remember? Mama said he's the one that killed Haskell Day—with witchcraft. He's a *stiginnee!*"

"A *stiginnee?* Aw, you don't believe that, do you? Mama says you can tell them by the way they never have to go to the toilet, and that's where he's been. Look down there." She pointed to the little unpainted house that stood among the trees.

"I don't care *where* he's been! Come on, Shirley! Look! Oh my gosh! He saw you pointing!"

"I'm coming," she said and followed him quickly around the corner of the camp house.

They sat on the porch. Almost everyone was in for the afternoon service and they felt alone. The wind was hot and it blew from the southwest. It blew past them across the dry fields of yellow weeds that spread before them up to the low hills that wavered in the heat and distance. They could smell the dry harshness of the grass and they felt the porch boards hot underneath them. Shirley bent over and wiped her face with the skirt of her dress.

"Come on," she said. "Let's go down to the creek branch before that deacon comes back." She pulled at his sleeve and they stood up.

"Okay," he said and they skirted the outer camp houses and followed the dusty road to the bridge, stepping from tuft to tuft of scorched grass.

Toward evening and suppertime they climbed out of the dry bed of the branch, over the huge boulders to the road and started for the camp grounds. The sun was in their eyes as they trudged up the steep road from the bridge. They had found no water in the branch so they had gone on down to the creek. For the most part it too was dry.

Suddenly they saw a shadow move into the dust before them. They looked up and saw old Ansul Middlecreek shuffling toward them. His cracked shoes raised little clouds of dust that rose around his ankles and made whispering sounds as he moved along.

"Don't look when you go by," the boy whispered intently, and he pushed her behind him. But as they passed by Shirley looked up.

"Hey, Ansul Middlecreek," she said cheerfully. "*Henkschay!*" Then with a swish of her skirt she grabbed her brother and they ran. The old man stopped and the puffs of dust around his feet moved ahead as he grumbled, his face still in shadow because he did not turn around. The two didn't stop until they had reached the first gate. Then they slowed down and the boy scolded his sister all the way to their camp. And all through supper he looked at the dark opening of the door and then at Shirley who sat beside him, helping herself with childish appetite to the heavy, greasy food that was set before her.

"You better eat some," she told her brother. "Next meetin's not 'til next month."

Soon after they had left the table she began to complain that her head hurt and their mother got them ready to go home. They took the two little girls and the baby boy from where they were playing under the arbor and cleaned them up before they started out. Their uncle, George Hulegy, would go with them and carry the biggest girl. The mother carried the other one while the boy struggled in the rear with the baby. Shirley followed morosely behind them all as they started down the road that lay white and pale under the rising moon.

She began to fall further behind and shuffled her bare feet into the warm underlayer of dust. The boy gave to his uncle the sleeping child he carried and took Shirley by the hand, surprised that it was so hot and limp.

"Come on, Shirley, come on. Mama, Shirley's got a fever. Don't walk so fast—we can't keep up. Come on, Shirley," he coaxed. "Hurry."

They turned into their lane and followed it until they were on the little hill above the last stretch of road and started down its rocky slope to the sandy road below. Ahead, the house sat wanly under the stars, and Rey, the dog, came out to greet them, sniffing and wriggling his black body and tail.

George Hulegy and the mother were already on the porch as the boy led his sister into the yard. As they reached the porch they saw the lamp begin to glow orange in the window. Then Shirley took hold of the boy's arm and pointed weakly toward the back yard and the form of the storehouse.

"Look, Sonny! Over there, by the storehouse." The boy froze with fear but he saw nothing. "They were three little men," she said vaguely and then she collapsed.

"Mama!" But as he screamed he saw a great yellow dog with large brown spots jump off the other end of the porch with a click of it heavy nails and disappear into the shadows that led to the creek. The boy could hear the brush rustle and a few pebbles scatter as it went. Rey only whined uneasily and did not even look to where the creature had gone.

"What is it? What's wrong?" The two older persons had come quickly onto the porch and the mother bent immediately to help her daughter.

"Oh, Shirley! George! Help me. Oh gosh! She's burning up. Sonny, put back the covers of the big bed. Quick now!"

They were inside now and the boy spoke.

"She saw dwarfs," he said solemnly and the mother looked at George Hulegy. "And there was a big yellow dog that Rey didn't even see."

"Oh, no, no," the mother wailed and leaned over Shirley who had begun to writhe and moan. "Hush, baby, hush. Mama's here. Hush, baby, your Mama's here." She began to sing softly a very old song while George Hulegy took a lantern from behind the stove.

"I'm going to the creek and get some pebbles where the water still runs," he said. "I have to hurry." He closed the screen quietly behind him and the boy watched him as he disappeared with the swinging lantern through the brush and trees, down into the darkness to the ford. Behind him the mother still sang softly as Shirley's voice began to rise, high and thin like a very small child's. The boy shivered in the heat and sat down in the corner to wait helplessly as he tried not to look at the dark space of the window. He grew stiff and tired trying to control his trembling muscles as they began to jump.

Then George Hulegy came in with some pebbles that still were dripping and they left little wet spots of dark on the floor as he placed them above all the doors and windows throughout the house. Finally he placed three round ones at the foot of the bed where Shirley lay twisting and crying with pain and fever.

The mother had managed to start a small fire in the kitchen stove and told the boy to go out and bring in a few pieces of cook wood from the woodpile. He looked at her and couldn't move. He stood stiff and alert and heard George Hulegy, who was bending close over Shirley, muttering some words that he could not understand. He looked at the door but the sagging screen only reflected the yellow lamplight so that he couldn't see through into the darkness; he froze even tighter.

"Hurry, son!"

He looked at Shirley lying on the bed and moving from side to side.

"Sonny, I have to make Shirley some medicine!" His body shook from a spasm. The mother saw and turned to the door. "I'll get them," she said.

"Mama!"

She stopped and he barged through the door and found the darkness envelop him. As he fixed his wide-open gaze on the woodpile that faintly reflected the starlight and that of the moon which had risen above the trees, he couldn't look to either side nor could he run. When he reached for the first piece of wood, the hysteria that was building inside him hardened into an aching bitter core. He squeezed the rough cool wood to his chest and felt the fibers press into his bare arms as he staggered toward the house and the two rectangles of light. The closer he came the higher the tension inside him stretched until he could scarcely breathe. Then he was inside again and he sat limply in the corner, light and drained of any support. He could feel nothing except that Shirley was lying in the big feather bed across the room, wailing with hurt and a scalding fever.

His mother was hurrying from the kitchen with a tin cup of grass tea when Shirley began to scream, louder and louder until the boy thought that he would never hear another sound as he stood straight and hard, not leaning at all.

She stopped.

In the silence he saw his mother standing above and behind the lamp, casting a shadow on the ceiling, stopped with fear as they heard the other sound. The little girls had come into the room from their bedroom and were standing whimpering in their nightgowns by the door. The mother signaled and they became still and quiet, their mouths slightly open and their eyes wide. They heard nothing.

Then like a great, beating heart the sound rose steadily until they could smell the heat of a monstrous flesh, raw and hot. Steadily it grew to a gagging, stifling crescendo—then stopped. They heard the click of dog's nails on the porch's wooden planks, and afterwards, nothing. In the complete silence the air became cold for an instant and Shirley was quiet.

It was three days now since Shirley had begun to die and everyone knew how and had given up any hope. Even the white doctor could find nothing wrong and all the old Indians nodded their solemn heads when he went away saying that Shirley would be up in a few days, for now, to them, her manner of death was confirmed. He said to send for him if there was any "real" change. No need to move her—

there was nothing wrong—nothing physically wrong, he had said. He could not even feel her raging fever. To him Shirley was only sleeping.

Everyone had accepted that Shirley was going to die and they were all afraid to go near her. "There is evil around her," they said. They even convinced the mother to put her in the back room and close off all light and only open it after three days. She would not die until the third day's night, nor would she live to see the fourth day's dawn. This they could know. A very old woman spoke these words to the mother and she could not disbelieve.

On this third day the boy sat and watched the flies as they crawled over the dirty floor, over the specks and splotches, the dust and crumbs. They buzzed and droned about some drops of water, rubbing their legs against themselves, nibbling, strutting, until the drops dried into meaningless little rings while the hot wind blew softly through the open window, stirring particles of dust from the torn screen. A droplet of sweat broke away from above his eyebrow and ran a crooked rivulet down his temple until he wiped it away. In his emptiness the boy did not want his sister to die.

"Mama?"

"What is it, son?"

"Is Shirley going to die?"

"Yes, son."

He watched her as she stood with her back to him. She moved the heavy skillet away from the direct heat and turned the damper so that the flames would begin to die. She moved automatically, as if faster movement would cause her to breathe in too much of the stifling heat. And as she moved the floor groaned under the shift in weight and her feet made whispering sounds against the sagging boards. The flies still flitted about, mindless and nasty, as the boy looked away from them to his mother.

"Does she have to, Mama?"

"Shirley is dying, son."

Again he saw how the flies went about, unaware of the heat, himself, his mother across the room or that Shirley lay in her silence in the back room. He splashed some more water from his glass and they knew he was there but immediately forgot and settled back to their patternless walking about. And even though the table was clean they walked jerkily among the dishes and inspected his tableware. The boy had lived all his life among these creatures but now he could not stand their nature.

"Darn flies!"

"Well, we won't have to worry when cold weather gets here," she said. "Now go call the kids and eat. I want to get some sewing done this afternoon."

He said nothing and watched her as she went into the other room. He went to the door and leaned out to call the small children. Then he slipped quietly into the back room and closed the door behind him, fastening the latch in the dark. The heat was almost choking and he blinked away the saltiness that stung his eyes. He stood by the door until he could see a little better. High above his head a crack in the shingles filtered down a star of daylight and he stepped to the bed that stood low against the rough planks of the wall. There were no flies in this room and there was no sound.

The boy sat down on a crate and watched the face of his sister emerge from the gloom where she lay. Straining his eyes he finally saw the rough army blanket rise and fall, but so slight was the movement that when his eyes lost their focus he could not see it and he quickly put out his hand but stopped. Air caught in his throat and he stifled a cough, still letting his hand hover over the motionless face. Then he touched the smooth forehead and jerked his hand away as if he had been burned.

He sat and watched his sister's well-formed profile and saw how the skin of the nose and forehead had become taut and dry and now gleamed pale and smooth like old ivory in the semi-darkness. A smell like that of hot wood filled the room but underneath it the boy could smell the odor of something raw, something evil—something that was making Shirley die.

The boy sat on the empty crate in the darkness through the late afternoon and did not answer when his mother called him. He knew that she would not even try the door to this room. He waited patiently for his thoughts to come together, not moving in the lifeless heat, and let the sweat flow from his body. He smelled the raw smell and when it became too strong he touched the smooth, round pebbles that had come from the creek where it still flowed, and the smell receded.

For many hours he sat, and then he got up and took down the heavy blanket that had covered the single window and let the moonlight fall across the face of his sister through the opening. He began to force his thoughts to remember, to relive every living moment of his life and every part that Shirley had lived in it with him. And then he spoke softly, saying what they had done, and how they would do again what they had done because he had not given up, for he was alive, and she was alive, and they had lived and would *still* live. And so he prayed to his will and forced his will out through his thoughts and spoke softly his words and was not afraid to look out through the window into the darkness through which came the coolness of the summer night. He smelled its scents and let them touch his flesh and come to rest around the "only sleeping" face of his sister. He stood, watching, listening, living.

Then they came, silently, dark-bellied clouds drifting up from the south, and the wind, increasing, swept in the heavy scent of the approaching storm. Lightning flashed over the low, distant hills and the clouds closed quietly around the moon as the thunder rumbled and the heavy drops began to fall, slowly at first, then irregularly, then increasing to a rhythmic rush of noise as the gusts of wind forced the rain in vertical waves across the shingled roof.

Much later, when the rain had moved ahead and the room became chilly when the water began to drip from the roof and the countless leaves, the boy slipped out of his worn denim pants and took off his shirt and lay down beside his sister. She felt him and woke up.

"You just now gettin' to bed?" she asked. "It's pretty late for that, ain't it?"

"No, Shirley," he said. "Go on back to sleep. It'll be morning pretty soon and when it gets light again we'll go see how high the water's risen in the creek."

He pulled the cover over him and drew his bare arms beneath the blanket and pulled it over their shoulders as he turned onto his side. Lying thus he could see in the darkness the even darker shapes of the trees and the storehouse his father had built.

When Simon J. Ortiz supplied biographical material to the editor of The South Dakota Review, where this story first appeared, he said, "I write about Indians mainly because I am Indian and do not feel apart from my people. In fact . . . it would not be possible for me to write as an individual but only as part of a people." That statement is proof in itself that he is very much a part of his people, for it is the mark of his heritage.

Woman Singing

Simon J. Ortiz

"Yessir, pretty good stuff," Willie said. He handed the bottle of Thunderbird wine to Clyde.

Clyde took a drink and then another before he said anything. He looked out the window of their wooden shack. Gray and brown land outside. Snow soon, but hope not, Clyde thought.

"Yes," Clyde said. But he didn't like it. He didn't drink wine very much, maybe some sometimes, but none very much.

Willie reached for the bottle, and Clyde thought that Willie didn't mind drinking anything. Any wine was just another drink. But he knew, too, that Willie liked whiskey, and he liked beer too. It didn't make any difference to Willie. Clyde wished he had some beer.

They had come from the potato fields a few minutes before. It was cold outside and Willie threw some wood into the kitchen stove as soon as they came in. He poured in kerosene from a mason jar and threw in a match. After a moment, the kerosene caught the small fire and exploded with a muffled sound. Willie jumped back and laughed. Clyde hung up his coat and then put it back on when he saw there were only a few pieces of wood in the woodbox. He looked over at Willie, but Willie was taking his coat off and so Clyde went on out to get the wood. Willie didn't do anything he didn't have to.

There was singing from the shack across from theirs. Singing, The People singing, Clyde said to himself in his native Indian tongue. It was a woman. Sad kind of, but not lonely, just something which bothered him, made him think of Arizona, his homeland. Brown and red land. Piñon, yucca, and his father's sheep, the dogs too around the door of the hogan at evening. Smoke and smell of stew and bread, and the older smell of the juniper mingled with the sheep. His heart and thoughts were lonely. Woman singing, The People singing, here and now, Clyde thought to himself. He stood for a while and listened and then looked over at the shack. The door was tightly shut, but the walls were thin, just scrap lumber and roofing paper, and the woman's voice was almost clear. Clyde was tempted to approach the shack and listen closer, his loneliness now pressed him, but he would not because it was broad daylight and it was not the way to do things. The woman was Joe Shorty's wife, and she was the mother of two children. Clyde picked up an armful of wood and returned to his own shack.

"Have some more, son," Willie said. Willie was only a few years older than Clyde, but he called him son sometimes. Just for fun, and Clyde would call him father in return. Willie was married and the father of two children. They lived in New Mexico while he worked in the Idaho potato fields.

"I think I'll fix us something to eat," Clyde said after he had taken a drink. He began to peel some potatoes. Willie's going to get drunk again, he thought. Yessir. They had gotten paid, and Willie had been fidgety since morning when they had received their money from Wheeler, their boss. He had told the Indians who worked for him, "Now I know that some of you are leaving as soon as you get paid, well that's okay with me because they ain't much to do around here until next year. But some of you are staying for a while longer, and I'm telling those guys who are staying that they better stay sober. Besides, it's getting colder out, and we don't want no froze Indians around." Wheeler laughed, and Willie laughed with him. Clyde didn't like the boss, and he didn't look at him or say anything when he received his pay. He was going to stay for at least another month, but he didn't want to. But he figured he had to since he wasn't sure whether he could get a job around home right off or even at all. Willie was staying too, because he didn't feel like going home just yet, besides the fact that his family needed money.

"I think I'm gonna go to town tonight," Willie said. He was casual in saying it, but he was excited and he had been planning for it since morning. "Joe Shorty and his wife are coming along. You want to come?"

"I'm not sure," Clyde said. He didn't know Joe Shorty too well, and he had only said Hello to his wife and children.

"Come on," Willie insisted. "We'll go to a show and then to the Elkhorn Bar. Dancing there. And all the drunks have left, so it'll be okay now. Come with us."

"Yeah, I might," Clyde said. He listened for the woman's singing while they ate, but the fire crackling in the stove was loud and Willie kept talking about going to town. "Isn't Joe Shorty and his family going back home?" Clyde asked.

"I don't know," Willie answered. He pushed back his chair and carried the dishes to the sink. Clyde began to wash the dishes but Willie stopped him. "Come on, let's go."

When they knocked on Joe Shorty's door, a boy answered. He looked at the two men and then ran back inside. Joe came to the door.

"Okay, just a little while," Joe said.

Willie and Clyde sat down on the front step. They could hear movement and mumbled talk inside. Clyde thought about the singing woman again. He felt uncomfortable because he was thinking of another man's woman. It was a healing song, strong mountains in it, strong and sharp and clear, and far up. Women always make songs strong, he thought. He almost told Willie about the song.

Joe and his wife and children, two boys, came out and they all began to walk on the road towards town. It was five miles away, and usually someone was driving into town and would give them a ride. If not, they would walk all the way. The children ran and walked ahead. They talked quietly with each other, but the grownups didn't say anything.

When they had walked a mile, a pickup truck stopped for them. It was Wheeler. "Hey, Willie. Joe. Everybody going to town, huh? Come," Wheeler called.

Willie and Clyde got in front with Wheeler, and Joe and his family got in the back.

"Well, gonna go have a good time, huh? Drink and raise hell," Wheeler said loudly and laughed. He punched Willie in the side playfully. He drove pretty fast along the gravel road.

Willie smiled. The wine he had finished off was warm in him. He wished he had another bottle. Out of the corners of his eyes, he searched the cab, and wondered if Wheeler might have a drink to offer.

"You Indians are the best damn workers," Wheeler said. "And I don't mind giving you a ride in my truck. Place down the road's got a bunch of Mexicans, had them up at my place several years back, but they ain't no good. Lazier than any Indian anytime, them Mexicans are. Couldn't nothing move them once they sit down. But you people— and for this reason I don't mind giving you a lift to town—Willie and your friend there do your work when I tell you, and that means you're okay for my farm."

Clyde felt the wine move in his belly. It made him swallow and he turned his head a little and saw that the woman's scarf had fallen away from her head. She was trying to put it back on.

"That Joe's got a pretty woman," Wheeler said to Willie. He looked at Clyde for comment, but Clyde would not look at him. Willie smiled and nodded.

"Yeah, don't get to see too many pretty Indian women around the camps, but she's a pretty one. You think so, Willie? Wheeler nudged Willie with his elbow.

"Yes," Willie said and he shrunk down in his seat. He wished that Wheeler would offer him a drink if he had any. But he knew that he probably wouldn't.

"Hey, Clyde, you married? A woman at home?" Wheeler asked, but he didn't look at Clyde. They were approaching the town and Clyde stared straight ahead at it but he decided to answer.

"No," Clyde said. "Not yet, maybe when I get enough money." He smiled faintly to show that he was making a minor joke.

"Someday you'll get a woman, maybe a pretty one like Joe's, with or without money." Wheeler said. And he laughed loudly. He pulled the pickup truck over to a curb in the center of the small town. "Well, take it easy. Don't over do it. Or else you'll land in jail or freeze out in the cold or something," Wheeler said with no special concern.

"We're going to the show," Willie said, and he smiled at Wheeler.

"Okay," Wheeler said, gave a quick laugh, and turned to watch Joe's wife climb out of the truck. He wanted to catch her eye, maybe to wink at her, but she didn't look at him. He watched the Indians walk up the street towards the town theater. The woman and her children followed behind the men. Wheeler thought about all the drunk Indians he'd seen in his life. He shrugged his shoulders and turned down the street in the opposite direction.

The movie was about a singer. Hank Williams was the singer's name. Clyde knew who he was, used to be on the Grand Ole Opry on radio, he remembered, sang songs he remembered too. Clyde thought about the singers back home. The singers of the land, the people, the rain, the good things of his home. His uncle on his mother's side was a medicine man, and he used to listen to him sing. In the quiet and cold winter evenings, lying on his sheepskin beside the fire, he would listen and sing under his breath with his uncle. Sing with me, his uncle would say, and Clyde would sing. But he had a long ways to go in truly learning the songs; he could not sing many of them and could only remember the feeling of them.

Willie laughed at the funny incidents in the movie, and he laughed about the drunk Hank Williams. That made him wish he had a drink again, and he tried to persuade Joe to go with him, but Joe didn't want to leave. Joe's wife and children watched the movie and the people around them, and they watched Willie fidget around in his seat. They figured he wanted to go drink.

At the end of the movie, they walked to a small cafe. On the way Willie ran into a liquor store and bought a pint of whiskey.

"Come on, son," he said to Clyde. "Help your father drink this medicine." Joe followed along into an alley where they quickly gulped some of the liquor.

"Call your woman and ask if she wants some," Willie said to Joe. He was in good spirit now. The whiskey ran through him quickly and lightly.

"Emma, come here," Joe called to his wife. She hesitated, looked up the street, and stepped into the alley. Her husband handed her the bottle and she drank quickly. She coughed and gasped for a moment, and Willie and Joe laughed.

Clyde saw the two children watching them. They stood in the weak overhead glare of a streetlight. Traffic barely moved, and a few people from the movies were walking on the streets. The children waited patiently for their parents.

They ate a quick dinner of hamburgers and cokes. And when they finished, they paid up and walked to the Elkhorn Bar a couple of blocks away.

"Do se doe," Willie said when he heard the music coming from the bar. Saturday night was always a busy night, but most of the Indian potato pickers were gone now. There were only a few cars and trucks; some men and women stood by the door. A small fire blazed several yards from the bar, and around it were a few Indians quietly talking.

Willie walked over to the fire, and Clyde followed him because he didn't want to be left alone. Joe and his family stood beside the door of the bar and peered in.

"Here comes a drunk," someone in the circle of Indians said as Willie and Clyde walked up. They laughed, but it was not meant in harm. For a moment, as he did upon entering a crowd away from his home, Clyde felt a small tension, but he relaxed quickly and he talked with an acquaintance. Willie passed him a bottle, and he made a small joke, and Clyde laughed. He felt better and took a long drink. Whiskey went down into the belly harder than wine but it made him feel warmer. And when he thought that it didn't make any difference to Willie what he drank he laughed to himself. The men talked.

The talk was mostly about their home and about The People at home. Clyde again felt the thought travel into his heart. It made him long for his home. He didn't belong here even though he had friends here, and he had money in his pocket and a job. He was from another place, where his people came from and belonged. Yet here some of them were around this fire, outside the Elkhorn Bar, and they worked in the Idaho potato fields cultivating, irrigating, and picking potatoes. Someone began a song. It was the season for sings back in The People's land. The song was about a moving people.

When no one passed a bottle for a while, Clyde decided to go get a drink at the bar. The liquor in him made him sleepy, but he was getting cold too. There was no wind, but it was getting colder. He remembered Wheeler's words, thought about them for a moment, but he knew it would not freeze tonight. The bar was crowded. Someone was on the floor near the doorway, and others stepped over him without taking much notice.

Clyde met Joe Shorty and his wife, and they drank some beer together. Joe was getting drunk and his wife was drinking quietly. It was too noisy for Clyde to remember the song anymore. The children were standing by the jukebox, watching the revolving discs. Clyde wondered when they were going back to the camp by the potato fields, and he went to look for Willie.

"So there you are, son," Willie said when Clyde found him. He was with the men around the fire. "Come join us." He was drunk, and he handed Clyde another bottle.

The Indians, who were very few now, were singing in the high voice of The People. Like the wind blowing through clefts in the mountains. Clyde wondered if it was only that he was getting drunk with the liquor that he could make out the wind and the mountains in the song. But it was the men getting drunk too, which didn't make it sound like the wind, he thought. He drank some more, but he was getting tired and colder, and he told Willie he wanted to go.

"No, stay," Willie said. "It is still a long night. These nights are long, and at home the sings last all night long."

This Idaho was not where The People's home was, Clyde thought. And he wanted to tell Willie that. He wanted to tell the others that, but they wouldn't pay attention to him, he knew.

The women would sit or stand quietly by the singing men at home. The fire would be big, and when it got smaller someone would bring an armload of wood and throw it in. Children would hurry through the crowd of The People until they were tired and sleepy. Here there were no children except by the jukebox, watching it play records. In the morning, there would be newly built fires before camps of families. In the mountains of The People. And the light beginning in the East would show that maybe it will snow sometime soon, but here by the Elkhorn Bar there would be no fires and no one to see the light in the East. Maybe, like Wheeler talked, there'd be some frozen Indian left lying around.

Clyde walked away. The town was quiet. A police cruiser went in the direction of the bar and the officer looked at Clyde. When he got to the edge of town, he lengthened his stride.

When he had walked for a while, he saw that someone was walking in front of him. He slowed down, and he saw that it was a woman and two children. Joe Shorty's family. Joe must have stayed, drunk I guess, Clyde thought, and his family had left without him. Clyde didn't want to talk with them because they were another man's wife and children. They heard him and one of the boys said loudly, "It's Clyde, come walk with us."

The woman was slightly drunk. Clyde could see her smile. She staggered some. "It's cold," she said. "We left Joe Shorty. He's going to come home in the morning."

Joe Shorty's wife and sons and Clyde walked quietly and steadily. The children stepped carefully in the dark. Once, Clyde looked back, and he could barely make out a pale light over the town. He thought about Willie and thought he would be all right. It was cold and Clyde let his hand out of his pocket to test the cold. Willie would be all right. Joe Shorty and Willie would probably come back to the camp together in the morning.

The lights of a truck lit them up and Clyde said, "We better get on this side of the road." The younger boy stumbled and grabbed for Clyde's hand. The boy's hand was cold, and Clyde felt funny with Joe Shorty's son's hand in his.

The truck was Wheeler's. It passed them and then slowed to a stop fifty yards ahead. Wheeler honked his horn. Clyde and Joe Shorty's family walked toward the truck as it backed towards them.

"It's Wheeler, the potato boss," Clyde said to the woman. She did not look at him or say anything. The younger boy clung to his mother's skirt.

The pickup truck drew back alongside of them and stopped. Wheeler rolled down his window and studied them for a moment. He looked at Clyde and winked. Clyde felt a small panic begin in him. He realized that he still held the child's hand in his. What did this mean to the potato boss, Clyde asked himself.

"Well come on," Wheeler said. "Get in, but just a minute," and he got out. He stood by the side of the truck and urinated. The woman and her children and then Clyde climbed into the back of the truck.

When Wheeler saw that they had climbed in back, he said gruffly, "Come on, get in front." And then with a softer tone, "There's enough room and it's colder than hell out," and he reached out a hand to one of the boys. But the boy hung back. Wheeler grabbed the other and swung him over the side. The woman and the other boy had no choice but to follow.

Clyde felt his feelings empty for a while and then he slowly felt himself burning. He watched the woman climb out of the back into the front. It was not cold as before and it was the liquor, he thought. When he jumped down from the back and got into the front he felt light and springy. He smiled at Wheeler.

Joe Shorty's wife did not say anything. She was looking at the dashboard and her children huddled against her.

"Well, Joe Shorty must be having a good time," Wheeler said. He laughed and steered wildly to keep the truck on the road.

The woman did not say anything. She held one of her children, and the other huddled against her tightly. Clyde was on the side against the door. He could feel her movement and her warmth. But he looked straight ahead until Wheeler spoke to him.

"Weren't you having a good time, Clyde? Maybe there's good times other places, huh?"

Clyde felt a hot liquid move in him. It was warm in the truck. The heater was blowing on his ankles. It's the whiskey, he thought. What does this man think of this, he thought. And then he thought of what all white men in the world thought about all the Indians in the world. I'm drunk, he thought, and he wanted to sing that in his own language, The People's language, but there didn't seem to be any words for it. When he thought about it in English and in song, it was silly, and he felt uncomfortable. Clyde smiled at Wheeler, but Wheeler wasn't paying attention to him now.

Wheeler drove with one hand and with the other he patted Joe Shorty's older son on the head and smiled at Joe Shorty's wife.

"Nice, nice kid," Wheeler said. The woman fidgeted, and she held her other son tightly to her.

Clyde felt her move against him and he tensed. He tried to think of the song then. The People singing, he thought, the woman singing. The mountains, the living, the women strong, the men strong. But he was tense in his mind, and there was no clear path between his mind and heart. Finally, he said to himself, Okay, potato boss, okay.

They drove into the camp and stopped in front of Clyde's and Willie's shack. Clyde thought, Okay, Potato boss, okay. He opened the door and began to climb out. The woman and her children began to follow him.

"Wait, Wheeler said. "I'll drive you home. I'm going your way." His voice was almost angry.

Wheeler grabbed her arm, but she wrenched away. Clyde stopped and looked at Wheeler.

"She lives over there," Clyde said, pointing to Joe Shorty's shack, but he knew that Wheeler knew that.

Wheeler scowled at him and then he searched for a bottle under the seat. The woman did not move away anymore. She watched Wheeler and then said something to her children. Clyde looked at her. The song, he thought, and he tried very hard to think of the woman singing. The children ran to the shack, and Joe Shorty's woman and Wheeler followed.

For a long time, Clyde stood behind the door of his and Willie's shack. Listening and thinking quiet angry thoughts. He thought of Willie, Joe Shorty, the Elkhorn Bar, Hank Williams, potatoes, the woman and her sons. And he thought of Wheeler and himself, and he asked himself what he was listening for. He knew that he was not listening for the song, because he had decided that the woman singing was something a long time ago and would not happen anymore. If it did, he would not believe it. He would not listen. Finally, he moved away from the door and began to search through Willie's things for a bottle. But there was no bottle of anything except the kerosene and for a moment he thought of drinking kerosene. It was a silly thought, and so he laughed.

When the bus pulled out of the town in the morning, Clyde thought of Willie again. Willie had come in when the sun was coming up. He was red-eyed and sick.

"We had a time, son," Willie said. He sat at the table woodenly. He did not notice that Clyde was putting clothes into a grip bag.

"That Wheeler, he sure gets up early. Joe Shorty and I met him outside his house. 'The early bird gets the worms,' he said. Sure funny guy. And he gave us some drinks," Willie mumbled. He was about to fall asleep with his head on the table.

"I'm going home," Clyde said. He had finished putting his clothes in the bag.

"You never have a good time," Willie said. Clyde thought about that and asked in his mind whether that was true or not.

When Clyde thought about the woman's singing he knew that it had been real. Later on he would hear it someplace again and he would believe it. There was a large hurt in his throat and he began to make a song, like those of The People, in his mind.

Old Injustices; New Protests

In November of 1969, a group of Indians occupied the island of Alcatraz as a pan-tribal effort. Their beleaguered forces, their determined members, their articulate arguments were ultimately dispossessed of the land they would have purchased in the "fair" tradition of white land purchases. The pan-tribal proclamation, the explanations of Richard Oakes (Mohawk) and Carol Williams (Yurok) were all for naught—or were they? If they accomplished nothing else, they made the Indian visible! He was also made visible by the National Day of Mourning declared by the United American Indians of New England. Clyde Warrior (Ponca) had been making him visible for some time, and Buffy Sainte-Marie (Cree) has been lending her voice for several years. The works that close this book are not the defeated words of a people who have lost their identity. As Vine Deloria, Jr. declares in We Talk, You Listen, "An undeveloped land created tribes and a fully developed land is creating tribes. In essence, Indians have really won the battle for cultural survival. It remains only for years to go by and the rise of youth to continue, and everyone will be in the real mainstream of American life—the tribe."

Proclamation to the Great White Father and All His People

Indians of all Tribes, San Francisco, California

We, the native Americans, re-claim the land known as Alcatraz Island in the name of all American Indians by right of discovery.

We wish to be fair and honorable in our dealings with the Caucasian inhabitants of this land, and hereby offer the following treaty:

We will purchase said Alcatraz Island for twenty-four dollars ($24) in glass beads and red cloth, a precedent set by the white man's purchase of a similar island about 300 years ago. We know that $24 in trade goods for these 16 acres is more than was paid when Manhattan Island was sold, but we know that land values have risen over the years. Our offer of $1.24 per acre is greater than the 47¢ per acre that the white men are now paying the California Indians for their land.

We will give to the inhabitants of this island a portion of that land for their own, to be held in trust by the American Indian Affairs and by the bureau of Caucasian Affairs to hold in perpetuity— for as long as the sun shall rise and the rivers go down to the sea. We will further guide the inhabitants in the proper way of living. We will offer them our religion, our education, our life-ways, in order to help them achieve our level of civilization and thus raise them and all their white brothers up from their savage and unhappy state. We offer this treaty in good faith and wish to be fair and honorable in our dealings with all white men.

We feel that this so-called Alcatraz Island is more than suitable for an Indian Reservation, as determined by the white man's own standards. By this we mean that this place resembles most Indian reservations in that:

1. It is isolated from modern facilities, and without adequate means of transportation.
2. It has no fresh running water.

3. It has inadequate sanitation facilities.
4. There are no oil or mineral rights.
5. There is no industry and so unemployment is very great.
6. There are no health care facilities.
7. The soil is rocky and non-productive; and the land does not support game.
8. There are no educational facilities.
9. The population has always exceeded the land base.
10. The population has always been held as prisoners and kept dependent upon others.

Further, it would be fitting and symbolic that ships from all over the world, entering the Golden Gate, would first see Indian land, and thus be reminded of the true history of this nation. This tiny island would be a symbol of the great lands once ruled by free and noble Indians.

Statements on the Alcatraz action. From the newspaper El Grito, an interview with Richard Oakes, the 27-year-old Mohawk leader and with Carol Williams, a Yurok Indian and mother of four.

RICHARD OAKES: There's a sad neglect of all the different tribal cultures. Ten years from now, there may not be anybody out on the reservation to retain our culture and to be able to relate it. So this is actually a move, not so much to liberate the island, but to liberate ourselves for the sake of cultural survival...

For the most part, you find that the people coming here are here for the knowledge they can acquire. We hope we've been instrumental in bringing about an awareness in young people, an awareness that there is something good in the traditional aspect of Indian life. And we hope that the young people begin to respond to the old people, not coming from the high schools, which are white oriented, and trying to teach the old people, when in fact the old people can teach them much more...

One of the basic tenets of Indian life is humbleness, though, it's true, for instance, that the Chicano people don't identify with the Indian part of their life. It's the invisible side for them; or it's the pagan side for them; or it's the side of them that's very savage. They rationalize, so far away from the Indian part of their lives; and I think all their lives try to believe in something they're not, trying to be more and more American.

The sad fact about the non-Indian world is that most of it is not based on the truth, and that's why it's going to fall, to crumble. It's crumbling now, it's falling apart...

Here on this island, we've got so much more. It has so much more in the way of promise, hope, for our own people. Our people are slow to react to something of this nature, and they want to find out how much truth there is in it. It's hard to live a lie.

I speak as a youth, and I speak as a spokesman for the people on the island here, and we are ready to start listening to the old people. Leave the land that has caused so much trouble and heartbreak and come to a neutral area; and leave with us the knowledge so we can go back and teach your children.

CAROL WILLIAMS: When we claimed Alcatraz Island for Indians of all tribes, we meant exactly that. It's so very important for the people to realize that we're never going to get the island unless the Indian people are going to come here, and represent the Indians of all tribes. We need to have Indian people that know the Indian culture, to begin now teaching it to the younger people here on Alcatraz.

This is why we want a cultural center and a college that represents young people learning the forgotten culture they left to learn the white man's culture. The young Indians want to come back. They want to learn. Because out there in the white man's culture, you learn that we no longer need the white man's culture. The white man's culture needs our culture...

I have four children of my own. I want them to learn what the Indian people represented on this whole earth. What their heritage is—not just of their tribe, but of all tribes.

And what we want to accomplish on Alcatraz Island is only symbolic of what we hope, in the future, will be the way that all mankind will live in harmony, without the prison...

We need more people. We need people with Indian ways to teach. We need people to teach languages, to tell what the different dances mean. The standards of how the college will be set up will not be white man's standards. It'll be the standards that the Indians had before the white man came...

I think throughout the years the older people began to be slighted because the younger people were going into a modern world and the older people didn't want to hold them back. And I think now that the younger people have come back and said, "I want my culture." We want to come back. We see out there in the world many, many people. Lost people; unhappy people; people that are wandering around lost and homeless and needing spiritual guidance. We can give it to them, if they want it. We have to go home. We have to learn...

National Day of Mourning

BROTHERS:

In September of 1970, the State of Massachusetts officially opened their 15-month long celebration of the 350th anniversary of the Landing of the Pilgrims with a state dinner with all sorts of dignitaries on hand. To foster the image of the "benevolent Christian Pilgrim," they even asked a descendant of the Wampanoag Tribe who met the Pilgrims to be the keynote speaker at their state dinner. When State officials found that the chosen Indian speaker, Frank Wamsutta James, was not the puppet they were looking for, they felt it necessary to censor his speech, which they found much too honest for the occasion.

Once the censorship took place, the United American Indians of New England sent out appeals across the country asking for support of Native Americans in a massive protest at Plymouth Rock. The response was gratifying! We had at least 500 Native Americans on hand that day when we buried Plymouth Rock as thousands of present-day Americans feasted on turkey dinners. Those of us who were there can never forget what a beautiful thing that was to have 500 Native Americans working together!

Now the Pilgrim Celebration is still continuing through to this Thanksgiving and we have heard that even the assistant "Great White Father," Spiro Agnew, is to be on hand Thanksgiving Day at Plymouth. Since the "Pilgrims" began celebrating their arrival last September, the Menominees in Wisconsin have continued losing their lands, the Iroquois in New York still do not have their wampum belts back, the Chippewa in Wisconsin, the Sioux in South Dakota, Pit River Indians in California—all are struggling for their lands. Poor Indian fishermen in Michigan are being harrassed by white sportsmen, and in the racist state of Washington, a native leader has been shot. Our people have been forced to leave Alcatraz! Black Mesa, sacred shrine of the Hopi and Navajo is still being destroyed! Up in Alaska, Big Business, U. S. Government, and the State of Alaska are still trying to cheat the natives and destroy their land. Even in Massachusetts, the Indians of Boston are still trying, with no success, to get an Indian Center for the 2,000 or more Indians in the area.

And the Pilgrims at Plymouth still expect us to join their celebration of a giant Hypocrisy. The 350th anniversary of the Landing of the Pilgrims! Where is that "Better Way of Life" that they came for? Where is the "Freedom from Oppression"? How can they expect us to sit and smile and eat turkey as they continue to dig up our graves and display our bones? Where is "Liberty and Justice for All"?

As the Pilgrims continue their exercise in nostalgia, we are calling once again for Native Americans to come together at the one time out of the year when people remember that Indians gave something to this country, and officially begin the TRUTH NETWORK that our Navajo brother, Peter MacDonald spoke of in September. There are people here in our land who have to hear our voices and this is the one day they will all listen. If you can't be with us in body, be with us in spirit and hold some public observance in your own community, to demonstrate support and unity with your brothers and sisters from across the country who will be gathering at Plymouth, Massachusetts, and together we can all shatter the myths that retard this country's spiritual growth. Advertise this in your area. Participation will be limited to Native Americans only, but if any non-Indian would like to support us, they could do so financially by sending their contribution to National Day of Mourning at the address below. People who join us should remember blankets and warm clothing—late November can be pretty chilly in New England.

Because we anticipate a much larger attendance than we had last year, we are asking for a reply from all who are planning to attend so that we can be better prepared to provide what help we are able to. We are doing our best to find sleeping space for those who need it, and a place to prepare a feast for our brothers when we break our fast in the evening. Come and dance the dance of unity!

We mourn: the removal of our brothers and sisters from Alcatraz!
We mourn: the continued desecration of our graves!
We mourn: the continued destruction of our mother earth by the "Pilgrim's Progress" at Black Mesa, Pyramid Lake, Alaska, and elsewhere.
We mourn: most of all, the fact that we live in a country where the people who have been so inhuman can now be honored by so many.

The UNITED AMERICAN INDIANS OF NEW ENGLAND HAVE DECLARED THANKSGIVING DAY TO BE A NATIONAL DAY OF MOURNING FOR NATIVE AMERICANS AT PLYMOUTH ROCK, MASS.

for more information, call or write: Tall Oak, P.O. Box 154
　　　　　　　　　　　　　　　　　Charleston, R.I. 02813
　　　　　　　　　　　　　　　　　(401) 364-8859
　　　　　　　　　　　　　　　　　Frank James (617) 945-0618
　　　　　　　　　　　　　　　　　Phillip Young (617) 266-1649

Which One Are You?
Five Types of
Young Indians

Clyde Warrior

Among American Indian youth today there exists a rather pathetic scene, in fact, a very sick, sad, sorry scene. This scene consists of the various types of Indian students found in various institutions of learning throughout American society. It is very sad that these institutions, and whatever conditioning takes place, creates these types. For these types are just what they are, types, and not full, real human beings, or people.

Many of you probably already know these types. Many of you probably know the reasons why these types exist. This writer does not pretend to know why. This writer can only offer an opinion as to names and types, define their characteristics, and offer a possible alternative; notice alternative — not a definite solution. All this writer is merely saying is he does not like Indian youth being turned into something that is not real, and that somebody needs to offer a better alternative:

Type A — SLOB or HOOD. This is the individual who receives his definition of self from the dominant society, and unfortunately, sees this kind in his daily relationships and associations with his own kind. Thus, he becomes this type by dropping out of school, becomes a wino, steals, eventually becomes a court case, and is usually sent off. If lucky, he marries, mistreats his family, and becomes a real pain to his tribal community as he attempts to cram that definition [of himself] down the society's throat. In doing this, he becomes a Super-Slob. Another Indian hits the dust through no fault of his own.

Type B — JOKER. This type has defined himself that to be an Indian is a joke. An Indian does stupid, funny things. After defining himself, from cues society gave him, he proceeds to act as such. Sometimes he accidentally goofs-up, sometimes unconsciously on purpose, after which he laughs, and usually says, "Well, that's Indian." And he goes through life a bungling clown.

Type C — REDSKIN "WHITE-NOSER" or THE SELL-OUT. This type has accepted and sold out to the dominant society. He has accepted that definition that anything Indian is dumb, usually filthy, and immoral, and to avoid this is to become a "LITTLE BROWN AMERICAN" by associating with everything that is white. He may mingle with Indians, but only when it is to his advantage, and not a second longer than is necessary. Thus, society has created the fink of finks.

Type D—ULTRA-PSEUDO-INDIAN. This type is proud that he is Indian, but for some reason does not know how one acts. Therefore he takes his cues from non-Indian sources, books, shows, etc., and proceeds to act "Indian." With each action, which is phony, we have a person becoming unconsciously phonier and phonier. Hence, we have a proud, phony Indian.

Type E—ANGRY NATIONALIST. Although abstract and ideological, this type is generally closer to true Indianness than the other types, and he resents the others for being ashamed of their own kind. Also, this type tends to dislike the older generation for being "Uncle Tomahawks" and "yes men" to the Bureau of Indian Affairs and whites in general. The "Angry Nationalist" wants to stop the current trend toward personality disappearance, and institute changes that will bring Indians into contemporary society as real human beings; but he views this, and other problems, with bitter abstract and ideological thinking. For thinking this [he] is termed radical, and [he] tends to alienate himself from the general masses of Indians, for speaking what appears, to him, to be truths.

None of these types is the ideal Indian. . . .

It appears that what is needed is genuine contemporary creative thinking, democratic leadership to set guidelines, cues and goals for the average Indian. The guidelines and cues have to be *based on true Indian philosophy geared to modern times.* This will not come about without nationalistic pride in one's self and one's own kind.

This group can evolve only from today's college youth. Not from those who are ashamed, or those who have sold out, or those who do not understand true Indianism. Only from those with pride and love and understanding of the People and the People's ways from which they come can this evolve. And this appears to be the major task of the National Indian Youth Council—for without a people, how can one have a cause?

This writer says this because he is fed up with religious workers and educationalists incapable of understanding, and pseudo-social scientists who are consciously creating social and cultural genocide among American Indian youth.

I am fed up with bureaucrats who try to pass off "rules and regulations" for organizational programs that will bring progress.

I am sick and tired of seeing my elders stripped of dignity and low-rated in the eyes of their young.

I am disturbed to the point of screaming when I see American Indian youth accepting the horror of "American conformity," as being the only way for Indian progress. While those who do not join the great American mainstream of personalityless neurotics are regarded as "incompetents and problems."

The National Indian Youth Council must introduce to this sick room of stench and anonymity some fresh air of new Indianness. A fresh air of new honesty, and integrity, a fresh air of new Indian idealism, a fresh air of a new Greater Indian America.

How about it? Let's raise some hell!

Now Speed the Day

The flag of the United States is not necessarily a unified symbol for all Americans. Some see the stars as the symbol of unfettered aspiration, the bars as confining reality. Perhaps the most difficult part of surviving in "one nation, under God, indivisible" is constantly realizing that freedom is as fragile as negotiated peace, and justice is not only blind but also bigoted. Gabriel Horn, an Onondaga of the Iroquois, has always been a displaced person in his own land. Born to parents afraid to be Indian, he drifted from identity crisis to identity crisis, from temporary home to temporary home, from school to school, always searching for some tie to his own past, some acceptance of his own present—an unreal, fragmented present in which he became the focal point of dissatisfied and alienated white peers because he represented the ultimate loss to them. But their needs were, possibly, greater than his own, for one day he met a brother, Bobby, the grandson of Quanah Parker. Together they renewed old faiths, made new pledges. Gabriel's identity was restored. In a few months, he will receive his college degree and his Indian name, the first from the University of South Florida, the second from Princess Red Wing of the Seven Crescents, who feels Gabriel has earned bestowal. Perhaps his last test came when he asked to participate in a week-long mock-United Nations session on the campus of his school. Wishing to join those contemporaries who seek a universal law of great peace, he was greeted with a firmly delivered truth: "You can't be a representative in the United Nations; you don't have a country." Gabriel's song is a gift in the old tradition. It was granted at that moment; it was realized in being cast as a chant to lure the hearer to the freedom Gabriel desires for the white man.

A Chant to Lure Honor

Gabriel Horn

Comes the need to the white man
Comes that need of bright honor
Comes the need to the white man

From the sands of Gulf waters
From the grove-dappled shoreline
Down the ridges of time, coming fast, coming faster
Comes that need, comes that need now

From the land of my fathers
Through the pines and the chestnuts
Comes the need to the white man
Comes the urge on my song

Down the slopes of Mount Ranier
Past its glacier and meadows
Through its flowers at snow line
That need sings in my song

Up from Baja, past Salt Lake
On the wide Mississippi
Down the winds of the great plains
Comes the need, comes my song

Drifting slow in the pollens of Sakoiatisan
Whispering wet in the rains gusting wide on the winds
Laughing bright as fall flowers in mists of the morning
Comes the need to the white man
Comes the need on my song

On the dust of the thundering herds of the bison
Their gray, ghosted manes flowing free in the wind
On the fog drifting softly like spirits of dead leaves
In the sunpools and shadows warming, cooling the ghosts
Of my people all waiting, waiting now for my song
Comes the need of bright honor, the need of the white man,
Comes the urge to the white man, comes the need,
          comes the need now

Up from sad Osamekun's old kindness, old largess
Through the ant-eaten sockets of Metacom's skull
Past the memories of Sand Creek, ruins of Pueblo Bonito
Out of kivas and longhouses rotting in time
Comes the need of the white man, the need and the urge
Comes the bright shining honor, comes its need,
    comes its urge

From the halls of Montezuma, from the shores of Tripoli
Oh beautiful for spacious skies
Can't you see, can't you see, oh say can't you see
What you've done to my people, my land, and to me?
Comes the urge, comes the need
Past your hate, past your greed
Through your minted and printed your coinaged lust
That I perjure myself with your "In God we trust"
As The Great Holy Mystery inhabits the dust
Of your glassed Constitution, your framed Bill of Rights
That proud Declaration and all the dark nights
You have rained on the world with your bombs from the
    heights
You have scaled and the depths of delights
You have plumbed in your extirpative fights
My country 'tis of thy Pequot and Heuchi
Thy Beothuk, Cayuse, Calusa, Caloucha
Thy Inkpa, Ihasha, thy Ika, Henuti
Peoria, Secawgo, Carises, Cajuenche
All, all the forgotten dead tribes and dead nations
You killed with your guns and your handkerchief rations
And smallpox-rich blankets, your Fort Pitt donations
Oh, my country 'tis of thy sermons, orations
that deny us God's grace shed on thee
Can't you see, can't you see, oh say can't can't you see
What you've done to my people, my land, and to me?
May your God and Sakoiatisan both let it be
That the need of bright honor may yet come to free
Us from you, from your justice, your freedom, and last
From our own dismal error: forgetting our past
In our present forgetting to still hear the word
Sakoiatisan sent us: Sakoiatisan heard.

Comes the need to the white man
Comes that need of bright honor
Comes the need to the white man
Comes that need now from me

Index